FROM PATRIARCH TO PRIEST
The Levi-Priestly Tradition from
Aramaic Levi to *Testament of Levi*

SOCIETY OF BIBLICAL LITERATURE

EARLY JUDAISM AND ITS LITERATURE

Number 09

FROM PATRIARCH TO PRIEST
The Levi-Priestly Tradition from
Aramaic Levi to *Testament of Levi*

by
Robert A. Kugler

FROM PATRIARCH TO PRIEST
The Levi-Priestly Tradition from
Aramaic Levi to *Testament of Levi*

by
Robert A. Kugler

Scholars Press
Atlanta, Georgia

FROM PATRIARCH TO PRIEST
The Levi-Priestly Tradition from
Aramaic Levi to *Testament of Levi*

by
Robert A. Kugler

Library of Congress Cataloging-in-Publication Data
Kugler, Robert A.
    The Levi-Priestly tradition : from Aramaic Levi to Testament of
Levi ; by Robert A. Kugler.
        p.   cm. — (Early Judaism and its literature ; no. 09)
    Includes bibliographical references and indexes.
    ISBN 0-7885-0177-1 (cloth : alk. paper). — ISBN 0-7885-0178-X
(pbk. : alk. paper)
    1. Testament of Levi—Criticism, interpretation, etc. I. Title.
II. Series.
BS830.T56K84   1996
229'.914—dc20   96-4354
                                           CIP

Printed in the United States of America
on acid-free paper

For my mother, blessed be her memory, and my father,
who encouraged the life of the intellect;
and for my wife and children,
who remind me daily of the joy of life in family.

TABLE OF CONTENTS

PREFACE

This book is a revised dissertation defended at the University of Notre Dame in May 1994. My advisor, James VanderKam, is to be thanked heartily for his kind, persistent, and encouraging direction. I also thank Joseph Blenkinsopp, John J. Collins, and Eugene Ulrich, the other readers of the work when it was still a dissertation, who all offered wisdom and insight from their particular perspectives; Bill Adler, editor of the Early Judaism and its Literature series, who encouraged submission of this manuscript for publication; the Novak family for their contributions to a scholarship fund at the University of Notre Dame which provided financial assistance for my study of the Qumran fragments of *Aramaic Levi* in Jerusalem; and the American Philosophical Society for a grant which enabled me to examine the Cairo Geniza fragments of *Aramaic Levi* in Cambridge and Oxford England. Thanks also to my graduate student assistant, Ian Bubenik, for assistance with the indexes.

Robert A. Kugler
Gonzaga University

INTRODUCTION

The consensus in nineteenth-century study of early Judaism was essentially that the period amounted to the long history of rabbinic Judaism's nascence. The prevalence of the view, even up to the middle of the twentieth century, was sustained, however, largely because so little literary data was available to historians of the era. But the discovery of the scrolls from the Judean desert, and the subsequent rebirth of interest in the Pseudepigrapha, have served in recent years to expand the literary data base and erode confidence in the old consensus. Where once there was general agreement that from the late Persian period to the second century CE Judaism was growing inexorably toward the form it would take in the Mishnah, the Talmudim, and the Midrashim, there is now a bewildering range of opinions about the nature of Judaism in that period, corresponding in large part to the equally perplexing array of literary artifacts from the time. Where there was once a clear portrait of a homogeneous Judaism in antiquity, there are now only fragmentary pictures of what appears a much more complex phenomenon.

In light of these circumstances it is clear that there is a critical need to develop a new synthesis respecting the wide range of evidence for the history of early Judaism. However, that objective has eluded scholarship precisely because of the breadth of literary evidence, and because of its fragmented and tortured history of transmission. To further complicate the matter, much of the literature that illuminates Judaism in antiquity was not preserved by Jews, but by Christians who redacted the material—making additions, deletions, and revisions—to suit their own interests. Other texts were not preserved by any living community of faith, but have survived only as scraps of leather and papyrus placed in storage by ancient preservationists and rediscovered by chance, centuries later. As a result, any attempt to draw historical conclusions regarding early Judaism from the extant texts must proceed first from extensive textual reconstruction and analysis. Answering the

1

challenge of creating a new history must begin at the level of working with ancient texts from the foundation up.[1]

Beyond the availability of individual texts historians have another resource for understanding Judaism in antiquity. In early Judaism there are also literary trajectories comprised of multiple texts, composed over the course of a century or more, dealing with a common theme or traditions. Descriptions and analyses of these literary trajectories are helpful in reconstructing the world of early Judaism. For instance, studies on literary traditions concerned with Adam, Melchizedek, Enoch, and other figures have been successfully undertaken.[2] Such studies illustrate the special value of working with literary traditions. They often link a figure from Israel's past with an institution or phenomenon of the author's time. The ancient figure functions like a magnet, drawing the expression of ideas and attitudes about a given reality toward himself.[3] When such a literary tradition is reconstructed, described, and analyzed the ideas expressed throughout its life give a continuous record of various views regarding the phenomenon or institution with which the tradition is concerned. Each tradition, discovered and analyzed, swells the pool of textual evidence for a more complete picture of Judaism in antiquity.[4]

0.1. Introducing the Levi-Priestly Tradition and the purpose of the study

One literary tradition of early Judaism that has curiously attracted little attention centers on Levi and the priesthood. Proceeding from a retelling of Levi's act of vengeance at Shechem (Genesis 34), the texts in the tradition depict Levi as God's ideal priest. Hence it may be called the Levi-Priestly tradition (henceforth LPT). Throughout the tradition's life Levi is depicted as an individual who was selected for

---

[1] For a similar analysis of the current situation with respect to the study of early Judaism, see G. W. E. Nickelsburg, with Robert A. Kraft, "Introduction: The Modern Study of Early Judaism," in *Early Judaism and its Interpreters* (ed. R. A. Kraft and G. W. E. Nickelsburg; Philadelphia: Fortress, 1986) 2, 22-23.

[2] See the study focused on Enoch traditions by James C. VanderKam, *Enoch and the Growth of an Apocalyptic Tradition* (CBQMS 16; Washington, D. C.: Catholic Biblical Association of America, 1984); and the studies on the Melchizedek traditions by F. L. Horton, *The Melchizedek Tradition* (Cambridge: Cambridge University, 1976); and Paul Kobelski, *Melchizedek and Melkireša^c* (CBQMS 10; Washington, D. C.: Catholic Biblical Association of America, 1981).

[3] VanderKam establishes the connection between Enoch traditions and the growth of apocalyptic and the various Melchizedek studies point to the obvious connection made in the literature between Melchizedek and the priesthood.

[4] When we speak of a *literary* tradition throughout this study we refer to a particular set of themes articulated textually that reappear in several distinct documents over a span of some years.

the priestly office by God precisely because of his zeal for Israel's purity. In turn, his priesthood is characterized by an intense passion for communal and cultic purity, and by a unique interest in the exercise of wisdom.

The tradition's first extant phase appears in *Aramaic Levi*.[5] It is attested in three fragmentary manuscripts from Qumran (1Q21; 4Q213; 4Q214), in two pieces of a single manuscript from the Cairo Geniza, and in additions to the Mt. Athos manuscript of the *Testaments of the Twelve Patriarchs* (*T. Levi* 2:3; 18:2). According to our reconstruction the text probably begins with a retelling of Genesis 34 (*Ar. Levi* 1-3), and continues with Levi's prayerful plea to serve as God's agent in the battle against evil and impurity (*Ar. Levi* supp. 1-19). Then follows Levi's dream in which angels address him regarding the evil of exogamy (supp. 20-27) and appoint him a priest (*Ar. Levi* 4-7). After he awakens Levi travels first to Isaac where he is blessed by his grandfather (8), then to Bethel where Jacob consecrates and ordains him to the priesthood (9-12). Levi takes to the road once more for yet another visit to Isaac; on this occasion Isaac lectures Levi on proper cultic procedures (13-61). A narration of Levi's family history follows (62-81), and the extant text concludes with Levi's speech in which he commends wisdom to his children and foretells the apostasy of some of his descendants from the model priesthood he himself embodies (82-106).[6]

The second phase of the tradition occurs in *Jub.* 30:1-32:9. This passage also depicts Levi as an ideal priest who was elevated to the office because of his violence at Shechem. Although it begins with a retelling of Genesis 34, as does *Aramaic Levi* (30:1-4, 24-26; cf. *Ar. Levi* 1-3), inserted in the middle of the account is the angelic address regarding exogamous practices (30:5-23; cf. *Ar. Levi* supp. 22-27). *Jubilees* 31 provides also a much fuller account than *Aramaic Levi* of Isaac's blessing, and probably preserves added material relating specifically to Jacob and Isaac. Then in *Jub.* 32:1-9 the reader is informed that Levi had a vision, that he was elevated to the priestly office by his father Jacob, and that he made sacrifice on his father's behalf. At this point the parallel with *Aramaic Levi* breaks off. Only in Isaac's cultic instructions in *Ar. Levi* 13-61 is there a loose parallel with *Jub.* 21:6-14.

---

[5] The text is also designated the *Aramaic Levi Document* (so Jonas Greenfield and Michael Stone, "Remarks on the Aramaic Testament of Levi from the Geniza," *RB* 86 [1979] 215), or an Aramaic *Testament of Levi* (see, for example, H. L. Pass and J. Arendzen, "Fragment of an Aramaic Text of the Testament of Levi," *JQR* 12 [1900] 651-61). For our choice of the title *Aramaic Levi*, see the introductory section of chapter two.

[6] Chapter two explicates more fully this understanding of *Aramaic Levi*'s contents, order, and versification.

Testament of Levi fills out the literary tradition. Unlike *Aramaic Levi* and *Jub.* 30:1–32:9 it does not start with a retelling of Genesis 34. Instead it begins with Levi's plea that God deliver him from evil, and continues with a first dream in which Levi's prayer is answered with his appointment to the priesthood and he is commissioned to avenge his sister's rape (*T. Levi* 2:3-6; 4:2–6:2). After an account of Levi's fulfillment of the angel's violent directive, of Jacob's negative reaction, and of Levi's self-defense (6:3–7:4), Levi dreams again, and his elevation to the sacerdotal office is accomplished once more by heavenly agents (8:1-19). Following his second dream Levi travels to Isaac where he is blessed by his grandfather (9:1-2a). Then he travels to Bethel where Jacob pays his tithes through Levi after having his own vision concerning Levi (9:2b-4). The family returns to Isaac where Levi receives priestly instruction (9:5-14). Finally Levi's life history is narrated (11:1–12:7) and he delivers a long speech regarding wisdom and his descendants' fate (13:1–15:4; 16:1–18:14).[7]

Given the clarity with which these individual texts present and develop their common theme, and considering the unquestionable connections among them, it is surprising that so little study has been devoted to them as *related texts*. One would think that this tradition would have long since been treated fully, especially the relationships among the three texts. But in fact, few studies have been devoted to the topic, and the attention that has been given to the relationships among the three documents has provided only a bewildering array of varying opinions regarding the character of the connections. Some think that *Testament of Levi* is directly dependent on *Aramaic Levi*. J. T. Milik holds this view,[8] as did Marinus de Jonge, at least in the early stages of his career-long study of *Testaments of the Twelve Patriarchs*.[9] Anders

---

[7] We understand *Testament of Levi* to have existed independently prior to its incorporation into *Testaments of the Twelve Patriarchs*. This outline of its contents reflects our judgment regarding the scope of that document. Our argument for this particular shape is in chapter five, below.

[8] J. T. Milik, "Le Testament de Lévi en araméen: Fragment de la Grotte 4 de Qumrân," *RB* 62 (1955) 404-406. See also Charles' pre-Qumran view in R. H. Charles and A. Cowley, "An Early Source of the Testaments of the Patriarchs," *JQR* 19 (1907) 566-69; and *The Greek Versions of the Testaments of the Twelve Patriarchs* (Oxford: Oxford University, 1908) liii-lviii. He believed then that *Aramaic Levi*, known to him only from the Cairo Geniza manuscript and the Mt. Athos additions, was "a work which formed a common source both of the Testaments and the Book of Jubilees" (*Greek Versions*, liv).

[9] Marinus de Jonge, *The Testaments of the Twelve Patriarchs. A Study of their Text, Composition, and Origin* (Assen: Van Gorcum, 1953) 38-52, 129-31. However, in his more recent statements on the matter, de Jonge has backed away from that view, opting for a more tentative assessment of the degree of actual dependence (see for example, Marinus de Jonge, "Main Issues in the Study of the Testaments of the Twelve Patriarchs," *NTS* 26 [1980] 515).

Hultgård claims that *Testament of Levi* exhibits literary dependence on *Aramaic Levi*, and that the detailed differences between the two documents merely demonstrate that the author of *Testaments of the Twelve Patriarchs* was not simply an abbreviator of his source, but adapted a Levi-apocryphon for his own aims, and added to it from other written and oral sources.[10] Detlev Haupt conceives of *Aramaic Levi* as the *Vorlage* of *Testament of Levi*, but in a text-form different from that preserved in any of its manuscript witnesses.[11] Other commentators think that the relationships among *Aramaic Levi*, *Jub.* 30:1–32:9, and *Testament of Levi* are less direct. Recently Jarl Henning Ulrichsen assessed all of the *Aramaic Levi* material available to him and concluded that there is only a *traditionsgeschichtliche Verwandschaft* between *Aramaic Levi* and *Testament of Levi*, and that *Jubilees* stands at an even greater distance from the other two.[12] Jürgen Becker holds a similar view, claiming that *Aramaic Levi*, *Jubilees*, and *Testament of Levi* relied independently on a common oral tradition.[13] Pierre Grelot posits a common midrash "de la Genèse élaboré dans des cercles lévitiques et centré sur la personne de Lévi, l'ancêtre éponyme," which the authors of *Aramaic Levi*, *Jubilees*, and *Testament of Levi* used independently from one another.[14] And Chr. Burchard insists that *Aramaic*

---

[10] Anders Hultgård, *L'eschatologie des Testaments des Douze Patriarches*, vol. 2, *Composition de l'ouvrage textes et traductions* (Acta Universitatis Upsaliensis; Historia Religionum 7; Uppsala: Almqvist & Wiksell, 1982) 106. Hultgård calls the document "l'*Apocryphe de Lévi*."

[11] Detlev Haupt, "Das Testament des Levi. Untersuchungen zu seiner Entstehung und Überlieferungsgeschichte" (Ph.D. diss., Halle, 1969) 123.

[12] Jarl Henning Ulrichsen, *Die Grundschrift der Testamente der zwölf Patriarchen: Eine Untersuchung zu Umfang, Inhalt und Eigenart der ursprünglichen Schrift* (Acta Universitatis Upsaliensis; Historia Religionum 10; Uppsala: Almqvist & Wiksell, 1991) 177-86. He states with respect to *Aramaic Levi* and *Testament of Levi*, "Sie schöpfen alle beide aus den vorliegenden Levitraditionen, die sie je getrennt verwenden und gestalten" (186). This judgment speaks for his view of *Jubilees'* relationship to *Testament of Levi* as well. Especially noteworthy is Ulrichsen's separate treatment of *Aramaic Levi*'s individual manuscript witnesses. He also seems to share Becker's opinion that the common tradition was oral (see next note), because, with respect to *Jubilees*, *Aramaic Levi*, and *Testament of Levi* on Levi's encounter with Jacob he says, "Die Versionen sind alleinstehende Darstellungen einer mündlichen Tradition" (*Grundschrift*, 182); and again, about Isaac's instructions in *Aramaic Levi* and *Testament of Levi* he says, "Man darf eher damit rechnen, daß die drei Texte (TL 9:6–14; Jub; der aramäisch-griechische Text) schriftliche Fixierungen verwandter mündlicher Traditionen sind" (ibid., 184). Yet he does not apply that judgment consistently to all of the *Aramaic Levi* texts which he examines, and avoids such language in his concluding statement.

[13] Jürgen Becker, *Untersuchungen zur Entstehungsgeschichte der Testamente der zwölf Patriarchen* (AGJU 8; Leiden: Brill, 1970) 103-5.

[14] Pierre Grelot, "Notes sur le Testament araméen de Lévi," *RB* 63 (1956) 404. See also Pierre Grelot, "Le Livre des Jubilés et le Testament de Lévi," in *Mélanges*

Levi and *Testament of Levi* share no close connections, and contain similar traditions only.[15]

There are clear reasons for the failure to reach a consensus regarding the contours of the LPT. The bygone inaccessibility of the Qumran manuscripts of *Aramaic Levi* long prohibited complete assessment of its scope and shape.[16] As a result efforts to reconstruct *Aramaic Levi* have remained tentative, relying for the most part on the close parallels it shares with *Testament of Levi*. And not knowing the proper shape of *Aramaic Levi* scholars could not be certain of its relationships to *Jubilees* and *Testament of Levi*.[17]

Now, however, the major obstacle to a complete reconstruction of *Aramaic Levi* and the LPT has been removed. Free access to the unpublished Dead Sea Scrolls allows one to solve the problem of *Aramaic Levi*'s scope and shape.[18] When that is accomplished it becomes at last possible to assess more completely the contents of the three texts and the relationships among them. Therefore the principal aims of this study are the reconstruction of *Aramaic Levi*, an assessment of that document and the other texts of the tradition, and a definition of the relationships among the three. In short, this study is intended as a contribution to the expansion of the textual foundation for rewriting the history of early Judaism. Only insofar as it will be a byproduct of and assist in attaining the study's primary goals, a secondary objective is to draw provisional conclusions regarding the documents' dates and their views respecting the proper character of the priestly office.

Lest one doubt the significance of recovering the LPT, it is important to recall that one of the central institutions throughout the life of early Judaism was the priesthood. It held the power to define Judaism, and to control much of the economic and social life of ordinary Jews. Hence, although not addressing the history of the office di-

---

Dominique Barthélemy: études bibliques offertes a l'occasion de son 60e anniversaire (ed. P. Casetti, O. Keel and Adrian Schenker; OBO 38; Göttingen: Vandenhoeck & Ruprecht, 1981) 110-33, especially 111.

[15] Chr. Burchard, "Zur armenischen Überlieferung der Testamente der Zwölf Patriarchen," *BZNW* 36 (1969) 4-5, n. 25. See also Burchard's review of an edition of *T12P* from Marinus de Jonge in *RevQ* 5 (1964/66) 283, n. 2.

[16] Indeed, some have eschewed full studies of *Aramaic Levi*, vowing to wait until the Qumran manuscripts are published in full. See, for example, Greenfield and Stone, "Remarks," 215.

[17] See chapter two, below, for a complete accounting of previous attempts to determine the contents and shape of *Aramaic Levi*; for a review of earlier treatments of *Aramaic Levi*'s relationship to *Jub.* 30:1–32:9 and *Testament of Levi*, see the appropriate sections in chapters four and five.

[18] For a convenient survey of recently available resources for study of the scrolls, see Lawrence Schiffman, "New Tools for the Study of the Dead Sea Scrolls," *RSR* 20 (1994) 113-116.

rectly, our reconstruction of *Aramaic Levi* will expand the textual foundation for comprehending this important institution in early Judaism, and our definition of the relationships among the three texts will assist future studies of how views on the office changed over time, and from one group to another.

0.2. Plan of the study

The first chapter is devoted to tracing the biblical roots of the notion that Levi was rewarded with the priesthood for his violence at Shechem. We determine that a synoptic reading of Genesis 34; Exod 32:25-29; Num 25:6-13; and Deut 33:8-11 served probably as the scriptural basis for the idea. We suggest also that the four Pentateuchal texts were used already in that fashion by the author of Mal 2:4-7.

The second chapter tackles the complex issue of the contents and structure of *Aramaic Levi*. We begin with a survey of the publication history of the witnesses to *Aramaic Levi* and the scholarly attempts to reconstruct its contents and shape. The survey shows that all of the evidence for the document has only now become available, and that its scope and structure remain highly disputed. In light of such observations we go on to propose a new definition of its contents and organization, relying for the first time on the complete body of textual witnesses. The result of this undertaking is essentially the recovery of a document of early Judaism heretofore unknown to scholarship, at least in the shape that we propose for it.

The third chapter shoulders the task of commenting on the text of *Aramaic Levi* as it has been reconstructed in chapter two. The scope of our commentary is limited by the tasks we seek to accomplish with it. In addition to developing a sense of what the text says, we are particularly interested in determining its content so as to provide a foundation for assessing its relationship to *Jub.* 30:1–32:9 and *Testament of Levi*. Prior even to this, however, it is necessary to establish the text of *Aramaic Levi*, using the wide variety of textual witnesses available to us. So the chapter will consist of a section-by-section presentation of the text with translation and notes, followed by comment on its contents. The commentary will focus on clarifying the progression of events and the purpose of their narration within *Aramaic Levi*, ascertaining the biblical traditions used by the author, and assessing the relationships among the sections of *Aramaic Levi* and between the individual sections and similar parts of the other texts of the LPT. The chapter concludes with a general statement regarding the apparent relationships *Aramaic Levi* shares with *Jub.* 30:1–32:9 and *Testament of Levi*, and a short provisional discussion of the document's date and purpose.

The fourth chapter describes and analyzes the LPT as it appears in *Jub.* 30:1-32:9. As will become apparent, it is important to address the possibility, raised only recently, that *Aramaic Levi* had *Jubilees* as one of several sources, and so we begin with consideration of *Jubilees'* date, concluding that it was composed well after *Aramaic Levi*. We also take time to consider its likely purpose so as to set the context for understanding *Jub.* 30:1–32:9 as part of the larger book. After those issues have been dealt with the chapter continues with analysis of *Jub.* 30:1–32:9 in relationship to *Aramaic Levi* and *Testament of Levi*. From this we conclude that *Jub.* 30:1–32:9 was based on a text similar to or identical with a source used also by the author of *Aramaic Levi*. Brief commentary on the individual sections of the *Jubilees* passage follows; the comments support our hypothesis about the relationship *Jubilees* shares with *Aramaic Levi*, and assist in establishing a sense of the LPT's purpose in *Jubilees* as a whole.

The fifth chapter concerns *Testament of Levi*. Accepting the notion that *Testament of Levi*, as it appears in *Testaments of the Twelve Patriarchs*, is a Christian document, we begin by establishing tentatively its scope prior to its incorporation in the *Testaments*. We then assess the relationship of what we call "Original *Testament of Levi*" to *Aramaic Levi* and *Jub.* 30:1–32:9, agreeing with those who say that it relied directly on *Aramaic Levi*. Following is commentary on Original *Testament of Levi* that focuses narrowly on the differences between it and *Aramaic Levi* and their value for understanding its date and purpose, both of which are addressed in preliminary fashion at the end of the chapter.

The conclusion offers an overview of the study's literary results. It also provides brief reflections on the implications of the LPT for our future study of the priesthood in the Second Temple period, and for our comprehension of the history of early Judaism.

CHAPTER 1 THE HEBREW BIBLE SOURCES FOR THE LEVI-PRIESTLY TRADITION

At first sight it appears the Levi-Priestly tradition's fundamental notion, that God selected Levi for the priesthood as a reward for his zeal at Shechem, is purely a product of authorial imagination: no single biblical text relating to Levi leads one to such a conclusion about him.[1] However, a synoptic reading of four Pentateuchal passages, Genesis 34; Exod 32:25-29; Num 25:6-13; and Deut 33:8-11, does supply the necessary biblical foundation. Inasmuch as they were significant in shaping the LPT, it is fruitful to begin our study of the tradition with a short chapter devoted to tracing the thematic developments in the respective texts. Observing the themes addressed in the Pentateuchal passages, we see that together they provided the biblical foundation for the tradition's portrait of Levi as the divinely ordained priest whose chief characteristics were his violent zeal for communal and cultic purity and his possession of great wisdom and insight into the law. Additionally, a look at Mal 2:4-7 proves that these four passages functioned already before the completion of the Hebrew Bible in the manner described.

---

[1] Apart from genealogical notices, the only texts undoubtedly relating to the patriarch include the explanation of his name in Gen 29:34; the account of the sack of Shechem in Genesis 34, at the end of which he is scolded by his father for his actions; and Jacob's non-blessing for him in Gen 49:5-7. One might add Deut 33:8-11, although most consider the blessing of Moses to refer to the tribe of Levi (see 1.4 below). And Mal 2:4-7, a text we understand to refer to Levi, is an exceptional case (see 1.5 below).

9

1.1. Genesis 34[2]

The story of Levi's vengeful attack on Shechem after the rape of Dinah is at the heart of *Aramaic Levi*, and it is a key ingredient in *Jub.* 30:1-32:9 and *Testament of Levi*.[3] The account is set within the cycle of narratives about Jacob, and appears intrusive since it shifts the focus from Jacob's generation to that of his sons.[4] While some think that the story was composed from several traditions,[5] as it stands now it is a coherent account depicting a violent incident involving Dinah, Levi (and Simeon and the rest of his brothers), and the men of Shechem.

Gen 34:1-4 records the events that set the stage for Levi's violent behavior. Levi's sister, Dinah, ventured out "to see the women of the land" (v. 1). While on her tour she was raped by Shechem, son of the chief of the region, Hamor (v. 2). Although we hear nothing of Dinah's response to the deed, readers are told that Shechem was smitten with his victim, and fell in love with her (v. 3). To make good on his

---

[2] For a very complete review of past scholarship on Genesis 34, and a full discussion of the basic critical issues associated with it, see Erhard Blum, *Die Komposition der Vätergeschichte* (WMANT 57; Neukirchen: Neukirchener, 1984) 210-23. See also the older studies in A. Cody, *A History of the Old Testament Priesthood* (AnBib 35; Rome: Pontifical Biblical Institute, 1969) 36-38; A. Gunneweg, *Leviten und Priester: Hauptlinien der Traditionsbildung und Geschichte des israelitisch-jüdischen Kultpersonals* (Göttingen: Vandenhoeck & Ruprecht, 1965) 47-52; S. Lehming, "Zur Überlieferungsgeschichte von Genesis 34," *ZAW* 70 (1958) 228-50. The question of the story's origin and purpose in the Genesis narrative is disputed. Perhaps most intriguing of the possibilities is that proposed by A. Kuenen, "Dina und Sichem," in *Gesammelte Abhandlungen zur biblischen Wissenschaft* (Freiburg: J. C. B. Mohr, 1894) 255-76. Kuenen associates the passage with Ezra 9–10. However, his thesis is speculative, and receives what appears to be fatal treatment by Blum, *Komposition*, 222-23. See now also the brief treatment by A. Soggin, "Genesis Kapitel 34. Eros und Thanatos," in *History and Tradition of Early Israel: Studies Presented to Eduard Nielsen* (ed. André Lemaire and Benedikt Otzen; VTSup 50; Leiden: Brill, 1993) 133-35, in which he suggests the story is post-P, or perhaps even from the Hasmonean era; it is at least, he claims, from a time when Gentiles were converting to Judaism.

[3] *Ar. Levi* 1-3; *Jub.* 30:1-4, 24-25; *T. Levi* 6:3–7:4. It is worth noting that the story of Levi, Simeon, and the Shechemites attracted attention elsewhere in Second Temple Judaism. For example, the matter is taken up in the Epic of Theodotus, as well as in Judith 9, and *Ant.* 1 §§ 337-40. For this listing, and a discussion of the Epic of Theodotus material, see John J. Collins, "The Epic of Theodotus and the Hellenism of the Hasmoneans," *HTR* 73 (1980) 91-104; see also T. Baarda, "The Shechem Episode in the Testament of Levi," in *Sacred History and Sacred Texts* (ed. J. N. Bremmer and Florentino Florentino García Martínez; Kampen: Pharos, 1992) 11-73.

[4] Blum, *Komposition*, 210-11.

[5] For discussions of the unity or disunity of the chapter, see Blum, *Komposition*, 213-16; and Claus Westermann, *Genesis 37-50* (Minneapolis: Augsburg, 1986) 535-37.

love for Dinah he asked his father to arrange their marriage (v. 4). For our purposes it is especially noteworthy that, although the encounter between Shechem and Dinah began with violence and violation, it ended with Shechem's statement of good intentions. As offensive as it may be to modern sensibilities, the narrative appeared intent on transforming the scalawag into a somewhat sympathetic figure.[6]

In Gen 34:5-17 one reads of Jacob's reaction, Shechem and Hamor's proposal, and the response of Jacob's sons. For his part, Jacob reacted laconically, holding his silence on the matter in order to await his sons' return from the field (v. 5). But before they could reach home, Hamor and Shechem arrived to make their proposal of marriage between Shechem and Dinah, and to suggest a business partnership between Jacob's clan and their own people (vv. 6, 8-12). Apparently Jacob's sons overheard the conversation, and were angered to violence by the news that Shechem had raped their sister (v. 7).[7] It is apparent that Shechem and Hamor told the truth about the situation, because it was precisely the knowledge that Dinah and Shechem had had intercourse that angered the sons (vv. 7, 13; cf. vv. 27, 31).[8] And so they hatched their plot, requiring the Shechemites to submit to circumcision, so that they could catch them unprepared to defend themselves against attack (vv. 13-17). Note once more the cooperative behavior of Hamor, and the contrasting action of Jacob's sons.

Gen 34:18-24 recounts Hamor and Shechem's persuasion of their fellow countrymen to accept the Israelite plan. Once again the generally good intentions of the Shechemites are highlighted. Only the reference in v. 23a to their hope that Israelite possessions would become their own betrays a note of greed or mercenary intent; otherwise they sounded like reasonable men who sought to make the best of the horrible misdeed of one of their own.

After the Shechemites submitted to circumcision, Levi and Simeon (mentioned by name for the first time[9]) killed them and removed Dinah from the city, and the rest of Jacob's sons pillaged the city and its inhabitants (vv. 25-29). The dishonor of their action is

---

[6] Cf. Gen 34:12, 19.

[7] We translate וידבר at the beginning of v. 8 "And he said . . . ," not "But he said . . . ," as it appears in the NRSV. Thus Hamor's words in vv. 8-12 are what angered Jacob's sons (v. 7).

[8] For this reason Genesis 34 is appropriately linked with Deut 22:28-29, the law regarding the rape of an unbetrothed woman (cf. the works cited in Blum, *Komposition*, 210-23). Meanwhile, that the brothers were angry over the proposed plan to marry Dinah to Shechem, a violation of Deuteronomic law (Deut 7:3), is not certain from the story itself.

[9] Some commentators see the late appearance of the two names as evidence that an existing narrative of a general Israelite response to the rape of Dinah was made into an explanation of tension between the tribes of Levi and Simeon, and Shechem (see the works cited by Blum, *Komposition*, 210-23).

spotlighted by Jacob's petulant retort to his sons that they had soured his business deal with the Shechemites, and had endangered him and the rest of his family (v. 30). The sons responded once more, saying that they were justified because of the wrong done to their sister (v. 31).

The story does not provide a basis for glorification of Levi. Throughout the account the sons of Jacob are portrayed as having acted deceitfully, while the Shechemites, although having begun their relationship with Jacob and his clan on an ugly note, sought to make amends as best they could. Moreover, judged strictly according to one view in Israelite law on the matter, Shechem's rape of Dinah was punishable only by payment of a fine and forced marriage with Dinah (Deut 22:28-29). Shechem's offer was essentially to do just that. Yet Jacob's sons sought a punishment not prescribed by the law, and Levi was the leader of the pack that inflicted it. In short, Genesis 34 hardly works alone as the cornerstone for a portrait of Levi as a priest who merited his office because of his ferocious attack on Shechem. On the basis of the recorded account, with its relatively sympathetic portrayal of Shechem and negative depiction of Levi and his brothers, Levi was more deserving of the non-blessing his father gave to him according to Gen 49:5-7.[10]

1.2. Exod 32:25-29[11]

In Exod 32:25-29, a passage that turns up in the LPT on occasion, Levites upheld their ancestor's reputation for aggressive behavior.[12] However, this time they were rewarded rather than cursed for their zeal, inasmuch as they were encouraged to take up the priestly profession for their trouble.

Exod 32:25-29 concludes the episode of the golden calf at Mt. Sinai. Because Moses was delayed in coming down from the mountain

---

[10] The disparity between the details of Genesis 34 and 49:5-7 has been noted by scholars, resulting in the suggestion that Gen 49:5-7 refers to a tradition about Levi that does not survive in the Hebrew Bible (see Westermann, *Genesis 37–50*, 226, and the bibliography he gives there; see also Blum, *Komposition*, 216-21).

[11] Most think that Exodus 32 is a composite work. See, for example, the extreme views of S. Lehming, "Versuch zu Ex XXXII," *VT* 10 (1960) 16-50; and Jaques Vermeylen, "L'affaire du veau d'or (Ex 32–34). Une clé pour la 'question deutéronomiste'?" *ZAW* 97 (1983) 1-23; for references to other examples of this approach to the chapter see John I. Durham, *Exodus* (WBC 3; Waco, TX: Word Books, 1987) 427-28. But also consult Lothar Perlitt, *Bundestheologie im Alten Testament* (WMANT 36; Neukirchen: Neukirchener, 1969) 203-32, who considers the whole pericope to be essentially a Deuteronomic composition. Meanwhile, vv. 25-29 are thought by different scholars to be from the hand of the Deuteronomist, the Yahwist, the so-called Elohist, and even yet another, unnamed contributor to the biblical record (see those cited by Durham, *Exodus*, 423). On vv. 25-29, see Cody, *History*, 151-56; and Gunneweg, *Leviten und Priester*, 29-37.

[12] See Mal 2:4-7; *Ar. Levi* 6; *Jub.* 30:18-20; 31:12-17.

where he had received the law from God, the people convinced Aaron to make a calf of gold that they might worship it and revel before it (32:1-6). On hearing from God of the people's apostasy, Moses first convinced God to repent of a plan for their punishment (vv. 7-14). Then Moses descended from the mountain and heard the noise of the people's merrymaking. He became angry, destroyed the tablets of the covenant, and burned the golden calf. Lastly he inflicted his own first measure of punishment on the people, forcing them to drink water mixed with the ground ashes of the calf (vv. 15-20). Then after he questioned Aaron regarding the matter (vv. 21-24), the passage under consideration commences. According to v. 25 Moses noted once more the failure of restraint among the people, and then invited all those who would side with him to identify themselves. Without missing a step, the Levites gathered around Moses (v. 26). Then Moses instructed them to go through the camp, killing brothers, neighbors, and friends as punishment for the act of apostasy (v. 27). The Levites did Moses' bidding with unexpected readiness. They willingly separated themselves from kith and kin to preserve the religious purity of the community (v. 28). As a consequence of their commitment, Moses instructed them to seize for themselves the priesthood that they might have a blessing that very day.[13]

This passage casts a new light on the use of violence by members of Levi's family. The biblical record can be read as saying that Levi's act of revenge for the sexual violation of his sister was condemned twice (Gen 34:30; 49:5-7); but his descendants' zealous punishment of those who had engaged in cultic sin that involved sexual misbehavior was rewarded with Moses' command that they take for themselves the office of the priesthood.[14] So when they are read together, Genesis 34 and Exod 32:25-29 provide some of the foundation on which one could develop a picture of Levi as a priest chosen for God's service due to his

---

[13] We accept the מלאו (2nd person plural imperative) of 𝔐 ωυ 4QpalaeoExod^m, against επληρωσατε in 𝔊 and *consecrastis* in 𝔙. For a discussion of 4QpalaeoExod^m, see Judith Sanderson, *An Exodus Scroll from Qumran: 4QpaleoExod^m and the Samaritan Tradition* (HSS 30; Atlanta: Scholars Press, 1986). For the text itself see the *editio princeps*, in *DJD* 9.52-130. However, compare Dominique Barthélemy, et al., *Preliminary Interim Report on the Hebrew Old Testament Text Project* (2nd rev. ed.; vol. 1; New York: United Bible Society, 1979-80) 145, where מלאו is taken as a 3rd common plural *qal* perfect, with the subject being impersonal. This represents one of the many attempts to get around the appearance 𝔐 gives of the Levites having assumed the priestly office for themselves (cf. the RSV and the NEB, and now the NRSV and the REB, where the 𝔊𝔙 reading is followed). For a discussion of the phrase מלא יד as it pertains to priestly ordination, see J. P. Hyatt, *Exodus* (NCBC; London: Oliphant, 1971) 310.

[14] The sexual character of worshipping the golden calf is betrayed by the use in v. 6 of the verb צחק, "to laugh, play," which is used in Gen 26:6-11; 39:6-20 to refer to sexual play.

passion for cultic and communal purity. However, two key elements are still missing: Levi, the individual, remains unrehabilitated; and the priestly office attained by the Levites' action at Sinai was not granted to them by God—rather Moses said of them that they earned the right to take it by their zealous behavior. Still more resources would be required to establish the biblical basis for the LPT.

1.3. Num 25:6-13[15]

The eternal priestly covenant Phinehas won for himself and his descendants in Num 25:6-13 also features prominently in the LPT.[16] The story follows an account of Israel's apostasy in worshipping Baal of Peor at Shittim (Num 25:1-5). The passage adds to the traditions about Levi and Levites the idea that God directly rewarded them with a priestly covenant for their violent faith.

Verse 6 sets the scene. The people of Israel wept at the door of the tent of meeting as they mourned the consequences of their worship of Baal of Peor. Into the midst of the repentant community an Israelite man brought a Midianite woman.[17] The sinful character of this act was apparently marriage and intercourse with a non-Israelite, and the concomitant introduction of foreign gods.[18] That act threatened the purity

---

[15] This is apparently a Priestly addition to an existing Yahwist account. While vv. 1-5 use terms and notions typical of the Yahwist in Numbers (e.g., the reference to the people of Israel with the word עם, and the interest in the שפטי ישראל), vv. 6-18 use terminology familiar from the Priestly Work (e.g., בני ישראל and עדה). It is also evident that the author of this text knew Ps 106:28-31, which is datable to the exilic or post-exilic period (see W. Beyerlin, "Der *nervus rerum* in Psalm 106," *ZAW* 86 [1974] 50-64); therefore the likelihood that the passage is from the Priestly Writer is strengthened (so Philip J. Budd, *Numbers* [WBC 5; Waco, TX: Word Books, 1984] 181; and Martin Noth, *Numbers: A Commentary* [OTL; London: SCM Press, 1968] 277; *pace* Milgrom, *Numbers* [JPS Torah Commentary; Philadelphia: Jewish Publication Society, 1990] 215, who also notes the connection between Psalm 106 and this passage, but who rejects the influence of the former on the latter, reversing the relationship, in keeping with his view of the Priestly Work as a pre-exilic document).

[16] Even though the hero in the story is a grandson of Aaron (Num 25:7, 10), his levitical lineage was apparently enough for the authors of the LPT to warrant the inclusion of his story among the foundational biblical passages in the tradition; see Mal 2:5-7; *Ar. Levi* 4-7; *Jub.* 30:18-20; 31:12-17; *T. Levi* 8:3.

[17] 𝕲 seems to have read this as an Israelite who brought his brother to the Midianite woman. The reading found in 𝔐 is preferable.

[18] So Budd, *Numbers*, 280; B. Baentsch, *Exodus, Leviticus, Numeri* (HKAT 2; Göttingen: Vandenhoeck & Ruprecht, 1903) 624-25; L. E. Binns, *The Book of Numbers* (London: Methuen, 1927) 178. But what precisely is it that Zimri and Cozbi did that was so objectionable? The answer to that question rests largely on one's conclusions regarding the meaning of הקבה and קבתה in v. 8. The usual view is to understand each word to refer to something like a tent, thus presumably the dwelling of Zimri and Cozbi. With some reading between the lines it is possible to arrive at the

of the community and its cult, and required a quick and decisive response. So in vv. 7-9 Phinehas entered the scene. He acted as the avenging agent and the guardian of purity without delay, slaying Zimri and Cozbi with one well-placed thrust of the spear. Phinehas' violent action succeeded in abating the plague, and his zeal for the purity of God's sanctuary delivered the people. Then vv. 11-13 record the reward Phinehas earned for himself and his descendants by his willingness to shed others' blood. Because he atoned (כפר) for the sin of the Israelites (v. 13),[19] and because he was impassioned (קנא) for God

---

conclusion that Phinehas caught the pair in the midst of intercourse, dispatching them for their violation of prohibitions against such sexual liaisons. For a listing of those who have taken this approach up to 1970, see S. C. Reif, "What Enraged Phinehas?— A Study of Numbers 25:8," *JBL* 90 (1971) 100-6. Reif notes that the Jewish exegetical tradition up to the Medieval exegetes tended to read the second word (קבתה) as a reference to the woman's "inner parts" (on occasion implying, perhaps, her genitalia). Thus the translation of the second half of the phrase speaks nothing about a tent, but about where Phinehas' spear did its damage. From that inference comes most easily and logically the notion that Phinehas caught the pair in sexual intercourse. For a contemporary preservation of that reading see the *Revised English Bible* with its subtle, but pointed rendering v. 8, "and [Phinehas] went into the nuptial tent after the Israelite, where he transfixed the two of them, pinning them together." Frank Moore Cross adds to this the notion that the sin was also cultic in nature, rendering קבה as "domed tent" and קבתה as the same word with a locative enclitic. He takes the reference to a domed tent to refer to the sanctuary itself, and therefore sees Zimri and Cozbi engaged in sacral prostitution before Moses and the people. Thus, according to Cross, Phinehas avenges not only the sin of exogamous relationships, but also the pollution of the cult (Cross, *Canaanite Myth*, 202, n. 32; without Cross' sophistication of argument, this is also the view of de Vaulx, *Nombres*, 299). Alternatively, one can see the tent as a brothel brought into the community by one of its male members (Zimri), and Cozbi as a prostitute without cultic significance. This is the opinion of Ibn Ezra. It is echoed by ᵭ which reads *lupanar* (brothel). Or, as in the case of yet another attempt to explain the words, one can hold that the tent is Cozbi's cult-tent which she brought with her as a part of her Midianite religion. By this reading the sin is the introduction of cultic impurity (S. C. Reif "What Enraged Phinehas?" 105-6). The possibilities are not exhausted by this brief listing. For example, see Noth, *Numbers*, 198-99, who despairs of clarifying the word, but assumes that it refers to something like the wedding chamber of the woman. He mixes this with the assumption that the sin was ultimately cultic, insofar as marriage with a non-Israelite presumed adoption of the non-Israelite's gods. Or, see George Mendenhall, *The Tenth Generation* (Baltimore, MD: Johns Hopkins University, 1973), 114-16, who suggests that the cult the Midianite woman brought with her was a cult of the dead. Mendenhall bases this notion on Ps 106:28b, where the people eat the sacrifices of the dead. However, see Milgrom's critique of this view (*Numbers*, 480). The importance of the nature of the sin vis-à-vis the LPT, at any rate, is its sexual and cultic character.

[19] Milgrom, *Numbers*, 217, points out that on another occasion in the Hebrew Bible impaling someone served to atone for the sins of the whole nation (cf. 2 Sam 21:1-14, esp. v. 3, where the word כפר is used).

(v. 11), he received from God ברית שלום, "my covenant of peace,"[20] and בריתכהנתעולם, a "covenant of eternal priesthood" (vv. 12-13).

With the addition of this passage a further building block for the LPT appears. In addition to Genesis 34 and Exod 32:25-29, which proved the zeal of Levi and Levites, and which showed that Levites were entitled to seek the priesthood, Num 25:6-13 demonstrated God's *choice* of the Levites for priestly service because of their ferocious commitment. Moreover, just as Genesis 34 and Exod 32:25-29 told tales of aggressive responses to acts of sexual indiscretion, Num 25:6-13 also focused on the sexual misbehavior of an Israelite. At any rate, all that was still necessary for the creators of the LPT was evidence that Levi, the individual, was also chosen for the priesthood because of his zealous opposition to sexual indiscretion in cult and community.

1.4. Deut 33:8-11[21]

Moses' blessing for the tribe of Levi is spoken at first as though it were meant for the Levi alone. For this reason the exegete who sought evidence that Levi was rewarded with a sacerdotal appointment because he exhibited passion for cultic and communal purity would have been particularly drawn to this passage. While Genesis 34 presents Levi as such a zealot, and Exod 32:25-29 and Num 25:6-13 indicate that his descendants won the office by their sword-bearing action, only this passage brings together Levi the individual, a violent passion for purity, and a consequent elevation to priestly leadership. And it adds to the resources for the LPT the notion that Levi was especially occupied with the law and wisdom in its instruction.[22]

---

[20] N. H. Snaith, *Leviticus and Numbers* (London: Nelson, 1967) 303-4, points out that a change in the pointing of שָׁלוֹם to שִׁלּוּם results in the phrase "a covenant of reward." There is a certain attractiveness to this suggestion, as it only strengthens the notion that God *rewards* Phinehas with the priesthood. However there is no versional support for such an emendation, leaving it a rather tenuous proposition. Moreover, as we will see, subsequent authors undoubtedly understood the word "peace" here.

[21] The critical issues associated with this text are immense. Ranging from the date of the blessing, to its placement next to a blessing of Judah in Deut 33:7, to its variant text form in 4QTestimonia, much has been written about it. For older detailed studies, see Cody, *History*, 114-20; A. Gunneweg, *Leviten und Priester*, 37-44; and L. Ruppert, "Das Motiv der Versuchung durch Gott in vordeuteronomischer Tradition," *VT* 22 (1972) 56-69. More recent commentaries include Peter Craigie, *The Book of Deuteronomy* (NICOT; Grand Rapids, MI: Eerdmans, 1976) 395-96; A. D. H. Mayes, *Deuteronomy* (NCBC; Grand Rapids, MI: Eerdmans, 1981) 402-404; André Caquot, "Les bénédictions de Moïse (Deutéonome 33, 6-25)," *Sem* 32 (1982) 75-79.

[22] In addition to its significance for supplying the general notion of Levi as a warrior-priest, the influence of Deut 33:8-11 is apparent in *Ar. Levi* 4, 6; *Jub.* 30:18-20; 31:12-17; *T. Levi* 4:3a, 6; 8:17. Inasmuch as Deut 4:5-8 identifies law with wisdom, Moses' assignment of the teaching of the law to Levi's tribe in 33:10 associates them

· There are textual variants in the Qumran witnesses to this passage which are of particular interest to us; it is important to determine how to treat them before proceeding any further. The first is the addition of הבו ללוי, "Give to Levi," in v. 8 before the word תמיך, "your Thummim." The command is absent in 𝔐, but is present in 𝔮𝔊.[23] It is generally accepted without discussion, and may be so here as well.[24] More problematic is the failure of 4QDeut^h to shift to the plural in vv. 9c-10, as does 𝔐. For 𝔐's plural forms, שמרו, "they observed," ינצרו, "they kept," יורו, "they teach," and ישימו, "they place," the Qumran manuscript provides singular verbs.[25] It is very difficult to decide which is the more primitive reading, 𝔮 or 𝔐. In view of the use of singular verbs throughout the rest of Moses' blessings (with the exception of Deut 33:19, the second half of the blessing of Zebulun), one could conclude that the 𝔮 reading is more primitive, and that the scribes responsible for the 𝔐 tradition made the verbs in vv. 9c-10 plural to reflect the behavior of Levites in Exod 32:25-29 and as sacerdotal functionaries. But then one must ask why the job was not completed, so that the verbs in v. 9ab were made plural as well. The alternative is to consider 𝔐 as the more primitive textual tradition, and imagine that the scribes of Qumran rendered all verbs in the singular. They might have done so because of their enthusiasm for Levi as a model priest. After all, they kept multiple copies of *Aramaic Levi* and *Jubilees* in their library, and they authored a text that suggests they anticipated Levi's appearance as a messianic priest (4QTestimonia).[26] As a result it would have been tempting to secure completely the basis for the LPT with a blessing from Moses that was spoken to Levi, and to Levi alone. But if that were the case one wonders why the scribe of 4QTestimonia did not complete the task either, leaving plural forms in v. 10. In short, no firm decision is possible. For now it is perhaps best to follow the reading preserved by 𝔐, and acknowledge that other possibilities exist.

---

with the sapiential tradition. Hence one might say that Levi's wisdom speech in *Ar. Levi* 82-106 and *T. Levi* 13:1-9 springs also, at least in part, from reflection on this passage.

[23] See 4QDeut^h and 4QTestimonia for the Qumran reading. The text of 4QDeut^h is available in Julie Duncan, "New Readings for the 'Blessing of Moses' From Qumran," *JBL* 114 (1995) 273-90, and 4QTestimonia is available in *DJD* 5.60; but also consult John Strugnell, "Notes en marge du Volume 5 des 'Discoveries in the Judaean Desert of Jordan'," *RevQ* 7 (1970) 225.

[24] See the NRSV where the addition has been incorporated.

[25] 4QTestimonia and 𝔊, however, give singular forms only in v. 9c, switching to the plural in v. 10. In fact, in 4QTestimonia ישימו seems to have been written over the singular form; a scribe corrected 4QTestimonia toward the reading found in 𝔐𝔊. See Allegro's opposing view on the matter in *DJD* 5.60, and Strugnell's correction in the article cited above, note 23.

[26] See *DJD* 5.60.

The passage begins with God instructing Moses to say "Give to
Levi your Thummim, and your Urim to your loyal one whom you
tested at Massah, with whom you contended at the waters of Meribah"
(v. 8; NRSV).[27] Then in v. 9 Levi and his descendants are lauded for
not allowing regard for kinship ties to diminish their commitment to
the Lord.[28] Following in v. 10 Levites are described as teachers and
keepers of the law, and the officiants at the Lord's altar. Then v. 11
reverts to singular verb forms, drawing the blessing to a close with a
general plea to God that Levi's actions be fruitful, and his adversaries
be cursed.[29]

With these verses the connection is finally made among the
Levi/Levite texts of the Hebrew Bible between Levi's violent past and
his appointment to the priesthood. The references to Levi alone in
Deut 33:8-9a, 11 are sufficient evidence for his own divine election to
the priesthood. The bonus is that Deut 33:8, 10a also link Levi with the
priestly roles of making judgment and teaching the law; thus the passage contributes a new element to the biblical material available for a
portrait of Levi, the priest.

1.5. The case of Mal 2:4-7

Reading Genesis 34; Exod 32:25-29; Num 25:6-13; and Deut 33:8-11
together an author could plausibly construct a portrait of Levi wherein
he was elevated to the priesthood as a reward for his aggression aimed
at preserving communal and cultic purity, and in which he was depicted
as a teacher, judge, and proponent of the law and of wisdom. In this
way these texts provided the necessary building blocks from which the
authors of the LPT constructed their tradition.

That these Pentateuchal resources functioned in the fashion just
described is evident already from a text in the Hebrew Bible, Mal
2:4-7. Declaring that God had a priestly covenant with Levi, the passage depicts Levi as an ideal priest. In 2:4bα and 5aα we encounter the
phrases, בריתי את לוי, "My covenant with Levi," and בריתי היתה אתו, "My
covenant was with him." Discerning the background for this covenant
has occupied the attention of many critics. In the absence of any biblical precedent for a covenant with Levi, some have sought the antecedent in covenants connected with Levites,[30] and have asserted that

---

[27] It is not certain to what the names Massah and Meribah refer; passages containing those place-names include Exod 15:25; 17:1-7; Deut 32:51; Pss 81:8; 106:32.

[28] Some speculate that the latter half of the verse refers to Exod 32:25-29.

[29] Mays, *Deuteronomy*, 402, 404, thinks that v. 11 is the displaced conclusion to
Judah's blessing. Although that may be the case, the ample use of the verse by the
authors who contributed to the LPT (*Ar. Levi* 4, 6; *Jub.* 30:18-20; 31:12-17) indicates
that by the time Deut 33:8-11 arrived in their hands any such displacement had already
taken effect.

[30] Covenants with Levites are mentioned in Jer 33:21 and Neh 13:29.

the anarthrous use of לוי actually refers to the individual's descendants.[31] But the most reasonable reading leaves us with the conundrum of a covenant with the *individual named Levi*. And it is only by admitting the influence on Mal 2:4-7 of all four Pentateuchal passages addressed above that we can comprehend the origin of such a covenant.[32]

Certain terms and concepts in Mal 2:4-7 lead one to believe that Malachi used Deut 33:8-11 to construct a covenant with Levi. Although the two texts share only the words ברית, "covenant," and תורה, "law" (Mal 2:5a and Deut 33:9c; Mal 2:6a and Deut 33:10a), both highlight Levi's teaching function (Mal 2:6a; Deut 33:10a), and both associate Levi with a covenant. Concentration of the factors in a single place is unique to these two texts in the Hebrew Bible.[33]

Meanwhile, Num 25:6-13 readily commends itself on the basis of the common vocabulary, theme, and structure it shares with Mal

---

[31] See, for example, Théophane Chary, *Aggée-Zacharie, Malachie* (Paris: Gabalda, 1969) 250; C. F. Keil, *Die zwölf kleinen Propheten* (Leipzig: Dörflin und Franke, 1888) 696; Karl Marti, *Dodekapropheton* (KHAT XIII; Tübingen: J. C. B. Mohr, 1904) 467; J. M. P. Smith, *Malachi* (ICC; Edinburgh: T. & T. Clark, 1912) 38; Pieter Verhoef, *The Books of Haggai and Malachi* (NICOT; Grand Rapids: Eerdmans, 1987) 244, all of whom think the covenant described in Mal 2:4-7 is related to Levites, not to Levi alone. Were that the case, one would expect הלוי, "the Levite," where לוי appears. Only in Deut 10:9; Judg 17:7, 9; 19:1, does לוי clearly refer to the tribe of Levi. Yet the contexts shared by those verses make it clear that the tribe, not the individual, is the referent; and in the passages from Judges לוי appears nearby with the article, and is used with reference to the same person. Neither condition applies in the case of Mal 2:4-7. Otherwise, one expects הלוי to refer to the tribe; see Exod 4:14; 6:19; Num 3:20, 32; 18:23; 26:57; Deut 10:8; 12:12, 18, 19; 14:27, 29; 16:11, 14; 18:6; 26:11, 12, 13; Josh 13:14, 33; Judg 17:10, 11, 12, 13; 18:3, 15; 20:4; Mal 2:8; Ps 135:20; Ezra 10:15; Neh 10:40; 1 Chron 6:4; 12:26; 23:4; 24:6; 2 Chron 20:14; 31:12, 14. The occurrence of הלוי in Mal 2:8 is expected, as attention shifts in that verse to the descendants of Levi who violated the covenant God made with their ancestor.

[32] Others who accept the premise that multiple texts stand in the background of Mal 2:4-7 are Julia O'Brien, *Priest and Levite* (SBLDS 121; Atlanta: Scholars, 1990) 104-6; and Helmut Utzschneider, *Künder oder Schreiber? Eine These zum Problem der "Schriftprophetie" auf Grund von Maleachi 1,6–2,9* (Beiträge zur Erforschung des Alten Testaments und des Antiken Judentums 19; Frankfurt am Main: Lang, 1989) 64-70.

[33] For some who see the exclusive influence of Deuteronomy 33, see Blenkinsopp, *A History of Prophecy in Israel* (Philadelphia: Westminster, 1983) 242; Chary, *Aggée—Zacharie—Malachie*, 251; Wilhelm Rudolph, *Haggai—Sacharja 1–8—Sacharja 9–14—Maleachi* (KAT XIII.4; Gütersloh: Gütersloher Verlagshaus, 1976) 266; J. M. P. Smith, *Malachi*, 38-39; R. Smith, *Micha–Malachi*, 317. Alexander von Bulmerincq, *Der Prophet Maleachi* (2 vols.; Tartu: J. G. Krüger, 1926/1932) 2:204, thinks that Deut 33:8-11 and a missing narrative that belonged with Deut 10:6-9 stand behind the Levi-covenant in Mal 2:4-7.

2:4-7.[34] The words ברית, "covenant"; שלום, "peace";[35] רבים, "many"; and השיב, "deliver," appear in both texts, as does the theme of a priestly covenant, and there is considerable structural similarity between the passages.[36]

Deut 33:8-11 and Num 25:6-13 are not the only texts that Malachi had in mind when he developed his notion of a priestly covenant with Levi. Although lexical similarities are absent, it is possible that he hoped also to call Exod 32:25-29 and Genesis 34 to mind with the words of this passage. Just as Exod 32:25-29 is associated in medieval and modern scholarship with the reference to the Levites' violent behavior in Deut 33:9,[37] it is probable that ancient exegetes like Malachi also understood the verse to refer to the Levites' zeal. Therefore, when he invoked Deut 33:8-11, Malachi also knew he would bring before his audience's attention the Exodus passage. Indeed, there Levi's descendants were rewarded with the priesthood because of their concern for the community's purity, a theme dear to Malachi.

Malachi also might have attempted to draw Genesis 34 into the orbit of his discourse. The phrase that most effectively reminds one of Numbers 25—ורבים השיב מעון, "And he delivered many from iniquity"— is actually off the mark in relationship to the Phinehas episode. It is said of Levi in Mal 2:5, while it was Phinehas about whom the language was used in Numbers 25. Moreover, Phinehas did not deliver anyone from evil action; the sin had already been committed when Zimri brought the Midianite woman into the camp, and when the rest of the Israelite men had had relations with Moabite women. Phinehas delivered them only from the further consequences of their errant action, and none too effectively, since twenty-four thousand died all the same. Meanwhile, in Genesis 34 Levi acted before the sinful behavior could be undertaken, forestalling the fulfillment of what he understood to be evil intentions. By slaying the Shechemites he not only avenged his

---

[34] Adherents to the view that only Num 25:6-13 influenced Mal 2:4-7 include Kimchi; Rashi; Beth Glazier-McDonald, *Malachi: The Divine Messenger* (SBLDS 98; Atlanta: Scholars, 1987) 77-80; Eric Meyers, "Priestly Language in the Book of Malachi," *HAR* 10 (1986) 232.

[35] שלום also appears in conjunction with ברית in Isa 54:10; Ezek 34:25; 37:26. But in each of these passages priesthood is not at issue as well.

[36] The shared vocabulary is noted by Utzschneider, *Künder*, 65; for a fuller discussion, and attention to the same three factors (vocabulary, theme, and structure), see Glazier-McDonald, *Malachi*, 77-80. Especially useful is her parallel alignment of the texts that provides convincing evidence of their structural relationship.

[37] For studies of the passage that include reflection on the relationship between it and Exod 32:25-29, see Cody, *History*, 114-20; Gunneweg, *Leviten und Priester*, 37-44; and L. Ruppert, "Das Motiv der Versuchung durch Gott in vordeuteronomischer Tradition," *VT* 22 (1972) 56-69. More recent commentaries include Craigie, *The Book of Deuteronomy*, 395-96; Mayes, *Deuteronomy*, 402-404; and Caquot, "Les bénédictions de Moïse," 75-79. For a medieval commentator, see Rashi on Mal 2:4-7.

sister's rape; he also saved the people of Israel from indulging in marriage (and business) alliances that would have polluted the community. So, in view of Genesis 34 the phrase ורבים השיב מעון, "And he delivered many from iniquity," makes good sense when said with respect to Levi. He delivered the people from wrongdoing by his faithfulness to God's cause.[38] While reminding his readers of Numbers 25, Malachi may also have brought this key text among the Levi-traditions into use as well.[39]

Malachi's use of Genesis 34; Exod 32:25-29; Num 25:6-13; and Deut 33:8-11 to create a covenant between God and Levi also indicates the character of the agreement. It entailed Levi's commitment to the offices of altar-service and teaching (Deut 33:8-11; Num 25:6-13), and to vigilance for communal and cultic purity (Genesis 34; Exod 32:25-29; Num 25:6-13).[40] As will soon become evident, these are also the themes characteristic of the LPT; and so it will not be surprising to see Mal 2:4-7 utilized in the tradition as well.[41]

---

[38] For this insight see Helmut Utzschneider, *Künder*, 67-68. However Utzschneider does not draw the conclusion that Malachi had Genesis 34 in mind, apparently because he believes that shared vocabulary must be present to make such an argument.

[39] It is worth noting that by doing so Malachi began a long history of attempting to rehabilitate Levi and affirm his action, in spite of his father's curse in Gen 49:5-7. For complete references to other texts that undertake this task, see T. Baarda, "The Shechem Episode," 11-73. Of course, the texts we examine in the following chapters form a central part of this tradition.

[40] For different approaches to the issue of the covenant in Malachi, see Steven L. McKenzie and Howard N. Wallace, "Covenant Themes in Malachi" *CBQ* 45 (1983) 549-63; and Alwin Renker, *Die Tora bei Maleachi* (FTS 112; Freiburg, 1979) 117-21.

[41] Before leaving the question of Malachi's understanding of the priestly covenant it is important to address another possible interpretation of the evidence. It can be argued, especially by those who reject Malachi's awareness of the Priestly Work, that his notion of a covenant with Levi came exclusively from the Deuteronomic tradition. Thus the texts that supported Malachi's notion of covenant would have included Deut 33:8-11; Exod 32:25-29 (see Perlitt, *Bundestheologie,* 203-32, for the view that Exodus 32–34 is Deuteronomic); Jer 33:18 (a text attributed to a student of the Deuteronomic school of thought; cf. Jer 33:17; 1 Kgs 2:4; 8:25; 9:5; see, for example, D. R. Jones, *Jeremiah* [NCBC; Grand Rapids: Eerdmans, 1992] 423; William Holladay, *Jeremiah 2. A Commentary on the Book of the Prophet Jeremiah, Chapters 26–52* [Hermeneia; Minneapolis: Fortress, 1989] 229-30); and 1 Kings 12:31. In support of this view one can cite Rivkin's claim that Malachi did not know the Priestly Work because the book does not evince awareness of a conflict between Aaronites and Levites, a dispute Rivkin thinks is known largely from the Priestly Work (E. Rivkin, "Aaron, Aaronites," *IDBSup*, 1-3). Likewise, Blenkinsopp notes the absence of the priestly designation, בני אהרון, "Aaronites," in any literature datable before the late Persian period, including Malachi, as evidence that the Priestly Work was not yet available when Malachi was composed (private conversation with Prof. Blenkinsopp, June 1993). Indeed, from these things one could conclude that Malachi, clearly influ-

1.6. Conclusion

There ought to be little doubt now that the LPT stands on a firm biblical foundation. When Genesis 34; Exod 32:25-29; Num 25:6-13; and
Deut 33:8-11 are read together they produce the basis for the notion
that Levi could have appointed God's first priest as a response to and
reward for his violent zeal for the purity of cult and community at
Shechem.   Analysis of the scriptural background for the priestly
covenant between God and Levi announced in Mal 2:4-7 underscores
the four texts' joint power to reshape the biblical image of Levi.   And
with Malachi's reading of these texts the groundwork was in place for
development of the Levi-Priestly tradition.

---

enced by Deuteronomic thought and language, derived his notion of a priestly
covenant solely from Deuteronomic sources. However, this approach labors under
several difficulties. The first is the fact that it is based, at least in part, on an argument
from silence. While it is true that the term בני אהרון, "the sons of Aaron," is missing
in texts datable prior to the Priestly Work, it does not necessarily mean that the authors
of the earlier works did not know of the designation. They may simply have chosen
not to use it, either because it was of no interest to them, or because they wanted to
eliminate it by their silence. Indeed, the fact that the term appears only in the Priestly
Work and in the Chronicler may indicate the peculiarity of that point of view to those
authors. Moreover, there is another possible explanation of the absence of בני אהרון in
Malachi, one advocated also by O'Brien and Meyers (O'Brien, *Priest and Levite*, 87-
106; Meyers, "Priestly Language," 235). It is possible that Malachi knew the Priestly
Work and Deuteronomy, but only in a nearly complete form of the Pentateuch in
which the distinction between Levites and Aaronites would have been blurred. And so
the prophet could have easily spoken generally of "priests," referring to them without
using the source-based designations of which modern, critical readers of the
Pentateuch are so acutely aware. There is a second, greater difficulty with the idea that
Malachi relied exclusively on the Deuteronomic Collection to develop his idea of a
covenant between Levi and God. Malachi seems to have been aware of Num 25:12-
13, a text from the Priestly tradition (see above). Without positing Malachi's knowledge of the account, it is difficult to explain the appearance, together, of the terms
ברית, "covenant"; שלום, "peace"; רבים, "many"; and השיב, "deliver."

CHAPTER 2 RECONSTRUCTING *ARAMAIC LEVI*

Aramaic Levi is devoted entirely to the theme of the LPT, dealing solely with Levi and his elevation to the priesthood. It is a document of considerable interest to students of early Judaism, since it was probably composed in the third century BCE, a period of Jewish life for which little evidence is otherwise available. Moreover, it is understood by most to have been a source for *Testament of Levi*. Yet it has received very little attention in its own right, and has engaged scholarly interest mostly because of its significance for the study of *Testament of Levi*.[1] In addition critics have taken little interest in reconstructing its scope and structure apart from the model provided by the Greek testament. Consequently our study of *Aramaic Levi* must begin with the basic tasks of establishing its contents and fixing its shape.

A word about terminology is necessary. The document is usually called *Aramaic Testament of Levi*.[2] The nomenclature requires ad-

---

[1] The exceptions to this generalization are few. After initial interest demonstrated by H. L. Pass and J. Arendzen (see next note), R. H. Charles and A. Cowley ("An Early Source of the Testaments of the Patriarchs," *JQR* 19 [1907] 566-83), and Israel Lévi (see next note), it took the discovery of the Qumran fragments to arouse any new excitement about the text in its own right.

[2] The origin of the practice probably lies in the title of the first publication of one of its fragments. H. L. Pass and J. Arendzen entitled their publication of the Cambridge fragment from the Cairo Geniza manuscript, "Fragment of an Aramaic Text of the Testament of Levi," *JQR* 12 (1900) 651-61. Since then it has been customary to call the document an Aramaic *Testament of Levi*. For instance, Israel Lévi designated it an Aramaic testament in his work issued shortly after Pass and Arendzen's publication (Israel Lévi, "Notes sur le texte araméen du Testament de Lévi récemment découvert," *REJ* 54 [1907] 166-80). J. T. Milik called 1Q21, 4Q213 and 4Q214, 1QTestLevi and 4QTestLevi[a, b] (for 1Q21 see D. Barthélemy, O.P. and J. T. Milik, *Discoveries in the Judaean Desert I: Qumran Cave 1* [Oxford: Clarendon Press, 1955] 87-91 [henceforth *DJD*]; for 4Q213, see his "Le Testament de Lévi en araméen: Fragment de la Grotte 4 de Qumrân," *RB* 62 [1955] 398-406). The few departures from this approach include Anders Hultgård, *L'eschatologie des Testaments des Douze Patriarches*, vol. 2, *Composition de l'ouvrage textes et traductions* (Acta Universitatis Upsaliensis;

justment for two reasons. First, as it turns out, *Aramaic Levi* is probably not a testament, lacking as it does the formal characteristics of that genre, most conspicuously a deathbed context for Levi's words.[3] Second, it is misleading to call it by the name of the document for which it served as a source. The designation betrays the bias built into most study of *Aramaic Levi*, and obscures its independent existence prior to *Testament of Levi*. Therefore it is necessary to adopt a new term. The difficulty in doing so lies in *Aramaic Levi*'s fragmentary nature, and the concomitant uncertainty whether we possess its beginning and conclusion. Because those parts of a document are essential for defining positively its genre, and thus classifying it accurately, a name that includes genre designation must be avoided. We settle on the name *Aramaic Levi*, since it captures the document's character—an Aramaic text about Levi, son of Jacob—and avoids the use of genre terminology.

2.1. Previous study of the scope and shape of *Aramaic Levi*

Among the issues addressed in the study of *Aramaic Levi*, none is as pressing as the determination of its contents and its organization.[4]

Historia Religionum 7; Uppsala: Almqvist & Wiksell, 1982) 93, who calls it an "apocryphon," and more recently Jonas Greenfield and Michael Stone, "Remarks on the Aramaic Testament of Levi from the Geniza," *RB* 86 (1979) 214-30, who abandon the term "testament."

[3] While we could construe Levi's call to his children to hear his speech in vv. 82-106 as an address from his sickbed, one would have to posit a rather lengthy sickness-unto-death: after telling the reader in v. 81 that he died at age 137, in v. 82 he says that he summoned his children to hear his words when he was but 118. The one absolutely certain requirement of a testament—the imminent death of the speaker—is ill-served by this document as well. When Levi says in v. 81 that he died at 137, and that he saw three generations before he passed away, we are given to believe that he speaks from *beyond* the grave. One searches known testaments in vain for a parallel to this remarkable first-person disclosure of the speaker's date of death.

[4] Other topics that have drawn attention include the questions of *Aramaic Levi*'s original language, unity, genre, relationship to *Jubilees*, and connection to other priestly-testamentary texts found at Qumran. Opinion is divided rather unevenly on the subject of the text's original language. Since Charles and Cowley's first attempt to answer this question in 1908 ("An Early Source"), the majority of critics have followed them in positing a Hebrew original (see, for instance, Lévi, "Notes" passim). However, J. T. Milik thinks that the text was always in Aramaic (J. T. Milik, "Écrits préesséniens de Qumrân; d'Hénoch à ʿAmram," in *Qumrân. Sa piété, sa théologie et son milieu* [ed. M. Delcor; BEThL 46; Gembloux: Duculot, 1978] 106). The question of its unity is raised by the repetitive nature of Isaac's instructions to Levi and by the awkward shift between the life history and the wisdom speech in the Cambridge fragment. On the matter of genre, although early on scholars simply assumed it to be a testament, a growing number of critics reject that facile definition, controlled as it is by the assumption that *Aramaic Levi* is the same as *Testament of Levi* (see the discussion

Nevertheless, as the following overview of previous studies shows, little careful attention has been given to the matter. Instead, scholarship has been content to presume a nearly complete similarity of content and structure between *Aramaic Levi* and *Testament of Levi*. Perhaps one reason for this is the sporadic and incomplete publication of the witnesses to *Aramaic Levi*. So we begin with a history of the process through which the parts of the text have been published.

2.1.1. Publication of *Aramaic Levi* texts[5]

Before the turn of the century *Aramaic Levi* was unknown, either through ancient references, or through manuscript witnesses. Then in 1896 fragments of a document similar to *Testament of Levi* were discovered in the Cairo Geniza. In 1900 Pass and Arendzen published a Geniza fragment housed in the Taylor-Schechter Collection in the library at Cambridge University.[6] The scrap was one and one-half leaves of vellum, part of a medieval manuscript. Because they recognized the full leaf of the fragment as source material for *Testament of Levi* 11–13,[7] Pass and Arendzen heralded the find as support for those who thought that *Testaments of the Twelve Patriarchs* (henceforth *T12P*) was a Jewish composition.[8] Hence they dubbed the text an Aramaic version of *Testament of Levi*. Oddly, they associated the partial leaf, which has a clear relationship to Genesis 34 and its events, with *Testament of Judah* 5, rather than with *Testament of Levi* 6–7.[9]

Only in 1907 was the remaining fragment of the Cairo Geniza manuscript brought to light. Charles and Cowley published the single leaf located in the Bodleian Library at Oxford, and provided improved readings of Pass and Arendzen's fragment.[10] They too identified the text with *Testament of Levi*, indicating that it covered material similar

---

above). The question of *Aramaic Levi*'s relationship to *Jubilees* has been discussed by numerous commentators and receives renewed attention in chapters three and four of this study. For now, see Pierre Grelot, "Notes sur le Testament araméen de Lévi," *RB* 63 (1956) 391-406. Finally, the relationship between *Aramaic Levi* and other testamentary literature from Qumran attributed to priestly figures has been noted by Milik, "Écrits préesséniens de Qumrân," 103; and by Marinus de Jonge, "The Testament of Levi and 'Aramaic Levi'," 13 (1988) 370-73.

[5] For an overview of texts and editions of *Aramaic Levi* manuscripts currently available see Appendix 1.

[6] H. L. Pass and J. Arendzen, "Fragment."

[7] Ibid., 651.

[8] For a convenient summary of the debate over the Christian or Jewish origins of *T12P*, see H. Dixon Slingerland, *The Testaments of the Twelve Patriarchs: A Critical History of Research* (SBLMS 21; Missoula, MT: Scholars Press, 1977).

[9] Pass and Arendzen, 652.

[10] Charles and Cowley, "An Early Source," 566-83.

to chapters 8–9. They concluded, like Pass and Arendzen, that the text was used as a source by the author of *Testament of Levi*.[11]

In the same article where he produced the Bodleian fragment Charles announced the discovery of additions to the Mt. Athos manuscript of *T12P* which matched some of the Aramaic material quite closely.[12] He published all the Mt. Athos additions[13] in his 1908 critical edition of the Greek versions of *T12P*.[14] The additions include a prayer inserted in the middle of *T. Levi* 2:3, a sentence placed after 5:2, and a lengthy section covering Isaac's instructions to Levi and some of Levi's family history added after 18:2. He recognized Mt. Athos 18:2 as *Aramaic Levi* material because its beginning and conclusion correspond with the Cairo Geniza fragments. But Charles lacked any parallel Aramaic evidence for Mt. Athos 2:3; 5:2, so he did not detect in their case any connection to *Aramaic Levi*.[15]

In 1947 additional fragments of *Aramaic Levi* were discovered in Cave 1 at Qumran. J. T. Milik identified 1Q21 as a manuscript of *Aramaic Levi*, and published it in 1955.[16] He rightly recognized a correspondence between 1Q21 3 and the Cairo Geniza fragment located at Cambridge, column a, lines 1-9.[17] But because of the small size and poor condition of the fragments he could make few additional connections between 1Q21 and the Geniza manuscript. Yet, since by the time *DJD* 1 went to press Milik had identified more substantial manuscripts of *Aramaic Levi* from Cave 4, he could say confidently that 1Q21 was also a copy of the document that served as a source for *Testament of Levi*.[18] His confidence was expressed in the title he gave to the manuscript, "Testament de Lévi."

---

[11] Ibid., 569.

[12] Ibid., 566. In this article Charles printed the portions of the addition that parallel the Bodleian fragment (571-75).

[13] Henceforth cited by the title "Mt. Athos," followed by the point in *Testament of Levi* at which the addition is inserted; e.g., Mt. Athos 2:3.

[14] R. H. Charles, *The Greek Versions of the Testaments of the Twelve Patriarchs* (Oxford: Oxford University, 1908) 29, 37, 245-56.

[15] Greenfield and Stone note that Charles failed to include the prayer of Mt. Athos 2:3 as *Aramaic Levi* material in Appendix III of *Greek Versions* (Michael Stone and Jonas Greenfield, "The Prayer of Levi," *JBL* 112 [1993] 247). Yet without the Qumran evidence—not to be discovered until 1952 and published in 1955—he had no way of knowing or guessing that the prayer of Levi preserved in Mt. Athos 2:3 was genuine *Aramaic Levi* material.

[16] *DJD* 1.87-91.

[17] Henceforth the Cairo Geniza fragments will be cited by the location of the fragment, the column letter and line numbers. For example, Cambridge a 1-9; or Bodl. d 11-18.

[18] Several times Milik notes in his presentation of 1Q21 his awareness then of the 4Q fragments; cf. his comments on 1Q21 4, 32, 37, *DJD* 1.89-90.

In the same year Milik published an important portion of 4Q213. Proving that Mt. Athos 2:3 is part of *Aramaic Levi*, Milik presented the well-known two-column fragment inscribed with Levi's prayer.[19] The parallel between Mt. Athos 2:3 and 4Q213 1 i, ii certified the identification, and it supported the view that a source text for *Testament of Levi* existed in Aramaic among Jewish circles before the testament's composition. It is also noteworthy that at this point Milik identified three Cave 4 manuscripts of the document.[20] He would later reduce the count to just two manuscripts, 4Q213 and 4Q214 (or, 4QTestLevi[a] and 4QTestLevi[b]),[21] only to increase it later to four, 4Q213, 4Q214, 4Q540, and 4Q548.[22]

No additional Qumran manuscripts were published until 1971 when Milik provided a translation of 4Q213 8–9. In the context of a study devoted to the Aramaic Enochic literature from Qumran he cited two *Aramaic Levi* fragments that correspond with *Testament of Levi* 14–15.[23] Then in 1976 Milik produced a transcription of the same material in a fuller study of the Qumran Enoch fragments.[24]

The remaining fragments of *Aramaic Levi* from the Dead Sea scrolls are not published in full. The unfortunate furor over the delay in publication of the Cave 4 scrolls at the beginning of this decade led to the reassignment of the manuscripts to Michael Stone and Jonas Greenfield. Greenfield and Stone have provided some useful preliminary publications.[25] We await the official edition of the manuscripts from Qumran, to be published in a forthcoming *DJD* volume.

---

[19] Milik, "Fragment," 398-406.

[20] Ibid., 399.

[21] J. T. Milik, "Fragment d'une source du Psautier (4Q Ps 89)," *RB* 73 (1976) 95, n. 2.

[22] See Milik, "Écrits préesséniens de Qumrân," 95, where he states that there are five scrolls of *Aramaic Levi* at Qumran. Milik published the fragment of 4Q548 originally as the remnant of a Testament of Amram, in "4Q Visions de ʿAmram et une citation d'Origène," *RB* 79 (1972) 90. It was in private conversation with the author that Milik clarified which scrolls he meant with the reference in the "Écrits" article. For further details and an assessment of Milik's views regarding 4Q540 and 4Q548, see 2.2.6.

[23] J. T. Milik, "Problèmes de la littérature hénochique à la lumière des fragments araméen de Qumrân," *HTR* 64 (1971) 345.

[24] J. T. Milik, *The Books of Enoch: Aramaic Fragments of Qumrân Cave 4* (Oxford: Clarendon, 1976) 23-25.

[25] For Greenfield and Stone's preliminary publications, see Michael Stone and Jonas Greenfield, "The Prayer of Levi," *JBL* 112 (1993) 247-66; and "The First Manuscript of *Aramaic Levi Document* from Qumran," *Museon* 107 (1994) 257-81. In the first they present the fragment known since 1955 when Milik published it in "Fragment," 398-406. The second publication provides their treatment of most of what is classified as 4Q213 material here. For reference to their division of the

2.1.2. Study of the scope and shape of *Aramaic Levi*

The debate about the origins of *T12P* has largely shaped the effort to determine *Aramaic Levi*'s contents and order. From the beginning the key issue in the critical study of *T12P* has been whether it was originally a Jewish or Christian composition. By the turn of the last century the view that it was a Christian composition, dominant since the end of the sixteenth century, had collapsed. Friedrich Schnapp's conclusion that *T12P* came from a Jewish author had won the day.[26] What he required to complete his case was textual evidence that supported his view. The discovery of the Cairo Geniza manuscript of *Aramaic Levi* appeared to be the necessary proof. But what was a boon to Schnapp's adherents was a detriment to any who hoped that the Aramaic document would be studied in its own right, since many simply observed the similarities between *Aramaic Levi* and *Testament of Levi*, and concluded that *Aramaic Levi* was a nearly identical Semitic precursor of the Greek work. As a result *Aramaic Levi* has yet to be reconstructed on the basis of the extant textual evidence for it alone.[27]

In 1900 Wilhelm Bousset made the first contribution to a long line of studies that closely identify *Aramaic Levi* with *Testament of Levi*. Involved in producing a series of articles on *T12P* at the time of Pass and Arendzen's publication, Bousset devoted one of his essays to a discussion of the importance of the Cambridge fragment for understanding *Testament of Levi*'s origins.[28] He argued that the fragment proved the Jewish roots of *Testament of Levi*. Then he demonstrated the close relationship between the explanations of the names of Levi's children in *Testament of Levi* and the etymologies offered in *Aramaic Levi*. He concluded that the testament relied on *Aramaic Levi*, and that the latter ought therefore to be considered in light of the former.

Qumran fragments into more than the three manuscripts we allow here, see 2.2.1 and Appendix 1 below.

[26] Friedrich Schnapp, *Die Testamente der zwölf Patriarchen untersucht* (Halle: Max Niemeyer, 1884).

[27] One must add that its fragmentary state has also been a serious obstacle. While the Cairo Geniza fragments (and the Mt. Athos additions) provide evidence for a Jewish text like *Testament of Levi*, they are only fragments, and leave open the question of what additional material the Jewish text may have contained. To confuse matters further, the discovery of the Qumran fragments introduced material that was not contained within the continuous order of events constituted by the Cairo Geniza fragments and the Mt. Athos additions.

[28] Wilhelm Bousset, "Die Testamente der XII Patriarchen: I. Die Ausscheidung der christlichen Interpolationen," *ZNW* 1 (1900) 187-209; "Die Testamente der XII Patriarchen: II. Composition und Zeit der jüdischen Grundschrift," *ZNW* 1 (1900) 187-209; "Ein aramäisches Fragment des Testamentum Levi," *ZNW* 1 (1900) 344-46. The last article pertains to this discussion.

Charles' subsequent treatment of the Aramaic fragments also made much of the similarities between *Testament of Levi* and *Aramaic Levi*.[29] He felt that *Aramaic Levi* probably served as a direct source for the author of the testament.[30] From that conclusion Charles reached a second, that where the Geniza text of *Aramaic Levi* was faulty it could be reconstructed with the help of *Testament of Levi*. For instance, he apparently called upon *T. Levi* 9:3 to emend הוה, "was," of Bodl. a 15 to read חזה, "saw"; and he relied on *T. Levi* 8:18 to understand the Aramaic of Bodl. a 10-13.[31]

Marinus de Jonge's 1953 dissertation on *T12P* advocates the view that the testaments originated in Christian circles.[32] The thesis allows him to posit a distance between *Aramaic Levi* and *Testament of Levi*, such as one would expect between Jewish and Christian documents. One would also expect, then, that de Jonge's view of the original scope of the Aramaic fragments would be influenced less heavily by *Testament of Levi*. Nevertheless, he determines that what he calls "Original Levi" was itself a text very similar in content to *Testament of Levi*, and that it was adapted by the Christian author of *T12P* for use in his composition.[33] So, for instance, de Jonge argues that the "fragments presuppose a first vision which has been lost and which will have corresponded to the vision found in Testament of Levi ii–v."[34]

De Jonge also advocates using *Testament of Levi*'s shape to determine the structure of *Aramaic Levi*. As the Qumran fragments came to light, the issue of *Aramaic Levi*'s proper arrangement was first introduced. Since the scrolls proved the prayer in Mt. Athos 2:3 to be genuine *Aramaic Levi* material, and since its proper place in the work is not evident from the other manuscript witnesses, critics had to address the question of *Aramaic Levi*'s overall shape for the first time. De Jonge hypothesizes that the prayer's placement in the Mt. Athos manuscript at the beginning of the document and before the Shechem

---

[29] Charles' treatment of the Aramaic material can be found in *Greek Versions*, liii-lxii; "An Early Source," passim; and *The Testaments of the Twelve Patriarchs* (London: Adam and Charles Black, 1908) lxviii-lxxiv.

[30] Charles and Cowley, "An Early Source," 567.

[31] Charles, *Greek Versions*, 246. Yet as demonstrated below such reliance is unwarranted. The Qumran fragments prove Charles' emendation of Bodl. a 15 to be unnecessary, and translation of Bodl. a 10-12 independently of *T. Levi* 8:18 provides a very different reading from that of Charles. See 2.2.5.

[32] Marinus de Jonge, *Testaments of the Twelve Patriarchs* (Assen: Van Gorcum, 1953).

[33] Ibid., 39. De Jonge moderated his position in 1980, in "The Main Issues in the Study of the Testaments of the Twelve Patriarchs," *NTS* 26 (1980) 515. He now accepts the view that the author of *Testament of Levi* did not rely directly on *Aramaic Levi*. Nevertheless, de Jonge's estimate of *Aramaic Levi*'s shape and scope continues to be determined by its correspondences with *Testament of Levi*.

[34] De Jonge, *Testaments*, 38.

incident is an indication of its place in Original Levi, and therefore in
Aramaic Levi.[35] Not surprisingly such an inference, paired with the
assumption of two visions in so-called Original Levi, results in a document remarkably like *Testament of Levi*.

> It is generally accepted that the various Aramaic and Greek
> fragments go back to one document. This will have contained a
> prayer and a vision (comparable to what we find in *Testament of
> Levi* 2–5) and a report on the expedition to Shechem (*Testament
> of Levi* 6). There is a reference to a second vision (cor-
> responding to that in *Testament of Levi* 8), and a very extended
> counterpart of the priestly instructions found in *Testament of
> Levi* 9, but no parallel to *Testament of Levi* 10. The existing
> fragments contain an equivalent to the autobiographical account
> in *Testament of Levi* 11–12 and break off somewhere in a
> passage singing the praise of Wisdom and the wise man
> (corresponding to *Testament of Levi* 13). After that there is
> only a small fragment that can be compared to *Testament of Levi*
> 14,3-4.[36]

When he published the prayer of Levi from Qumran in 1955, J.
T. Milik stated his agreement with de Jonge on the Christian origin of
the testaments.[37] Milik and de Jonge share also the view that *Aramaic
Levi* was a source for the author of *Testament of Levi*, and that the two
documents are therefore comparable in content and structure. Indeed,
his contention that *Aramaic Levi* must have contained at one time material like *Testament of Levi* 16–17 suggests that he thinks *Testament of
Levi* is, in large part, a mirror image of *Aramaic Levi*.[38] Milik's view
that 4Q540 and 4Q548 resemble *Testament of Levi* 17 and 19:1 respectively also implies his adherence to the principle that *Aramaic Levi*
and *Testament of Levi* are similar in content and structure.[39]

In 1956 Pierre Grelot undertook a careful analysis of the relationships among Bodl. a, *Jub.* 30:1–32:9, and *Testament of Levi* 8–9.[40]
He notes that while on occasion one witness is expansive in its narration
and the others are abbreviated, in other places the situation is re-

---

[35] Marinus de Jonge, "Notes on Testament of Levi II-VII," in *Travels in the World
of the Old Testament* (eds. H. van Voss, H. ten Cate, and N. A. van Uchelen; Assen:
Van Gorcum, 1974) 132-45.

[36] Marinus de Jonge, "The Testament of Levi and 'Aramaic Levi'," 369.

[37] Milik, "Le Testament," 405-406.

[38] J. T. Milik, *The Books of Enoch*, 252-53.

[39] See 2.2.6.

[40] Grelot, "Notes," 393-97.

versed.[41] From this he concludes that the Aramaic fragments, *Jubilees*, and *Testament of Levi* all relied independently on a Genesis-midrash centered on the figure of Levi.[42] From the contents of the three texts that depended on it, but especially from *Testament of Levi*, he reconstructs the apocryphon, saying that it contained (1) a prayer followed by (2) a vision, (3) the Shechem incident, (4) another vision, (5) a series of visits to Bethel and Isaac in which Isaac blesses Levi, Jacob invests Levi with the priesthood, and Isaac instructs Levi in proper cultic administration, (6) a life history, and (7) a wisdom speech.[43] Hence Grelot concludes that *Aramaic Levi*, like its source, included two visions.[44] And so like the reconstructions offered by others, Grelot's is in large part controlled by the paradigm of *Testament of Levi*.[45]

Detlev Haupt's 1969 dissertation also concludes that *Testament of Levi* relied on a text very close to *Aramaic Levi* as source material. Of particular interest is Haupt's evaluation of the scope and structure of *Aramaic Levi*. While Haupt's principal aim is to discriminate between the two documents in terms of their content and shape, like the others discussed here he still understands *Aramaic Levi* to contain two visions, basing his conclusion on a reading of *Ar. Levi* 7.[46] He too is largely controlled in his decisions by the model provided by *Testament of Levi*.[47]

In 1970 Jürgen Becker published his dissertation on the origins of *T12P*.[48] He includes an extended discussion of the relationship between the parallel Semitic texts for *Testament of Levi*, *Testament of Naphtali*, and *Testament of Judah*.[49] With Grelot he observes that

---

[41] For example, Bodl. a 14-15 fails to mention that Levi and his entourage had to move from one place to another first to be with Isaac, and then with Jacob. Meanwhile *Jub* 30:26-30 and *Testament of Levi* 9:2b-3a indicate the movement.

[42] Ibid., 406.

[43] Ibid., 405.

[44] Ibid., 395.

[45] Oddly, not only does Grelot have the difficulty of arguing for the existence of a vision for which there is no evidence, but his own analysis encourages a conclusion different from the one that he reaches. If *Aramaic Levi*, *Jubilees*, and *Testament of Levi* relied independently on a single midrash on Genesis, it does not necessarily follow that the episodes which appear in the three separate witnesses must all occur in the hypothetical midrash, much less in one of the witnesses that is incompletely preserved (*Aramaic Levi*). It is more logical to assume that each witness could have developed the midrash in its own way, with additions and deletions reflective of the author's interests.

[46] Detlev Haupt, "Das Testament des Levi. Untersuchungen zu seiner Entstehung und Überlieferungsgeschichte" (Ph.D. diss., Halle, 1969) 51.

[47] For his understanding of *Aramaic Levi* see "Testament," 123.

[48] Jürgen Becker, *Untersuchungen zur Entstehungsgeschichte der Testamente der Zwölf Patriarchen* (AGJU VIII; Leiden: Brill, 1970).

[49] Ibid., 69-128.

Jubilees, *Testament of Levi*, and *Aramaic Levi* differ from one another in expansiveness and brevity, and even omit items that the others contain.[50] He decides that all three go back to a common oral tradition which probably contained two visions, two trips to Isaac, one set of cultic instructions, a genealogy, and a wisdom speech.[51] To infer that at one time there were two visions in *Aramaic Levi* he relies on Grelot's reading of Bodl. a 10-13.[52]

In 1982 Anders Hultgård produced the second volume of his two-volume work on the eschatology of the *T12P*.[53] He includes a discussion of the relationship between *Aramaic Levi* and *Testament of Levi*, and argues that the latter relied on the former.[54] Because he assumes a rather direct relationship between them, he reconstructs *Aramaic Levi* by a simple parallel alignment with *Testament of Levi*. The result is predictable: he posits a text nearly identical with *Testament of Levi* in content and structure.[55]

A departure from the common practice appears in the contribution of Jonas Greenfield and Michael Stone to the Strugnell *Festschrift* of 1991.[56] They suggest that the usual placement of the prayer of Levi at the beginning of *Aramaic Levi* on the basis of its location in the Mt. Athos manuscript is not a reliable procedure.[57] They object that *T. Levi* 4:2, usually cited as evidence that the author had before him a prayer like the one found in Mt. Athos 2:3 and 4Q213 1 i, ii, does not necessarily presuppose that particular prayer. Thus the placement of the prayer remains an open question for Greenfield and Stone.

In a lecture given at the 1991 Madrid Congress on the Dead Sea Scrolls, Émile Puech aligned himself with the view that *Aramaic Levi* can be reconstructed by comparison with *Testament of Levi*.[58] Like

---

[50] Ibid., 82.

[51] Ibid., 86.

[52] Ibid., 77, n. 4.

[53] Anders Hultgård, *L'eschatologie des Testaments des Douze Patriarches* (2 vols.; Acta Universitatis Upsaliensis; Historia Religionum 6 & 7; Uppsala: Almqvist & Wiksell, 1977, 1982).

[54] Ibid., 2:106. Hultgård calls *Aramaic Levi* "l'*Apocryphe de Lévi*."

[55] Ibid., 2:94. Hultgård includes Mt. Athos 5:2 in his reconstructed *Aramaic Levi*. He thinks it corresponds to *T. Levi* 2:10-12 or 4:4, and gives it the title "La fonction expiatoire du sacerdoce de Lévi."

[56] Jonas Greenfield and Michael Stone, "Two Notes on the Aramaic Levi Document," in *Of Scribes and Scrolls* (ed. Harold Attridge, John J. Collins, and Thomas Tobin; Lanham, MD: University Press of America, 1991) 153-61.

[57] Ibid., 154-58.

[58] Émile Puech, "Fragments d'un apocryphe de Lévi et le personnage eschatologique. 4QTestLévi^c-d(?) et 4QAJa," in *The Madrid Congress: Proceedings of the International Congress on the Dead Sea Scrolls, Madrid 18-21 March 1991* (ed. Julio Trebolle Barrera and Luis Vegas Montaner; Studies on the Texts of the Desert of Judah 11; Leiden: Brill, 1993) 2:490-91.

Milik he believes that *Aramaic Levi* can be expanded by acknowledging further Cave 4 manuscripts as *Aramaic Levi* textual material. However he exceeds Milik's count by saying that in addition to 4Q540 and 4Q548, at least one fragment from 4Q541 may reflect something from *T. Levi* 18:2ff.[59] He suggests that 4Q540 be renamed 4QTestLevi[c], 4Q541 be given the title 4QTestLevi[d], and 4Q548 receive the designation 4QTestLevi[e].[60]

Another recent contribution to the discussion highlights the persistent reliance on *Testament of Levi* for defining the scope and order of *Aramaic Levi*. Jarl Henning Ulrichsen attempts to establish the origins of *T12P*, focusing in particular on determining its *Grundschrift*.[61] Within that context he is inevitably caught up in the question of *Aramaic Levi*'s relationship to *Testament of Levi*.[62] Although he dismisses *Aramaic Levi* as being of little use in establishing the *Grundschrift* of *Testament of Levi*,[63] he presents the *Aramaic Levi* material as though it replicates the general contours of *Testament of Levi*. Thus he too assumes that *Aramaic Levi* once contained two visions, the first having simply been lost.[64] His position is especially surprising in light of his view that *Testament of Levi* did not contain two visions early in its existence.[65]

Finally, James Kugel provides a unique perspective in the history of investigation into *Aramaic Levi*'s scope and structure, at least with respect to the question of how it achieved its shape.[66] He takes the unusual approach of positing *Jubilees* as one of *Aramaic Levi*'s three sources; the other two separately contained Levi's two visions known from *Testament of Levi*. Kugel thinks that the two vision sources were merged to create *Aramaic Levi*, and that details from *Jubilees* were also integrated into it to complete its present scope. Like others before him, Kugel assumes that *Aramaic Levi* contained two visions on the basis of a comparison with *Testament of Levi* (which Kugel thinks had *Aramaic Levi* as its source) and on the basis of Bodl. a 10-13.[67]

---

[59] Ibid.

[60] Ibid., 468-69, 490-91.

[61] Jarl Henning Ulrichsen, *Die Grundschrift der Testamente der zwölf Patriarchen: Eine Untersuchung zu Umfang, Inhalt und Eigenart der ursprünglichen Schrift* (Acta Universitatis Upsaliensis; Historia Religionum 10; Uppsala: Almqvist & Wiksell, 1991).

[62] Ibid., 176-87.

[63] Ibid., 186

[64] Ibid., 180-81.

[65] Ibid., 193.

[66] James Kugel, "Levi's Elevation to the Priesthood in Second Temple Writings," *HTR* 86 (1993) 1-64.

[67] Ibid., 12, 27-46, 52-58.

2.2. Reconstructing the scope of *Aramaic Levi*

As the foregoing history of research demonstrates, the little consensus that exists regarding *Aramaic Levi*'s scope and arrangement relies on the general contours of *Testament of Levi*. Now, however, with access to all of the Qumran manuscripts of *Aramaic Levi* it is possible to attain more critical insight on the matter. We begin by establishing *Aramaic Levi*'s contents through an assessment of the textual witnesses and resources usually employed to reconstruct it. They include 4Q213, 4Q214, the Cairo Geniza fragments, the Mt. Athos manuscript additions, 1Q21, *Testament of Levi*, and several other Cave 4 manuscripts.

2.2.1. 4Q213 and 4Q214[68]

We begin with 4Q213-214 since they are the only unquestioned witnesses to *Aramaic Levi*. The Cave 4 fragments hold the preeminent claim to antiquity and reliability, while the youthfulness of the Cairo Geniza manuscript impairs its reliability, philological considerations raise doubts about the Mt. Athos manuscript additions, and the minuscule size of the 1Q21 fragments undermine their usefulness.

4Q213 is a mid- to late second-century manuscript which preserves fifteen fragments of *Aramaic Levi*.[69] At the present time eight fragments have been published in a reliable form.[70] Milik presented the prayer of Levi in 1955,[71] and in 1976 he published two fragments

---

[68] See Appendix 1 for a list of texts and editions of the material from these manuscripts published to date. Find there also a correlation of our fragment assignments and numbering in 4Q213 with the assignments and numbering offered by Greenfield and Stone for a large part of 4Q213 in their recent publication "The First Manuscript," 257-81. As the Appendix explains, it seems Greenfield and Stone divided the two manuscripts, 4Q213 and 4Q214, into at least five. We retain the assignment of fragments made by Milik, trusting in his paleographic judgment. In any case, the fragments' content is the same no matter what manuscript one assigns them to, and they all require arrangement in a reconstructed document. So how one assigns them to manuscripts is in the end largely immaterial to the task of making sense of the whole.

[69] Milik, "Fragment," 397. Milik's paleographic dating of 4Q213 has now been supported by recent Carbon-14 tests. With very accurate methods of testing, 4Q213 was determined to have been written on leather prepared between 190 and 120 BCE; cf. G. Bonani, M. Broshi, I. Carmi, S. Ivy, J. Strugnell, and W. Wölfi, "Radiocarbon Dating of the Dead Sea Scrolls," *Atiqot* 20 (1991) 27-32.

[70] It is true that Robert Eisenman and Michael Wise, *The Dead Sea Scrolls Uncovered* Rockport, MA: Element, 1992) 136-141, have published the majority of the fragments of 4Q213 and 4Q214. However their incomplete treatment of the manuscripts and the errors of transcription and translation prohibit reliance on their work.

[71] Milik, "Fragment," 398-406.

bearing text similar to *Testament of Levi* 14–15.[72] In 1994 Greenfield and Stone published what they label 4QLevi[a] aram; it contains the fragments we label 4Q213 6-8 i, 9–10, Levi's wisdom speech and warnings to his children.[73] In addition to these there are seven more fragments. We can be reasonably sure that parts of at least nine columns of the manuscript have been preserved.

Fragment	Column
1 i	1
1 ii	2
2	3
3	4
4–5	5
6 i	6
6 ii–7	7
8 i, 9–10	8
8 ii	9

Unfortunately fragments 11 through 15 remain unidentified and do not allow any determination regarding their placement in columns.[74]

The ten identifiable fragments of 4Q213 contain a wide range of material, including, among other things, Levi's prayer and the beginning of a vision (frg. 1 i, ii), a speech against exogamous relationships (frg. 2), the conclusion of a vision, Jacob's gift of a tithe to Levi and the ordination and investiture of Levi by Jacob (frg. 3), portions of Isaac's instructions to Levi regarding the cult (frgs. 4–5), Levi's wisdom speech (frgs. 6–7), and words of condemnation for Levi's descendants who pollute the priesthood (frgs. 8–10). Only fragment 2 provides text that is entirely unknown from other witnesses to *Aramaic Levi*, or that has no significant parallel in *Testament of Levi*.

---

[72] Milik, *The Books of Enoch*, 23-25.

[73] Michael Stone and Jonas Greenfield, "The First Manuscript," 257-81.

[74] Fragments 11–14 are the four located at the bottom of PAM 43.260. Fragment 15 is located on PAM 43.242, next to the fragment we label 4Q213 2 (see immediately following). Milik apparently considered our fragment 15, bearing the words כהנות עלמא, to be properly joined to fragment 2; but our own inspection of the fragments leads us to reject his placement; see 3.1.3 for additional discussion of Milik's proposal.

4Q213 2[75]

א וכען ∘[ ]לו מכת[ש]י גבריא	[מן נק[ב]תא ל[ ] 16
]אנתה ותחלל שמה ושם אבוה	[חאבין חוב] 17
]ובההתא וכל	[ב(עליה למש[ר]פה[ ]∘[ ]∘ דה בח[ ] 18
	[בתו]לה זי חבלת שמה ושם אבהתה ואבהתת לכל אחיה 19
	]ול[אבוה ולא מתמחא שם חסדה מן כול עמהא לעלם 20
[זע קדיש∘ מן עמא∘	]ש לכל דרי עלמא ומ[ ]∘∘[ ]∘∘ 21
]מעשר קודש קרבן לאל מן	[ל וח[ ] 22

bottom margin

"from the wom[a]n to [ ]∘. And now ∘[ ]∘∘ the pla[g]ues of men [ ]
[17]the ones incurring guilt [ ] you (or wife?). And she profanes her
name and the name of her father [18][ ] husband(s?) to bu[r]n her [ ]∘ ∘∘
∘∘[ ] and (the?) shame. And every [19]virgin who ruins her name, and
the name of her fathers, she also causes shame to all her brothers [20][and
to] her father. And the reputation of her revilement will not be wiped
out from among all her people forever. [21][ ]∘ for all the generations
of eternity. ∘∘[ ]∘∘ holier (purer?) than the people [22][ ]∘ ∘∘[ ] a holy
tithe, an offering to God from . . . ."

The fragment records a speech, directed probably to Levi, regarding
the impropriety of exogamous relationships.[76] The view taken by the
speaker is clearly hostile to such unions, commanding, perhaps, the
burning of the female (line 18), and referring to the shame of such a
woman. Indeed, after condemning marriage between Jews and non-
Jews the speaker promises that the woman's bad reputation will never
be forgotten (lines 20 and 21). Then the speaker mentions a holy tithe
and an offering to God. The fragment shares a good deal with *Jub.*
30:5-17, the record of an angelic address to Moses.[77] In that text also
the speaker roundly condemns exogamous relationships (30:5-17) after
an account of the sack of Shechem (30:1-4). Since *Jubilees* is widely
understood to have relied on *Aramaic Levi* (or a Levi-literature common to both authors), it is fair to assume that 4Q213 2 reflects *Aramaic*

---

[75] For notes on the readings and an explanation of the translation, see 3.1.3.

[76] Thanks are due to J. T. Milik for a December 1992 conversation with the author
in which he confirmed our reading of the fragment. He also enlarged our understanding of its scope by pointing out that a scrap from a plate of unidentified fragments may
be joined to this fragment; it gives all or part of words in the first portion of lines 16-18.

[77] That it is the speech of angels is clear from 30:18 where the narrator says Levi
will do what "we" do when he serves in God's presence.

Levi's version of what appears in *Jub.* 30:5-17.[78] And we would probably be correct to say that the fragment preserves part of a vision. Of
the three possible places for such an address in *Aramaic Levi*—the
speech of angels to Levi in a dream, Isaac's instructions to Levi, and
Levi's address to his children—this is the most likely context. While
Isaac addresses the issue of marriage (*Ar. Levi* 22-25a), the well-preserved, continuous version of Isaac's teaching in the combined witnesses of the Cairo Geniza manuscript and Mt. Athos 18:2 lacks this
material, and it would be thematically dissonant in Levi's wisdom-oriented speech to his children. Meanwhile it would not be out of place in
an angelic elevation of Levi to the priesthood as a reward for his zeal at
Shechem. And *Jub.* 30:18-20 shows that the source used by its author
closely associated the angel's speech against exogamy with angelic designation of Levi as a priest. In *Aramaic Levi*, as we will see, such an
elevation occurs within a post-Shechem vision. So 4Q213 2 is almost
certainly from a vision that occurred after the Shechem incident.[79]

4Q214 is a second-century BCE manuscript which preserves six
fragments of *Aramaic Levi*.[80] None of them has been published officially. Nevertheless, examination of the fragments in the museum and
on the photograph confirms Milik's identification of 4Q214 as a witness
to *Aramaic Levi*.[81] The six fragments preserve portions of five
columns.

Fragment	*Column*
1–4 i	1
4 ii	2
5	3
6 i	4
6 ii	5

---

[78] For the details of the relationship between *Jub* 30:5-17 and 4Q213 2 (*Aramaic Levi* supp. 22-27), see 3.1.3. That *Jub.* 30:5-17 (and Levi's elevation in 30:18-20) were derived from a vision, see 4.3.2.

[79] Yet another possibility is that the speech is from an extended account of the Shechem incident. In that location one would expect the speaker to be Levi and the address to be part of his self-justification to Jacob. However this seems unlikely in light of the vitriol reserved for the woman who has relations with a foreigner (lines 17-20). One can hardly imagine Levi giving such a speech in the wake of his sister's vio-lation (cf. *T. Levi* 6:8).

[80] Milik, *Books of Enoch*, 244. Milik notes that 4QEn^f and 4Q214 are from the same scribe. Greenfield and Stone will apparently divide this manuscript into two; see Appendix 2 below.

[81] PAM 43.260. To say this manuscript contains six fragments is somewhat mis-leading. Milik had to piece together about twenty different scraps of leather to recon-struct this small manuscript. The photo and the plate in the museum are testimony to a painstaking and brilliant reconstruction.

4Q214 includes a section of Isaac's priestly instructions (frgs. 1–4), a tiny fragment that reflects the instructional material otherwise extant only in Mt. Athos 18:2 (frg. 5), and a larger fragment that provides small portions of the right and left margins of two successive columns, one probably from the life history, and one from the wisdom speech (frg. 6).

2.2.2. The Cairo Geniza manuscript[82]

The Cairo Geniza manuscript preserves two and one-half leaves of a single codex, inscribed on both sides of the vellum.[83] The leaves are not presently located in the same place. A single leaf is held by the Bodleian Library at Oxford, and a one and one-half leaf piece of vellum is located in the University Library at Cambridge. Only after the fragments had been assigned to the two libraries was it discovered that they belong to the same manuscript.[84]

Pass and Arendzen describe the Cambridge fragment as "one complete leaf, and attaching to it a very small portion of a second leaf of a two-column vellum MS."[85] The complete leaf is the left side of a double leaf, and the "small portion of a second leaf" is the right side of the same double leaf. The "one complete leaf" is actually heavily damaged at the top of the interior half, and lacks large pieces of vellum from the exterior half.[86] The preserved "portion of a second leaf" is approximately the bottom third of the interior half; the exterior half is missing completely. As a whole the Cambridge fragment preserves small portions of two columns from early in the document, and four nearly complete columns from a later portion of *Aramaic Levi*.

---

[82] See Appendix 1 for a list of the texts and editions of the Cairo Geniza manuscript.

[83] For a brief description of the Bodleian manuscript see O. Neubauer and A. E. Cowley, *Catalogue of the Hebrew Manuscripts in the Bodleian Library* (Oxford: Clarendon, 1906) 2:274. We preface further description of the fragments by clarifying terminology. One piece of vellum is folded in the middle to provide two equally-sized leaves. Thus a single piece of vellum may also be referred to as a double leaf. In this manuscript a single leaf contains four columns, two on each side of the leather, and a double leaf contains eight columns, four on each side of the leather. The leaf on the right side of a double leaf gives text from the early portion of the document, and the left leaf presents text from the later part. A quire is an assemblage of double leaves, laid one on top of the other, and folded in the middle. A codex is made up of several quires bound together. For terminology and additional details regarding the character of medieval Hebrew manuscripts, see Malachi Beit-Arié, *Hebrew Codicology: Tentative Typology of Technical Practices Employed in Hebrew Dated Medieval Manuscripts* (Jerusalem: Israel Academy of Sciences and Humanities, 1981).

[84] R. H. Charles and A. Cowley, "An Early Source," 566.

[85] H. L. Pass and J. Arendzen, "Fragment," 651.

[86] See the photo provided by Jonas C. Greenfield and Michael E. Stone, "Remarks," 224-25.

The Bodleian fragment is a single leaf, broken on one side and cut nicely on the other.[87] It preserves four columns, almost all of which are visible, apart from some marginal loss of text. It is from the same scribe as the one responsible for the Cambridge fragment, and Charles and Cowley determined it to be from the same manuscript.[88]

The hand is uniform, and suggests an early medieval date for the manuscript, although the dates proposed have varied. Pass and Arendzen assign it a date "scarcely . . . later than the eleventh century."[89] Charles and Cowley add simply, "Possibly it is even earlier."[90] Citing Malachi Beit-Arié, Greenfield and Stone say it is pre-1000.[91] Beit-Arié makes the judgment on the basis of the similarity of the forms of ʾ*aleph* and *mem* in relationship to the "palimpsest fragments of the Palestinian Talmud and of Genesis Rabba."[92]

The manuscript contains a variety of material. The two partial columns of the damaged half leaf in the University Library at Cambridge rehearse the events of Genesis 34. Although the remains are very sketchy, the identification seems certain, since such key words as מילה, "circumcision" (a 23) and חמס, "violence" (b 19) are legible. The columns on the full leaf of the Cambridge fragment come from a later part of the document. They provide Levi's family history (c 1–d 14), a short life history (d 15–e 3), and Levi's speech in praise of wisdom (e 3–f 23). The single leaf stored in the Bodleian Library at Oxford begins with the conclusion of Levi's vision (a 1-13), an account of Isaac's blessing of Levi, his ordination to the priesthood by Jacob, Levi's first priestly action, and a trip from Bethel to Isaac (a 14–b 3). Then follow Isaac's extensive priestly instructions (b 3–d 23). The text breaks off before the conclusion of the instructions.[93]

Certainly prior to the discovery of the Qumran fragments it was only natural to wonder about the degree to which the medieval manuscript contained revisions, expansions, or corruptions introduced over the years; so one might be concerned about its reliability as a source for reconstructing *Aramaic Levi*'s contents. But when the Cairo Geniza manuscript is compared with the Qumran fragments it is clear that the scribe responsible for it worked from a *Vorlage* very similar to the older Qumran text form, and was faithful to it. One significant

---

[87] It is certain that the break indicates this was once a double leaf. See Appendix 2 below for a detailed description of the physical characteristics of the fragment which allow such certainty.

[88] Charles and Cowley, "An Early Source," 566.

[89] Ibid.

[90] Charles and Cowley, "An Early Source," 566.

[91] Greenfield and Stone, "Remarks," 216.

[92] Ibid.

[93] See 2.3 and Appendix 2 for the order of the fragments in the Cairo Geniza manuscript.

indication of the close textual relationship between 4Q213 and the Cairo Geniza manuscript is their shared account of Jacob's gift of a tithe to Levi. Bodl. a 15-16 has the following.

Bodl. a 15-16

15 ‹[ברכ]ני› אדין כדי הוה יעקב

16 [ ] עשר כל מה דיהוה לה כנדרה

"Then when Jacob was [   ]°°° all that was his according to his vow."

Charles filled the lacuna on line 16 with [עשר]בתרי, "with respect to the twelve," and emended הוה, "was," of the previous line to read חזה, "saw," on the basis of *T. Levi* 9:3, which states that Jacob had a vision on this occasion.[94] Greenfield and Stone approve of Charles' emendation of line 15, but supply הוה in the lacuna in line 16 instead of Charles' בתרי.[95] As a result Greenfield and Stone's reconstruction creates a reading in which Jacob has a vision, and as a result tithes his possessions, just as is the case in *T. Levi* 9:3-4. Grelot opposes Charles' emendation, and would clearly reject Greenfield and Stone's thesis. Instead he supplies אבי, "my father," in the lacuna and leaves the הוה of the previous line unchanged.[96] Now, one of the unpublished Qumran fragments proves Grelot correct. 4Q213 3 4 clearly shows the following reading: כ[ד]י הוה יעקב אבי מעשר, "When my father Jacob was tithing." The scribe responsible for the Cairo Geniza manuscript appears to have relied faithfully on a text form like the one found at Qumran.

Another sign of the close relationship between the Geniza Aramaic and 4Q213 are the minimal differences between Isaac's priestly instructions as they appear in both manuscripts. See, for example, the following partial reconstruction of 4Q213 4–5 19-22 on the basis of the corresponding Cairo Geniza material.

---

[94] Charles, *The Greek Versions*, 246.
[95] Greenfield and Stone, "Remarks," 219.
[96] Grelot, "Notes," 404-405.

4Q213 4–5 19-22/Bodl. d 8-15

19 ‏[ובתר ירכאתא רגלין רחי]ען עם קרביא וכלא‎

20 ‏[מליחין במלח כדי חזה לה]ן [כ]מסתן   ובת[ר]‎

21 ‏[נישפא בליל במשחא ו]בת[ר]כלא חמר [נסך]‎

22 ‏[והקטיר עליהון לבנה]להוא עבדך בס[ו]רך‎

["And after the haunches the hindquarters was]hed with the inner parts. And all of them ²⁰salted with salt as is fitting for them, [as much as] they require. And after [this ²¹(the) fine meal mixed with (the) oil. And]afte[r]everything [pour] wine, ²²[and burn over them incense.] Let whatever you do be according to or[der.]"

Filling in the material surrounding the extant Qumran text with the corresponding Geniza Aramaic results in an almost perfect fit.

Of course, some caution must still be exercised when using the Cairo Geniza manuscript to reconstruct *Aramaic Levi*'s contents. In at least two instances the Geniza and Qumran manuscripts differ. For example, although 4Q213 3 2-6 matches Bodl. a 10-16 word-for-word, 4Q213 3 1 also gives ‏כהנותך‎, "your priesthood," a word not found nearby in the Bodleian fragment. The Cairo Geniza text seems to have undergone some change, or relied on a variant text for its *Vorlage*.⁹⁷ In another case reconstruction of 4Q213 6 i 4-6 (a portion of the Levi's hymn in praise of wisdom) using the corresponding Cairo Geniza material (Cambridge e) would require more space than the physical remains allow.⁹⁸

2.2.3. The Mt. Athos manuscript additions⁹⁹

We turn now to the additions to the Mt. Athos manuscript of *Testament of Levi*.¹⁰⁰ The expansions are fully integrated into the Mt. Athos text of the testament, testimony either to the fact that the scribe's *Vorlage* already incorporated the additional material, or he had reason to consider it fitting for inclusion in *Testament of Levi*.¹⁰¹ Charles tells us that the manuscript itself is written "in a good hand of the tenth century."¹⁰²

---

⁹⁷ See 3.1.4 for a discussion of possible reasons for the variation.

⁹⁸ See 3.1.7 for the Geniza text alone. For an attempt to integrate the two witnesses, see Stone and Greenfield, "The First Manuscript," 264.

⁹⁹ See Appendix 1 for the texts and editions of the Mt. Athos additions.

¹⁰⁰ R. H. Charles, *The Greek Versions*, 29, 37, 247-53.

¹⁰¹ Marinus de Jonge, *The Testaments of the Twelve Patriarchs: A Critical Edition of the Greek Text* (PVTG I, 2; Leiden: Brill, 1978) xvii.

¹⁰² R. H. Charles, *The Greek Versions*, xi.

From the moment of their identification scholars suspected that the expansions belonged to the same document extant in the Aramaic fragments from the Cairo Geniza, and with good reason. The first part of the expansion inserted at *T. Levi* 18:2 corresponds with Bodl. b–d, part of Isaac's instructions on proper cultic practice. The last portion matches Cambridge c 3-10, which contains some of Levi's family history. The middle section, equal to four columns of the Geniza Aramaic, gives more of Isaac's instructions and exhortations, and the first part of Levi's family history. Because they are matched by Aramaic material, the opening and closing sections were immediately accepted as Greek witnesses to the corresponding parts of *Aramaic Levi*.[103] And now one of the newly available fragments of 4Q214 offers a very small amount of text matching the middle of the addition at Mt. Athos 18:2.[104] Though the fragment is very small, there can be little doubt about the similarity of the two witnesses. The words preserved on 4Q214 5, תכל בשר, "you will consume meat,"and בשרא, "the meat," fit nowhere else in the extant portions of *Aramaic Levi*. Only in vv. 51-56 of the Greek does the word "flesh" occur.[105] The unpublished Qumran fragment corroborates the reliability of at least a small section of the previously unparalleled middle-portion of the the Mt. Athos expansion at *T. Levi* 18:2.

Mt. Athos 2:3 is a prayer of Levi. Its status as a witness to *Aramaic Levi* was confirmed with Milik's publication in 1955 of two columns of 4Q213 containing the same text in Aramaic. Indication of the close relationship between the Aramaic version and the Greek is the way in which an oddity in the Greek text is explained, and a lacuna in the Aramaic is filled by comparing the two. In the Greek of Levi's prayer he states abruptly, και νυν τεκνα μου μετ εμου. και δος μοι πασας οδους αληθειας, "And now my children are with me. And make all my paths straight." Although it makes *Aramaic Levi* appear to be a testament, the first sentence is nonsense in the context, intruding as it does in a section that is otherwise a general plea for God's guidance and assistance. The Aramaic words preserved at this point are ארחת קשט, "a straight path" (4Q213 1 i 12). If one assumes that the translator misread בני לי, "build for me," as "my children are with me," the odd

---

[103] Charles included it in Appendix III of *Greek Versions*. He correctly excluded Mt. Athos 2:3; 5:2 at the time, since he lacked any evidence that there ever existed an Aramaic form of the same texts.

[104] In "A Preliminary Concordance to the Hebrew and Aramaic Fragments from Qumran Caves II–X Including Especially the Unpublished Material from Cave IV" (Privately printed, Göttingen, 1988), the words on 4Q214 5 are identified as *Ar. Levi* 56, a verse from Mt. Athos 18:2 that lacks Aramaic parallel. This is apparently the fragment Milik mentioned in *Books of Enoch*, 214.

[105] A sign of the Greek translator's frequently free translation is the variation in the term used for flesh; in vv. 51-55 σαρκος is used; κρεας is used only in v. 56.

phrase in the Greek is understandable, and the verb that accompanied the expression "a straight path" becomes apparent.[106] It appears that the Greek translator had an Aramaic *Vorlage* with the words וכען בני לי והב לי (כל) ארחת קשט, "And now, build for me, and make for me every path straight," but misunderstood the first part of the phrase to refer to the presence of Levi's children.

Unfortunately the authenticity of the addition at 5:2 remains in question, lacking as it does parallel Aramaic material. The full text reads (σοι) δοθησεται η ιερατεια και τω σπερματι σου του λειτουργειν τω υψιστω εν μεσω της γης και εξιλασκεσθαι σε επι ταις αγνοιαις της γης.[107] It reminds the reader of the Melchizedek-connection made elsewhere in *Aramaic Levi* with its allusion to Jerusalem/Salem in the phrase εν μεσος της γης, "in the middle of the earth," and with its name for God, a translation of אל עליון, "the Most High God."[108] Although there is no comparable sentence in the Aramaic witnesses to *Aramaic Levi*, given the tenor of the statement, one suspects that there was at one time.[109] Nevertheless, without any Aramaic parallel it is impossible to include it as a witness to *Aramaic Levi*. It is also troubling that we lack any indication regarding its proper place in a reconstructed text of *Aramaic Levi*.[110]

2.2.4. 1Q21

The sixty fragments of 1Q21 were published by J. T. Milik in 1955.[111] He determines that only very few of the fragments can be securely identified as *Aramaic Levi*, at least as it was known already from the Cairo Geniza, and as he knew it from the 4Q fragments at the time.[112] The remaining fragments are so small as to defy identification.

Milik assigns all the fragments to the same manuscript, largely on the basis of their paleographic homogeneity.[113] The letters are al-

---

[106] We owe this insight to Klaus Beyer, *Die aramäischen Texten vom Toten Meer* (Göttingen: Vandenhoeck & Ruprecht, 1984) 193, n. 1.

[107] De Jonge, *Testaments*, 30.

[108] See אל עליון, or its Greek equivalent, in 4Q213 4 ₆; Bodl. b 5-6; d 16; Mt. Athos 18:2, 51. In Bodl. a 20 it appears that אל עלמיא has been written over אל עליון (see 3.1.4; cf. Greenfield and Stone, "Remarks," 220; Grelot, "Notes," 405, also thinks the text originally read עליון).

[109] See the comments of Marinus de Jonge in this regard, in "Notes on Testament of Levi II-VII," 139, n. 24.

[110] In spite of such concerns Hultgård, *L'eschatologie*, 2:94 includes the passage.

[111] *DJD* 1.87-91.

[112] *DJD* 1.87. That Milik had already identified the 4Q material by then is evident in his general comment regarding the relationship of 1Q21 to other material from Qumran (88), and his indication that 1Q21 4 can be linked with a 4Q fragment, and with Bodl. a 15-16.

[113] *DJD* 1.87.

most invisible. Visible letters are fairly uniform. Because of their size it is difficult to use paleography as a means of dating the manuscript. None of the fragments exceeds 4.5 cm in width or 2.5 cm in height. The majority are considerably smaller.

In lieu of a description of the fragments' content—a nearly impossible task due to their minuscule size—attention is directed to those Milik managed to link to existing *Aramaic Levi* material. This will assist in determining the degree to which it is possible to use 1Q21 as a witness to *Aramaic Levi*.

Fragment	*Corresponding Location*
1-2	Bodl. c 3, Mt. Athos 18:2 65-67
3	Bodl. a 1-9
4	4Q213 3, Bodl. a 15-16
5	Bodl. a 14
6	Bodl. a 17
8	Cambridge a–b
26	Bodl. a 1
30	Bodl. b 16
32, 37	4Q213 1 ii 15-18

Milik is not able to relate frgs. 1–2 with certainty to other extant Aramaic text; he does, however, suggest that they relate well to Bodl. c 3 and to Mt. Athos 18:2, 65-67.[114] But in fact, of the three witnesses only Mt. Athos 18:2, 67 contains both key words "kingdom," and "priesthood," though in a sentence that is probably secondary and the result of scribal confusion.[115] Meanwhile Grelot has suggested that frg. 1, which contains the words מלכות כהנותא, precedes Bodl. a 1-7.[116] In his view the match between the two allows one to posit a two-part account by the heavenly angels of the kingdoms Levi will inherit—one of the sword, and one of the priesthood. Grelot's speculative reconstruction has met with generally skeptical reception. Chief among his critics has been Jürgen Becker.[117] He notes that it is not certain that 1Q21 1 is *Aramaic Levi* material, and that the kingdom of the sword could just as easily have been given to Judah. Becker rightly decides that Grelot's reconstruction ought to be received with proper skepticism. Anyway, another reading of the fragment in conjunction with Bodl. a 1-7 is pos-

---

[114] 1Q21 1 2 contains the phrase מלכות כהנותא רבא מן מלכות], "The kingdom of the priesthood is greater than the kingdom of . . . ," while Bodl. c 3 has only the word כהנותא. The Greek text of Mt. Athos 18:2, 67 contains the sentence αυτος και το σπερμα αυτου εσονται αρχη βασιλεων ιερατευμα τω Ισραηλ, "He and his seed will be the beginning of kings, a priesthood for Israel." On the latter, see the discussion cited in the following note.

[115] See the NOTE on this phrase in 3.1.6.

[116] Grelot, "Notes," 393-97.

[117] Becker, *Untersuchungen*, 78-79.

sible. 1Q21 1 may be the remnant of a statement about the comparative
strengths and weaknesses of the kingdoms of the sword and the priesthood, with the latter faring decidedly better in the end. Indeed, that *is*
the sense of what remains at the beginning of Bodl. a.[118] Nevertheless,
without a more certain placement, 1Q21 1 has only a very tentative
place in a reconstructed text of *Aramaic Levi.*

Fragment 3 is the single piece of *Aramaic Levi* that Milik identifies firmly with other *Aramaic Levi* material. The letters on the tiny
scrap of leather match nicely the text of Bodl. a 1-9, especially the appearance of the word זמנין(ו) "times." It can be included among the witnesses to the text of *Aramaic Levi.*

From frg. 4 onward the connections between the fragments and
known *Aramaic Levi* material are tenuous at best. Fragment 4 1 preserves יע[קב מעשר, "Jacob, tithing." Milik thinks it relates to Bodl. a
15-16 and 4Q213 4. However in both of those places the word אבי, "my
father," intervenes between the two words preserved on the fragment.
In frg. 5 there is only יצחק, "Isaac," a name appearing on numerous
other occasions in Bodl. a–b. Fragment 6 gives only וכדי, "And when,"
which Milik aligns with Bodl. a 17. Yet the same consonant cluster appears also at Bodl. b 5; c 1, 22. Milik associates frg. 8—which preserves tantalizing evidence for the final letters of the word
"Jerusalem"—with Cambridge a–b, an account of Genesis 34; yet the
name never occurs in the remains of those two columns. Fragment 26,
bearing the word ארעא, "the land," can be associated with many
manuscripts other than *Aramaic Levi.* The partial remains of a word
that hints at זנות, "harlotry," in frg. 30 does not qualify it for a role in
reconstructing *Aramaic Levi.* Finally, שמיא, "heavens," in frgs. 32 and
37 may link them with 4Q213 1 ii 15-18, but the other letters extant on
frg. 37 do not match the surrounding material of 4Q213 1 ii. In short,
only 1Q21 3 assists one in reconstructing *Aramaic Levi,* and 1Q21 1
may be used to suggest an understanding of the end of Levi's vision,
preserved in Bodl. a 1-9.

2.2.5. *Testament of Levi*

While all of the manuscripts described thus far are textual *witnesses* to
Aramaic Levi, Testament of Levi should be called only a textual *resource* for reconstructing it. Yet most critics, seeing that the author of
Testament of Levi relied on *Aramaic Levi* as a source, conclude that
what appears in the testament can be presumed to have been part of
Aramaic Levi. As a result scholars have consistently used the Greek
testament to supplement the Aramaic document, and to determine its
structure. Most significantly scholars have assumed that the two visions

---

[118] See 3.1.3.

of *Testament of Levi* 2–5; 8 were a part of *Aramaic Levi*.[119]   And
Milik has expressed the view that *Aramaic Levi* contained something
like *Testament of Levi* 16–18, a passage that periodizes the history of
the priesthood according to seventy-weeks and seven-jubilees periods,
and announces the coming of a priestly messiah.[120]   Of course, those
who adhere to these views do not actually attach the additional material
to *Aramaic Levi*.[121]   Instead they only assume that two visions and the
future-oriented material in *Testament of Levi* 16–18 were once a part
of *Aramaic Levi*, but are now lost through the vagaries of time and de-
cay.

The character of the reconstructed document is especially affected if one assumes the Aramaic text contained material like
Testament of Levi 2–5; 16-18. Indeed, the vision in *Testament of Levi*
2–5 is rightly described by one commentator as a "full-blown apocalypse,"[122] and no one who accepts the Christian origin of the present
version of *T12P* disputes the eschatological character of much that appears in *Testament of Levi* 16–18. Assuming the existence of something like *Testament of Levi* 2–5; 16–18 in *Aramaic Levi* would lead
one to view it as an apocalyptic work, at least in part. Yet the indis-
putably authentic portions of *Aramaic Levi* are hardly apocalyptic in
character. The only hints of the genre are Levi's vision, and his
warnings about future apostasy on the part of his descendants.
However, the little of the vision report that has survived does not
record the revelation of heavenly secrets to Levi. At most it announces
Levi's ordination to the priesthood, and gives instruction regarding the
impropriety of exogamy.[123]   Furthermore, the report is only a small
part of a much larger document that is mostly concerned with proper
teaching and cultic practice.[124]   As for Levi's warnings about the future, they are probably the author's proof that Levi predicted the failure of the priesthood in the author's day, not apocalyptic reflections on
the end of time.[125]   For these reasons it is imperative that one conclude
with some certainty whether it is legitimate to posit two visions in

---

[119] See the history of research on the scope of *Aramaic Levi* above for the scholars
associated with this view.

[120] Milik, *Books of Enoch*, 253. See also Puech, "Fragments d'un apocryphe de
Lévi," passim.

[121] See, for example, Marinus de Jonge, "The Testament of Levi and 'Aramaic
Levi,'" 369, quoted above in 2.1.2, who says that *Aramaic Levi* "*will have* contained"
such items (italics ours).

[122] John J. Collins, *The Apocalyptic Imagination* (New York: Crossroad, 1987)
109.

[123] See 3.1.3.

[124] For the passages concerned with the cult and with wisdom, see 3.1.5 and
3.1.7.

[125] For this interpretation of that part of *Aramaic Levi*, see 3.1.7.

Aramaic Levi like those in *Testament of Levi* 2–5; 8 and the existence at one time of material like *Testament of Levi* 16–18.

The notion that *Aramaic Levi* contained material corresponding to *Testament of Levi* 16–18 can be disposed of quickly because it founders on a lack of significant manuscript evidence.[126] Meanwhile the textual witnesses do, at first sight, appear to lend credence to the notion that there were two visions in *Aramaic Levi*. Many think that 4Q213 1 ii 15-18 reflects the beginning of Levi's first vision (especially since it follows Levi's prayer as does the first vision in *T. Levi* 2:4-5), and Bodl. a 1-13 gives the end of the second. In fact, by the reckoning of some, the content of these two passages in *Aramaic Levi* demonstrates the affinity between them and the two visions in *Testament of Levi* 2–5; 8.[127] Moreover, Levi's expression of surprise in Bodl. a 10-13 at having a dream and statement that he hid it in his heart are usually taken to imply that he had not one, but two visions. Yet this list of arguments for positing a double vision in *Aramaic Levi* by comparison with *Testament of Levi*, although impressive at first, evanesces under scrutiny.

But even before considering these arguments we note that the first vision of *Testament of Levi*, at least in its present form, could not have been a part of *Aramaic Levi*. *T. Levi* 2:5–5:7 contains a seven-heaven cosmology. Such an expanded cosmology first appeared in Jewish literature only in the first century CE, well after *Aramaic Levi* was composed, and even after the date of the Qumran fragments of the document.[128] So whatever one's decision regarding the number of dreams in *Aramaic Levi*, it is certain that the very one reported in *T. Levi* 2:5–5:7 may not be attributed also to *Aramaic Levi*.

To return to the arguments for two visions, we begin with the popular notion that the characteristics of the vision reports in 4Q213 1 ii 15-18 and Bodl. a 1-13 reflect the beginning of the first and end of the second visions in *Testament of Levi*. Items often noted include the following.[129] (1) While the first vision of *Testament of Levi* takes

---

[126] But see the view of Puech and Milik, noted in 2.1.2 above.

[127] See virtually all those surveyed in 2.1.2 who posit two visions in *Aramaic Levi* on the basis of comparison with *Testament of Levi*.

[128] For the view that the seven-heaven cosmology first entered Jewish thought in the first century, see Martha Himmelfarb, *Ascent to Heaven in Jewish and Christian Apocalypses* (Oxford: Oxford University, 1993) 32-33, and the works cited there. For the date of the fragments, see above in this section. It is necessary to concede that the seven-heaven cosmology may be a late addition to *Testament of Levi*, leaving open the possibility that the rest of the report was inherited from *Aramaic Levi*. However, that too is unlikely, as the following discussion demonstrates.

[129] James Kugel, "Levi's Elevation to the Priesthood in Second Temple Writings," *HTR* 86 (1993) 27, provides essentially this same list, but as differences between the two visions in *Testament of Levi*. Nevertheless, it is clear that he assumes much the same two dreams appeared also in *Aramaic Levi*.

place at or near Abelmaul and the second occurs at Bethel, 4Q213 1 ii 13 places Levi near Abelmain and Bodl. a 1-13 apparently puts Levi at Bethel. (2) Just as the first vision in *Testament of Levi* mentions one angel and the second includes seven beings, 4Q213 1 ii 18 refers to a single angel and Bodl. a 9 recalls seven heavenly figures. (3) *Testament of Levi* portrays Levi as a celestial voyager who passes through heaven's portals to gather heavenly secrets in his first vision and as the passive recipient of priestly ordination in his second dream, while 4Q213 1 ii 16-18 describes his apparent passage through heaven's gates and his vision of the heavens and their physical characteristics and Bodl. a 1-13 depicts him as the ordinand in a priestly elevation. With respect to the first item, it is true that the first vision of *Testament of Levi* takes place in Abelmaul (*T. Levi* 2:3), and the second occurs in Bethel (*T. Levi* 7:4). But 4Q213 1 ii 13, מן אבל מין, "from Abelmain," makes it clear that in the Aramaic work Levi has left that location before he settles down to dream (line 14).[130] In fact it seems possible that in line 12 Levi announces his intention to travel to his father Jacob (על אבי יעקוב) and only narrates his departure from Abelmain in line 13. Thus he may already be in Bethel for the beginning of the dream narrated after the prayer, which is probably the location in which he finds himself upon waking from a dream in Bodl. a 1-13.[131] As for the contrast between one angel and seven beings, indeed only a single angel appears in 4Q213 1 ii 18 and seven are referenced in Bodl. a 9; but little should be made of this since it is precisely at the point of saying "one angel" that 4Q213 1 breaks off; the other six beings we hear of later could well have appeared in subsequent text. And the language of 4Q213 1 ii 16-18, although suggestive of heavenly travels and the revelation of celestial secrets, can just as easily be understood as a dream Levi had while earthbound; and what little is preserved in this fragment is in no way incompatible with an eventual ordination to the priesthood at the hands of seven heavenly beings in the same vision (Bodl. a 1-13). In short, these often-noted differences between the visions in *Testament of Levi* and between the vision-report texts of *Aramaic Levi* may not be used so readily to posit the existence of two visions in the latter work.[132] In fact, apart from knowledge of *Testament of Levi* it would not necessarily occur to one that the surviving vision-report material in *Aramaic Levi* entails any more than one dream.

---

[130] Kugel, "Levi's Elevation," 10-11, rightly acknowledges this fact.

[131] Unfortunately the truncated report of Levi's movements after his dream in Oxford a does not allow certainty on this score. For more on this possible reading of 4Q213 1 ii 12-13, see 3.1.3 below.

[132] In fact, as we shall see below (5.4.1 and 5.4.3), it is equally likely that all of these indications suggest the author of *Testament of Levi* took an existing single vision and broke it into two.

Having said this, advocates of the two-vision reconstruction of *Aramaic Levi* will hold their ground, saying that comparison of Bodl. a 10-13 with *T. Levi* 8:18-19 demands that one accept two visions in *Aramaic Levi*. Levi says in the testament "When I awoke, I understood that this was like the former. And I hid this also in my heart, and I did not report it to any human being on earth." Meanwhile Bodl. a 10-13 is as follows.

Bodl. a 10-13

10 ‹ואנה אתעירת מן שנתי› אדין

11 אמרת חזוא הוא דן וכדן אנה

12 מתמה די יהוי לה כל חזוא וטמרת

13 אף דן בלבי ולכל אינש לא גליתה

Charles rendered the section beginning with the last word of line 10, "Then I said: 'The one vision is even as the other (?).' I wondered that every vision should be given to him, and I hid this one also in my heart and revealed it to no man." He made the translation by relying on *T. Levi* 8:18-19.[133] Adopting Charles' translation, commentators have assumed that חזוא הוא דן וכדן implies, and אף דן proves that two visions came to Levi in *Aramaic Levi*. Yet when one translates the first Aramaic phrase apart from reliance on *T. Levi* 8:18, as have Greenfield and Stone, the result is far different: "Then I said, 'This is a vision, and thus I am amazed that I should have any vision at all.'" This rendering is clearly superior to Charles' translation. Besides eliminating any strong indication that Levi refers here to a second dream, it respects the syntax of the sentence, not ignoring the *waw* before כדן(ו) as did Charles,[134] and it avoids the awkward circumstance of relying on a Greek text to make sense of the Aramaic.[135] And if one translates וטמרת אף דן בלבי ולכל אינש לא גליתה apart from *T. Levi* 8:19, and without assuming two visions, a translation quite different from Charles' suggests itself. Instead of meaning "also," the particle אף may be used here to emphasize what Levi hid, while the second clause ex-

---

[133] Charles and Cowley, "An Early Source," 578. Charles placed a question mark in parentheses after the first phrase, indicating his own uncertainty regarding its proper translation. For further evidence of the struggle over adequately rendering this phrase, see Grelot, "Notes," 399-400.

[134] See Grelot, "Notes," 400, who dismisses the *waw* as a scribal error.

[135] Jonas Greenfield and Michael Stone, "Remarks," 219. Note that Greenfield and Stone explain לה, "to him," which they emend to לי, "to me," saying that the scribe deliberately transposed the *he* of יהוה with the *yod* of לי to avoid a homograph of the Divine Name. See Joseph Baumgarten, "A New Qumran Substitute for the Divine Name and Mishnah Sukkah 4.5," *JQR* 83 (1992) 1-5, for additional discussion of the Qumran and early Jewish habit of avoiding the production in print of the Divine Name.

pands on and explicates the emphatic statement.[136] The sentence thus reads, "And I hid this very thing in my heart, and I revealed it to no one." On this understanding the sentence, like the one before it, may in no way be taken as conclusive evidence for the presence of two visions in *Aramaic Levi*.[137] And even if we do retain the meaning of "also" for אף, it is not immediately apparent that Levi is referring to a second dream. He may refer to his prayer, or to still another event or disclosure not known to us because of the fragmentary condition of *Aramaic Levi*'s textual witnesses. In any case, had the author wanted to indicate that it was a second dream Levi hid in his heart, the sentence in question was a rather oblique way to make that point. And as we shall see, reconstruction of *Aramaic Levi*'s structure and the physical evidence of the Cairo Geniza manuscript almost completely assure us that the surviving textual evidence allows only one vision in *Aramaic Levi*.

Another reason to hesitate before using *Testament of Levi* as evidence for the content of *Aramaic Levi* is the undeniable penchant on the part of the testament's author for adjusting what he took over from the earlier work.[138] For instance, *T. Levi* 9:3-4 undoubtedly goes back to 4Q213 3 4 (כ[די הוה יעקוב אבי מעשר), "When my father Jacob was tithing") and Bodl. a 15-16 (אדין כדי הוה יעקב [אבי מ[עשר), "Now when my father Jacob was tithing"), yet it differs from *Aramaic Levi* in two important details. *T. Levi* 9:3-4 records Jacob's reception of Levi by noting only that he pays his tithes through Levi. But in the same encounter with Jacob in *Aramaic Levi* Jacob pays his tithes through Levi, then ordains him and invests him with the signs of the priesthood. Similarly, in *Aramaic Levi* Jacob decides of his own accord to make good on his vow to tithe his possessions (4Q213 3 4; Bodl. a 15-16), while according to *Testament of Levi* a vision is required to prompt Jacob's fulfillment of the vow. These examples of *Testament of Levi*'s exegetical appropriation of *Aramaic Levi* caution against accepting *Testament of Levi* as a reliable model for *Aramaic Levi*'s content.[139]

---

136 For similar use of אף, see 11QtgJob 12 1, 9, and the translation of Joseph Fitzmyer and Daniel Harrington, *A Manual of Palestinian Aramaic Texts* (BibOr 34; Rome: Biblical Institute, 1978) 26-29. In at least those two instances—as in our text—אף within a sentence or clause and before a pronoun serves to emphasize the pronoun's referent. Meanwhile a check of other occurrences of אף in Fitzmyer and Harrington's *Manual* also shows that when it occurs at the beginning of a sentence or clause it does mean "also."

137 Perhaps a reading of the sentence like that given it by modern critics was the exegetical hook on which the doubling of visions we see in *Testament of Levi* was hung. For more on this see 5.4.3 below.

138 See 5.1 and 5.3 for the argument that *Testament of Levi* had *Aramaic Levi* as its chief source.

139 See 5.4 for other examples of the way the author of *Testament of Levi* transformed *Aramaic Levi*. For the significance of the particular difference mentioned here, see 3.1.4 and 5.4.4.

For now we are compelled to eschew the long-standing practice of reconstructing *Aramaic Levi*'s contents on the basis of *Testament of Levi*, and of insisting thereby that *Aramaic Levi* contained two visions. There is insufficient textual evidence for two visions, and the view that Levi refers to two dreams in Bodl. a 10-13 rests too precariously on comparison with *T. Levi* 8:18-19 and assumptions about word meanings and referents. We are compelled under these conditions to reconstruct *Aramaic Levi*'s contents not on the basis of comparison with *Testament of Levi*, but on the evidence of its own textual witnesses.

2.2.6. 4Q540, 4Q541, and 4Q548

Other manuscripts from Qumran have been employed as textual resources for reconstructing the scope of *Aramaic Levi*. Most recently Émile Puech has tentatively renamed 4Q540 and 4Q541 as 4QTestLevi[c, d]. Puech finds similarities between the ideas in the latter two manuscripts and those of *Testament of Levi* 17–18.[140] In 4Q541 9 3-4 there is language opposing light and dark, and Puech likens it to *T. Levi* 18:2, 4, 9.[141] In 4Q540 1 he identifies references to fifty-two weeks, and the rebuilding of a house; this he compares with *T. Levi* 17:8-10.[142] Milik agrees with Puech that 4Q540 bears some resemblance to *Testament of Levi* 17, but he rejects the association of 4Q541 with *Testament of Levi* 18.[143] Milik adds 4Q548 as a possible witness to *T. Levi* 19:1.[144]

Milik and Puech make intriguing proposals. However, some difficulties discourage their acceptance.[145] While 4Q540 1, 4Q541 9 3-4, and 4Q548 may resemble *T. Levi* 17:8-10; 18:2, 4, 9; and 19:1, the remaining twenty-three fragments of the second manuscript lack a clear nexus with the Greek testament, and the other two manuscripts share only vague connections with *Testament of Levi*. In addition, Milik's and Puech's suggestions are subject to the same objection raised against all who reconstruct otherwise non-extant *Aramaic Levi* material on the basis of *Testament of Levi*. Their proposals are based on what *Testament of Levi* contains, not on what is known to be part of *Aramaic Levi* from unquestioned witnesses to it. We suggest that it is

---

[140] Puech, "Fragments d'un apocryphe de Lévi," 490-91.

[141] Ibid., 468-69.

[142] Ibid., 482.

[143] Private conversation with the author, 3 December 1992.

[144] Oral communication to Puech, noted in Puech, "Fragments d'un apocryphe de Lévi," 491, n. 48.

[145] Puech seems to acknowledge the difficulties with the question mark in the title of his article; see note 58 above.

perhaps best to reconstruct *Aramaic Levi*, for now, using only the manuscript witnesses that attest, without any doubt, to the document.[146]

2.2.7. Conclusion

Only 1Q21 3, 4Q213, 4Q214, the Cairo Geniza fragments, and the Mt. Athos additions remain as valid textual witnesses to the contents of *Aramaic Levi*. They provide the following items.

Event	*Textual Witness*
The Shechem incident	Cambridge a–b
Prayer of Levi	4Q213 1 i 1–ii 14, Mt. Athos 2:3
Vision	1Q21 3, 4Q213 1 ii 15-18, 4Q213 2, 3 1-3, Bodl. a 1-13
Isaac and Jacob	4Q213 3 4-6, Bodl. a 14–b 1
Isaac's instructions	4Q213 4–5, 4Q214 1–4, 5, Bodl. b 2–d 23, Mt. Athos 18:2
Family and personal history	4Q214 6 i, Cambridge c 3–e 3, Mt. Athos 18:2
Wisdom speech	4Q213 6–7, 4Q214 6 ii, Cambridge e 3–f 23
Warnings to descendants	4Q213 8–10

2.3. Reconstructing the shape of *Aramaic Levi*

As a result of the overlap between the Cairo Geniza fragments and Mt. Athos 18:2 the order of *Aramaic Levi* from the end of the vision to Levi's warnings to his descendants has long been known, and we can be certain that the Shechem episode preceded the foregoing stretch of continuous text.[147] Bodl. a–d gives the end of Levi's vision, his encounter with Isaac and with Jacob, and the beginning of Isaac's instructions. Mt. Athos 18:2 provides Greek text that runs parallel with Bodl. b–d; it continues after Bodl. d breaks off, giving, in Greek, the equivalent of four and one-half columns of Geniza Aramaic. The section records the remainder of Isaac's instructions and the first part of Levi's life history. Before it discontinues, Mt. Athos 18:2 runs parallel with Cambridge c 3-13. Then, after Mt. Athos 18:2 breaks off, Cambridge c 14–f 23 provides the remainder of Levi's life history and much of his wisdom speech. And since Cambridge a–b, the Shechem episode, is located on the right half of the double-leaf Cambridge fragment, we

---

[146] In their favor one can say that Milik and Puech have successfully isolated a body of literature from Qumran that focuses on priestly concerns. It includes, among other manuscripts, 4QQahat, 4QVisions of Amram, 1Q21, 4Q213, 4Q214, and the material just addressed.

[147] See Appendix 2 for a reconstruction of the Cairo Geniza manuscript based on the following observations.

know that it precedes the continuous text that begins with Bodl. a. Additionally, most place 4Q213 8–10 following the wisdom speech, since the fragments give text like *Testament of Levi* 14–15, which follows a similar wisdom address in *Testament of Levi* 13.[148] The order of events resulting from this arrangement follows.

Event	*Textual Witness*
Shechem incident	Cambridge a–b
Unknown	Columns missing[149]
End of the vision	4Q213 3 1-3, Bodl. a 1–13
Isaac and Jacob	4Q213 3 4-6, Bodl. a 14–b 1
Isaac's instructions	4Q213 4–5, 4Q214 1–4, 5, Bodl. b 2–d 23, Mt. Athos 18:2
Family history	4Q214 6 i, Cambridge c 3–e 3, Mt. Athos 18:2
Wisdom speech	4Q213 6–7, 4Q214 6 ii, Cambridge e 3–f 23
Levi's warnings	4Q213 8–10

All that remains is to determine the place of Levi's prayer recorded in Mt. Athos 2:3 and 4Q213 1 i 5–ii 14, and the beginning of the vision that follows the prayer in 4Q213 ii 15-18. 4Q213 2, additional vision report material, also requires placement. Given the order indicated above, the choices are limited: we can either place the prayer and the beginning of the vision before the Shechem incident, or after it. If the former option is taken, *Aramaic Levi* contained two visions, just like *Testament of Levi*; if the latter path is followed, it contained only one vision.

2.3.1. The standard approach to reconstructing the shape of *Aramaic Levi*

The conventional view is that the prayer and the following vision are to be placed before the Shechem incident. This approach rests on three assumptions: there are two visions in *Aramaic Levi*; the placement of the prayer in the Mt. Athos manuscript at the beginning of *Testament of Levi* is indicative of its place in the Aramaic work; and the order of events in the testament may be used reliably as a paradigm for the order of *Aramaic Levi*. Guided by these three assumptions critics con-

---

[148] In spite of reservations about reconstructing *Aramaic Levi* on the basis of *Testament of Levi*, one may accept Milik's judgment in this regard. Moreover, the fragments which preserve the text have a strong physical resemblance to those of the preceding column. In any case, the material in 4Q213 8–10 follows naturally after the wisdom speech.

[149] It is almost certain that this gap amounts to eight columns of Cairo Geniza manuscript Aramaic text. See Appendix 2.

clude that the prayer is the first element in *Aramaic Levi*, followed by the first vision, the Shechem incident, and the second vision.[150]

The principal difficulties with this arrangement are associated with the assumptions on which it is based. Given the conclusion above that the vision-report texts in *Aramaic Levi* (4Q213 1 ii 15-18; Bodl. a 1-13) provide evidence for only one vision, it is unwise to predicate an arrangement of the fragments on the view that there are two. And Greenfield and Stone effectively undermined the presumption that the placement of the prayer in the Mt. Athos manuscript indicates something of its location in *Aramaic Levi*.[151] But most questionable is the premise that one can rely on the shape of the testament to determine the structure of *Aramaic Levi*. In addition to the exegetical differences between the two noted above,[152] a most significant indication that *Testament of Levi* may not be used as a pattern for the *structure* of *Aramaic Levi* is the relationship between Cambridge d 16-19 and *T. Levi* 12:5, and *T. Levi* 5:2-4. The first two passages are nearly identical, each stating briefly the order in which Levi sacked Shechem and was made a priest.

Cambridge d 16-19 (*Ar. Levi* 78)

16 ‹כלארע כנען› ובר שנין [חמ]נה עשרה

17 כדי קטלית אנה לש[כם] ונמרת

18 לעבדי חמסא ובר שנין תשע

19 עשרה כהנית ‹ובר שנין תמנה›

"I was eighteen when I killed Shechem and when I destroyed the doers of violence, and I was nineteen when I became a priest."

T. Levi 12:5

και οκτωκαιδεκα ετων οτε απεκτεινα το Συχεμ. και εννεακαιδεκα ετων ιερατευσα.

"I was eighteen when I killed Shechem, and nineteen when I became a priest."

Aramaic Levi and *T. Levi* 12:5 preserve the same order of events: the sack of Shechem was followed by elevation to the priesthood. *Testament of Levi* adopted Levi's summary statement regarding key events in his life without adjusting it. Yet the order of events presented

---

150 For an example of the standard approach and its results, see Hultgård, *L'eschatologie*, 2:94. For others, see the history of scholarship in 2.1.2.

151 Stone and Greenfield, "The Prayer of Levi," 249-51; "Two Notes," 156-58.

152 See 2.2.5 above.

otherwise by the testament diverges considerably—Levi is elevated to the priesthood (4:2-6; 5:2-4) *before* the Shechem incident (6:3-5).[153] By faithfully reproducing Bodl. d 16-19, *T. Levi* 12:5 proves that its author used *Aramaic Levi*.[154] Then by recounting the substance of the events listed in 12:5 and Bodl. d 16-19 in a different order, *Testament of Levi* also demonstrates its author's tendency to rearrange sources to suit his own purposes. This recognition certainly discourages one from relying on *Testament of Levi* for direction in deciding where to place Levi's prayer and the vision that follows it.

2.3.2. A new understanding of the shape of *Aramaic Levi*

Using only the unquestioned textual evidence for *Aramaic Levi*, the problem of where Levi's prayer and vision belong is easily solved. If we begin by accepting the view that the evidence suggests *Aramaic Levi* contained but one vision, the prayer and the vision may only follow the Shechem incident. Since 4Q213 1 i, ii breaks off after reporting the beginning of a vision,[155] it must precede the end of the vision in Bodl.

---

153 Kugel, "Levi's Elevation," 8, 12, draws attention to this discrepancy as well. He later argues (39-40) that the order of events in Bodl. d 16-19; *T. Levi* 12:5 is explained by *Testament of Levi's* (and by comparison, *Aramaic Levi's*) adoption of "*Jubilees* view on this matter" (39), since the latter document posits Levi's elevation to the priesthood as a reward for his zeal at Shechem, while in Levi's first vision from *Testament of Levi* the covenant of the priesthood is given as a result of prayer to God, and therefore need not have followed the Shechem account. He also notes that *T. Levi* 2:2 gives Levi's age upon arrival at Shechem as "about twenty years old," and suggests that this is "an editorial attempt to blur somewhat the obvious contradiction between *T. Levi* 12.5 . . . and *T. Levi* 5.3" (40, n. 39). His arguments on this matter presuppose that *Aramaic Levi's* author was acquainted with *Jubilees*, and that *T. Levi* 2:2 was part of the earliest form of the document. For our contrary views on the first topic, see 3.2 and 4.2.1; for our judgment that *T. Levi* 2:2 is a late addition meant to bring Original *Testament of Levi* into line with the format of the other testaments, see 5.2.2.

154 The only difference is the absence of the phrase "doers of violence" in *T. Levi* 12:5. This may be a late gloss in the Aramaic textual tradition represented by the Cairo Geniza manuscript, based, perhaps, on *Ar. Levi* 3, where the term עב[ד]י חמסא appears also.

155 The beginning of the vision, 4Q213 1 ii 15-18, is as follows. For a full discussion of the fragment, see 3.1.3.

15 אדין חזיון אחזית]

16 בחזית חזיוא וחזית שמ[יא

17 תחותי רם עד דבק לשמי]א

18 לי תרעי שמיא ומלאך חד]

bottom margin

a.[156] Furthermore, only additional vision-report text may come between the two fragments; hence 4Q213 2, determined to be angelic discourse from a vision report,[157] may be placed somewhere between the beginning of the vision in 4Q213 1 i, ii and its conclusion in Bodl. a. We may also be sure that the Shechem incident precedes the vision, since the angelic speech in 4Q213 2 presumes the reader's knowledge of the event. Moreover, the location of the Shechem incident on the right leaf of the double-leaf Cambridge fragment also requires that it precede the vision. One will recall that the left leaf of the same double-leaf (Cambridge c–f) is the end of the continuous text that begins with the conclusion of the vision in Bodl. a; and since the rest of the vision must immediately precede Bodl. a, the Shechem incident can only come before the vision.[158]

The order of events in *Aramaic Levi* that results from this reconstruction is as follows.

"Then I was shown a vision [   ] [16]when I saw the vision. And I saw heav[en   ] [17]below me, reaching up until (it) touched heave[n   ] [18]to me the gates of heaven, and an angel."

[156] The end of the vision in Bodl. a 1-9 follows. For a full discussion of the fragment, especially of the translation, see 3.1.3.

1   שלמא וכל חמדת בכורי ארעא

2   כולא למאכל ולמלכות חרבא פגשא

3   וקרבא ונחשירותא ועמלא

4   ונצפתא וקטלא וכפנא זמנין תאכול

5   וזמנין תכפן וזמנין תעמול וזמנין

6   תנוח וזמנין תדמוך וזמנין תנוד

7   שנת עינא כען חזי לך הכין רבינך

8   מן כולא והך יהבנא לך רבות שלם

9   עלמא   ונגדו שבעתין מן לותי

"'Peace and all choice first fruits of the [2]whole earth to eat. The reign of the sword has fighting, [3]the battle, the chase, exertion, [4]conflict, and killing and hunger. Sometimes it (the kingdom of the sword) will eat, [5]sometimes it will go hungry; sometimes it will labor, sometimes [6]it will rest; sometimes it will sleep, and sometimes the [7]sleep of the eye will flee. Now see, we established your greatness [8]over all, and how we gave you the anointing of [9]eternal peace.'"

[157] For the text and translation of the fragment, and an explanation of the view that it is part of a vision report, see 2.2.1. For a fuller discussion of the fragment see 3.1.3.

[158] See Appendix 2 for a complete discussion of the Cairo Geniza's scope and shape.

Event	Textual Witness
Shechem incident	Cambridge a–b
Prayer of Levi	4Q213 1 i 1–ii 14, Mt. Athos 2:3
Vision	1Q21 3, 4Q213 1 ii 15-18, 4Q213 2–3 3, Bodl. a 1-13
Isaac and Jacob	4Q213 3 4-6, Bodl. a 14–b 1
Isaac's instructions	4Q213 4–5, 4Q214 1–4, 5, Bodl. b 2–d 23, Mt. Athos 18:2
Family history	4Q214 6 i, Cambridge c 3–e 3, Mt. Athos 18:2
Wisdom speech	4Q213 6–7, 4Q214 6 ii, Cambridge e 3–f 23
Levi's warnings	4Q213 8–10

For all of this, some might object that, apart from the assertion that *Aramaic Levi* contained only one vision, there is nothing in the proposal we have just put forward prohibiting placement of the prayer and the beginning of the vision in 4Q213 1 i, ii before the Shechem episode, and assigning 4Q213 2 to a second dream that follows the sack and that concludes in Bodl. a 1-9. This would match the pattern apparent in *Testament of Levi.* Yet there is a small but significant reference at the beginning of the Greek version of the prayer that requires its placement *after* the violent incident. Before praying, Levi washes his clothing in pure water and his body in running water.[159]

Mt. Athos 2:3, 1-2

[1]Τοτε εγω επλυνα τα ιματια μου, και καθαρισας αυτα εν υδατι καθαρω· [2]και ολος ελουσαμην εν υδατι ζωντι.

"[1]Then I washed my clothing, and I purified them in pure water; [2]and I cleansed my entire self in living water."

According to Lev 15:13 this is the standard self-purification requirement for the זב, a person afflicted with a genital discharge. The combination of garment-laundering and self-purification in running water

---

[159] 4Q213 1 i preserves enough of this line to reassure the reader that it contained this information also. Greenfield and Stone want to detach the ablution from the rest of the prayer in the Greek text. They think the use of τοτε at the beginning of the cleansing and again at the beginning of the prayer suggests two unrelated events are being retold (Stone and Greenfield, "The Prayer of Levi," 249-50). It is more likely that the actions are related—the first, in response to a previous event, prepares for the second.

occurs nowhere else in the Hebrew Bible. But one does not expect Levi to be described as a זר. However, Num 5:2 classifies the leper, the זב, and the corpse-contaminated together as persons too impure for cultic participation. In the context of *Aramaic Levi*, corpse-contamination surely resulted from Levi's attack on Shechem. He was rendered impure because of the inevitable contact he had with the dead while slaying his share of Shechemites. Reading Lev 15:13 and Num 5:2 synoptically, the author arrived at his prescription for self-cleansing.[160] Beginning in such a fashion, it is certain that the prayer must follow Levi's attack on Shechem, not precede it as has been thought. The order proposed above is confirmed.

Some may still object to this limitation of *Aramaic Levi* to one vision, saying that even though the vision following the prayer may be the beginning of the one that concludes in Bodl. a 1-13, it is still possible that the remains of the vision before the Shechem incident, known from *T. Levi* 2:5–5:7, are simply lost to us. Apart from the fact that an argument for the existence of something for which we have no evidence is not particularly convincing, it is to be remembered that the characteristics of the vision introduced after the prayer lead most commentators to identify it as precisely the one we find in *T. Levi* 2:5–5:7.[161] And as we have just demonstrated, that vision report *must* follow the Shechem incident and the prayer.

A last attempt at salvaging two visions for *Aramaic Levi* could come in the claim, then, that what we have are two visions back to back, situated between the prayer and Levi's encounters with Isaac and Jacob. This proposal would also fail, since reconstruction of the Cairo Geniza manuscript makes it nearly certain that there would not be enough room for all that would need to fit between those two points in the narrative.[162] There is an eight-column gap between the narration of the Shechem incident in Cambridge b and the conclusion of the vision in Bodl. a. The prayer in 4Q213 1 i 1–ii 14 and the vision-report

---

160 See also Num 31:20, 23-24, where the requirements for purification after corpse contamination seem to be in effect. Harmonizing readings of the biblical text are common in *Aramaic Levi*. For example, at the end of the vision the angels tell Levi he has received רבות שלם עלמא. This recalls Exod 40:15; Num 25:12-13; and Mal 2:4-7 (see Greenfield and Stone, "Remarks," 218, for their explanation of רבות which legitimates the link with Exod 40:15). Greenfield and Stone connect Levi's act of self-purification to Num 8:21 and suggest that the cleansing referred to in 4Q213 1 i has to do with levitical purity requirements ("The Prayer of Levi," 250). However the unique requirement that the water for self-purification be living or running water is missing from Num 8:21. In fact it is not clear that the Levites' act of purifying themselves "from sin" was actually meant to be an ablution. And if it was, Num 8:7—which indicates that the Levites' washing is to consist of water being sprinkled on them—shows that it was quite different from what Levi did in 4Q213 1 i 6.

161 See 2.2.5 above.

162 For full details, see Appendix 2.

material in 4Q213 1 i 15–2 22 provide already about three and one-half of the missing columns. Allowing for about three more columns to complete the account of the Shechem incident and narrate the transition to Levi's prayer, and another one and one-half columns to complete the vision report, the eight column gap is easily filled. There is no room for two visions with the length and character of those found in *T. Levi* 2:5–5:7; 8:1-19.

2.4. Conclusion

The product of the foregoing chapter is essentially a newly discovered document from Second Temple Judaism. *Aramaic Levi*, as we reconstruct it, is considerably different from the Aramaic *Testament of Levi* known to past scholarship. It contains a single vision, and, as will become evident in the course of our investigation of it and of *Testament of Levi*, many smaller, but no less significant differences vis-à-vis *Testament of Levi*. We turn now to closer examination of *Aramaic Levi* so as to establish its text and determine more completely the character of its contents, to assess the internal evidence for its date and apparent purpose, and to set the stage for understanding its relationship to *Jub.* 30:1–32:9 and *Testament of Levi*, the remaining texts in the Levi-Priestly tradition.

CHAPTER 3 THE LEVI-PRIESTLY TRADITION IN
ARAMAIC LEVI

The center of attention in this chapter is the reconstructed text of
Aramaic Levi. In keeping with the study's overall objective of establishing the shape of the LPT, we limit the scope of our analysis of the
document to a section-by-section clarification of its text, description of
its contents, and assessment of its relationships with other texts in the
LPT. However, we also offer analysis of the apocryphon's reliance on
and differences from the Hebrew Bible and reflection on its author's
purpose as an additional means of sharpening our comprehension of tits
contents. So after presentation of the TEXT and TRANSLATION of each
section of *Aramaic Levi* appears a discussion of text-critical and trans-
lational problems, entitled NOTES ON THE TEXT AND TRANSLATION.
Then follows COMMENT on the text. The COMMENT provides a description of the section's contents; analysis of the biblical sources used
in the section and the manner of their use; reflection on the section's
probable intent; and discussion of its relationship to the whole of
Aramaic Levi and with other texts in the LPT. After treating all of the
extant portions we offer a provisional thesis regarding the relationships
among *Aramaic Levi*, *Jub.* 30:1–32:9, and *Testament of Levi*.[1] Only at
the end of the chapter do we provide some preliminary reflections regarding *Aramaic Levi*'s date, provenance, and purpose.

Having made clear what the chapter is about, it is also necessary
to indicate what it refrains from accomplishing. First, as noted above,
it does not attempt to exhaust all of the issues normally touched upon in
commentaries on ancient texts; instead we restrict ourselves to just
those items mentioned in the last paragraph. Secondly, discussion is
limited to the extant portions of *Aramaic Levi*. Although some speculate that there was at one time considerably more to it, the temptation

---

[1] Only by closer inspection of the contents of *Jub.* 30:1–32:9 and *Testament of
Levi*, in comparison with *Aramaic Levi* (see chapters four and five) can our thesis
move from the domain of speculation to that of probability.

to include reflection on the hypothetical contribution of equally conjectural parts of the document must be resisted.[2]

One other caveat is in order. The purpose here is not to produce an edition of the Cave 4 manuscripts of *Aramaic Levi*, nor a critical edition of all its textual witnesses. That task is left for another occasion. Instead, our aim is only to establish a basic form of the text that may serve further research. So each text section will be represented by the best witness or witnesses to it.[3] The existence of parallel witnesses is indicated in the introduction to each section.[4] Of course, significant differences among the witnesses to a given section will be indicated in the NOTES ON THE TEXT.

3.1. The LPT in *Aramaic Levi*

The versification of the following text of *Aramaic Levi* follows and supplements the standard developed by R. H. Charles in his 1908 publication of the Cairo Geniza and Mt. Athos witnesses.[5] It is necessary to supplement Charles' verse-numbering on two occasions. In keeping with the reconstruction of *Aramaic Levi* developed in chapter two, Levi's prayer and vision are inserted after the Shechem incident (*Ar. Levi* 1-3) and before the end of the vision known from the Cairo Geniza fragments (*Ar. Levi* 4ff). The additional material is cited as *Ar. Levi* supp., followed by the verse number of the supplementary section. Since the supplementary section begins with Levi's prayer, and its versification was established by Milik's 1955 publication of the Aramaic and Greek texts of the prayer, we use his numeration; because the visionary material provided by 4Q213 2 follows the prayer and completes the supplementary section, Milik's versification of the prayer is simply extended by several numbers to cover the additional material.

---

[2] As indicated in chapter two, comparison with *Testament of Levi* has greatly encouraged the view that *Aramaic Levi* included material like that found in *Testament of Levi* 2–5; 16–18.

[3] The principle that guides selection of witnesses for each section is completeness. Often a section of text is covered by several witnesses, but almost always one is more complete than the others. Where the Aramaic and Greek are equally full the Semitic text always takes precedence. On occasion only one witness gives testimony to a section, and then no decision need be made.

[4] In the single instance where the Greek text is the "majority" witness—the prayer of Levi—we also provide the corresponding Aramaic text in parentheses next to its Greek counterpart. In addition, on those occasions when one of the Qumran witnesses provides exceptionally close parallel material to the Cairo Geniza manuscript, the Mt. Athos manuscript additions, or the other Qumran manuscript we indicate such commonalties by underlining the parallel text.

[5] R. H. Charles, *The Greek Versions of the Testaments of the Twelve Patriarchs* (Oxford: Oxford University, 1908) 245-56.

The second place where it is necessary to extend Charles' verse-numbering begins immediately after the last verse of his text, *Ar. Levi* 95. Here 4Q213 continues Levi's wisdom speech after the Cairo Geniza text breaks off. Therefore at this point we add to Charles' versification to account for the additional material provided by the Qumran fragments.

3.1.1. *Ar. Levi* 1-3: The Shechem incident

The Shechem episode appears only in Cambridge a and b, and is very fragmentary. Unfortunately, there are no other manuscript witnesses to this section of *Aramaic Levi*.

TEXT[6]

[למעבד כדין בכל]   [דברת די כלא]   ¹[ו]ממאת למ[

ינח ר°°] [צביין אינון בברתן ונהוי   [ואמרן להון ב]   יעקב אבי וראו[בן

כולן א[ח]ין] וחברין ²גזורו[ ]עורלת בשרכון והתחמיין כו[אתנ] ותהון חתימין כואתן במילת

[°ס ונהוי לכ[ון]

Two and a half columns missing

אחי ואחוי דן   [די הוו בשכם   [א די הוו בשכם   [אחי בכל עדן   ]³

עב[די חמסא ואחוי אינו[נ] יהודה די אנה ושמעון אחי   [°°° ומה מ°°°ס]   [בשכם ומה מ°°°ס   ]

אזלנא לה [ ] [°ד לראובן אחונן די למד°] [שר ושור יהודה קדמא [למ]שבק עאנא

TRANSLATION

¹°°°°°°[ ]°°°that all [ ] to do according to the determination in all[ ] Jacob, my father, and Reu[ben,] and we said to them °[ ]°°° °°°[ ] they found pleasure in our daughter, and we will all be bro[thers] and friends. ²Circumcise the foreskin of your flesh and appear like [us], and you will be sealed like us with the circumcision of [ ]°° and we will be for y[ou]

Two and a half columns missing

³[ ] my brother(s) in every time [ ]° who were in Shechem [ ] my brother(s), and he showed this [ ] in Shechem, and what °°°°[do]ers

---

[6] Since we do not provide here an edition of the text of *Aramaic Levi*—only an attempt to establish its general contours—throughout the transcription we avoid the use of marks above letters denoting the degree of certainty regarding them. Where uncertainty is great enough, and has significant bearing on determining the meaning of the text, it is discussed in the NOTES on the text. Additionally, we only discuss variations in our transcriptions from those offered by other commentators when the meaning of the text is effected. It is to be reiterated that we made our own firsthand examinations of the Cairo Geniza manuscript and of the Qumran fragments.

of violence and Judah told them that I and Simeon my brother had gone to [ ]∘∘ to Reuben our brother who ∘∘∘∘[ ]∘∘ Judah started forward [to le]ave the sheep.

NOTES ON THE TEXT AND TRANSLATION

Ar. Levi 1.]למ ממאת[ו]. Beyer reads לכל מאת, and after it ומד]ינה.[7] Meanwhile Greenfield and Stone provide]שי after מאת.[8] The surviving ink traces support neither Beyer's intriguing proposal, nor Greenfield and Stone's two letters. Rather inspection of the manuscript suggests מ immediately before מאת and לם after מאת and a single space. The ink traces are very faint, though, and prohibit sufficient trust to render the letters in the translation.

Ar. Levi 1.] דברת די כלא [. Beyer provides here על] דברת די כלא אינון, translating " . . . weil er sie hinderten . . . ."[9] Neither the suggestion for the lacuna, nor his discovery of traces of ʾ*aleph* and *yod* at the end of the lemma are convincing. Were one confident that דברת were a Hebraism, it would be possible to translate, "I (you?) said that all . . . ." But that seems an unwarranted treatment of the word. The phrase remains a puzzle.[10]

Ar. Levi 1. כדין. דין is translated by Greenfield and Stone as "law," and by Charles as "right."[11] However, דין in line 32 of Papyrus 7 from Elephantine (entitled "The marriage of Anniah b. Haggai and Yehoyishma") means "judgment" or "stipulation" in a context describing marital obligations. The text reads ויעבד [לה] דין ספרא דנה, "And he shall do to her the law of this document."[12] Although Kraeling rendered דין with "law," the meaning is something like "stipulation." The same may be true in this passage.[13] One suspects that the story uses the term to describe the agreement reached between the Shechemites and the sons of Jacob.

---

[7] Klaus Beyer, *Die aramäischen Texten vom Toten Meer* (Göttingen: Vandenhoeck & Ruprecht, 1984) 195.

[8] Jonas Greenfield and Michael Stone, "Remarks on the Aramaic Testament of Levi from the Geniza," *RB* 86 (1979) 216.

[9] Beyer, *Die aramäischen Texten*, 195.

[10] See also the translation of Jonas Greenfield and Michael Stone, "Appendix III," in H. W. Hollander and M. de Jonge, *The Testaments of the Twelve Patriarchs: A Commentary* (SVTP 8; Leiden: Brill, 1985) 461 (henceforth cited as Greenfield and Stone, "Appendix III"), "according to the manner of all." Previously, in their translation of the same section in "Remarks," 217, they left the entire phrase untranslated.

[11] Greenfield and Stone, "Remarks," 217; R. H. Charles and A. Cowley, "An Early Source of the Testaments of the Patriarchs," *JQR* 19 (1907) 577.

[12] *The Brooklyn Museum Aramaic Papyri* (ed. E. G. Kraeling; New Haven: Yale University, 1953) 204.

[13] See *T. Levi* 6:8, where Levi claims to have acted according to God's determination in the matter of the Shechemites.

Ar. Levi 2. והתחמיון. An imperfect is expected, expressing as it does the consequence of the Shechemites' assent to circumcision. However, it is probably to be read as an imperative, following the previous imperative, גזורו, with the consequence of the action being expressed by the following verb, ותהון.[14]

Ar. Levi 2.]°ס .במילח[. Beyer reads here במילח קושט, " . . . durch die wahre Beschneidung."[15] The word קושט would fit quite comfortably were there leather to reveal its presence. Hence what appears from his transcription to be the actual text is no more than Beyer's good attempt the fill a lacuna.

Ar. Levi 3. אחי ואחוי דן. Charles translates this as "my brother and Dan showed."[16] Without additional evidence we ought to avoid the introduction of still another of Levi's brothers into this retelling of Genesis 34, and translate instead with the more likely "this."

Ar. Levi 3. די למד[°ן שר[. Beyer gives די למד]נח א[שר, "der sich im Osten von Aser aufhalten."[17] Although it is an intriguing proposal, it is too speculative to accept.

Ar. Levi 3. קדמא [למ]שבק עאנא. Charles transcribes thus: קדמא [רי] שבק.[18] There is insufficient space for his reconstruction. Meanwhile Beyer transcribes the phrase as קדמאה ושבק עאנא, and translates it thus: "Und Juda (der älteste anwesende Sohn Jakobs) sprang als erster auf und ließ das Kleinvieh zurück."[19] What he reads as the *he* at the end of קדמא may be ink, but it is of the first letter in the following word.

---

[14] See Greenfield and Stone, "Remarks," 218, where they say that the phrase ought to be rendered "'circumcise the foreskin of your flesh and you will look l[ike us]'—this is based on Gen., 34:15 and התחמיון כואתן matches אם תהיו כמונו" (first noted by Israel Lévi, "Notes sur le texte araméen du Testament de Lévi récemment découvert," *REJ* 54 [1907] 175, n. 5). They seem to assume that the verb is to be translated as an imperfect. Yet in their translation for Appendix III of Hollander and de Jonge's commentary on *Testament of the Twelve Patriarchs* they translate as though they read the verb as an imperative ("Appendix III," 461).

[15] Beyer, *Die aramäischen Texten*, 195. Beyer's markings, however, indicate that he finds the first three letters of the second word to be very faint. Greenfield and Stone, "Appendix III," 461, translate as though they have accepted Beyer's view, although they leave a portion of the words "of truth" in brackets, denoting their recognition that not all of the word remains visible.

[16] R. H. Charles, *APOT* II, 364. See also Anders Hultgård, *L'eschatologie des Testaments des Douze Patriarches*, vol. 2, *Composition de l'ouvrage textes et traductions* (Acta Universitatis Upsaliensis; Historia Religionum 6; Uppsala: Almqvist & Wiksell, 1982) 97, who thinks the name of Dan appears here.

[17] Beyer, *Die aramäischen Texten*, 195.

[18] Charles, *Greek Versions*, 245.

[19] Beyer, *Die aramäischen Texten*, 195.

COMMENT

Due to the fragmentary state of the sole witness to this section (Cambridge a and b), it is difficult to describe its precise contents. However, it is nearly certain that it retells the events of Genesis 34. References to Shechem, Simeon, desire for "our daughter,"[20] circumcision, and deeds of violence suggest that much. Also, comparison with Genesis 34, and with *Testament of Levi* 6–7, for which *Aramaic Levi* probably served as a source,[21] allows one to draw a number of conclusions about the account. First, mention of Jacob and Reuben in *Ar. Levi* 1 exceeds the details of Genesis 34 and probably parallels *T. Levi* 6:3 where Levi suggests negotiating the Shechemites' circumcision.[22] Second, unlike *Testament of Levi* 6–7 this account seems to dwell at some length on the proposal that the Shechemites become like Jacob and his sons (vv. 1-2), and so evinces none of the tentativeness regarding the deceit of later retellings.[23] Third, this account may have provided a more detailed description of the actual sack of Shechem than the one found in *Testament of Levi* (cf. *Ar. Levi* 3; *T. Levi* 6:4-5).[24] Nevertheless, and lastly, the two accounts are still probably connected by the use of the Aramaic tradition on the part of the author of the Greek testament; see, for example, the parallels among the references to the finishing off of "doers of violence" in *Ar. Levi* 3 and 78 and *T. Levi* 5:4a and 12:5. Unfortunately, because the text breaks off so soon it cannot be known whether *Aramaic Levi* preserves Jacob's reproof and Levi's self-justification (cf. *T. Levi* 6:6–7:4).

Due to the poor preservation of the section it is also difficult to say much concerning *Aramaic Levi*'s use of sources. Certainly Genesis 34 stands behind this account, but the biblical story is embellished here

---

[20] This is the text's circumlocution for Dinah, Levi's *sister*, and Jacob's *daughter*.

[21] For discussion of the relationship between *Aramaic Levi* and *Testament of Levi*, see 3.3 and 5.2.

[22] Cf. the ᵐ text of Gen 34:13-17, where Jacob's sons make the deal; the ᵰ text of Gen 34:14, where Levi and Simeon are the negotiators; and Theodotus in Eusebius, *Praeparatio evangelica* 9.22.5-7, where Jacob makes the arrangements.

[23] The Shechem incident is recounted not only here, and in *Jubilees* and *Testament of Levi*, but appears also in Josephus, *Ant.* 1 §§ 337-340; Theodotus in Eusebius, *Praeparatio Evangelica* 9.22.4-12; Judith 9:2-4; Philo, *De migratione Abrahami* 224; *De mutatione nominum* 193-95; 199-200; Pseudo-Philo, *Liber antiquitam biblicarum* 8:7. For a study of the Theodotus account, see John J. Collins, "The Epic of Theodotus and the Hellenism of the Hasmoneans," *HTR* 73 (1980) 91-104. See also Reinhard Pummer, "Genesis 34 in Jewish Writings of the Hellenistic and Roman Periods," *HTR* 75 (1982) 177-88; and T. Baarda, "The Shechem Episode in the Testament of Levi," in *Sacred History and Sacred Texts* (eds. J. N. Bremmer and Florentino García Martínez; Kampen: Pharos, 1992) 11-73.

[24] This is also the view of Jürgen Becker, *Untersuchungen zur Entstehungsgeschichte der Testamente der zwölf Patriarchen* (AGJU VIII; Leiden: Brill, 1970) 77; and Hultgård, *L'eschatologie*, 2:96.

with considerable detail. The appearance of Jacob and Reuben at the beginning (*Ar. Levi* 1), and of Reuben and Judah at the end (*Ar. Levi* 3) prove that to be the case.[25] These indications that the account exceeds the details of the biblical narrative do suggest that *Aramaic Levi* relied on another tradition as well, one in which the story had been developed already beyond Genesis 34.[26]

Judging from the way Levi is treated subsequently in *Aramaic Levi*—as a hero of Israel for his zealous protection of communal purity—it is fair to say that the author's intent in reshaping Genesis 34 was to depict Levi as justified and righteous in his action against Shechem. Like the brief account in *Jub.* 30:1-4, 24-25 and the longer version in *T. Levi* 6:3–7:4, the aim of the narrative is to elevate Levi from the biblical role of the deceitful and intemperate son of Jacob to his pseudepigraphical position of the archetypal defender of Jewish communal integrity.

Comment on subsequent sections of *Aramaic Levi* shows that the portion fits well with Levi's prayer in which he articulates his concern for purity and his sense that the world is divisible between those who maintain purity and those who pursue evil ends (*Ar. Levi* supp. 7ff.). The prayer is also linked to the account of the incident at Shechem since it amounts to a bold claim to the priestly office as a position from which Levi can continue to exercise his zeal for communal integrity (*Ar. Levi* supp. 17ff.). The Shechem episode blends well with Levi's vision in which he is elevated to the priesthood, apparently as a result of his action at Shechem and his plea for the office (*Ar. Levi* supp. 20-27, 4-7). It is also nicely supplemented by Isaac's recognition of Levi as a priest in his blessing (*Ar. Levi* 8), by Jacob's similar acknowledgement expressed in his appointment of Levi as a priest (*Ar. Levi* 9-11), and by Isaac's instructions which also emphasize purity (*Ar. Levi* 13-61). Levi's life history is connected with the story of Shechem's sack by the mention of it in *Ar. Levi* 78, and especially by the apparent

---

[25] Perhaps it is this fragment to which Milik refers when he says that he thinks *Aramaic Levi* records the gift of pasturage to the sons of Jacob, mentioning Levi, Reuben, Judah, and one other unidentified brother (J. T. Milik, "Écrits préesséniens de Qumrân; d'Hénoch à ꞌAmram," in *Qumrân. Sa piété, sa théologie et son milieu* [ed. M. Delcor, BEThL 46; Gembloux: Duculot, 1978] 96). It is strange that we hear of Reuben and Judah, since Genesis 34 mentions explicitly only Simeon and Levi's part in the slaughter. Nevertheless it is hard to see how the phrase in *Ar. Levi* 3, "Judah hastened to leave the sheep," fits the context Milik proposes. It seems more likely that the reference continues an elaboration of the story from Genesis, an expansion in which Judah has become a named partner in the battle.

[26] In fact, when *Jub.* 30:1–32:9 is compared with *Aramaic Levi*, it seems likely that *Aramaic Levi* (and *Jubilees*) had a Levi-apocryphon as a source for this section of the text. See 3.2 and 4.3.1.

quotation of *Ar. Levi* 3 in the same verse.[27] Less obvious is the connection between this first passage and Levi's speech to his children.[28]

From the little of the account that survives, it can be linked to similar material in *T. Levi* 6:3–7:4.[29] However, the similarities with *Jub.* 30:1-4, 24-25 are not as striking, the latter text being the briefest report of the Shechem episode among the LPT texts which appear after Malachi.

3.1.2. *Ar. Levi* supp. 1-19: Levi's Prayer

Levi's prayer is attested in 4Q213 1 i 1–ii 10 and Mt. Athos 2:3. The Qumran text, though generous at this point, is still quite fragmentary in comparison with the full version of the prayer in the Mt. Athos manuscript. Thus the text of Mt. Athos 2:3 is presented with the Aramaic material inserted within parentheses after the corresponding Greek text, which is underlined. For the differences between the two versions, see the NOTES below.

TEXT

[s1]Τοτε <u>εγω</u> (אנה) επλυνα τα ιματια μου, και καθαρισας αυτα εν υδατι καθαρω [s2]και ολος <u>ελουσαμην</u> (אתרחע[ת) εν υδατι ζωντι· <u>και πασας</u> (וכל) τας οδους μου εποιησα ευθειας. [s3]τοτε τους οφθαλμους μου και το προσωπον μου <u>πρα</u> <u>προς τον ουρανον</u> (נטלת לשמיא), και το στομα μου ηνοιξα και ελαλησα [s4]<u>και</u> <u>τους δακτυλους των χειρων μου και τας χειρας μου</u> (ואצבעת כפי ידי) ανεπετασα εις αληθειαν κατεναντι των αγιων. και ηυξαμην και <u>ειπα</u>· [s5]<u>Κυριε</u> (ו[אמרת מרי אנתה) γινωσκεις πασας τας καρδιας και παντας τους διαλογισμους εννοιων· <u>συ μονος επιστασαι</u> (א[נתה בלחודיך ידע). [s6]<u>και</u> νυν τεκνα μου μετ εμου. και δος μοι πασας <u>οδους αληθειας</u>· [s7]<u>μακρυνον</u> (ארחק קשט ארחת) απ εμου, Κυριε, το πνευμα το αδικον και διαλογισμον τον <u>πονηρον (ms ων των</u> <u>πονηρων) και πορνειαν</u> (וב[אישא וזנותא), και υβριν <u>αποστρεψον</u> (דחא) απ εμου.

---

[27] As it turns out, this may be an important indication that the author of *Aramaic Levi*, while relying on a source for the Shechem episode, and for a good bit of the entire document, supplemented the source with another, or with his own composition reciting Levi's major deeds. For more on this, see below, the closing section of 3.1.6 and 3.2.

[28] As we indicate in 3.2 below, this turns out to be a hint that the speech is an addition to an existing source adapted by the author of *Aramaic Levi*.

[29] See especially *T. Levi* 5:4a and 12:5, and their relationship to *Ar. Levi* 3 and 78. See the comments above. It is worth noting that one of the opponents of the notion that *Testament of Levi* relied on *Aramaic Levi*, Jürgen Becker, says about this whole section of the Aramaic document that it is too fragmentary to permit any conclusions; yet he completes his brief remarks on *Ar. Levi* 1-3 with the observation that the passage *cannot* be directly related to *Testament of Levi* 6–7 (*Untersuchungen*, 77).

[s8]Δειχθητω μοι, Δεσποτα, το πνευμα το αγιον, και βουλην και <u>σοφιαν και</u>
<u>γνωσιν και ισχυν</u> (ח[כמה ומדע ובורה]) δος μοι [s9]ποιησαι τα (ms το) αρεσκοντα
σοι και <u>ευρειν χαριν ενωπιον σου</u> (לא[שכחה רחמיך קדמי]ך) και αινειν τους
λογους σου μετ εμου, Κυριε· [s10]και <u>μη κατισχυσατω με πας σατανας</u>
(א[ל תשלם בי כל שטן]) πλανησαι με απο της οδου σου. [s11]και ελεησον <u>με και</u>
<u>προσαγαγε με ειναι σου</u> (ע[לי מרי וקרבני למהוא לכה]) δουλος και λατρευσαι σοι
καλως· [s12]τειχος ειρηνης σου γενεσθαι κυκλω μου· και σκεπη σου της
δυναστειας σκεπασατω απο παντος κακου. [s13]παραδους διο δη και την
ανομιαν εξαλειψον υπο κατωθεν του ουρανου· και συντελεσαι την ανομιαν
απο προσωπου της γης [s14]καθαρισον την καρδιαν μου, Δεσποτα, απο πασης
ακαθαρσιας, και προσαρωμαι προς σε αυτος· [s15]και μη αποστρεψεις το
προσωπον σου απο του υιου παιδος σου Ιακωβ. συ, <u>Κυριε, ευλογησας</u> (ברכ[ת]
מרי·) τον Αβρααμ πατερα μου και Σαρραν μητερα μου, [s16]και ειπας δουναι
αυτοις <u>σπερμα δικαιον</u> (זרע דק]שטא[) ευλογημενον εις τους αιωνας.
[s17]εισακουσον δε και <u>της φωνης του παιδος σου</u> (צלות עבד]ך[) Λευι γενεσθαι
σοι εγγυς, [s18]και μετοχον ποιησον τοις λογοις σου ποιειν <u>κρισιν αληθινην</u>
<u>εις παντα</u> (דין קשט לכ]ל[) τον αιωνα, εμε και τους υιους μου εις πασας τας
γενεας των αιωνων· [s19]και μη αποστησης <u>τον υιον του παιδος σου απο του</u>
<u>προσωπου</u> (לבר עבדך מן קד]מי]ך) σου πασας τας ημερας του αιωνος. και
εσιωπησα ετι δεομενος.

TRANSLATION

[s1]Then I washed my garments and I was cleansing them in pure water.
[s2]And my whole body I washed in living water, and I made all my paths
straight. [s3]Then I lifted my eyes and face toward heaven, and I opened
my mouth and I spoke. [s4]And I spread out the fingers of my hands and
my hands truly before the holy ones. And I prayed and I said,
[s5]"Lord, you know all the hearts, and all the plans of the [Greek text
corrupt?] thoughts you alone know. [s6]And now, my children are with
me, and give me all the paths of truth. [s7]Remove from me, Lord, the
unrighteous spirit, wicked thought, and fornication; and turn away
pride from me. [s8]Show me, Lord, the holy spirit, and give to me counsel, wisdom, knowledge and strength [s9]to do that which is pleasing to
you and find favor before you, and to tell your words [text corrupt?]
with me, Lord. [s10]And do not allow any satan to have dominion over
me, to lead me from your path. [s11]Have mercy on me [Aramaic adds:
"Lord"], and draw me near to be your servant, and to serve you well.
[s12]Let the wall of your peace surround me, and let the covering of your
power protect (me) from every evil. [s13]On which account, handing

over even lawlessness, eliminate (it) from under heaven, and bring to an end lawlessness from the face of the earth. [s14]Purify my heart, Lord, from all impurity, and let me be raised to you. [s15]And do not turn your face from the son of your servant, Jacob, you, Lord, who blessed my father Abraham and Sarah my mother. [s16]And you said (you would) give them a righteous seed, blessed forever. [s17]Listen also to the voice [Aramaic reads: prayer] of your servant, Levi, to be near to you, [s18]and make (me) a partner with your words, to do true judgment forever, me and my sons, for all the generations of the ages. [s19]And do not remove the son of your servant from before your presence all the days of eternity." And I grew silent, still praying.

NOTES ON THE TEXT AND TRANSLATION[30]

Ar. Levi supp. 1. Prior to the first verse of the prayer 4Q213 1 i preserves part of one line. It reads ןֵה.

Ar. Levi supp. 4. και τους δακτυλους των χειρων μου και τας χειρας μου (ואצבעת כפי ידי) ανεπετασα εις αληθειαν κατεναντι των αγιων. There are two difficulties in the verse.[31] The first is the meaning of εις αληθειαν, "toward truth." The second is the meaning of των αγιων, "the holy ones." The phrase "toward truth" is without satisfactory explanation in the secondary literature, in spite of Jacobson's attempt to clarify it in light of rabbinic texts of a much later period.[32] As for the proper translation of των αγιων—whether it is "the holy ones" or "holy things"—little can be said with certainty, although treating it as a personal designation is most sensible in the context.[33] As a whole the verse is perplexing, and there seems to be little basis for clarity on these two questions.

---

[30] Only the most significant textual difficulties are addressed here. For a recent treatment of the text of the Aramaic fragment and the Greek text, see Michael Stone and Jonas Greenfield, "The Prayer of Levi," *JBL* 112 (1993) 247-66.

[31] Stone and Greenfield, "Prayer," 260-61, count a third difficulty in the double-occurrence of χειρ. However, as Detlev Haupt, "Das Testament des Levi. Untersuchungen zu seiner Entstehung und Überlieferungsgeschichte" (Ph.D. diss., Halle, 1969) 9, n. 28, points out, the twofold use of the Greek word may reflect an Aramaic *Vorlage* that included כף and יד.

[32] Howard Jacobson, "The Position of the Fingers During the Priestly Blessing," *RevQ* 9 (1977) 259, n. 2, suggests that "truth" may be a circumlocution for God, as it is in *y. Sanh.* 1.18a; *b. Ber.* 14a-b. The well known difficulty with citing later texts from rabbinic literature to illuminate documents of a much earlier provenance makes this an uncertain explanation.

[33] Stone and Greenfield, "Prayer of Levi," 261, n. 24, suggest that comparison with 11QPsᵃ 24 3-7 (=Syriac Psalm 3:3-4) indicates των αγιων might derive from a Semitic *Vorlage* like קדישין or קודשין, with the implication that it read "holy habitations," like the Syriac Psalm.

Ar. Levi supp. 5. εννοιων. Stone and Greenfield suggest רעיוניא, "thoughts," as an Aramaic *Vorlage* for this problematic word.[34] Another possibility is that εν νοω, "in mind(s)," is what the translator intended.[35] In the end, however, any translation can be only a best guess.

Ar. Levi supp. 6. και νυν τεκνα μου μετ εμου. και δος μοι πασας οδους αληθειας. While the first part of the verse (και νυν τεκνα μου μετ εμου) might be taken as evidence of the testamentary character of the work, it is almost certainly a misreading of וכען בני לי, "And now, build for me . . ."[36] The rest of the line is easily retroverted into Aramaic, והב לי כל ארחת קשט, reading, "and give to me all straight paths [or: every straight path]."[37] The question is whether the misreading was intentional, or simply amounted to a translator's failure to understand the Aramaic. The last option seems more probable; indeed, it is possible that the scribe responsible for the merger of the prayer with the rest of *Testament of Levi*, thinking in testamentary categories, easily misread בני לי, "Build for me," as "My children are with me."[38]

Ar. Levi supp. 9. רחמיך. Stone and Greenfield rightly emend this to read רחמין, "mercy, favor," with the Greek text.[39]

Ar. Levi supp. 9. και αινειν τους λογους σου μετ εμου, κυριε. There is no room in the Aramaic fragment for the phrase.[40]

Ar. Levi supp. 9. דשפיר ודטב קדמיך. The phrase, translated as "which is of value and good before you," does not appear in the Greek, but is present in the Aramaic. It was probably lost through scribal homoioteleuton (קדמיך1°∩2°; the first occurrence of the word appears at the end of the preceding Aramaic lemma).

Ar. Levi supp. 11. מרי. The word is omitted in the Greek.

Ar. Levi supp. 12-15a. The absence of parallel Aramaic material reflects the fact that the top portions of the two columns in 4Q213 1 i, ii are missing. In fact 4Q213 1 ii 4 preserves לען, but it may

---

[34] Stone and Greenfield, "Prayer of Levi," 261. They make the proposal by comparison with the Theodotionic text of Dan 2:29, 30; 4:16.

[35] The suggestion of Prof. James VanderKam, University of Notre Dame.

[36] Oddly, few have noted the disruptive and unusual character of the interjection; however, see Haupt, "Testament," 9, n. 32, who simply says, "Die Wendung is unklar. Offenbar is der Text zerstört."

[37] Beyer, *Die aramäischen Texten*,193, n. 1.

[38] Jonas Greenfield and Michael Stone, "Two Notes on the Aramaic Levi Document," in *Of Scribes and Scrolls* (eds. H. Attridge, John Collins, and T. Tobin; Lanham, MD: University Press of America, 1990) 155-56; and "Prayer of Levi," 249, 251, 259, read with the Greek text.

[39] Stone and Greenfield, "Prayer of Levi," 261.

[40] So also Stone and Greenfield, "Prayer of Levi," 262.

not be reliably placed in relationship to any corresponding text in the Greek version of the prayer.[41]

Ar. Levi supp. 15. Ιακωβ. συ. Stone and Greenfield point out that there is room for a hemistych between these two words in the Aramaic text.[42]

COMMENT

Levi's prayer exhibits a loose structure. In *Ar. Levi* supp. 1-4 he readies himself for prayer in a manner reminiscent of preparation for cultic-sacrificial service after a person incurs impurity.[43] He washes himself and his garments, he corrects his own ways, and he positions himself for prayer, with face lifted heavenward, and hands and fingers properly positioned. Then in *Ar. Levi* supp. 5-9 his prayer begins with a section that pleads for God's purification from evil and wickedness, and for an infusion of the divine gifts of counsel, wisdom, knowledge, and strength; it concludes with Levi's reason for requesting these things—he wants to serve God and find favor in God's eyes. Then in *Ar. Levi* supp. 10 Levi expresses his desire to be protected from external evil. Following that *Ar. Levi* supp. 11-19 gives a litany of the three themes articulated to that point, namely that Levi be purified, that the evil of the world be conquered, and that Levi be elevated to God's service in the battle against impurity in creation.

The text is rich in biblical allusions.[44] Prior to beginning his prayer Levi washes himself and his clothing in a fashion that suggests the purification procedures one might undertake to alleviate corpse-contamination (*Ar. Levi* supp. 1; cf. Lev 15:13ff and Num 5:2; see also Num 31:20, 23-24, where the rules for cleansing after corpse-contamination seem to be in effect, if one assumes that bodily washing was required as well).[45] The prayer itself appears to "derive from a

---

[41] This is the view also of Stone and Greenfield, "Prayer," 264; however, see Joseph Fitzmyer and D. J. Harrington, *A Manual of Palestinian Aramaic Texts* (Rome: Biblical Institute Press, 1978) 88-89, and Robert Eisenman and Michael Wise, *The Dead Sea Scrolls Uncovered* (Rockport, MA: Element, 1992) 137, who think one can reconstruct thus: לעׂ]ינׁיך.

[42] Ibid., 264. See also Fitzmyer and Harrington, *Manual*, 90.

[43] See below, in this section, for the view that Levi's washing is the proper action after corpse-contamination.

[44] For many more such illusions, and for a very complete listing of nonbiblical parallels, see Haupt, "Testament," 8-11, nn. 13-55. It must be admitted, however, that many of the allusions and/or parallels adduced by Haupt are vague at best.

[45] Just enough remains in the Aramaic to suggest that it too contained the purity measures Levi takes before prayer. Note that Greenfield and Stone think that the washing has nothing to do with the following prayer ("Two Notes," 156-57; "Prayer of Levi," 249-50, 251, 260). They say it relates to another incident separate from the prayer, for which we have no record, an incident in which Levi was already a priestly figure. In support of their view they cite the appearance of τοτε, "then," at the

common midrashic tradition, based on the Priestly Benediction."[46] The practice of extending one's hands in prayer is known from Pss 28:2; 134:2.[47] Mention of the "holy ones" (*Ar. Levi* supp. 4) reminds the reader of Zech 3:1-10 where the first post-exilic high priest, Joshua, stands in the company of the heavenly angels to be cleansed, and is promised access to them should he fulfill his commission as cultic leader. The list of attributes Levi requests in *Ar. Levi* supp. 8 is usually interpreted as an allusion to Isa 11:2.[48] *Ar. Levi* supp. 10 relies on Ps 119:133b, but changes עון, "iniquity" in the psalm to שטן, "satan."[49] Greenfield and Stone note that the blessing of Abraham and

---

beginning of the washing account and again at the outset of the prayer, saying that it would be unusual to mark the continuation of a thought or conclusion of an action with that word. Having thus separated Levi's act of self-cleansing from the prayer, they suggest that it is an act of levitical purity like that prescribed in Num 8:21 where Levites purify themselves by washing their clothing ("Prayer of Levi," 261). To complete their argument they offer a phrase from Philo's *Vita Mosis* 2.143, saying that there the "high priest is washed in υδατι πηγης καθαρωτατω και ζωτικωτατως" (260). For all of their arguments, one remains unconvinced that the ablution and the prayer do not belong together. The double use of τοτε is no certain sign that they are separate incidents; the ablution prescribed by Num 8:21 does not match the washing Levi undertakes in this text; and one would be loathe to draw too firm a conclusion from any similarities of language between Philo and *Aramaic Levi*.

[46] David Flusser, "Qumran and Jewish 'Apotropaic' Prayers," *IEJ* 16 (1966) 197. Flusser also lists 1QS 2 3 and 11QPsᵃ Plea as other exegeses of the Priestly Benediction.

[47] Positioning of the fingers is discussed in *b. Sotah* 39b, "R. Hisda said, 'The priests are not permitted to bend the joints of their fingers until they turn their faces from the congregation'" (quoted by Jacobson, "The Position of the Fingers During the Priestly Blessing," 259).

[48] See, for example, Flusser, "Prayers," 196; Beyer, *Die aramäischen Texten*, 193; Stone and Greenfield, "Prayer of Levi," 261 (note also Stone and Greenfield's citation of 1QS 4:3-4, where similar language appears; but see Haupt, "Testament," 9, n. 38, where he treats each of the terms individually, linking them to separate biblical and nonbiblical texts). However, the equally attractive possibility of Prov 8:10-14 has been overlooked. It also contains the equivalent Hebrew words for the traits listed in the phrase. Moreover, it has the added appeal of being a passage in which Lady Wisdom describes them as items worthy to be sought after, just as Levi requests them in his prayer. Meanwhile Isa 11:2 only uses the terms to describe the predetermined characteristics of an anticipated figure. Another argument in favor of Prov 8:10-14 is the appearance of the wisdom speech later in the document—in *Aramaic Levi* Levi proves himself to be a devotee of Wisdom as one aspect of his priestly character. So it would not be surprising to find him pleading with God for the gifts promised in Prov 8:10-14.

[49] Flusser, "Prayers," 197. Flusser shows that the phrase in the prayer, and its counterpart in 11QPsᵃ Plea 15, are not the only occurrences of "every satan" in the Qumran corpus; see also 1QH 4 6; 43 3; 1QSb 1 8 (197, n. 15). Flusser also notes that the plural, "satans," appears in *Enoch* 40:7; 65:6 (197, n. 16). See also Stone and

Sarah in *Ar. Levi* supp. 15 "draws on Gen 18:10," and v. 16 reflects Gen 22:17-18.[50] Finally *Ar. Levi* supp. 18, making reference to "true judgment," recalls Mal 2:4-7 and Deut 33:8-11 (esp. v. 10).

The most striking thing about the way these biblical texts have been put to use is the fact that several of them pertain to priestly figures, although Levi is not yet a priest in this narrative. In other words, the author gives Levi priestly characteristics *before* his elevation to that role, lending credence to his plea to serve in that capacity: Levi, it seems, is especially fit for the office of the priesthood.

As for the purpose of the passage, David Flusser has suggested that it is an "apotropaic" prayer.[51] Comparing it with 11QPs^a Plea 13-16,[52] Flusser thinks it alternates between a request for God's deliverance from evil and a request for spiritual bliss. However, in the broader context of *Aramaic Levi*, what Levi actually seeks in the prayer is not merely spiritual bliss and deliverance from evil, but partnership with God in the task of opposing evil. At the heart of the prayer is the statement, "lead me forward to be your servant and to serve you well" (*Ar. Levi* supp. 11), a sentiment repeated in v. 14. Similarly, *Ar. Levi* supp. 17-19 is without doubt a plea for alliance with God. Therefore it might be better to call this a prayer for deliverance and appointment. In fact, much of what is present in the prayer suggests that its speaker wishes to be appointed a priest for God, and even considers himself already to be one. By including priestly elements the author claims for Levi, even before the office has been bestowed upon him, the special qualifications necessary to fill it as the author would have it filled. That Levi prays in the fashion of the Priestly Benediction, that his posture is one of praise in God's presence, and that he claims to be before the "holy ones," all suggest the act of ritual service on behalf of the people of Israel. Additionally, the positioning of the hands and fingers probably reflects priestly practice, and the closing section of the Greek text gives language that comes very close to an explicit request for the sacerdotal office.[53] All of this amounts to an impressive set of

---

Greenfield's discussion of the term and its parallels in nonbiblical literature and inscriptions, and their claim that the occurrence of שׁמן denotes "a category of evil spirit" ("Prayer of Levi," 262-64).

[50] Stone and Greenfield, "Prayer of Levi," 252.

[51] Flusser, "Prayers," 194-205.

[52] James A. Sanders, *Discoveries in the Judaean Desert* 4 (Oxford: Oxford University, 1965) 77.

[53] Noteworthy is the sapiential character of the priesthood sought by Levi (*Ar. Levi* supp. 8; cf. *Ar. Levi* 82-95).

indications that the petition is aimed at winning its speaker appointment as a priest.[54]

The prayer is also marked by a moderately dualistic perspective. It makes an effort to delineate between good and evil in the world, and includes the notion of satans as the embodiment of such evil (*Ar. Levi* supp. 10). This moderate dualism indicates that the text is a product of the Judaism that existed between the period of the formation of the Bible's prayer book and the founding of the Qumran community. On one hand, the dualism is not as sharp as that which appears in the "Discourse on the Two Spirits" of 1QS 3 13–4 26;[55] on the other hand, it is an advance on the mild dualism exhibited in Ps 119:133b.[56] The prayer's dualism also indicates the author's attitude toward those who are not on his side: they belong with all that is evil, and deserve utter rejection, even eradication (*Ar. Levi* supp. 13). But perhaps the most telling indication of the author's dualistic perspective is the faint trace of an early form of the יצר הרע ("evil inclination") doctrine of later Judaism (*Ar. Levi* supp. 5-7). Also significant is the author's view that dualism has its place in the human heart; this is a good indication of the pre-Qumran character of the prayer. Among the sectarians one finds the division between good and evil to have advanced from its place within human hearts to include a rift between kinds of persons as well, a rift that is determined by external forces of good and evil.[57]

So while the prayer is meant to demonstrate Levi's suitability and eagerness for the priestly office, it also shows that Levi was a figure fit for sacerdotal service even before he became a priest through divine and human appointment. Its rich appropriation of biblical texts and traditions concerning the priesthood, and its bestowal on Levi of many of the characteristics shared by holders of the office accomplish that

---

[54] One might argue that the presence in the prayer of actions and words typical of priests indicates that it ought to be placed after Levi's elevation to the priesthood. Of course that would mean moving it from its present location. However, both the unique character of the washing in *Ar. Levi* supp. 1 and the commencement of a vision at the conclusion of *Ar. Levi* supp. 21 indicate on the one hand that the prayer belongs immediately after the Shechem episode, and on the other that it must precede the remaining textual evidence for Levi's vision in *Ar. Levi* 4ff. Anyway, Levi's speech in the prayer itself indicates he is not yet a priest—rather he yearns to become one.

[55] Nevertheless, there is structural similarity between the prayer and the Discourse; Stone and Greenfield, "Prayer," 261, note that both are composed, at least in part, in balanced prose.

[56] Psalm 119 is typically dated anywhere from sometime during the exilic period to the early Hellenistic era. See most recently Will Soll, *Psalm 119: Matrix, Form, and Setting* (CBQMS 23; Washington: Catholic Biblical Association of America, 1991) 142-54.

[57] For example, see the War Scroll, passim, and the "Discourse on the Two Spirits." See also Haupt, "Testament," 9, n. 34, for a lengthy discussion of the dualism apparent in the prayer.

objective. Meanwhile Levi's dualistic outlook marks his desire to become a priest as a longing to be a guardian of purity and righteousness. Hence the ideal priest embodied by Levi is identified once more as a zealot for purity.

The prayer fits well within the broader context of *Aramaic Levi*. There are clear connections between it and the Shechem incident, the vision, the encounter with Isaac and Jacob beyond the vision, the priestly instructions Isaac gives to Levi, the life history, and the speech Levi gives his children. Assuming that Levi's behavior in the Shechem episode (*Ar. Levi* 1-3) was viewed positively by *Aramaic Levi*'s author, the dualism and plea for election to the priesthood in the prayer follow it quite naturally. Having taken upon himself the task of defending the community's purity by means of an act of violence, it is not surprising to find Levi identifying himself with a dualistic worldview, and intensifying his zeal by asking that he be appointed God's intermediary and partner in the battle against evil. The prayer is the liturgical reflex of the conquest of Shechem; both acts express the same ideal of a hyperbolic commitment to communal purity. The vision, with its appointment-scene (*Ar. Levi* 4-7) and angelic speech against exogamy (*Ar. Levi* supp. 22-27), also blends well with the prayer; in essence it is the answer to Levi's prayerful plea. Isaac's blessing of Levi (*Ar. Levi* 8), Jacob's ordination and investiture of Levi (9-12), and Isaac's instructions (13-61) confirm the vision's contents, and fulfill in the earthly realm Levi's entreaty. While Levi's life history (62-81) is not closely connected with the prayer, *Ar. Levi* 78 does note that his desire to become a priest was fulfilled. But the wisdom speech that Levi gives his children (82-101) carries forward his concern for integrity expressed here, and confirms Levi's interest in wisdom evident in *Ar. Levi* supp. 8. The last preserved portion of the speech (102-106) fits well also with the prayer, since there he warns that some of his own descendants will fall into the power of evil and impurity against which he allies himself with God in the prayer.

As for the prayer's relationship to the rest of the LPT, it does not appear in this form beyond *Aramaic Levi*. *Jubilees* has no trace of it, but *T. Levi* 2:4 does preserve a brief mention of the supplication, while 4:2-6 indicates that *Testament of Levi*'s author knew the prayer as it appears here.[58] From these facts one can say with confidence only

---

[58] So also Hultgård, *L'eschatologie*,2:95-96; but see the other opinions on the connection between the prayer and the Greek *Testament of Levi*; Haupt, "Testament," 7-17, concludes that a prayer like the one preserved in 4Q213 1 i, ii and the Mt. Athos manuscript was known to the author of *Testament of Levi*; but Becker, *Untersuchungen*, 75; and Jarl Henning Ulrichsen, *Die Grundschrift der Testamente der zwölf Patriarchen: eine Untersuchung zu Umfang, Inhalt und Eigenart der ursprünglichen Schrift* (Acta Universitatis Upsaliensis; Historia Religionum 10; Uppsala: Almqvist & Wiksell, 1991) 179, both think that there could only be a distant

that the author of *Testament of Levi* knew *Aramaic Levi* and the prayer, but chose to use the prayer sparingly, and that the prayer may have entered the literary tradition for the first time with the appearance of *Aramaic Levi*.[59]

3.1.3. *Ar. Levi* supp. 20-27, 4-7: Levi's vision

Levi's vision appears in 1Q21 3, 4Q213 1 ii 11-18, 4Q213 2, Bodl. a 1-13, and 4Q213 3 1-3. The Qumran manuscript is fragmentary, resulting in two gaps of unknown scope in the vision. 4Q213 3 2-3 gives text identical with Bodl. a 10, 12-13, while 4Q213 3 1 provides quite a different text from Bodl. a 6-7, where one expects it to parallel the Bodl. fragment (see NOTES ON THE TEXT AND TRANSLATION below). 1 Q21 3 matches only a portion of the vision recorded in Bodl. a.

TEXT

[מן אבל מין   [על אבי יעקוב וכד]י   [באדין נגדת ב]^{20}

[[אדין חזיון אחזית]^{21} [שכבת ויתבת אנה ע]   [אדין]

לי תרעי שמיא [תחותי רם עד דבק לשמי]א   בחזית חזיוא וחזית שמ]יא

[ומלאך חד]

Lost text

ואנתה ^{24}ותחלל[[חאבין חוב] [גבריא [לו מכת]ש[י [וכען י] [א [מן נק]ב[ב]חא ל] [^{22}

שמה ושם אבוה [בעליה למ]ש[ר]פ[ה [דהב] ובהתתא[וכל [בתו]לה זי חבלת שמה ושם ^{25}

[אבהתה ואבהתת לכל אחיה [ול]אבוה ולא מתמחא שם חסדה מן כול עמהא לעלם ^{26}

ל] מן קרבן לאל מן [מעשר קודש [ל וח] [תע קדיש]י מן עמא$^\circ$[ומ]^{27}ל לכל דרי עלמא[

Lost text

שלמא וכל חמדת בכורי ארעא כולא למאכל ולמלכות חרבא פגשא וקרבא ונחשירותא ועמלא ^{4}

ונצפתא וקטלא וכפנא ^{5}זמנין תאכול וזמנין תכפן וזמנין תעמול וזמנין תנוח וזמנין תדמוך וזמנין תנוד

שנת עינא^{6}כען חזי לך הכין רבינך מן כולה והיך יהבנא לך רבות שלם עלמא vacat ^{7}ונגדו שבעתון

מן לותי ואנה אתעירת מן שנתי אדין אמרת חזוא הוא דן וכדן אנה מתמה די יהוי לה כל חזוא

וטמרת אף דן בלבי ולכל אינש לא גליתה

---

traditio-historical connection between the *Aramaic Levi* prayer and the plea mentioned in *T. Levi* 2:4; 4:2-6.

[59] For the view that the older text served as a source for the younger text, and for possible reasons that the author of *Testament of Levi* was not inclined to preserve the prayer *in toto*, see 5.1, 5.3, and 5.4.1.

TRANSLATION

ˢ²⁰Then I continued on ∘[   ] to my father Jacob, and when [   ] from Abel Main. Then [   ] I lay down. And I remained ∘[   ] ˢ²¹Then I was shown a vision [   ] when I saw the visions. And I saw heav[en   ] below me, reaching up until (it) touched heave[n   ] to me the gates of heaven, and an angel [   ]

Lost text

ˢ²²[   ] "from the wom[a]n to [   ]∘. ˢ²³And now ∘[ ]∘∘ the pla[g]ues of men [   ] the ones incurring guilt [   ] you (or wife?). ˢ²⁴And she profanes her name and the name of her father [   ] husband(s?) to bu[r]n her [   ]∘ ∘∘∘∘[   ] and (the?) shame. ˢ²⁵And every virgin who ruins her name, and the name of her fathers, she also causes shame for all her brothers [and for] her father. ˢ²⁶And the reputation of her revilement will not be wiped out from among all her people forever. [   ]∘[ ]∘ for all the generations of eternity. ˢ²⁷∘∘[ ]∘∘ holy (pure?) from the people [   ]∘ ∘∘[   ] a holy tithe, an offering to God from"

Lost text

⁴"peace, and all choice first fruits of the whole earth to eat. The reign of the sword has fighting, the battle, the chase, exertion, conflict, and killing and hunger. ⁵Sometimes it (the kingdom of the sword) will eat, and sometimes it will go hungry; sometimes it will labor, sometimes it will rest; sometimes it will sleep, and sometimes the sleep of the eye will flee. ⁶Now see how we magnified you over all, and how we gave you the anointing of eternal peace." ⁷And the seven departed from me, and I awoke from my sleep. Then I said, "This was a vision," and thus I was amazed that I should have a vision at all. And I hid this very thing in my heart, and I revealed it to no one.

NOTES ON THE TEXT AND TRANSLATION

Ar. Levi supp. 20. ויתבה. Stone and Greenfield suggest that the word may mean "sat up," perhaps after a vision. Alternatively they say "remained" or "settled" might be appropriate.[60] The last possibility seems the most probable, since what precedes is a prayer, and what follows is visionary material.

Ar. Levi supp. 21. חזיון. Read this as "vision," not "visions."[61]

---

[60] Stone and Greenfield, "Prayer of Levi," 265.

[61] So also Milik, "Le Testament de Lévi en araméen: Fragment de la Grotte 4 de Qumrân," *RB* 62 (1955) 400. Fitzmyer and Harrington, *Manual*, 91, read the word as a plural, and are justified in doing so since they transcribe the letters on the fragment as

Ar. Levi supp. 21. חזיית בחזיא. The first word is the verb with a -ב prefix having the meaning of "as," or "when." Milik transcribes the word as we do, and translates it also as a plural. Yet the ending does not readily encourage such a translation. However, if we read the word as חזויא, the appropriate plural ending would be present. Nevertheless, that is not to be; Milik's and our reading of the ink seems certain. Thus it may be best to treat this as an instance of scribal metathesis.[62]

Ar. Levi supp. 21. רם. The word can be a verb or an adjective; in either case its meaning is clear.[63]

Ar. Levi supp. 23. ין]לו מכתֹ[שֹ]י גבריא. The transcription and translation of the text depend heavily on tenuous ink traces. They must be treated with proper caution.

Ar. Levi supp. 25. ואבהתת. Read as an ʾ*aphel* third feminine singular perfect of בהת.[64]

Ar. Levi supp. 26. חסדה. Read the word as "her revilement," with the *he* serving as a third person feminine singular possessive suffix, attached to חסדא, "revilement, shame."[65] The alternative rendering is "his piety," or even "his holiness," with the *he* serving as the third person masculine singular possessive suffix.[66] That is rather unlikely, since the pious person would then have to be either Levi, to whom angelic speech in the vision is probably addressed, or the offending father who gives his daughter in marriage to foreigners. If it were Levi, the possessive suffix ought to be second person, since the angelic announcement in the vision is direct speech (cf. *Ar. Levi* 6). If it were the father, the sentence would be nonsense, suggesting about a man

---

חזוין. However, Stone and Greenfield, "Prayer of Levi," 260 transcribe it as we do, yet translate the word with a plural form; cf. "Two Notes," 156; "Appendix III," 460.

[62] Nevertheless Fitzmyer and Harrington, *Manual*, 90, followed by Eisenman and Wise, *The Dead Sea Scrolls Uncovered*, 138 transcribe the word as חזויא, and translate with a plural. Meanwhile, Beyer, *Die aramäischen Texten*, 194, offers בחזוה חזוא for the two words. Although he marks the *nun* as very tentative, his transcription of the second word can not be entertained. There is clearly no *nun* present in the manuscript at that point, and the *waw* seems quite clear, especially when it is compared with the many other occurrences of the same letter in the manuscript.

[63] See Stone and Greenfield, "Prayer of Levi," 266; and Milik, "Fragment," 400, where he opts for the adjective "élevée."

[64] J. T. Milik, *The Books of Enoch* (Oxford; Oxford University, 1976) 263.

[65] Marcus Jastrow, *Dictionary of the Targumim, Talmud Babli, Yerushalmi and the Midrashic Literature* (New York: Judaica Press, 1989) 486. The ʾ*aleph* is lost when the suffix is attached.

[66] For another reading, see F. M. Cross, *The Ancient Library of Qumran* (3rd edition; Minneapolis: Fortress, 1995) 183, where the *dalet* is a *yod*, and the word is translated "his holy one." Cross attributes the reading to Jonas Greenfield and Michael Stone. It is, however, an impossible reading given the ink traces on the fragment.

condemned earlier in the passage that the reputation of his piety would
be preserved among his people forever.[67]

Ar. Levi supp. 26. עמהא. Translate as "her people," in keeping
with the reading of the previous noun.

Ar. Levi supp. 27. קדיש∘ מן עמא∘. Both midline circlets represent
what appear to be erasures or attempts to cross out existing ink.

Ar. Levi supp. 27 and *Ar. Levi* 4. 4Q213 15, an unidentified
fragment, may fit between these two parts of Levi's vision. The tiny
scrap preserves only two full words on the second of two lines of visible ink. The words are כהנות עלמא, "an eternal priesthood."
Comparison with *Jub.* 30:5-20 suggests this placement. In the latter
text the angelic speech against exogamy (30:5-17) is followed by commendation of Levi for his action at Shechem, and his elevation to the
priesthood (30:18-20). It is possible that 4Q213 15 is from the following portion of the manuscript, and reflects the material in *Jub.* 30:18-
20. Yet no convincing physical join can be made between the fragments, and lacking sufficient parallel evidence, the possibility must remain only in the realm of speculation.[68]

Ar. Levi 4. חרבא. The last three letters of the word appear in
1Q21 3 1.

Ar. Levi 5. תעמול וזמנין תנוח. Save for the last two letters, all three
words appear in 1Q21 3 2, although תעמול lacks the *waw*.

Ar. Levi 5. Greenfield and Stone think the subject of the series
of verbs in the verse is the kingdom of the sword.[69] The alternative, of
course, is that Levi is the subject. In either case, the point is clear: the
dominion of the sword, and those who undertake it, lead a variable existence, one less attractive than that of a priest who will enjoy the good
things of Israel (*Ar. Levi* 4).

Ar. Levi 6. הכין. The word is probably a scribal error for היך.[70]

Ar. Levi 6. רבינך מן כולה. While phrases from the Cairo Geniza
text of this and the next section (*Ar. Levi* 8-12) have exact parallels in
4Q213 3 2-3 (cf. the underlined TEXT of *Ar. Levi* 7, 9), in contrast
4Q213 3 1 reads כהונתך מן כל בשר, "Your priesthood is over all flesh," a
phrase not found in the Cairo Geniza manuscript. But a most likely
parallel in the Cairo Geniza manuscript is the text cited at the beginning

---

[67] One could read חסדה as "his shame." But the focus on the woman in the
preceding sentences argues in favor of the reading we adopt.

[68] In a private conversation on 3 December 1992 J. T. Milik expressed his view
that 4Q213 15 comes from the bottom of the column preceding what we have labelled
4Q213 2 (*Ar. Levi* supp. 22-27), and can be physically joined to the bottom right
corner of that fragment. We have been unable to make the join between the two
fragments that forms the basis for his view. See the COMMENT following.

[69] Greenfield and Stone, "Remarks," 218.

[70] But see the alternative suggested in the following NOTE.

of this NOTE. The word, רבינך, "we magnified you,"[71] is perhaps the remnant of an earlier direct reference to priesthood which has been lost. The difficulty, of course, is in relating "your priesthood" to רבינך, "we magnified you." However, as Greenfield and Stone have pointed out with respect to the use of the root in *Ar. Levi* 7, the verb רבי in Aramaic has the sense of "anointing" in the Targumim.[72] Hence it is conceivable that the younger manuscript witness simply expresses differently the same idea communicated in the older witness; in one text Levi's elevated status is indicated by a straightforward reference to priesthood, while the other is less direct, using a term for anointing to disclose Levi's lofty rank. Hence it may be better to translate, "We anointed you over all." An additional possibility is that the first two letters of the word preceding this phrase, הכין, suffered metathesis; then the text would have been כהין, "a priest."[73] The sentence would thus read, "Now see yourself, a priest! We magnified you over all." In spite of the apparent syntactical difficulties, the latter reconstruction is another way of understanding the relationship between the Qumran manuscript's כהונתך מן כל בשר and the surviving material in the Cairo Geniza manuscript.

Ar. Levi 6. שלם עלמא. The last two letters of the first word and the first two letters of the second word appear in 1Q21 3 3.

Ar. Levi 7. רבות שלם עלמא. Greenfield and Stone translate this as "an anointing of eternal peace." The basis for their translation is the connection they draw between this phrase and *T. Levi* 8:3ff and *Jub.* 32:1, and the fact that in the Targumim the root רבי corresponds to Hebrew משח, "anoint."[74] They conclude that "the idea should be compared with Ex., 40:15 'that their anointing be for an eternal priesthood' and Numb., 25:12-13 where to Phinehas' descendants are promised 'a covenant of peace' and 'a covenant of eternal priesthood.'"[75]

Ar. Levi 7. שבעתון. This is the reading offered by Greenfield and Stone.[76] They are probably correct, against Grelot, who reads שבעתין.[77] Their translation is almost assuredly superior to that of Charles and Cowley, and of Lévi.[78]

---

[71] See Grelot, "Notes sur le Testament araméen de Lévi," *RB* 63 (1956) 397-98, for this translation. Grelot is probably right in reading the word as a first-person plural with a second-person singular possessive suffix.

[72] See the NOTE on רבות שלם עלמא, *Ar. Levi* 7.

[73] For the same spelling in the Cairo Geniza manuscript, see *Ar. Levi* 9, 13.

[74] Greenfield and Stone, "Remarks," 218.

[75] Ibid.

[76] Ibid, 218-19.

[77] Grelot, "Notes," 398-99; Grelot is followed by Haupt, "Testament," 51. Grelot and Haupt nevertheless translate the word as "seven."

[78] Charles and Cowley, "An Early Source," 578, translate "two weeks"; Lévi, "Notes sur le texte araméen du Testament de Lévi," 175, renders the phrase as "deux semaines."

Ar. Levi 7. ואנה אתעירת מן שנתי. These words appear in 4Q213 3 2.

Ar. Levi 7 חזוא הוא דן וכדן אנה מתמה די יהוי לה כל חזוא. Read the sentence with Greenfield and Stone as "This was a vision, and thus I was amazed that I should have a vision at all."[79] The translation indicating that it was Levi's own vision which amazed him rests on the notion that לה in the present text results from scribal transposition of the final *he* of יהוה with the *yod* of לי to avoid a homograph of the divine name.[80]

Ar. Levi 7. וסמרת אף דן בלבי ולכל אינש לא. Everything from the last letter of וסמרת to לא occurs also in 4Q213 3 3. For an explanation of our translation see 2.2.5 above.

COMMENT

Before Levi's vision begins in *Ar. Levi* supp. 21, v. 20 gives evidence for his movements between the prayer and the vision. Commentators usually understand this to indicate that Levi first travels to his father Jacob, and then leaves a place called Abelmain[81] to go to yet another location.[82] But from what little survives of the text it is also possible to say that he was already at Abelmain at the time of the prayer. He may have first announced his intention to travel to Jacob, and then narrated the actual departure in the following line. The latter reading matches *T. Levi* 2:3-4, where Levi is said to be at Abelmaul when he prayed. As to the location where Levi settles prior to his vision, Bethel is the most likely possibility, since both *T. Levi* 8:1-2 and *Jub.* 32:1 indicate he had a vision there. At any rate, at the beginning of the vision Levi observes the heavens, and then we hear that he looks down and sees something reaching up to touch the celestial surface. Next there is mention of an angel. Regrettably at that point 4Q213 1 ii breaks off.

---

[79] Ibid., 219. See 2.2.5 above for the significance of the translation for laying to rest the notion that *Aramaic Levi* contained two visions. Note the intriguing alternative view of James Kugel, "Levi's Elevation to the Priesthood in Second Temple Writings," *HTR* 86 (1993) 57-58. He accepts the translation of Greenfield and Stone, yet, assuming still that *Aramaic Levi* contained two visions, understands the sentence as "a certain editorial sheepishness on the part of *ALD*'s creator at having presented these two texts [two visions] as separate 'visions'" (66).

[80] Greenfield and Stone, "Remarks," 219.

[81] Cf. 1 Kgs 15:26; 2 Chr 16:4. For our purpose it is not necessary to enter into the complex question of just where Abelmain/Abelmaul is. For now see Haupt, "Testament," 11-13, and his wide-ranging discussion of the possibilities; and Milik, "Fragment," 403-5. Milik has offered extensive reflections on the significance of the place name. He takes it as a significant indication of the document's northern origins. However, the evidence Milik has marshalled for his argument thus far is not sufficient to convince many regarding his views. Cf. G. W. E. Nickelsburg, "Enoch, Levi and Peter: Recipients of Revelation in Upper Galilee," *JBL* (100) 588-90; Marinus de Jonge, "Notes on Testament of Levi II-VII," in *Studies on the Testaments of the Twelve Patriarchs* (Leiden: Brill, 1975) 260, n. 45.

[82] See, for example, de Jonge, "Notes," 253; Haupt, "Testament," 11, n. 57.

The next evidence we have for the vision's content is probably 4Q213 2.[83] This large and very broken fragment tantalizes and frustrates in equal measures. There is enough extant text to allow considerable speculation as to its original content, but not enough to decide with complete confidence which of the many possibilities for its reconstruction and placement is correct. For example, it gives only one entire sentence (*Ar. Levi* supp. 26), yet it renders many complete words and even phrases. Further, one can compare the fragment with *Jub.* 30:5-17, insofar as both texts address exogamy and use much the same language; but this text seems to be an abbreviated version of what appears in *Jubilees*. Moreover, J. T. Milik proposes joining a fragment we leave unidentified, 4Q213 15, to the right edge of this one (see NOTES ON THE TEXT above). His join makes כהנות עלמא, "the eternal priesthood" (the only complete words on 4Q213 15), the last phrase of the preceding column. And it places the letters מח-, which are at the left edge of frg. 15, next to the first visible letters of line 21 of frg. 2, rendering the word מחלל[י]ם, "accursed."[84] Yet there are four dots of ink on line 1 of frg. 15 that extend beyond the beginning of Milik's putative line 20, which requires only ול- to fill out comfortably what one might expect (ולאבוה). Finally, in *Ar. Levi* supp. 26 it is said that a שם חסדה will not be removed from the people forever; unfortunately the word חסדה can have two different meanings—"his (or her) piety," or "her (or his) shame (or revilement)."[85] Given this plethora of difficulties and possibilities, we offer the following explanation of the fragment's proper placement and construal with the acknowledgement that it may only be, in the final analysis, a rather tentative explanation.

As noted already, what survives is material similar to *Jub.* 30:5-17. The latter text is an angelic speech against exogamous relationships, and a description of the punishment dealt to those who violate the prohibition of such unions.[86] Likewise, *Ar. Levi* supp. 22-27 condemns exogamy, and seems to describe the disciplinary measures brought against transgressors. Mention of plagues or blows and of guilty persons in *Ar. Levi* supp. 23 recalls *Jub.* 30:7, 15. Reference to a woman who profanes her own name, her father's name, and her

---

[83] In a private conversation on 3 December 1992 Milik suggested placing 4Q213 2 in Isaac's instructions to Levi, rather than in the vision as is done here. He may have done so on the premise that this resembles a midrash on Lev 21:7-9, where it is Moses who gives instruction to Aaron. But the continuous texts of Isaac's instructions in the Cairo Geniza manuscript and Mt. Athos 18:2 do not preserve this, nor does the parallel material in *Jubilees* 21. Moreover, it is material of a visionary nature in *Jubilees*. For more on the decision to place the fragment in Levi's vision, see 2.2.1.

[84] Note that the transcription provided here does not match Milik's reading of the edge of 4Q213 2 either. For his מ[י]ל[we read מ[ל[.

[85] For the view that the word is "her revilement," see the NOTE above.

[86] It is clear from *Jub.* 30:18, where the speaker says that Levi will minister continually "as we do," that the speech is spoken by the angelic narrator of *Jubilees*.

brothers' names, and to burning in *Ar. Levi* supp. 24-25 also remind the reader of *Jub.* 30:7, where the same language is used to describe what a woman's exogamy brings upon her family and herself. The enduring character of the woman's shameful reputation noted in *Ar. Levi* supp. 26 resonates with *Jub.* 30:14 where it is said that Israel will not be cleansed from the defilement stemming from the presence of such unions in its midst. References to a holy tithe and an offering to God in *Ar. Levi* supp. 27 probably are reflected in *Jub.* 30:16, where the angel announces that no sacrifices will be accepted from violators of the law against exogamy.[87] The two words for shame or revilement used in *Ar. Levi* supp. 24 and 26 (אבהתתא and חסדא) have mirror images in the use of the parallel Ethiopic term, *xafrat*, "shame," in *Jub.* 30:5, 7.

In light of these points of comparison this fragment is placed within the vision, and after the Shechem incident, and is understood as angelic speech to Levi. While *Jub.* 30:5-17 does not give the words of an angel to Levi in a vision, but part of the angelic narration to Moses, it does associate the speech closely with Levi's elevation to the priesthood at the hands of angels (*Jub.* 30:18-20), something which takes place in a vision in *Aramaic Levi*.[88] And, like *Jub.* 30:5-17, the section clearly relates to the Shechem incident, and can easily be understood to follow it. We recall also our earlier explanation for placing this fragment in Levi's vision.[89] Of the three possible places for such an address in *Aramaic Levi*—the speech of angels to Levi in a dream, Isaac's instructions to Levi, and Levi's address to his children— this is the only plausible context for it. While Isaac addresses the issue of marriage (*Ar. Levi* 22-25a), the well-preserved and continuous version of Isaac's teaching in Cairo Geniza manuscript and the addition at Mt. Athos 18:2 does not contain this material, and the speech would be thematically dissonant in Levi's wisdom-oriented speech to his children. Meanwhile it would be quite consonant with an angelic elevation of Levi to the priesthood as a reward for his zeal at Shechem. So we assume that the speaker is here an angel as in *Jubilees*, and that the subject matter of the speech indicates that the events at Shechem

---

[87] An alternative explanation of *Ar. Levi* supp. 27 is possible. It may be the beginning of the angelic elevation of Levi to the priesthood. While the language of sacrifice seems out of place in that respect, it could explain the origin of the tradition in *Jub.* 32:4 that Jacob ordained Levi to the priesthood as a tithe of his sons. Perhaps the phrase מעשר קודש קרבן לאל reflects angelic ordination of Levi to the priesthood as a "holy tithe, an offering to God," and the author of *Jubilees* derived the notion of Levi as a tithe from this text (cf. Num 3:44-45, were the Levites are set apart in place of the first born).

[88] On the reasons for *Jubilees*' removal of the speech from Levi's vision (*Jub.* 32:1), see 4.2.1 below.

[89] See 2.2.1 above.

stand in the background. Thus the fragment probably records angelic condemnation of exogamy, spoken to Levi in his vision.[90]

The final section of the vision, *Ar. Levi* 4-6, is variously interpreted. Grelot thinks the Bodl. fragment concluded a diptych that represented first the character of the priestly kingdom (1Q21 1 and Bodl. a 2a) and then the nature of the reign of the sword exercised by Levites charged with temple security (Bodl. a 2b-7a).[91] Although Grelot may be correct in his view that this text and the preceding material depict both kinds of dominion, the objective of the passage seems to be to make a comparison between the two, with priestly rule emerging more favorably than military dominion. From this perspective *Ar. Levi* 4a concludes a favorable description of priestly control, and *Ar. Levi* 4b-5 describes the reign of the sword in ambivalent terms. Following is the angelic proclamation that they have ordained Levi to the priesthood (*Ar. Levi* 6). On this reading Levi, it seems, receives the more profitable of the two types of sovereignty.[92]

Unfortunately, if reconstruction of the Cairo Geniza codex is correct, it is virtually certain that there was considerably more to the vision than the little that survives; it would have occupied a total of about three and a half columns of Geniza text, while the extant portion is slightly less than one and a half columns.[93] Therefore the full scope of the vision's contents remains elusive. To summarize that of which we can be certain, it is clear that it begins after Levi's prayer, and concludes before his first journey to Isaac. Within the vision there is evidence for a dream-ascent to heaven, a speech against exogamy, and an angelic ordination of Levi to the priesthood.

Many biblical traditions come into play here. Lev 21:9, which decrees that the sexually indiscreet daughter of a priest is to be burned,

---

[90] Another possibility, some might argue, is that the speech is part of the Shechem incident itself. However we lack any manuscript evidence that would support such a supposition, and there is no indication from the account of the event in *T. Levi* 6:3-7:4 that it ever contained this speech in an earlier form.

[91] Grelot, "Notes sur le Testament araméen de Lévi," *RB* 63 (1956) 393-97. He fills the gap between 1Q21 1 and *Ar. Levi* 4 with text from *T. Levi* 8:11-15. The absence of textual evidence to support his approach, and the degree of Christian redaction the *Testament of Levi* passage has undergone (see 5.2.6) militate against accepting Grelot's speculative reconstruction.

[92] The view is strengthened by assuming with Grelot that 1Q21 1, with its phrase מלכות כהנותא מן מלכות, "the kingdom of the priesthood is greater than the kingdom of," fits prior to the beginning of the Bodl. fragment. It certifies the notion that a comparison is being made between two types of dominion. However it is best not to rely too heavily on the placement, since there is no additional evidence to confirm it. Meanwhile, Kugel, "Levi's Elevation," 37, n. 37, accepts the placement, and seems to suggest that this reflects a comparison between Levi's priestly reign and Judah's royal dominion. See also Haupt, "Testament," 53.

[93] See Appendix 2.

stands behind much of *Ar. Levi* supp. 23-26, although it is not certain whether the woman to whom reference is made throughout the section is a priest's daughter or an ordinary Israelite.[94] *Ar. Levi* supp. 24 may also reflect Lev 20:2, where the man who gives his offspring to Molech is to be stoned. Like *Jub.* 30:9-10, this text equates giving one's daughter to a Gentile marriage partner with offering a child to Molech.

Another biblical tradition used by the author is far less obvious, but no less significant. With his usual keen exegetical insight, James Kugel has suggested that the notion of Levi's vision rests ultimately on Mal 2:4-7.[95] He begins by noting that the Malachi passage speaks of a covenant between God and the *individual* Levi. Kugel then asks when such a covenant could have been executed. An exegete of Malachi wanting to find the occasion for such an event would search the remainder of the Hebrew Bible in vain.[96] But the immediate text in Malachi accomplishes the purpose nicely: with speech from God proclaiming that Levi אתי הלך ובמישור בשלום, "walked with me in peace and uprightness," the interpreter could imply the notion of a vision—an ascent even—wherein Levi encountered God, and God made a covenant with Levi. On Kugel's reading of the text, one can well imagine that the author of *Aramaic Levi* relied on Mal 2:4-7 as the biblical basis for the notion that Levi had a vision in which God covenanted to make him a priest.

A biblical allusion is apparent in *Ar. Levi* 4 where Levi is promised the choice fruits and all the pleasant things of Israel to eat. The phrase echoes Num 18:8-32 and Deut 18:1-8 where priestly tithes are prescribed. Interestingly, the promise in *Ar. Levi* 4 places the biblical assertion that Levites would have a share in the temple's wealth in the distant past, giving it its origin with Levi himself. It implicitly contradicts the hierarchy of tithes in Numbers 18 where the Levites must give a tenth from their share to Aaron and his sons.

Finally, if Greenfield and Stone are correct in their view that the use of the root רבי, "to magnify," in *Ar. Levi* 6 is similar to the Targumim's use of it in place of משח, "to anoint," in Exod 40:15, then the allusion to that passage is also apparent.[97] But the verse from Exodus is not the only text that is called to mind by such a reference; one can include Exod 32:25-29; Num 25:12-13; Deut 33:8-11; and Mal 2:4-7 as further biblical traditions to which the phrase alludes.

---

[94] See *Jub.* 30:5-17, a related text that does generalize the law to cover all Israelite women.

[95] Kugel, "Levi's Elevation," 30-32. In fact, Kugel thinks the vision based on Mal 2:4-7 developed independently of any of the LPT documents addressed in this study; he says it arose as "Levi's Apocalypse," an entirely separate document.

[96] See 1.5 for a discussion of the Hebrew Bible textual background of the covenant intended by the *author* of Malachi.

[97] Greenfield and Stone, "Remarks," 218.

All of these biblical sources feature in the text to create a picture of Levi as the earliest, and therefore most authoritative priestly figure known to Israel. The text paints the portrait by placing the origin of the priestly office, rules concerning exogamy, and laws of the priestly tithe in the context of Levi's elevation to the priesthood. The author underscores the legitimacy of Levi's call to the priesthood and the laws regarding exogamy and tithes by setting them all within a vision-ascent.

Hence the intent of the passage appears to have been to legitimate its author's notion of the priestly office. Placing Levi's elevation in this context, along with laws regarding exogamy and tithes, makes a powerful statement that while there may be other traditions regarding these matters that come from a later time, more ancient and authoritative ones were already known and effective in the ancestral period. Moreover, those traditions related to Levi, a proven zealot for communal and cultic purity.

The last point indicates how this section of *Aramaic Levi* links with the rest of the document. There can be little doubt that *Aramaic Levi* intends to draw Levi's elevation to the priesthood into close connection with his ferocious act of devotion to God and to communal purity. Levi's appointment to the sacerdotal office is a reward for his zealotry (*Ar. Levi* 1-3), and is a response to his prayerful plea to become a servant of God in this capacity (*Ar. Levi* supp. 1-19). These connections ensure that the text communicates a coherent message regarding its view of the proper character of the priesthood: a holder of that office should be very concerned with communal integrity. At the same time the heavenly elevation of Levi is a forerunner of Jacob's human act of ordination (*Ar. Levi* 9-12), and Isaac's instruction in sacerdotal duties (*Ar. Levi* 13-61). It also legitimates Levi's claim to instruct his children and predict the fate of some of his descendants (*Ar. Levi* 82-106).

The vision's relationship to the rest of the texts in the LPT is also clear. A text prior to the LPT proper, Mal 2:4-7, may be the basis for depicting Levi as a visionary. There is, too, a clear parallel between *Jub.* 30:5-17 and *Ar. Levi* supp. 20-27. Also the mention in *Jub.* 32:1 that Levi was ordained a priest in a dream is surely a single-sentence summary of the material found in this vision. It is likewise probable that parts of the two visions in *Testament of Levi* derive from this one.[98] But on the whole, unfortunately, from these connections alone little can be concluded regarding the relationships among *Aramaic Levi*, *Jubilees*, and *Testament of Levi*, other than to say that they all treated the common idea of Levi's vision rather differently.

---

[98] For details regarding this view see 5.3, 5.4.1, and 5.4.3.

3.1.4. *Ar. Levi* 8-12: Levi's encounter with Isaac and Jacob

This section of *Aramaic Levi* is attested principally in Bodl. a 14–b 5a. The underlined text also occurs in 4Q213 3 4-6, and vv. 11 and 12 are paralleled by Mt. Athos 18:2. The few differences among these three witnesses are indicated in the NOTES below.

TEXT

‏[ע]לנא על אבי יצחק ואף הוא כדן [ברכ]ני⁸ ‏ אדין כדי הוה יעקב [אבי מ]עשר כל מה דיהוה⁹

לה כנדרה [וכ]ע[ן] אנה הוית קדמי בראש [כהונ]תה ולי מכל בנוהי יהב קרבן מעש[ר] לאל ואלבשי

לבוש כהונתא ומלי ידי והוית כהין לאל עלמיא וקרבית כל קרבנוהי וברכת לאבי בחיותי וברכת

לאחי¹⁰ אדין כולהון ברכוני ואף אבא ברכני ואשלמית להקרבה קורבנוהי בבית אל ¹¹ואזלנא מבית

אל ושרינא בבירת אברהם אבונן לות יצחק אבונה ¹²וחזא יצחק אבונא לכולנא וברכנא וחדי

TRANSLATION

⁸And we went up to my father Isaac, and he too blessed me thus. ⁹Then when Jacob [my father was ti]thing all that was his, according to his vow, [now] I was first, at the head [of the priestho]od, and to me of all his sons he gave a gift of a tit[he] to God. And he clothed me in the priestly clothing, [and he con]secrated me, and I became a priest of the eternal God. And I offered all his sacrifices, and I blessed my father during my lifetime, and I blessed my brothers. ¹⁰Then they all blessed me, and my father also blessed me. Then I finished offering his sacrifices in Bethel. ¹¹And we went from Bethel and we camped at the settlement of Abraham, our father, alongside Isaac our father. ¹²And Isaac our father saw all of us (and) he blessed us and he rejoiced.

NOTES ON THE TEXT AND TRANSLATION

Ar. Levi 9. ‏אדין כדי הוה יעקב [אבי מ]עשר‎. 4Q213 3 4 gives the underlined text *in toto*. Thus Grelot's reconstruction of the Bodl. fragment is confirmed.[99] It also disproves the reconstruction proposed by Charles (‏אדין כדי חזה יעקב [בתרי]עשר‎, "Then when Jacob saw concerning the twelve"),[100] and the one suggested more recently by Greenfield and

---

[99] Grelot, "Notes," 404. See also his article on the occurrence of the term ‏אבי‎, "Une mention inaperçue de 'Abba' dans le Testament araméen de Lévi," *Sem* 33 (1983) 101-108, esp. 106.

[100] Charles and Cowley, "An Early Source," 570, 578; Charles, *Greek Versions*, 246. Note that his reconstruction requires emendation of ‏הוה‎ as ‏חזה‎. Charles takes *T. Levi* 9:3 as the basis for the emendation. On the inadvisability of allowing the younger document to shape the older text, see 2.2.5 above.

Stone (אדין כדי חזה יעקב הוה מ[עשר], "Then when Jacob had a vision he tithed.").[101]

Ar. Levi 9. [וכ[ע[ן]. All that remains of the ʿ*ayin* is the left tip of the bottom stroke. In this hand the ʿ*ayin* often extends far to the left and low, even low enough to come under the bottom tip of a final *nun*.[102]

Ar. Levi 9. קדמי. The *yod* is not to be emended to *he* on the basis of *Jub.* 32:9 with Greenfield and Stone.[103] Instead Grelot's and Charles' explanation that the word is the ordinal number "first" stands.[104]

Ar. Levi 9. כהונ]תה ולי מכל בנוהי יהב]. 4Q213 3 5 gives ולי מן בנוהי יהב for the underlined section of text.

Ar. Levi 9. מעש[ר]. The reading concurs with Greenfield and Stone. Indeed, the left tip of the bottom stroke of *mem* is visible, as is the characteristically long and deep bottom stroke of ʿ*ayin*. The left bottom edge of the *śin* is evident as well.

Ar. Levi 9. לאל עלמיא. This is the present reading in the manuscript. However, the second word is written over what appears to be עליון.[105] The inverted "v" of the *yod* has been made into the top of a *mem* by the addition of a base-stroke; the *waw* of עליון doubles as the *yod* of עלמיא. And the short final *nun* has become the downstroke on the right side of *ʾaleph*. The reading עליון is supported by 4Q213 3 6, which preserves ink traces that lead one to believe that the manuscript reads לא[ל עליון.[106]

Ar. Levi 12. חזא. Charles thinks it necessary to emend the word so that it reads with a *zayin* instead of *waw*.[107] Comparison with other examples of each letter in this hand demonstrates an inconsistency of writing which allows one to read this as *zayin* without the necessity of an emendation.

---

[101] Greenfield and Stone, "Remarks," 219. Like Charles, Greenfield and Stone emend הוה to read חזה on the basis of *T. Levi* 9:3. They also introduce Jacob's vision mentioned in the same verse. Kugel, "Levi's Elevation," 11, n. 12, rejects the emendation offered first by Charles, and then expanded by Greenfield and Stone. For further discussion of the passage in the two books, see 2.2.2 and 5.4.4.

[102] Compare with Charles, *Greek Versions*, 246, who sees no legible ink, and provides [וכדי]; and Grelot, "Notes," 404, who suggests [כען].

[103] Greenfield and Stone, "Remarks," 219.

[104] Charles and Cowley, "An Early Source," 578; Charles, *APOT* II, 364; Grelot, "Une mention," 106. Note especially Grelot's remark that the sort of emdentation proposed by Greenfield and Stone's is grammatically indefensible.

[105] So also Grelot, "Notes," 405; Greenfield and Stone, "Remarks," 220. Cf. Lévi, "Le texte araméen du Testament de Lévi," 175. Firsthand examination of the manuscript makes this reading of the ink all but certain.

[106] Eisenman and Wise, *The Dead Sea Scrolls Uncovered*, 138, simply do not transcribe the line in question.

[107] Charles, *Greek Versions*, 247, n. a.

COMMENT

This brief passage gives a succinct account of a series of important events. The text begins with the shortest possible description of the family's trip to Isaac and the blessing he gives to Levi, stating simply that both things took place (*Ar. Levi* 8). Next Levi, Jacob, and the rest of Jacob's sons find themselves back in Bethel, although the reader does not know that until *Ar. Levi* 10, when Levi states that he completed sacrifices on Jacob's behalf *in Bethel*. While in Bethel Jacob tithes his belongings (*Ar. Levi* 9a), doing so through Levi, whom he recognized as a priest (*Ar. Levi* 9b), and whom he thus ordained and invested with the office (*Ar. Levi* 9c). Levi fulfills for his father his vowed tithe (cf. Gen 22:18), and extends to him and to his brothers the blessing characteristic of the newly-ordained priest (*Ar. Levi* 9d; cf. Lev 9:22). Levi's father and brothers then bless him (*Ar. Levi* 10a), and he concludes making sacrifices for his father (*Ar. Levi* 10b). After that the family leaves Bethel to travel once more to Isaac (*Ar. Levi* 11), who upon seeing them blesses them and rejoices (*Ar. Levi* 12).

Several texts from Scripture make an appearance in this section. One can imagine that the author hoped to remind readers of Isaac's single biblical benison, his blessing of Jacob in Gen 27:27-29. In Genesis Isaac's words aimed to ensure the addressee's prosperity, power, and supremacy. It is possible that the author sought to appropriate those promises for Levi by mentioning a blessing of Isaac for Levi.

Ar. Levi 9 also evinces rich reliance on biblical traditions, and it shows how the author read and used those texts in a synoptic fashion. First, it recalls Gen 28:22 where Jacob vowed to tithe all of his possessions. The vow went unfulfilled in the Hebrew Bible. *Aramaic Levi*, participating in a venerable tradition of concern over Jacob's failure to fulfill his vow, announces its completion (*Ar. Levi* 9a).[108] Because Num 18:21-28—surely yet another Torah-text present in the author's mind at this point—indicates that the only means of fulfilling a vowed tithe was by rendering the portion to a priest or to a Levite, Jacob's first opportunity to complete his promise to God was when his son was ordained a priest by the heavenly angels. Yet another text which the sentence calls to mind is Gen 14:18-20, where Abram encounters Melchizedek, priest of the Most High God, at Salem. On that occasion Abram tithes all his possessions to the mysterious figure. Similarly, Jacob tithes to Levi who also serves the Most High God.[109] It appears the author of our text wished to depict Levi's relationship to Jacob as similar to the one that existed between Abram and

---

[108] For other passages concerned with the matter, see Kugel, "Levi's Elevation," 4.

[109] See *Ar. Levi* 9b, where the unusual designation for God probably appears; see NOTE above.

Melchizedek, and to claim for Levi the sacerdotal role of the latter figure.

Two additional biblical texts shimmering through this narrative are Exod 28:41, the *locus classicus* for the notion that "filling the hands" of an individual amounts to ordination to the priesthood (*Ar. Levi* 9b); and Lev 9:22, which indicates that the proper response of the newly ordained priest is to bless his congregants, just as Levi blesses his father and brothers after his earthly ordination (*Ar. Levi* 9c).

James Kugel has suggested one additional connection between this passage and the Hebrew Bible. Noting that two trips to Hebron on the part of Jacob and his family are not found in the biblical narrative, he wonders about the scriptural basis for the second journey. Citing the presence of Deborah, Rebekah's nurse, at Bethel in Gen 35:7-8, Kugel supposes that the author took the reference to indicate that a trip to Hebron, on the occasion of which Deborah and Rebekah joined the family for the return to Bethel, is simply not mentioned in Genesis; it is only implied by the reference to Deborah's death. Seizing on this the author supplied an account of the unmentioned journey, including in it Isaac's blessing of Levi.[110]

The way in which the author of *Aramaic Levi* used sources in this instance demonstrates well the intent of the passage. By utilizing texts dealing with elevation to the priesthood (Exod 28:41), priestly actions and prerogatives (Gen 14:18-20; Num 18:21-28; and Lev 9:22), and Isaac's generous blessing (Gen 27:27-29), the author paints a picture of Levi as an eminently priestly figure. His visionary ordination is confirmed by human blessing and appointment at the hands of the forefathers of all Israel, and immediately upon ordination he knows how to act as clergy. The author wants to make certain that there is no doubt about the authenticity of Levi's priesthood; this first and ideal priest is shown to have had the best pedigree possible, and he proves himself immediately as a worthy occupant of the office.

The connection of this passage to the rest of *Aramaic Levi* is evident: it legitimates once more Levi's violence at Shechem, his prayerful plea for the priesthood, and his heavenly election to the office. All that remains is for Levi to be instructed in the rules of priestly conduct and to teach his children regarding proper thought and action.

Meanwhile the relationship between this passage and the other texts in the LPT is complex. It is probable that the author relied on a source for the passage, a source that is only incompletely preserved among the texts of the LPT. Supporting this contention is the way *Ar. Levi* 8 gives only a one-sentence resumé of the non-biblical material that appears in much fuller form in *Jub.* 31:4-32. In the latter text we

---

[110] Kugel, "Levi's Elevation," 24-27. Note, however, that Kugel thinks the author in question is the writer of *Jubilees*, and that *Aramaic Levi* relied on that work for this brief reference.

read a complete version of Isaac's blessing for Levi and a full explanation of how Levi and his family traveled to Isaac and back once more to Bethel. Meanwhile, *Ar. Levi* 8 only alludes to the blessing, and the trip from Isaac back to Bethel is omitted altogether, only to become apparent when we read later that it is in Bethel that Jacob acts on Levi's behalf and Levi sacrifices for Jacob (*Ar. Levi* 10b). At least one scholar has concluded from this that *Aramaic Levi* must have relied on *Jubilees*,[111] while the more usual view is that both authors shared, independently of one another, a common source.[112] The accepted date for *Jubilees'* composition (between 164 and 152 BCE) makes it difficult to believe that *Aramaic Levi* could have relied on it, since the oldest manuscripts of *Aramaic Levi* are nearly that age themselves. One must posit the near-autograph character of the Qumran manuscripts of *Aramaic Levi*, and considerable breadth of distribution of *Jubilees* within a decade of its composition in order to defend this view. Both circumstances seem unlikely. Moreover, as our discussion of *Aramaic Levi's* date of composition will indicate, it is probable that it originated sometime in the third century BCE. Thus the differences and similarities between *Ar. Levi* 8 and *Jub.* 31:4-32 support the view that both authors used a common source independently of one another, a source that contained a blessing of Levi from Isaac and a fuller description of the family's travel. *Jubilees* preserves the more complete form of the source, while *Aramaic Levi* has reduced it to a passing notice.

The latter conclusion is not without difficulties. It seems strange that *Aramaic Levi*, with its deep concern to elevate Levi in the eyes of its readers, would virtually eliminate Isaac's blessing which is so rich in praise for Levi. However, as analysis of Levi's wisdom speech and discourse on his children's' future indicates (see 3.1.7 below), the author of *Aramaic Levi* apparently reused elements of Isaac's blessing for that address. The blessing was not lost; it was simply utilized in a new way by the author of *Aramaic Levi*.

This version of Levi's encounter with Isaac and Jacob differs in other significant ways from the parallel accounts in *Jubilees* and *Testament of Levi*. The author of *Jubilees* 31 expands considerably the first sojourn in Hebron with additional material which gives a blessing of Isaac for Judah, and an exchange between Jacob and Isaac. *Jub.* 32:3-9, in keeping with the author's interest in narrative consistency, also rationalizes Jacob's selection of Levi as his priest by making Levi a

---

[111] Kugel, "Levi's Elevation," 52-58.

[112] See Grelot, "Notes," 405-6; Haupt, "Testament," 71; Anders Hultgård, *L'eschatologie des Testaments des Douze Patriarches*, vol. 1, *Interprétation des textes* (Acta Universitatis Upsaliensis; Historia Religionum 6; Uppsala: Almqvist & Wiksell, 1977) 24; 2:98; and de Jonge, *Testaments*, 39, 140, n. 10, 148, n. 167. But Becker, *Untersuchungen*, 104-5; and Ulrichsen, *Grundschrift*, 182, think that *Jubilees*, *Aramaic Levi*, and *Testament of Levi* were all based on a common oral tradition.

part of Jacob's tithe.[113] *T. Levi* 9:1-3 gives the most abbreviated account of these events, making two important changes.   In the report Jacob's vision, by means of which he knew Levi's priestly status, is added, and his ordination and investiture of Levi are omitted.[114]

3.1.5. *Ar. Levi* 13-61: Isaac's cultic instructions

After being ordained a priest by Jacob, Levi is instructed by his grandfather, Isaac, in proper cultic action.   An extraordinary and lengthy section of *Aramaic Levi* that makes up about a third of the extant portion of the document,[115] it is represented generously in all four witnesses to the text.   While Mt. Athos 18:2 preserves all of the cultic instructions, the Cairo Geniza fragment located in the Bodleian Library goes as far as *Ar. Levi* 32, 4Q213 4–5 contribute material matching *Ar. Levi* 24-30, and 4Q214 1–5 attest to *Ar. Levi* 22-27.   Because of the completeness of the Geniza and Mt. Athos texts, they are used here, with Bodl. b 5–d 23 providing the text for *Ar. Levi* 13-32,[116] and Mt. Athos 18:2 supplying the remainder.[117]

---

[113] For an extended discussion of this passage in *Jubilees*, see 4.3.5.

[114] For reflection on the reason for these differences between *Aramaic Levi* and *Testament of Levi*, see 5.4.4.

[115] The percentage is based on thirty-eight verses (*Ar. Levi* 13-61) of one hundred thirty-three being devoted to cultic instructions.   The total for *Aramaic Levi* derives from the merger of the Cairo Geniza and Mt. Athos manuscript total of ninety-five verses with the additional material supplied by 4Q213 between the Shechem incident and the conclusion of the vision, and at the end of Levi's instructions to his children.

[116] On several occasions the Cairo Geniza text reproduced here has been emended in line with the witness of 4Q213 or 4Q214.   Otherwise the Cairo Geniza text is printed without the conjectural emendations offered by previous commentators. Nevertheless, some of those emendations are discussed in the NOTES, and are adopted as readings which affect translation.

[117] The Greek text appears with the spelling and punctuation norms employed by Marinus de Jonge in *The Testaments of the Twelve Patriarchs: A Critical Edition of the Greek Text* (PVTG I, 2; Leiden: E. J. Brill, 1978).

T<small>EXT</small>

[13]וכדי ידע די אנה כהן לאל עליון למארי שמיא שארי לפקדה יתי ולאלפא יתי דין כהנותא

ואמר לי [14]לוי אזדהר לך ברי מן כל טומאה ומן כל חטא דינך רב הוא מן כל בישרא

[15]וכען ברי דין קושטא אחוינך ולא אטמר מינך כל פתגם לאלפותך דין כהנותא [16]לקדמין היזדהר

לך ברי מן כל פחז וטמאה ומן כל זנות [17]ואנת אנתתא מן משפחתי סב לך ולא תחל זרעך עם

זניאן ארי זרע קדיש אנת וקדיש זרעך היך קודשא ארו כהן קדיש אנת מתקרי לכל זרע אברהם

קריב אנת ל[אל]וקריב לכל קדישׁוהי כען אזדכי בבשרך מן כל טומאת כל גבר [18]

[19]כדי תהוי קאים למיעל לבית אל הוי סחי במיא ובאדין תהוי לביש לבוש כהנותא [20]וכדי תהוי

לביש הוי תאיב תוב ורחיע ידיך ורגליך עד דלא תקרב למדבחא כל דנה [21]וכדי תהוי נסב

להקרבה כל די חזה להנסקה למדבחה הוי עוד תאב ורחיע ידיך ורגליך [22]ומהקריב אעין מהצלחין

ובקר אינון לקודמין מן תולעא ובאדין הסק אינון ארי כדנה חזיתי לאברהם אבי מיזדהר

[23]מן כל תריעשר מיני אעין די די חזין להנסקה מינהון למדבחה די ריח תננהון בשים סליק

[24]ואלין אינון שמהתהון ארזא ודפרנא וסגדא ואטולא ושוחא ואדונא ברותא ותאנתא ואע משחא

ערא והדסה ואעי דקתא [25]אלין אינון די אמר לי די חזין להסקה מנהון ל[תחו]ת עלתא על

מדבחה וכדי [הסקת] מן אעי אלין על מדבחה ונורא ישרא להדלקא בהון והא באדין תשרא

למזרק דמא על כותלי מדבחה [26]ועוד רחע ידיך ורגליך מן דמא ושרי להנסקה אבריה מליחין

[27]וראשה הוי מהנסק לקדמין ועלוהי חפי תרבא ולא יתחזה לה דם נסבת תורא [28]ובתרוהי צוארה

ובתר צוארה ידוהי ובתר ידוהי ניעא עם כן דפנא ובתר ידיא ירכאתא עם שדרת חרצא ובתר

ירכאתא רגלין רחיען עם קרביא [29]וכולהון מליחין במלח כדי חזה להון כמסתהון [30]ובתר דנה

נישפא בליל במשחא ובתר כולא חמר נסך והקטיר עליהון לבונה ויהון [כל] עובדיך בסרך וכל

קורבניך [לרעו]א לריח ניחוח קודם אל עליון [31]ו[כל די] תהוה עביד בסרך הוי עב[יד במדה]

ובמתקל לא תותר צבו די לא [הזה] ולא תחסר מן חושבן הזה °° אע[ין] חזיק להקרבה לכל

די סליק למדבחא [32]לתורא רבא כבר אעין ליה במתקל ואם תרבא בלחודוהי סליק שיתה מנין

ואם פר תורין הוא די סליק

End of the Bodl. d; continue reading with Mt. Athos 18:2

[32b][και τω ταυρω τω δευτερω] πεντηκοντα μνας. και εις το στεαρ αυτου
μονον πεντε μνας. [33]και εις μοσχον τελειον μ μναι. [34]και ει κριος εκ
προβατων η τραγος εξ αιγων το προσφερομενον η, και τουτω λ μναι, και τω
στεατι τρεις μναι· [35]και ει αρνα εκ προβατων η εριφον εξ αιγων κ μναι, και
τω στεατι β μναι· [36]και ει αμνος τελειος ενιαυσιος η εριφος εξ αιγων ιε

μναι, και τω στεατι μιαν ημισυ μναν. ³⁷και αλας αποδεδεικτω τω ταυρω τω μεγαλω αλισαι το κρεας αυτου, και ανενεγκε επι τον βωμον. σατον καθηκει τω ταυρω· και ω αν περισσευση του αλος αλισον εν αυτω το δερμα· ³⁸και τω ταυρω τω δευτερω τα πεντε μερη απο των εξ μερων του σατου· και του μοσχου το διμοιρον του σατου. ³⁹και τω κριω το ημισυ του σατου και τω τραγω το ισον· ⁴⁰και τω αρνιω και τω εριφω το τριτον του σατου και σεμιδαλις καθηκουσα αυτοις· ⁴¹τω ταυρω τω μεγαλω και τω ταυρω β και τω μοσχαριω, σατον σεμιδαλιν· ⁴²και τω κριω και τω τραγω τα δου μερη του σατου και τω αρνιω και τω εριφω εξ αιγων το τριτον του σατου και το ελαιον· ⁴³και το τεταρτον του σατου τω ταυρω αναπεποιημενον εν τη σεμιδαλει ταυτη· ⁴⁴και τω κριω το εκτον του σατου και τω αρνιω το ογδοον του σατου και αμνου και οινον κατα το μετρον του ελαιου τω ταυρω και τω κριω και τω εριφω κατασπεισαι σπονδην. ⁴⁵Λιβανωτου σικλοι εξ τω ταυρω και το ημισυ αυτου τω κριω και το τριτον αυτου τω εριφω· και πασα η σεμιδαλις αναπεποιημενη· ⁴⁶η αν προσαγαγης μονον, ουκ επι στεατος, προσωχθισεται επ αυτην λιβανου ολκη σικλων δυο· και το τριτον του σατου το τριτον του υφη εστιν· ⁴⁷και τα δυο μερη του βατου και ολκης της μνας ν σικλων εστιν· και του σικλου το τεταρτον ολκη θερμων δ εστιν· γινεται ο σικλος ωσει ις θερμοι και ολκης μιας. ⁴⁸και νυν, τεκνον μου, ακουσον τους λογους μου και ενωτισαι τας εντολας μου, και μη αποστητωσαν οι λογοι μου ουτοι απο της καρδιας σου εν πασαις ταις ημεραις σου, οτι ιερευς συ αγιος κυριου, ⁴⁹και ιερεις εσονται παν το σπερμα σου· και τοις υιοις σου ουτως εντειλον ινα ποιησουσιν κατα την κρισιν ταυτην ως σοι υπεδειξα. ⁵⁰Ουτως γαρ μοι ενετειλατο ο πατηρ Αβρααμ ποιειν και εντελλεσθαι τοις υιοις μου. ⁵¹και νυν, τεκνον, χαιρω οτι εξελεχθης εις ιεροσυνην αγιαν και προσενεγκειν θυσιαν κυριω υψιστω, ως καθηκει κατα το προστεταγμενον τουτω ποιειν. ⁵²οταν παραλαμβανης θυσιαν ποιειν εναντι κυριου απο πασης σαρκος, κατα τον λογισμον των ξυλων επιδεχου ουτως, ως σοι εντελλομαι, και το αλας και την σεμιδαλιν και τον οινον και τον λιβανον επιδεχου εκ των χειρων αυτων επι παντα κτηνη. ⁵³και επι πασαν ωραν νιπτου τας χειρας και τους ποδας, οταν πορευη προς το θυσιαστηριον· και οταν εκπορευης εκ των αγιων, παν αιμα μη απτεσθω της στολης σου· ουκ ανηψης αυτω αυθημερον. ⁵⁴και τας χειρας και τους ποδας νιπτου δια παντος απο πασης της σαρκος· ⁵⁵και μη οφθητω επι σοι παν αιμα πασα ψυχη· το γαρ αιμα ψυχη εστιν εν τη σαρκι. ⁵⁶και ο εαν εν οικω ουσης σεαυτον παν κρεας φαγειν, καλυπτε το αιμα αυτου τη γη πρωτον πριν η φαγειν σε απο των κρεων και ουκετι εση εσθιων επι του αιματος. ⁵⁷ουτως γαρ μοι ενετειλατο ο πατηρ μου Αβρααμ, οτι ουτως ευρεν εν τη γραφη της βιβλου του Νωε περι

του αιματος. ⁵⁸και νυν ως σοι, τεκνον αγαπητον, εγω λεγω, ηγαπημενος συ
τω πατρι σου και αγιος κυριου υψιστου· και ηγαπημενος εση υπερ παντας
τους αδελφους σου. ⁵⁹τω σπερματι σου ευλογηθησεται εν τη γη και το
σπερμα σου εως παντων των αιωνων ενεχθησεται εν βιβλιω μνημοσυνου
ζωης· ⁶⁰και ουκ εξαλειφθησεται το ονομα σου και το ονομα σπερματος σου
εως των αιωνων. ⁶¹και νυν, τεκνον Λευι, ευλογημενον εσται το σπερμα σου
επι της γης εις πασας τας γενεας των αιωνων.

TRANSLATION

¹³When he knew that I was a priest of the Most High God, of the Lord
of heaven, he began to command me and to teach me the law of the
priesthood. And he said to me, ¹⁴"Levi, keep yourself pure, my son,
from all uncleanness, and from all sin. Your judgment is greater than
that of all flesh. ¹⁵And now, my son, the true law I will show you, and
I will not hide from you any word, so as to teach you the law of the
priesthood. ¹⁶First, keep yourself pure of all fornication and uncleanness, and of all harlotry. ¹⁷And you, take for yourself a wife from my
family so that you will not defile your seed with harlots. For you are
holy seed, and holy is your seed, like the holy place. For you are a
holy priest called for all the seed of Abraham. ¹⁸You are near to [God,
]and near to all his holy ones. Now be pure in your flesh from all uncleanness of any man. ¹⁹When you rise to enter the house of God wash
with water, and then put on the priestly clothing. ²⁰And when you are
clothed, once again wash your hands and your feet before you approach
the altar at all. ²¹And when you take to offer anything that is fitting to
sacrifice upon the altar, once again wash your hands and your feet.
²²And offer split wood, but inspect it first for worms. And then offer
it up, for thus I saw Abraham my father acting carefully. ²³Of any of
twelve kinds of wood he said to me that they are fitting for offering
upon the altar, for their smoke rises up with a pleasant odor. ²⁴These
are their names; cedar, and juniper, and almond, and fir, and pine, and
ash, cypress, and fig, and oleaster, laurel, and myrtle and asphaltos.
²⁵These are those that he told me are fitting to offer up from them
u[nd]er the burnt offering upon the altar. And when [you have offered
up] from the woods of these trees upon the altar, and the fire begins to
burn them, at that very time you will begin to sprinkle the blood on the
sides of the altar. ²⁶And once again wash your hands and your feet of
the blood, and begin to offer up the salted parts. ²⁷Let the head be offered up first, and cover it with fat, but do not let be seen upon it the

blood of the slaughtered bull. [28]And after it its neck, and after its neck its forequarters, and after its forequarters the breast with the base of the rib, and after this the haunches with the spine of the loins, and after the haunches the hindquarters washed with the inner parts. [29]And all of them salted with salt as is fitting for them, as much as they require. [30]And after this, the fine meal mixed with the oil, and after everything pour wine and burn over them incense. And let [all] your deeds be in order, and all your sacrifices [be acceptab]le for a pleasing odor before the Most High God. [31][And whatever] you do, let it be done in order, and let [it be done in measure] and by weight. Do not add anything whatsoever which is not [appropriate]. And do not diminish from the amount ∘∘∘∘ wo[od] fit for sacrifice for anything that is offered on the altar. [32]For a large bull, a talent's weight of wood for it; and if the fat alone is offered up, six minas; and if a bullock of oxen is offered

End of the Bodl. d; continue reading with Mt. Athos 18:2

(and for a second bull) fifty minas, and for its fat alone, five minas. [33]And for a heifer, forty minas. [34]And if that which is offered is a ram of the sheep or a he-goat out of the goats, for it thirty minas and for its fat three minas. [35]And if it is a lamb of the sheep or a kid of the goats, twenty minas, and for its fat two minas. [36]And if it is an unblemished lamb one year old or a kid of the goats fifteen minas, and for its fat one and a half minas. [37]And [untranslatable word] salt upon the large bull to salt its flesh and offer it up upon the altar. A saton is appropriate for the bull; and with whatever salt is left over salt the skin. [38]And for the second bull; five sixths of a saton; and for the heifer, two thirds of a saton; [39]and for the ram half a saton; and for the he-goat the equal amount; [40]and for the lamb and the kid a third of a saton. And the fine flour which is appropriate for them: [41]for the large bull and for the second bull and for the heifer, a saton of fine flour; [42]and for the ram and the he-goat two portions of a saton, and for the lamb and the kid of the goats a third of a saton. And the oil: [43]and the fourth of a saton for the bull mixed up in that fine flour; [44]and for the ram the sixth of a saton, and for the lamb the eighth of a saton, and of the lamb (?). And wine: according to the measure of the oil for the bull and for the ram and for the kid pour out a drink-offering. [45]Six shekels of frankincense for the bull, and half of that for the ram, and a third of that for the kid. And all the mixed up fine flour, [46]whenever you offer it up alone and not upon the fat, let two shekels' weight of frankincense be poured out

(?) upon it. And a third of a saton is a third of an ephah, [47]and two thirds of a bath, and of the weight of the mina, it is of fifty shekels (?). And the fourth of the shekel is the weight of four thermoi. The shekel comes to about sixteen thermoi and of one weight (?). [48]And now, my child, listen to my words and pay heed to my commandments, and let not these my words leave your heart all your days, for you are a holy priest of the Lord, [49]and all your seed will be priests. And command your sons thus, so that they do according to this determination as I have shown you. [50]For thus father Abraham commanded me to do and to command my sons. [51]And now, child, I rejoice that you were elected to the holy priesthood, and to offer sacrifice to the Most High Lord, to do as is appropriate, according to this instruction. [52]Whenever you receive a sacrifice to make before the Lord from any flesh, accept thus according to the figuring of the wood, as I commanded you, and the salt and the fine flour and the wine and the frankincense accept from their hands for all creatures. [53]And on each occasion wash (your) hands and feet whenever you go to the altar; and whenever you come out of the sanctuary, let no blood cling to your robe. Do not kindle it (?) on that same day. [54]And wash (your) hands and feet completely from all the flesh, [55]and let not any blood, any soul be seen upon you, for the blood is (the) soul in the flesh. [56]And if in your house [untranslatable word] yourself, to eat any flesh, hide its blood in the earth first, before you eat from the flesh so that you should no longer eat of the blood. [57]For thus my father Abraham commanded me, for thus he found in the writing of the book of Noah concerning the blood. [58]And now, as I say to you, beloved child, you are beloved to your father and holy of the Most High Lord. And you will be more beloved than all your brothers. [59]And blessing will be pronounced by your seed upon the earth and your seed will be entered in a book of a memorial of life for all eternity. [60]And your name and the name of your seed will not be blotted out for eternity. [61]And now, (my) child Levi, your seed will be blessed upon the earth for all generations of eternity.

NOTES ON THE TEXT AND TRANSLATION

Ar. Levi 13. לאל עליון. The Greek text reads κυριω.

Ar. Levi 14. ברי ברי. Most critics see the doublet as a scribal error.[118] We translate it as "[Keep yourself] *pure, my son.*" See v. 16
for the same use of ברי for "pure."

Ar. Levi 14. דינך. Charles translates the word as "rights."[119]
Greenfield and Stone prefer the word judgment, although they say
"liability" is "most likely on intrinsic grounds."[120] Grelot translates
"droit."[121] It seems clear that *judgment* regarding sacrifices and disputes is meant here, especially since "law" is what Isaac is about to
teach Levi.

Ar. Levi 16. פחז. Greenfield links this word, and the bulk of the
verse with the quotation of the words of Levi in CD 4 15-19.[122]

Ar. Levi 19, 20, 21. סחי/ורחע. Greenfield and Stone suggest that
the first verb is equivalent to λουω, "to bathe," and the second to νιζω,
"to wash part of the body."[123] Though the distinction would add further nuance to Levi's ablution requirements, which already exceed
those of the Pentateuch, unfortunately the distinction they suggest cannot be established with a sufficient degree of certainty.

Ar. Levi 20. עד דלא תקרב למדבחא כל דנה. Greenfield and Stone's
rendering of כל דנה, "at all," is preferable to that of Charles, who took
it as "anything," the direct object of תקרב, "offer."[124] Not until the next
phrase does attention shift to the material placed on the altar; this one
addresses the preliminary and more general issue of approaching the
altar in the first place. Note that the Greek omits כל דנה, replacing it
with προσενεγκαι ολοκαρπωσιν, "to offer a burnt offering."

Ar. Levi 22-30. The underlined text in this section appears in
either 4Q213 4-5 9-22 or 4Q214 1-4 1-9. The parallel material from
4Q214 1-4 begins in v. 22 and ends with the last word of v. 26.
Parallels with 4Q213 4-5 commence with ואע in v. 24 and conclude in
v. 30.[125] Double-underlined text appears in both Qumran manuscripts.
Apart from orthographic differences there are few substantive varia-

---

[118] For example, Greenfield and Stone, "Appendix III," 462, n. b, where they say
"Dittography of 'my son' in Greek. Omitted sometimes by Greek, cf. e.g., vv. 15
and 16." See also Charles, *Greek Versions*, 274, n. 6, where he states, "Aram.
repeats τεκνον."

[119] Charles, *APOT* II, 364.

[120] Greenfield and Stone, "Remarks," 220.

[121] P. Grelot, "Le coutumier sacerdotal ancien dans le Testament araméen de
Lévi," *RevQ* 15 (1991) 255.

[122] Jonas Greenfield, "The Words of Levi, Son of Jacob in Damascus Document
IV, 15-19," *RevQ* 13 (1988) 319-22.

[123] Greenfield and Stone, "Remarks," 221.

[124] Ibid.; Charles, *APOT* II, 364. Grelot, "Le coutumier," 255, translates "avant
que tu n'approches de l'autel".

[125] There is evidence of two additional lines visible in 4Q213 4-5 before line 9, but
they contain only one letter each.

tions among the three manuscripts. Those of interest are indicated in the following notes.

Ar. Levi 22. מַן_תולעא. 4Q214 4-5 2 adds the word כול between מן and תולעא.

Ar. Levi 23. 4Q213 adds לבוך ("grasp"?) between כל and תריעשר.

Ar. Levi 24. The names of the trees are not all known. Some appear in all four of the witnesses. 4Q214 is, for the most part, remarkably similar to the Cairo Geniza text.[126]

Ar. Levi 25. די חזין. 4Q214 1-4 6 adds אלן אנון before this phrase.

Ar. Levi 25. כדי [הסקת] מן אעי אלין על מדבחה. The Greek text omits the sentence. Greenfield and Stone indicate that its absence is due to homoioteleuton, while Charles thinks that the phrase is a later gloss in the Aramaic.[127] Added to this confusion is the fact that 4Q213 4-5 12 cannot be placed with certainty in this section, since it reads]לאסק[, the equivalent of which in the Cairo Geniza manuscript (להסקה in v. 25) appears *before* the parallel material from 4Q213 4-5 11. The most original form of the verse remains an unsolved mystery.

Ar. Levi 26. מליחין. Although the Cairo Geniza manuscript reads מליחי, it is appropriate to emend the text to read with a final *nun* since 4Q214 1–4 9, providing the same text, clearly reads with the final *nun*.[128]

Ar. Levi 27. וראשה. The Cairo Geniza manuscript reads ואשה. We have emended on the basis of 4Q214 1–4 9 and 4Q213 4-5 15, which confirm the Greek text, την κεφαλην, "the head," and in agreement with the emendation offered, without textual support, by Charles and by Greenfield and Stone.[129]

Ar. Levi 27. נסבת תורא. Read נכסת תורא, "slaughtered bull," with Greenfield and Stone, and before them, Lévi.[130]

Ar. Levi 28. בן דפנא. Read "base of the rib."

Ar. Levi 28. דפנא ובתר ידיא יכאתא עם שדרה. The dotted underlining highlights the considerable differences in this section between the Cairo Geniza manuscript and 4Q213 4-5 17-18. Line 17 reads א[, ובתרהן ידיא], probably where the Cairo Geniza manuscript has דפנא ובתר ידיא. Line 18

---

[126] See note 152 for the additional primary texts where wood for the sacrifice is mentioned, and for secondary literature on the subject.

[127] Greenfield and Stone, "Remarks," 221; Charles, *The Greek Versions*, 249, n. 13.

[128] Thus the emendation offered by Charles without textual support, *Greek Versions*, 250, n. a, is confirmed by the textual evidence of 4Q214. *Pace* Greenfield and Stone, "Remarks," 222, where they think the text ought to be emended to read מליחיה, to match with the preceding word, אבריה, "its parts." Compare with 4Q213 4–5 15.

[129] Charles, *Greek Versions*, 250, n. d; Greenfield and Stone, "Remarks," 222.

[130] Greenfield and Stone, "Remarks," 222; I. Lévi, "Notes sur le texte du Testament de Lévi," 170. Note that the Greek reads here επι της κεφαλης αυτης, "upon its head."

gives ובח‎ן‎רהן ירכחא ושדר‎ן‎ח, and seems to parallel the Cairo Geniza manuscript where ירכאחא appears. The lemmata of 4Q213 are thus too close together to match the geniza text very closely, and the use of בחרהן instead of בחר indicates variation between the texts in terms of the way in which they grouped the parts of the sacrifice being described. In addition, it appears that the scribe responsible for the geniza manuscript was confused, writing ידיא after ובחר and before ירכאחא, well after the complete description of the forequarters. Hence Charles was probably right to emend ובחר ידיא to read ובחר דנה, "and after this," in correspondence with the Greek, και μετα ταυτα, even though the evidence of 4Q213 4-5 17-18 suggests that the corruption was somewhat more complex.[131]

Ar. Levi 30. ‎[כל]‎ עובדיך בסרך ‎ויהון‎. Here 4Q213 4-5 22 reads ‎[להוא עבדך בס]‎.

Ar. Levi 31. חזיק. Read חזין, "fitting."[132]

Ar. Levi 32. ואם פר חורין. While the Aramaic can be translated "And if [it is] a bullock of oxen," the corresponding Greek text, repeated in vv. 38 and 41, refers to a ταυρω δευτερω, "a second bull." It is likely that the Greek translator misread פר חורין, "bullock of oxen," for פר תרין, "a second bullock."[133]

Ar. Levi 37. αποδεδεικτω. Charles suggests that this is a "corrupt form of αποδεικνυμι ['sprinkle']."[134] Although Charles' idea represents a rather remote possibility,[135] the path taken by Greenfield and Stone—of letting the mystery stand—is preferable. There is no manuscript evidence to support Charles' emendation.[136]

Ar. Levi 37. σατον. The Greek word for seah.[137]

Ar. Levi 44. και αμνου. The genitive case is not entirely explicable here. The most plausible explanation of the unattached phrase is Grelot's suggestion that it is an incomplete repetition of a previous portion of the verse.[138]

Ar. Levi 46. προσωχθισεται. Charles suggests that the word is corrupt for προσενεχθησεται, "to be dashed upon."[139] Like his suggestion for the untranslatable verb form in v. 37, this one is interesting, but in the absence of manuscript support is not acceptable.

---

[131] Charles and Cowley, "Early Source," 580, n. 8.

[132] Charles, *Greek Versions*, 250.

[133] Greenfield and Stone, "Appendix III," 464.

[134] Charles, *Greek Versions*, 251.

[135] The word is not otherwise translated as "sprinkle," usually having the meaning of "point out, indicate." See H. G. Liddell and Robert Scott, *A Greek-English Lexicon* (rev. ed.; Oxford: Clarendon, 1940 1968) 195.

[136] Greenfield and Stone, "Appendix III," 464.

[137] See 𝕲 Hag 2:16-17; Matt 13:33; Luke 13:21; cf. Josephus, *Ant.* 9 § 85.

[138] Grelot, "Le coutumier," 257, n. 15.

[139] Charles, *Greek Versions*, 251.

Ar. Levi 47. The entire verse seems to have been corrupted, either in the process of translation, or through the history of the text's transmission. The genitive οκλης, "of the weight," is not clear, nor is the meaning of the word θερμοι, and the concluding phrase seems incomplete.[140]

Ar. Levi 51 κυριω υψιστω. This name for God probably reflects a Greek translator's rendering of אל עליון, a frequent designation for the Divine throughout *Aramaic Levi*.[141] Cf. *Ar. Levi* 58.

Ar. Levi 53. ανηψης. Greenfield and Stone give, "be [not] connected," for this word.[142] The lexicon offers little support for their conjecture. However Charles' translation, "You shall not kindle it," does win support from the lexicon, if the verb is αναπτω, "to kindle."[143] However that suggestion offers little help, inasmuch as it is nonsensical in the context. Hence the meaning remains unclear.

Ar. Levi 56. ουσης. The Greek is corrupt and untranslatable.

COMMENT[144]

The instructions begin with an introductory section in which Isaac exhorts Levi to safeguard himself from contamination (*Ar. Levi* 13-18).[145] At the heart of the purity-centered introduction is Isaac's contention that Levi's judgment is superior to that of any other human being; hence it is necessary that Levi defend his own purity. With his claim Isaac implicitly asserts that Levi is especially fit for the role of the priest; it is that individual who determines the proper measures to be paid by worshipers for the atonement of sin, the fulfillment of vows, and thank-offerings. Levi, Isaac urges, should protect that privilege from taint.

There are several biblical traditions used in the introduction. First, this particular journey to Isaac appears to be the one referred to in Gen 35:27 on the occasion of which Isaac dies.[146] Rather than letting

---

[140] Greenfield and Stone, "Appendix III," 465, nn. e-g. For θερμοι, see also Grelot, "Le coutumier," 257, n. 16.

[141] See, for example, *Ar. Levi* 13, 30.

[142] Greenfield and Stone, "Appendix III," 465.

[143] Charles, *APOT* II, 365. See Liddell and Scott, *A Greek-English Lexicon*, 118.

[144] Due to the length of the section we integrate description of the content of separate sections of the instructions with the discussion of the biblical sources that appear in them. We also note that, although the unusual nature of many of the cultic prescriptions appearing in this extended passage invite more in-depth analysis, especially comparison with rabbinic, Qumran (e.g., the Temple Scroll), and other pseudepigraphic cultic texts, we restrict our search for parallels to the biblical tradition. It lies beyond the scope of this study to do more.

[145] The first segment of Isaac's instructions is preserved only in Bodl. b 5b-23 and in Mt. Athos 18:2.

[146] Kugel, "Levi's Elevation," 24, agrees with this assessment.

that come immediately to pass, the author uses the visit as Isaac's opportunity to educate Levi in cultic matters. The term in *Ar. Levi* 13 and 15, דין כהנותא, the "law of the priesthood," recalls Deut 18:3, משפט כהנים, "the customary due of the priests" (REB). But unlike the biblical passage which speaks of what is due to a priest, this one addresses what is expected of him. The notion of Levi's דין, "judgment," in *Ar. Levi* 14 draws Deut 33:10 to mind, with its admonition to Levi that he teach משפטיך, "your ordinances," to Isaac and תורתך, "your law," to Israel. The following sentence recalls Lev 21:7, 14-15, where the priests are prohibited from marrying women of questionable background, and thus from introducing exogamous marriages into the priestly bloodline.[147] The admonition, that Levi marry within the community, seems to imply that a woman's non-Israelite parentage would qualify her for the label זנה, "harlot." Such words from the mouth of Isaac recall Gen 28:1ff, where he instructs his sons not to marry Canaanite women. Finally, the reference in *Ar. Levi* 18 to Levi's closeness to God's "holy ones" recalls Zech 3:7.[148] All of these biblical allusions underscore the point of the section—Levi is holy unto God and must defend his sanctity against impurity.

After the general introduction the instructions begin with Isaac's explanation of the necessary ablutions in the context of sacrifice (*Ar. Levi* 19-21).[149] The section appears at first glance to be quite mundane. Yet when it is compared to corresponding biblical norms for ablution in association with sacrifice, it is an unusual passage, for Levi is instructed to exceed those demands considerably. He must wash before vesting (v. 19), after vesting and before approaching the altar (v. 20), and once more before undertaking the actual act of sacrifice (v. 21). And in v. 26 we learn that he must wash again after sprinkling the blood of the sacrifice on the sides of the altar.[150] In the corresponding biblical requirements, Exod 30:19-21, Moses instructs Aaron and his sons regarding proper ablutions for cultic servants. The passage has an envelope structure, stating at the beginning and conclusion that if they wash according to this rule they will not die. Between the two general admonitions two washings are mandated—one prior to entering the

[147] See Beyer, *Die aramäischen Texten*, 197, n. 1.

[148] There is also a non-biblical tradition which makes an appearance here and elsewhere in Second Temple literature. *Ar. Levi* 17b is very similar to 1QSb 4. Both texts liken a priestly figure to the heavenly angels, and draw the priestly figure into connection with the sanctuary. Similarly *Ar. Levi* 18 is related to *Jub.* 31:16 (cf. Greenfield and Stone, "Remarks," 221).

[149] The two witnesses that give this section of text are Mt. Athos 18:2 and Bodl. c 1-8.

[150] These very specific requirements stand in sharp contrast to the more general exhortation in vv. 53ff to wash before and after sacrifice to avoid having any blood of the sacrifice cling to one's body or garments.

sanctuary and one before bringing anything forward to sacrifice on the altar. *Aramaic Levi* does not differ from Exodus insofar as Isaac commands Levi to wash before he enters the sanctuary and immediately before he approaches the altar with a sacrifice (cf. *Ar. Levi* 19, 21 and Exod 30:20-21a). But it adds a second ablution to be accomplished after vesting, one which is absent in the Torah (*Ar. Levi* 20). Lev 8:6-7 does tell of Moses washing Aaron and his sons *before* they are vested for the first time; but otherwise there is no indication in the Pentateuch regarding the need to wash immediately *after* vesting.

The next section of Isaac's instructions gives a list of twelve kinds of wood acceptable for the fire on the altar under the sacrifice (*Ar. Levi* 22-25a).[151] It is difficult to imagine that the author of *Aramaic Levi* did not have some source for the list. But whatever the case, a tradition of naming and/or restricting the kinds of wood acceptable for use in the holocaust offering follows, appearing in *Jubilees* 21, and continuing in rabbinic literature.[152] The biblical foundation upon which the text rests is very narrow. Lev 1:7 simply instructs the priest to arrange the wood upon the altar in an orderly fashion (ערך). *Aramaic Levi* represents a considerable elaboration on the single verb, ערך, "to put in order, arrange," of Lev 1:7. The only other faint echo of an Hebrew Bible tradition is the requirement that the wood be free of worms. One suspects that the concern for worms arises from their place in the Priestly Work's categorization of "creeping things" as unclean. It would not do to have impure creatures infesting the wood used to kindle the fire for an offering to God.[153] Once again there is

---

[151] The list of the twelve kinds of wood that may be used for the holocaust fire is attested in 4Q213 4–5 7-12; 4Q214 1–4 1-7a; Bodl. c 9-21; and Mt. Athos 18:2, 22-25a. Note that the Greek text actually only gives the names of eleven trees. The fragments of 4Q213 are small, and preserve only a few words, while the many pieces of leather that Milik joined to make 4Q214 1–4 allow reconstruction of a considerable portion of the text. The section is most completely attested in the Bodl. fragment and in the Mt. Athos manuscript. There are minor differences among the witnesses, mostly owing, no doubt, to the obscurity of some of the tree names.

[152] See *Jub.* 21:12 (thirteen wood-types; see James C. VanderKam, *The Book of Jubilees* [Corpus Scriptorum Christianorum Orientalium 511; Louvain: E. Peeters, 1989] 124); *1 Enoch* 3:1 (fourteen wood-types); *T. Levi* 9:12. Rabbinic restrictions on the acceptable kinds of wood appear in *m. Tamid* 2:3; *t. Menah.* 9.14; *Sifra Nedaba Perek* 6:4; *b. Tamid* 29b; *b. Menah.* 22a; 85b. Also see the *Geoponica* 11:1. There is a considerable secondary literature dedicated to sorting out the relationships among the various witnesses to the list of acceptable wood-types. See, for example, Lévi, "Notes sur le texte araméen Testament de Lévi," 170-73; "Encore un mot sur le texte araméen du Testament de Lévi récemment découvert," *REJ* 55 (1908) 285-87; Ch. Albeck, *Das Buch der Jubiläen und die Halacha* (Berlin: Scholem, 1930) 23; R. H. Charles, *Greek Versions*, 249.

[153] Greenfield and Stone, "Remarks," 221, n. 3, note that the word used here for "inspect" in the Aramaic of the Bodl. fragment occurs regularly in rabbinic literature

an expansion of, or at least differentiation from the biblical mandates by the author.

Isaac next gives instruction regarding the order in which the parts of the sacrificial beast should be placed upon the fire (*Ar. Levi* 25b-30).[154] After sprinkling blood on the side of the altar and another ablution, Levi is told to place on the fire in order the head, fat, neck, forequarters, breast, haunches and spine of the loin, and the hindquarters washed with the inner parts. Each piece is to be salted. The sacrifice is to be followed with appropriately measured offerings of fine meal, oil, wine, and incense.

The biblical instructions regarding the holocaust offering in Leviticus 1 are probably the foundation for this order of sacrifice; nevertheless there are considerable differences between the two descriptions. While this passage states explicitly that the the blood of the sacrifice must be sprinkled *after* the fire has been laid on the altar, Lev 1:5 requires sprinkling of blood *before* laying the fire in v. 7. After that *Aramaic Levi* adds another ablution absent from Leviticus 1 (*Ar. Levi* 26). Then, according to Lev 1:8-9, the prescribed order in which the offering is to be laid on the altar is pieces, head, fat, the washed internal organs of the beast, and its legs; yet *Aramaic Levi* requires that the order be head, fat, and then the pieces and the inner parts washed with water, along with the hindquarters (*Ar. Levi* 27-28).[155] While the Torah requires that the meat offering be salted, only the קרבן is referred to (Lev 2:13; but see also Ezek 43:24), but *Aramaic Levi* states *explicitly* that the pieces of the holocaust offering are to be salted (*Ar. Levi* 26b, 29). It adds the demand that the blood of the beast not be

---

for examination of sacrificial animals. Only in *m. Mid.* 2:5 is it applied to wood, where the disqualified priests are instructed to search for worms. The expectation that it was to be free of worms also appears in *Jub* 21:13; *b. Menah.* 85b.

[154] All four witnesses to *Aramaic Levi* provide some part of the text. 4Q213 4-5 13-21 provides text from *Ar. Levi* 25bβ-30a; 4Q214 1-4 7b-9 gives text from *Ar. Levi* 25b-27a; and Mt. Athos 18:2 provides a complete witness that is virtually identical with Bodl. c 22-d 16a.

[155] While 𝔐 reserves certain actions in the rite of the burnt offering for the layman making sacrifice, *Aramaic Levi* makes no mention of the worshipper; all actions described are taken by the priest. Similarly the 𝔲 and 𝔊 texts explicitly shift some responsibilities to the priests; both provide masculine plural verbs in Lev 1:6, 12, giving the task of cutting the beast up for sacrifice to the priests. Perhaps *Aramaic Levi's* author relied on a "Samaritan" text-type. One ought not make too much of that possibility, however, since the evidence is slim and this passage only treats the actions of the priest. Moreover, we now know that the so-called Samaritan Pentateuch is not necessarily to be associated strictly with the Samaritan movement (see Judith Sanderson, *An Exodus Scroll from Qumran: 4QpaleoExod^m and the Samaritan Tradition* [HSS 30; Atlanta: Scholars Press, 1986]).

visible (*Ar. Levi* 27b), a concern absent from Leviticus 1.[156] The passage continues with the requirement that fine meal, mixed with oil, wine, and frankincense be offered with the holocaust; this is prescribed in Num 15:3, and is followed, both in *Aramaic Levi* and in the Numbers passage, by specific measures fitting for the different beasts. The section closes with a phrase that is very similar to Lev 1:13b, the final sentence in the Pentateuchal legislation for the holocaust offering; but it changes the designation for God from יהוה to אל עליון (*Ar. Levi* 30b).[157] Once again Isaac's cultic regulations differ from related Torah prescriptions.

After urging Levi to adhere strictly to the order of sacrifice he had just articulated, Isaac commands him to follow the sacrificial measures he provides in the next section of the instructions (*Ar. Levi* 31-48).[158] Isaac teaches Levi the specific amounts of wood, salt, fine flour, oil, wine, and incense to be used with each type of holocaust offering. Following is a comparative table of weights and measures.[159] As a whole the section lacks substantial connections with known Pentateuchal laws. There are no similar instructions for the amounts of wood to be offered up with the various types of holocaust offering. Likewise, there are no parallel requirements for set amounts of salt with the various types of holocaust offering. However, mention is made of the amounts of flour, oil, and wine that accompany a meat offering (e.g., Exod 29:40; Num 15:1-9; 28:3-8). Interestingly the Torah does not require frankincense with the meal offering that accompanies a meat offering (Num 15:1-9). Again *Aramaic Levi* offers a unique method of making sacrifice, at least vis-à-vis the Pentateuch.

Ar. Levi 48-50 gives Isaac's first conclusion to his instructions.[160] As in vv. 30-31 he admonishes Levi to comply with the regulations he has articulated. However, this time he adds a motive clause—Levi must obey the law of the cult because he is a holy priest to the Lord, as will his children be after him. Moreover, Isaac adds that these instructions come from the most ancient patriarchal figure, Abraham himself. Isaac frames his unusual cultic precepts with a firm

---

[156] It is necessary to admit, however, that one would expect the concern to be implicit in the holocaust offering, as the blood was of such significance, carrying as it did the life-force of the beast. At any rate, the same concern surfaces again in *Ar. Levi* 57 when Isaac mentions the "Book of Noah concerning the blood."

[157] The Greek preserves both names for God.

[158] Only a small part of the text is preserved at the end of the Bodl. fragment; for the rest one must rely on Mt. Athos 18:2. 4Q213 4–5 13 also gives enough to be certain that the exhortation to adherence was present there as well.

[159] For a full discussion of the Hebrew Bible's use of some of the terms that occur here see Marvin A. Powell, "Weights and Measures," in *Anchor Bible Dictionary* (ed. D. N. Freedman; New York: Doubleday, 1992) VI:897-908. See also the comments of Grelot, "Le coutumier," 257, nn. 14-16.

[160] This section is preserved only in Mt. Athos 18:2.

statement of their purpose, and links the conclusion with the introduction (*Ar. Levi* 13-18); what was implied in the introduction is made explicit now—Levi and his descendants are holy priests to the Lord, and the true heirs of the office.

Following the first conclusion to his instructions, Isaac resumes teaching Levi, this time in overview fashion (*Ar. Levi* 51-57).[161] These instructions summarize some of the preceding guidelines, touching on the issues of Levi's election to the priesthood, the wood requirements,[162] rules for washing, and the sacrificial measures. The new material in this set of instructions is Isaac's concern for the blood of the animal. The additional section on blood begins by repeating the command to wash before approaching the altar (*Ar. Levi* 53a; cf. *Ar. Levi* 20-22; Exod 30:20b), and adds that when leaving the sanctuary one must also wash, making sure that no blood of the sacrifice clings to the priestly vestments, or to one's hands or feet (*Ar. Levi* 53b-55). Apparently *Aramaic Levi* adopts the Priestly and Deuteronomic view that the blood of the beast is not to be eaten (*Ar. Levi* 56; Gen 9:4; Lev 3:17; 7:22-26; 19:26; Deut 12:24). The particular form the prohibition takes is most like the Priestly legislation on the matter, requiring as it does burial of the blood before consumption of the meat.[163] Yet reverence for the blood of the beast in *Aramaic Levi* is said to be based on the so-called "Book of Noah concerning the blood" (*Ar. Levi* 57).[164] Whatever that mysterious work may have been—if it ever existed—it must have dealt with the kinds of issues addressed by Leviticus 17, Deuteronomy 12, and the text under discussion.[165]

In the closing section Isaac summarizes Levi's affiliation with God as a priest, and the impact that has on his relationship to his brothers and on his children's future. He is holy to God, and superior to his brothers, while his children's name, as well as his own, will be memorialized for eternity, and his children will flourish on earth forever

---

[161] Only Mt. Athos 18:2 witnesses to this section.

[162] The reference to the wood requirements is a strong indication of the author's effort to integrate this section with the rest of the instructions, referring back to the previous exposition regarding provisions for the fire (*Ar. Levi* 22-25a).

[163] More precisely this particular prohibition of eating blood matches the Holiness Code's instructions for the consumption of meat gained from the hunt (Lev 17:13), in contrast to the Priestly Work's rules regarding the ingestion of sacrificial meat (Lev 3:17; 7:22-26).

[164] Other references to the "Book of Noah" occur in *Jub* 10:13; 21:10.

[165] The most recent attempt to address this elusive text is by Florentino García Martínez, "*4QMess Ar* and the *Book of Noah*," in *Qumran and Apocalyptic: Studies on the Aramaic Texts from Qumran* (Leiden: Brill, 1992) 24-44. He notes that there are additional references in the *Chronography* from Syncellus, and in other locations. His treatment provides a convenient bibliography of the most important attempts to deal with the document.

(*Ar. Levi* 58-61).[166] One possible biblical allusion is the promise that Levi's name, and his children's names would not be blotted out for eternity. In Exod 32:33 and Deut 9:14 God expresses the desire to blot out the names of those who were unfaithful in the matter of the golden calf. Similarly, Deut 25:19 promises that whoever ignores the covenant with God would have his or her name blotted out from under heaven. It is possible that the biblical texts, with their emphasis on the fate of the unfaithful and arrogant, serve as the backdrop for *Ar. Levi* 60. Levi and his descendants who are as faithful as he are assured that their names will never suffer that fate; the family of Levi is destined to be ever faithful to proper, righteous service of God.

Before addressing the purpose of Isaac's instructions it is important to note the debate regarding the integrity of the text. The issue is raised by the obvious repetition by *Ar. Levi* 51-60 of instructional material appearing in *Ar. Levi* 13-50, as well as by the introduction of new subject matter in the second section. Some claim that there was a late addition to an existing text; hence *Ar. Levi* 51-60 intruded on a more original set of instructions made up of *Ar. Levi* 13-50, 61.[167] Others defend the integrity of the text, suggesting, for instance, that *Ar. Levi* 13-47 is summarized and reiterated in vv. 48-61.[168] Both approaches hold some attraction. On the one hand the first more adequately explains the repetitive character of the instructions. On the other hand, the second option preserves the integrity of the text, suggesting that there was only an attempt to summarize and reiterate what had gone before. However, as tempting as it may be to linger over the question, the reality is that the text appears as it does now, and must be understood as such.[169]

What can the author's intention have been in including such a complex, detailed set of cultic instructions? The clues that lead to an

---

[166] Only Mt. Athos 18:2 survives for the text. The promise that Levi's seed will be entered in the book of eternity and that his name and that of his children will not be annihilated forever echoes 4Q213 2 20-21. In fact, one is tempted to place that fragment here; but the lack of any concern here with exogamy precludes that judgment.

[167] See Becker, *Untersuchungen*, 88-89. Becker cites in particular the apparent repetition of v. 59 in v. 61. This, he suggests, indicates that v. 61 was the original conclusion, and that vv. 51-60 separated it from its location following v. 50. See also Haupt, "Testament," 75

[168] This is the explanation offered by Marinus de Jonge, *Testaments*, 39. See also Hultgård, *L'eschatologie*, 1:27-28.

[169] Indeed, as Ulrichsen, *Grundschrift*, 183, points out, "Diese Zusammenarbeitung ist wahrscheinlich so alt, daß der aramäisch-griechische Text niemals anders aussah. Die Dubletten bedeuten also nur, daß zwei Traditionen zugrunde liegen. Sie zeigen nicht ohne weiteres von Mangel an literarischer Einheit." Nevertheless, the fact that *T. Levi* 9:6-14 (which, as we will see, used *Aramaic Levi* as its chief source) synthesized only *Ar. Levi* 13-47 does suggest that vv. 48-61 might have been a late addition to *Aramaic Levi*. See 5.4.5 below.

adequate answer to the question are the content and narrative context of the directions, and their relationship to corresponding Pentateuchal legislation. First, their content and narrative context underscore the author's central thesis that Levi was an ideal priest, and is therefore the model for all clergy. Although the detailed and complex nature of the instructions suggests that they were composed for actual use,[170] the limited scope of their content and their narrative context militate against the view. Indeed, the directions provide only advice on making a holocaust offering and its accompanying meal offering. Isaac offers no instruction in the other types of sacrifice required of a priest. From this it appears that they are not provided for practical use, but only to make a point. The narrative context indicates what the point may be. The real interest is not in providing instruction, but in proving that Levi was not only chosen a priest by heavenly agents and ordained by Judaism's ancestral fathers; he was also instructed in the ways of the cult, long before God gave the Pentateuchal rules for cultic service through Moses. Levi, as he is depicted in *Aramaic Levi*, may be trusted as the model for the priesthood in all times and places.

The relationship of these rules to the corresponding Pentateuchal legislation offers further indication of the author's intention. Comparison between the separate sections of *Ar. Levi* 13-61 with related Pentateuchal texts repeatedly shows *Aramaic Levi* to be at variance with the Torah. In some instances the rules for Levi's cultic behavior require a higher degree of purity than the similar regulations in the Pentateuch.[171] In a similar vein, throughout the instructions the demands placed on Levi differ from the corresponding rules for cultic service in the Pentateuch. It is possible that these contradictions of Pentateuchal legislation are a conscious attempt to set Levi and his priesthood apart from the clergy depicted by the Torah, and to demonstrate a deeper concern for purity than that communicated by the Pentateuch. Taken as a whole Isaac's instructions could be seen as an alternative to the existing priesthood and its practices. And so *Ar. Levi* 60 cogently summarizes the section; it states the author's certainty that Levi and any who follow his example are destined to be God's favored cultic servants, for they never turn away from faithful service. Implied in this, perhaps, is the notion that anyone who does not follow these rules, favoring instead another code, will be rejected from sacerdotal service for his lack of faithfulness.

---

[170] This is the view of J. T. Milik, expressed in conversation with the author in December 1992. Especially supportive of Milik's assessment of the rules as being meant for use, of course, are such things as the section on comparative weights and measurements, the intricate description of how to lay the pieces of the beast on the altar-fire, and the description of the types of wood acceptable for the fire.

[171] See, for example, the introductory reflections (vv. 13-18) and the additional ablutions required of Levi (vv. 19-21).

In addition one ought to remember that these rules offer a model of the priesthood that is grounded in antiquity and ancestral authority. Such a picture of the priesthood, bound by more stringent purity requirements than those appearing in the Pentateuch, instructed to act differently from the priests governed by the Torah, and rooted in a figure more ancient than Aaron, must have been created with two aims in mind: to polemicize against a priesthood that its author perceived to be inadequate, and to promote a more pure model of the office.

This understanding of the purpose of the instructions speaks equally to the question of their relationship to the rest of *Aramaic Levi*. By now it should be clear to the reader that *Aramaic Levi* is perhaps in part a protest document aimed at expressing dissatisfaction with the priesthood of the author's day, and at offering an alternative with roots in ancestral antiquity and divine election. In a sense the instructions are the pinnacle of that assertion, demonstrating in concrete fashion how the priesthood proposed by the author would differ from the temple-priesthood of his own day. Levi, the zealot, petitioner, visionary, and ordinand, is a priest unlike any other depicted by Pentateuchal legislation and narrative.

The question that remains is the nature of the relationship between this set of instructions and those given in *Jubilees* and *Testament of Levi*. As for *T. Levi* 9:6-14, it seems clear that it is an abbreviated version of *Ar. Levi* 13-61.[172] The theory that *Aramaic Levi* was a source for the author of *Testament of Levi* garners support from this observation. Meanwhile, Levi receives no instructions in *Jub.* 30:1–32:9, but Isaac accepts a somewhat related set of regulations from Abraham in *Jubilees* 21. It is important to note that Isaac says he received the instructions recorded in *Aramaic Levi* first from Abraham (*Ar. Levi* 22, 50, 57). Perhaps encountering the same set of instructions, the author of *Jubilees*—known to have been concerned with establishing narrative consistency among the sources he used for his composition[173]—might have felt compelled to move the instructions out

---

[172] Among those who share this view is de Jonge (*Testaments*, 91-92; cf. Ulrichsen, *Grundschrift*, 184). There are, however, other views. Becker insists that the authors of *Aramaic Levi*, *Testament of Levi*, and *Jubilees* relied independently on a common oral tradition (*Testaments*, 40), and Haupt thinks that *Testament of Levi* abbreviated the source used by *Aramaic Levi* (Haupt, "Testament," 75). See 5.4.5.

[173] For more on this characteristic of the author of *Jubilees* see chapter four. Note the alternative explanation offered by Kugel, "Levi's Elevation," 17-19, 54. He notes that *Jubilees* shared in a tradition of concern for the fact that biblical Israelite ancestors performed sacrifice without explicitly being designated as priests. *Jubilees'* author remedied that problem by making it clear that these figures participated in an unbroken chain of priests who were not only designated as such, but were instructed and skilled in priestly functions. So it was that in *Jubilees* Isaac received instruction from Abraham as next in the line of priestly succession. *Aramaic Levi* eschews the "chain-of-priests tradition" in favor of making Levi the first priest of all. But because, as

of the narrative about Levi and into a context that would allow Abraham to speak them to Isaac. *Jubilees* 21 offered that context, and required slightly different concerns, since Abraham prepares Isaac to make sacrifice on the occasion of the Feast of Shabuoth (cf. *Jubilees* 22). On this reading the relationship between *Aramaic Levi* and *Jubilees* that has been suggested is upheld.[174] It remains entirely plausible that *Aramaic Levi* and *Jubilees* used independently of one another a common source.

3.1.6. *Ar. Levi* 62-81: Levi's life history

Up to *Ar. Levi* 66b only Mt. Athos 18:2 provides text for this section. From there the Cambridge fragment resumes.[175] The Greek continues to v. 68 where it breaks off. It is necessary to rely on the Cambridge fragment for the remainder of the life history.

TEXT

[62]και οτε ανεπληρωθησαν μοι εβδομαδες τεσσαρες εν τοις ετεσιν της ζωης μου, εν ετει ογδοω και εικοστω ελαβον γυναικα εμαυτω εκ της συγγενειας Αβρααμ του πατρος μου, Μελχα, θυγατερα Βαθουηλ, υιου Λαβαν, αδελφου μητρος μου. [63]και εν γαστρι λαβουσα εξ εμου ετεκεν υιον πρωτον, και εκαλεσα το ονομα αυτου Γηρσαμ· ειπα γαρ οτι παροικον εσται το σπερμα μου εν γη, η εγεννηθην· παροικοι εσμεν ως τουτω εν τη γη η ημετερα νομιζομενη. [64]και επι του παιδαριου ιδον εγω εν τω οραματι μου οτι εκβεβλημενος εσται αυτος και το σπερμα αυτου απο της αρχης ιεροσυνης [εσται τω σπερμα αυτου]. [65]Λ ετων ημην οτε εγεννηθη εν τη ζωη μου, και εν τω ι μηνι εγεννηθη επι δυσμας ηλιου. [66]και παλιν συλλαβουσα ετεκεν εξ εμου κατα τον καιρον τον καθηκοντα των γυναικων

The Cambridge fragment resumes here; Mt. Athos 18:2 breaks off at v. 68

Kugel sees it, *Aramaic Levi* had *Jubilees* as one of its sources, we find vestigial remains of the chain-of-priests tradition in *Ar. Levi* 22, 50. 57. On the relationship between *Aramaic Levi* and *Jubilees*, see the sections cited in the next note.

[174] See 3.1.4, 3.2, and 4.2.

[175] It is possible that some of this section appears in 4Q214 6 i. The underlined Aramaic text represents the few words that appear on that fragment.

[וקרא]תי שמה [קהת 67וחזיתי] די לה [תהו]ח כנשת כל[עמא ודי] לה תהו[ה] כהנותא רבתא

[לכל יש]ראל 68בשנת ארב[א] ותל[תין לחיי יליד בירחא קמ]אה בח[ד לירח]א[עם מדנח שמש]א[

69ועוד א]וס[פת והוית ע]מ[ה] וילידת לי בר תליתוי וקראתי שמה מררי ארי ארי מר לי עלוהי לחדה

ארי <u>כד</u>י יליד הוא מית והוה מריר לי עלוהי סגיא מן די ימות ובעית והתחננת <u>עלוהי</u>

והיה בכל מרר   70בשנת ארבעין לחיי ילידת בייררחה תליתנ[י 71ועוד אוספת והוית עמהא והרת

וילידת לי ברתא <u>ושויתי</u> שמהא יוכב[ד] אמ[רת]כדי ילידת לי ליקר ילידת לי לכבוד לישראל

72<u>בשנת</u> שתין וארבע לי לחיי וילידת בחד בחודשא שביעיא מן בתר די ה[עלינא ל]מצרים

73בשנת שת עש[רה ה]עלינא <u>לארע</u> מצרים ולבנ[   ]° בנת אחי לעדן אשיות זמניהו[ן]   °[

להון בנין   74ושם בני גרשון ל[בני ו]שמעי ושם בני קה[ת ע]מ[ר]ם ויצהר וחברון ועוזיאל [ושם] בני

מררי מחלי ומושי 75[ונסב] לה עמרם אנתא ליוכבד ברתי עד די אנה חי בשנה תשעין וארב[ע]

לחיי76וקריתי שמה די עמרם כדי יליד עמרם ארי אמרת כדי יליד דנה [יפיק] עמא מן ארע

מ[צ]רים [כ]דן י[תקר]א [שמה עמ]א ראמא 77ביום חד יל[יד ה]וא ויוכבד ברתי 78בר שנין ת[מ]נ[ה

עשרה העלת   [לא]רע כנע[ן] ובר שנין תמנה עשרה כדי קטלית אנה לשכם וגמרת לעבדי חמסא

79ובר שנין תשע עשרה כהנית ובר שנין תמנה ועסרין נסבת לי אנתה   80ובר שנין תמנה

וארבעין הויתי כדי העלנא לארע מצרים ושנין תמנין ותשע הויתי חי במצר[ים] 81והוו כל יומי חיי

שבע ות[ליתין ו]מאה שנין וחזיתי לי בנין תל[יתאין] עד די לא מיתת

TRANSLATION

62And when four weeks were completed for me in the years of my life, in the twenty-eighth year I took a wife for myself from the family of Abraham my father, Milchah, daughter of Bathuel, son of Laban, my mother's brother. 63When she became pregnant by me, she bore a first son, and I called his name Gersam. For I said, "My seed shall be sojourners in the land in which I was born." We are sojourners like him in the land which is considered ours. 64And with respect to the youngster, I saw in my dream that he and his seed will be cast out of the high priesthood (his seed will be). 65I was thirty years old in my life when he was born, and he was born in the tenth month towards sunset. 66And once more she conceived and bore by me according to the proper time of women

The Cambridge fragment resumes here; Mt. Athos 18:2 breaks off at v. 68

[And I call]ed his name [Kohath. 67And I saw] that he would ha[ve] an assembly of all[the people, that] he would hav[e] the high priesthood, [for all Is]rael. ⁶⁸In the [thi]rty-four[th] year of my life he was born in the [fi]rst month [on the fi]rst of the mon[th] with the rising of the su[n]. ⁶⁹And again I was wi[th he]r and she bore for me a third son, and I called his name Merari, for I was bitter over him especially, for when he was born he was dying. And I was very bitter concerning him on account of the fact that he was about to die; and I begged and I be-seeched on his behalf, and there was bitterness in everything. ⁷⁰In the fortieth year of my life she gave birth in the thi[rd] month. ⁷¹And again I was with her, and she conceived and bore to me a daughter, and I named her Jocheb[ed]. I sa[id]when she was born to me "For glory she was born to me, for the glory of Israel." ⁷²In the sixty-fourth year (for me) of my life she gave birth on the first day of the seventh month, after he bro[ught us into] Egypt. ⁷³In the sixteen[th] year he had[b]rought us to the land of Egypt, and to my sons [ ] the daughters of my brothers at the time [untranslatable word] their times [ ] sons for them. ⁷⁴And the names of the sons of Gershom: [Libni, and]Shimei. And the names of the sons of Ko[hath: Amra]m and Yizhar and Hebron and Uzziel. [And the names] of the sons of Merari: Mahli and Mushi. ⁷⁵And Amram [took] for himself as a wife my daughter Jochebed while I was still living, in the ninety-f[ourth] year of my life. ⁷⁶And I called Amram's name, when he was born, Amram, since I said when he was born "This one [will lead] the people from the land of Eg[y]pt. Thus [his name] will be c[alle]d ["A peop]le exalted." ⁷⁷On the same day, he w[as born,] h[e] and Jochebed my daughter. ⁷⁸I was ei[g]hteen years old when I was brought [to the la]nd of Canaan; and I was eighteen years old when I killed Shechem and destroyed the doers of violence. ⁷⁹I was nineteen when I became a priest, and I was twenty-eight when I took for myself a wife. ⁸⁰And I was forty-eight when he brought us to the land of Egypt, and I lived eighty-nine years in Egyp[t]. ⁸¹And all the days of my life were one hundred [thirty]-seven years; and I saw my th[ird] generation before I died.

NOTES ON THE TEXT AND TRANSLATION

Ar. Levi 63. ως τουτω. We translate this as "like him." This may be a dative of standard of judgment.[176]

---

[176] See H. W. Smyth, *Greek Grammar* (Cambridge: Harvard University, 1920) §1512.

Ar. Levi 64. [εσται τω σπερμα αυτου]. The phrase appears in brackets since it seems to be a scribal error in the Greek text. It is likely a dittography.[177]

Ar. Levi 67. αυτος και το σπερμα αυτου εσονται αρχη βασιλεων ιερατευμα τω Ισραηλ. The sentence appears only in the Greek after αυτος εσται η αρχιεροσυνη η μεγαλη, "He will be the high priesthood" (matched by כהנותא [תהו|ה לה י|ד|ר], ". . . that he would have the high priest-hood"). One explanation for this variation is that the sentence was lost from the Aramaic by parablepsis,[178] but it is difficult to see how the parablepsis would have occurred. The Aramaic corresponding to the Greek as it is preserved would probably have been (ו)הוא וזרעו יהוו ראש מלכיא כהנות לישראל, "(And) he and his seed will be the beginning of kings, a priesthood for Israel." The single word in the extant Aramaic that provides a basis for the purported parablepsis is כהנותא; but it is followed by רבתא לכל, and would have been followed by לישראל in the supposedly lost Aramaic. A better explanation of the additional phrase in the Greek might be that it is a clumsy gloss reflecting the 𝔊 text of Exod 19:6, υμεις δε εσεσθε μοι βασιλειον ιερατευμα και εθνος αγιον, "You will be a priestly kingdom and a holy nation for me."[179] If that is the case the glossator was adding nothing about kings, but only sharpening the point regarding Kohath's relationship to the priesthood.[180]

Ar. Levi 68. The Greek text continues to this verse, and breaks off after the עלוהי that occurs before סניא.

Ar. Levi 69. It appears that the scribe or author has provided two explanations of Merari's name. The first says that Levi was bitter because from birth Merari "was dying." The second indicates that when he was born "he was about to die." It is probable that the first is a "hebraising" version, and the second reflects a better Aramaic rendi-tion.[181]

---

[177] Greenfield and Stone, "Appendix III," 466.

[178] Ibid.

[179] The basis for this insight is a similar, but more speculative and elaborate expla-nation of the Greek by T. Baarda, "Qehath—'What's in a name?'" *JSJ* 19 (1988) 220-21. See now also Grelot, "Le coutumier," 259, n. 22, where he suggests also that a clumsy use of Exod 19:6 may stand behind the additional material in the Greek.

[180] It is also worth noting that 1Q21 1 preserves the phrase מלכות כהנותא, "the kingdom of the priesthood." The phrase fits in well with the ideology expressed in Exod 19:6.

[181] So Pierre Grelot, "Le Testament araméen Lévi est-il traduit de l'hébreu?" *REJ* 14 (1955) 93. Before him Lévi, "Le Testament," 178, n. 1, suggested that the first et-ymology reflects Syriac influence in its use of לחדה. Grelot disproves that possibility, indicating that the same word is used in the Targumim for מאד in Gen 1:31; 17:20; Ps 99:8. Before Lévi, Charles and Cowley, "An Early Source," 568-69, already noted the double explanation of Merari's name. For other Hebraisms, see Beyer, *Die aramäischen Texten*, 189.

Ar. Levi 71. לכבוד ישראל. Grelot understands the double explanation of Jochebed's name as evidence that *Aramaic Levi* was originally
written in Hebrew.[182] This phrase would have been original, and יקר
would be the later gloss. Greenfield and Stone argue for the opposite
order of textual development, if any ever took place. They doubt that
any Jew in the Middle Ages would have felt it necessary to make such a
clarification, but they acknowledge that לכבוד may have been added to
make the "onomastic explanation explicit."[183] Anyway, the double explanation of the name is common in biblical tradition (Gen 30:30;
35:18; 49:8 [?]; and 49:19).[184]

Ar. Levi 72. לי. The superfluous prepositional possessive appears to be a corruption in the manuscript.

Ar. Levi 73. בנת אחי לעדן אשויות זמניהון. Among the difficulties presented by this phrase is the word אשויות. It is pronounced an "Unknown
word" by Greenfield and Stone,[185] translated with only a question mark
to indicate uncertainty by Charles and Cowley,[186] and Beyer appears to
think the word has something to do with coming of age.[187] Grelot offers the most extensive attempt to make sense of the word, but also despairs ultimately of solving the puzzle.[188]

Ar. Levi 76. [יפק]. We follow Charles' suggestion for the lacuna, in spite of the claim made by Greenfield and Stone that they can
see the top of a *lamed* at the left edge of the space that would be occupied by יפק.[189] The evidence for a *lamed* is slim indeed, and it is better
treated as part of the general distortion of the ink that was at one time
present on the vellum at this point. Likewise, Charles' suggestion may
be treated as only a best guess.[190]

Ar. Levi 77. ביום חד יל[יד ה]וא ה[ו]ה ויוכבד. We accept Greenfield and
Stone's suggested reconstruction for the gaps in the manuscript, although we do discern firm traces of a few more letters than do they.[191]

COMMENT

Levi's life history is given first as an account of the births of his children, the names of his sons' children, and information about the mar-

---

[182] Grelot, "Le Testament," 95.

[183] Greenfield and Stone, "Remarks," 225.

[184] Ibid.

[185] Greenfield and Stone, "Appendix III," 467, n. a. Moreover, they think the final word is מבניהון.

[186] Charles and Cowley, "An Early Source," 582. Charles reads the final word as
זבניהון.

[187] Beyer, *Die aramäischen Texten*, 204. For the last word Beyer reads מפניהון.

[188] Grelot, "Le Testament," 98-99; "Le coutumier," 260, n. 25. He suggests the
verb derives from the root שוי.

[189] Charles, *Greek Versions*, 254; Greenfield and Stone, "Remarks," 226.

[190] Beyer, *Die aramäischen Texten*, 203, gives an implausible יעיר for the lacuna.

[191] Greenfield and Stone, "Remarks," 226.

riage of Jochebed to Amram (*Ar. Levi* 62-77). Next there is a brief recitation of the principal events in Levi's life (*Ar. Levi* 78-82).

The highlight of the first part is the contrast between Gershom and Kohath and its implications for the author's calendrical interests. Levi notes that Gershom was fated to be driven out of the high priesthood (*Ar. Levi* 63-65). In contrast, Kohath is born at sunrise on the first day of the month, and Levi says that from birth he was destined to possess the high priesthood and to be glorious in his fulfillment of the role.[192] From this one most conclude that the author favored measuring time, like the Qumran sect, by the sun rather than by the moon.[193]

The second half of the life history (*Ar. Levi* 78-81) provides crucial evidence for the order of the events in Levi's life recorded by *Aramaic Levi*. An additional noteworthy item is the fact that at the close of the section Levi announces that he died at the age of one hundred thirty-seven, but then in *Ar. Levi* 82 he refers to events in his hundred eighteenth year. The statement in v. 81, followed as it is by reference to earlier events, suggests strongly that it marked the original ending of a source that was incompletely integrated with the rest of the text.[194]

As for the biblical texts used in Levi's life history, the author relied on the Levi genealogies in Gen 46:7, 11; Exod 6:16-25; Num 3:17-39; 26:57-62; 1 Chronicles 6.[195] Gen 46:7 gives the list of those whom Jacob took with him on his descent into Egypt, and 46:11 provides the names of Levi's sons (*Ar. Levi* 74). Most evidently in use, however, is Exod 6:16-25 which gives information about all three sons, mentions the marriage of Jochebed and Amram, and provides the text's structure. The author apparently drew from Num 26:57-62 only the fact that Jochebed was born in Egypt. In addition Gen 49:8-12 is called into

---

[192] As indicated in the NOTE above, we suggest that the addition in the Greek of *Ar. Levi* 67 regarding Kohath as "the beginning of kings, a priesthood for Israel" reflects only an awkward gloss in the Greek on the basis of Exod 19:6. In any event, such an addition adds nothing of a royalist character to the description of Kohath's fate. It only reinforces the document's judgment regarding the priestly character of his future.

[193] See S. Talmon, "The Calendar Reckoning of the Sect From the Judean Desert," *ScrHier* 4 (1958) 162-99. Indeed calendars similar to this one—with numbered (rather than named) months and according to which important events occur on the first day of the month—are found also in *Jubilees* and *1 Enoch* (cf. A. Jaubert, "Le calendrier des Jubilés et de la secte Qumrân: ses origines bibliques," *VT* 33 [1953] 210-64).

[194] For the full significance of this observation for understanding the composition of *Aramaic Levi* and for its relationship to other parts of the LPT, see below.

[195] For the same listing, and a very full treatment of the names, see Becker, *Untersuchungen*, 93-101.

service to describe Kohath's fate.[196] Exod 6:16 and Gen 50:23 are the sources for *Ar. Levi* 81. And Exod 19:6 seems to lie at the root of the the Greek addition in *Ar. Levi* 67.[197]

These two accounts of Levi's life serve distinct purposes. The first establishes Levi's lineage and indicates how his seed became a priestly family. The second rehearses the events narrated by the document up to this point. It reminds the reader that Levi's life has been dominated by zealous pursuit of the priestly office, and by the achievement of that aim through his own purity and the recognition of that personal trait by God, by angels, and by his father and grandfather. As a whole, the two-part life history is intended to summarize the narrative up to this point in the document, to support the aim of explaining the origins of Levi's priestly role, to legitimate his descendants' claim to the office, and to establish Levi's authority to speak as he does in the subsequent portions of *Aramaic Levi*.

The place of the life history within *Aramaic Levi* is twofold. First, it serves as a bridge connecting the action of the narrative to this point with Levi's speech to his children. Second, it assures the reader that Levi has the authority to teach as he is about to, and the right to warn about priestly abuses as he will in the following lines.

As for the relationship of the account to the rest of the LPT, much of it appears again in *T. Levi* 11:1–12:5.[198] This eliminates almost all doubt that *Aramaic Levi* was used as a source for *Testament of Levi*. More difficult to explain is the passage's absence in *Jubilees*. Already it has been suggested that *Aramaic Levi* and *Jubilees* both relied independently on a common source, perhaps a Levi-apocryphon.[199] *Jubilees'* failure to include the life history indicates that it was not part of the Levi-apocryphon. At the same time the history concludes so neatly with Levi's announcement of his own death, and the seam between it and the wisdom speech that follows is handled so poorly by the author of *Aramaic Levi*, that it seems certain that it marks the conclusion of an independent source employed by the author of *Aramaic Levi*. On the basis of these observations one may draw the tentative

---

[196] Greenfield and Stone, "Remarks," 219, 223-24, see this as a sign that the author sought to attach royal characteristics to Levi's lineage (see also de Jonge, *Testament*, 42). It is difficult, however, to accept their supposition that the use of the verb כוש is meant to recall the verb קהה in Gen 49:10. And even if it is the case that *Ar. Levi* 67 is a reuse of Gen 49:10, one ought not make too much of it: attaching royal characteristics to an exalted priestly figure is not unusual in early Judaism, and marks mostly the author's desire to elevate the sacerdotal office to preeminence in Jewish life. That is certainly the case for the author of *Aramaic Levi*.

[197] See NOTE on *Ar. Levi* 67 above.

[198] *Pace* Becker, *Untersuchungen*, 93-100; Ulrichsen, *Grundschrift*, 185. Haupt, "Testament," 82-84, only makes allowance for *Testament of Levi* having relied on an alternative textual tradition. For more on this see 5.4.6 below.

[199] See 3.1.4.

conclusion that the life history was not part of the Levi-apocryphon, and that the author of *Aramaic Levi* added it from yet another source. Its existence in an established form would help explain its tidy conclusion.[200]

3.1.7. *Ar. Levi* 82-106: Levi's speech to his children

Levi's speech to his children is preserved in the last two extant columns of the Cairo Geniza manuscript, 4Q213 6 i–10, and 4Q214 6 ii. The first large portion of the speech appears in Cambridge e 3b–f 23, with substantial parts of the same section occurring in 4Q213 6 i 1-20. Therefore we use the Cairo Geniza manuscript as the text for Levi's speech through *Ar. Levi* 95, where the geniza text breaks off.[201] From *Ar. Levi* 96 to the end 4Q213 provides the most complete witness, although the last five fragmentary lines of 4Q214 6 ii give some parallel material (see the underlining in *Ar. Levi* 96-98); thus the text of *Ar. Levi* 96-106 that appears here is from 4Q213, with corresponding material from 4Q214 6 ii underlined.[202]

---

[200] For consideration of the years in Levi's life indicated by the foregoing section, and their significance in relationship to Pentateuchal chronologies, see Grelot's two studies, "Quatre cents trente ans (Ex XII, 34): du Pentateuque au Testament araméen de Lévi," in *Hommages à André Dupont-Sommer* (eds. A. Caquot et M. Philonenko; Paris: Adrien-Maisonneuve, 1971) 383-94; and "Quatre cents trente ans (Ex 12,40): du Testament de Lévi aux visions de ʿAmram," in *Hommenaja a Juan Prado* (ed. Alvarez Verdes; Madrid, 1975) 559-70.

[201] The only exception is in *Ar. Levi* 90b-91c where the Cambridge fragment suffered considerable damage, and where 4Q213 6 i-ii is helpful; therefore for those verses we use the Qumran witness as the base text, and fill in the lacunae with information from the Cambridge witness where that is possible.

[202] Once again we only note the variations among the manuscript witnesses when they provide readings that differ in ways beyond orthography. Also note that Michael Stone and Jonas Greenfield, in their provisional publication of this material ("The First Manuscript of *Aramaic Levi Document* from Qumran," *Museon* 107 [1994] 257-81; they label it "4QLevi^a aram") give a rather complete reconstruction of the speech using both the Cairo Geniza manuscript and relevant sections of 4Q213 (264-65, 272).

TEXT

⁸²בש]נת מאה ות]מ[ני עשרה לחיי היא ש]תא] די מית בה יוסף אחי קריית לב]ני ול]בניהון

ושריית לפקדה הנון כל ד]י] הווה עם לבבי ⁸³עניית ואמרת לבנ]י שמעו] למאמר לוי אבוכון

והציתו לפקודי ידיד אל ⁸⁴אנה לכון מפקד בני ואנה קושטא לכון מהחוי חביבי

⁸⁵ראש כל עובדיכון יהוי קושטא ועד עלמ]א] י]הו]י קאים עמכן צדקתא ⁸⁶וקושט]א   כני עלון

עללה בריכה ו]זר[עא ⁸⁷די זרע טאב מהנעל ודי זרע ביש עלוהי תאיב זרעה

⁸⁸וכען בני ספר ומוסר וחוכמה אפילו לבניכון ותהוי חוכמתא עמכן ליקר עלם ⁸⁹די אליף

חוכמתא ויקר היא בה ודי שאים חוכמתא לבשרון מתיהב ⁹⁰חזו בני ליוסף אחי]ד]מאלפא

ספר ומוסר חכמא

End of Cambridge e; continue reading with 4Q213 6 i 11-14 supplemented by Cambridge f 4-11²⁰³

ליקר ולרבו ולמלכין כל   [גבר די אלף חכמה כל °°[[למאלף ⁹¹]אל תמחלו חכמתא [

]יומהי אריכין וסגה לה שמע]ה לכל מת מדינה די יהך לה [אח א°°° הוי בה ולא מתנכר הוא] בה

ולא דמא בה לנכרי ולא [דמא בה לכיל]י ( ) די כולהון י]הבין לה בה יקר בדי כלא צבין

Resume reading with Cambridge f 12

למאלף מן חוכמתה ⁹²רחמוה]י] סגיאין ושאל]י שלמיה רברבין ⁹³ועל כורסי ייקר מהותבין לה

בדיל למשמע מילי חוכמתה ⁹⁴עותר רב די יקר היא חכמתה וסימא טאבא לכל קניהא ⁹⁵הן

יאתון מלכין תקיפין ועם רב וחיל ופרשין ורתיכין סגיאין עמהון וינסבון נכסי מאת ומדינה

ויבזון כל די בהון אוצרי חוכמתא לא יבוזון ולא ישכחון מטמוריה

End of Cambridge f; continue reading with 4Q213 6 ii-7 1²⁰⁴

⁹⁶ולא יעלון תרעיה ולא ישכחון למכבש שוריה   °[[ ] ולא יחזון שידתה שימתה ב]

דמ[[ ] ולא איתי כל מחיר נגדה ⁹⁷כ]ל] אנ]ש די] בעא חכמת] לא]מתח]בא]ה מ]נה]ולא]

מטמרה מנ]ה]   [ ]ן כל בעין בקשט   [ ] ולא חסנ]י]ר]ה   [א לא]   [וכען בני ⁹⁸]

ספר ומוסר ח]כ]מה אלפו   [תרתין אנון ל°[[רבה תתנון]   י]קר

ארו⁹⁹   [אף בספריא קר]ל   ותה]וון ראשין ושפטין ודא]נין   [ב

ועבדין [   ]אף כהנין ומלכין תא]לפון¹⁰⁰ [   ]ל[   ]ן מלכותכן תהוא

[יק]ר ¹⁰¹ולא איתי סוף ליקרה   ולא]תעבר מנכן עד כל

---

²⁰³ The underlined text and that which appears in the brackets in this section is from the Cambridge fragment. Where parentheses are used within the brackets they denote a lacuna in the Cambridge fragment.

²⁰⁴ The underlined text in the following section is from 4Q214.

]◦   ]ן ביקר רב

End of 4Q213 6 ii–7; several lines lost; resume reading with 4Q213 8–10

ש]הרא וכוכביא   ]כל עממיא [102]ן [ל]   ]

]לשהרה   ]מן[   ]

נ]א   עממי]א הלא קבל חנוך ע]ל   [103]והן אנ]תן תחשכון[

א]רחת [105]   ]הלא עלי ועליכן בני ארו ידעתה [   ]ועל מן תהוא חובתא[

קשטא תשבקון וכל שבילי [צדקתא]תמחלון ותהכון בחשוך שטן [   ] עקה]ר[בה תתא עליכן

[   ]◦◦ר]שיע]יא [   ]◦[   ]ל תהוון לשכלין [   ]◦◦[   ]ומ[◦◦ [   ]◦◦[ו]תתי]ה]כון[

Several lines lost

]נאיכן אדין ירי]בון[בכן   ]ין ב]ר]שעא [◦◦◦[   ][106]

]שנון בכן מן כל ב[ ]◦[ ] כחכים אל   ]

TRANSLATION

[82]And in the [one hundred eighteen]th [year] of my life, the y[ear] in which my brother Joseph died, I called my chil[dren and] their children and I began to instruct them (about) all that was in my heart. [83]I began to speak and I said to my chil[dren, "Listen] to the word of Levi, your father, and pay heed to the instructions of God's friend. [84]I am instructing you, my children, and I reveal truth to you, my beloved ones. [85]Let the chief of all your deeds be truth, and fore[ver] m[ay it b]e established with you. Justice [86]and tru[th]◦◦ a blessed harvest. And w[hoever so]ws [87]good harvests goodness, and whoever sows evil, upon him returns what he sows. [88]And now, my children, teach reading and writing, and instruction, and wisdom to your children, and may wisdom be with you for eternal glory. [89]He who teaches wisdom, she is an honor in him, but whoever abandons wisdom, to disdain he is given. [90]Observe, my children, my brother Joseph [who] taught reading and writing and the instruction of wisdom

End of Cambridge e; continue reading with 4Q213 6 i 11-14 supplemented by Cambridge f 4-11

for glory, and for greatness, and for knowledge. [   ] [91]Do not forsake wisdom to learn [   ]◦◦ A man who learns wisdom, all [of his days will be long, and his reputatio]n [will be great]. For every foreign land and country to which he goes [there he will have a brother ◦◦ be in it and he will not be treated as a stranger] in it. And he will not be like a traveler there, nor [will he be like a scoundrel ∘∘. For all there g]ive to him glory, since they all wish

Resume reading with Cambridge f 12

to learn from his wisdom. ⁹²His friend[s] are many, and those wishing him well are numerous. ⁹³And people seat him on the seat of honor, so as to hear the words of his wisdom. ⁹⁴Great abundance of glory is wisdom, and it is a good treasure to all who acquire it. ⁹⁵Strong kings and a great people, and an army, and horsemen, and many chariots with them may come, and they may seize the possessions of the lands and countries and plunder everything that is in them, (but) the storehouses of wisdom they will not plunder, and they will not discover its hiding places.

*End of Cambridge f; continue reading with 4Q213 6 ii-7 1*²⁰⁵

⁹⁶And (they will) not enter its gates, and they will not succeed in conquering its walls. ∘[ ] And they do not see its treasure box ∘[ ]∘∘[ ] And it is priceless. ⁹⁷An[y] ma[n who] seeks wisdom, [it will not]be hid[d]e[n from] him, and it [will not] be concealed from him. [ ]∘∘∘[ ] And there is no la[c]k[of it]∘ all who seek in truth [⁹⁸And now my children,]reading and writing, and instruction in wisdom he (they?) lear[n(s)] these are two (?) ∘∘[ ] glory. You will give [gl]ory. ⁹⁹Fo[r] indeed, with the books ∘∘[And you will] be leaders, judges, and magis[trates]∘ and workers (works?) [ ] ¹⁰⁰Also priests and kings you will te[ach]∘[ ]∘ your kingdom will be[glor]y. ¹⁰¹And there will be no end to its g[lory. And it will not] pass from you until all ∘[ ]∘ in great glory.

End of 4Q213 6 ii-7; several lines lost; resume reading with 4Q213 8–10

∘[ ]∘ ¹⁰²All peoples [the m]oon and stars [ ] from [ ] for the moon. ¹⁰³And if you darken [the people]s. Did not Enoch accuse [ ]∘ ¹⁰⁴And upon whom will the blame be[ ] if not upon me and upon you, my children. For knowledge [¹⁰⁵The wa]y of truth you will abandon, and all paths of [righteousness]you will forsake. And you will walk in the darkness of satan. [ ] Gre[at] distress will come upon you, [and] you will wa[l]k about [ ]∘∘[ ]∘∘∘∘[ ]∘ you will become fools [ ]∘∘ [wi]cked o[nes]∘∘[ ]

---

²⁰⁵ The underlined material is from 4Q214 6 ii 2-5.

Several lines lost

[106][ ]∘∘∘∘ with wickedness [ ]∘∘∘∘ Then they will in[crease] thus [ ]∘∘∘∘ Therefore from all ∘[ ]∘[ ] like a wise one of God.

NOTES ON THE TEXT AND TRANSLATION

Ar. Levi 82. מיח בה. 4Q213 6 i 1-2 preserves this phrase, as well as הנון later in the verse, although there it may read אנון.

Ar. Levi 83. לבני. 4Q213 6 i 3 shows this word.

Ar. Levi 84. אנה לכון. The extant portion of 4Q213 6 i 4 gives these words, but without the *waw* in לכון.

Ar. Levi 85. ראש כל עובדיכון. 4Q213 6 i 5 adds the word כל, "all." The Cambridge fragment lacks it.

Ar. Levi 85-86. קאים עמכון צדקתא וקושטא. There is scarcely enough space between קאים and צדקתה in 4Q213 6 i 6 for the word עמכון. Perhaps it follows וקושטא in the lacuna; thus the proper translation of the whole sentence would begin with the earlier ועד, and a new sentence would not begin with צדקתה.[206] Note also that the Qumran fragment reads צדקתא for צדקה of the Cambridge fragment; the determined state of the noun supports our translation, which treats "righteousness" and "truth" as an associated pair.

Ar. Levi 86.]כני עלון. There is wide variety in the treatment of this section. Charles transcribes it as מלכני עלון, but does not offer a translation.[207] Beyer says that is is ותהנעלון, and translates, "so werdet ihr einbringen."[208] Greenfield and Stone read כני עלון.[209] Beyer's reading is without foundation, while that of Charles is unlikely, at least with respect to the first two letters. The most acceptable reading, by the measure of the photographs of the manuscript and the manuscript itself, is Greenfield and Stone's.

Ar. Levi 86-87. ו]זר[עא די זרע טאב מאב מהנעל. 4Q213 6 i 7 provides the underlined portion of the text. However, it is necessary to note that the first two letters are not entirely clear, and the ʿ*ayin* is particularly suspect. Also noteworthy is the variation in spelling between the two manuscripts. The Qumran manuscript gives דזרע טב טב מעל, with its shorter forms throughout.

Ar. Levi 87-88. זרעה וכען בני ספר ומוסר וחוכמה אפילו. 4Q213 6 i 8 lacks בני. Note also that the word ספר is translated with the phrase

---

[206] Compare with Greenfield and Stone, "Appendix III," 468, where they translate וקושטא, as the beginning of the following sentence. But now see Stone and Greenfield, "The First Manuscript," 265, where they say that a new sentence does begin with צדקתא. We concur with their latest view on the matter.

[207] Charles, *Greek Versions*, 255.

[208] Beyer, *Die aramäischen Texte*, 206-7.

[209] Greenfield and Stone, "Remarks," 226. In "Appendix," 468, they translate the full word with the word "harvest."

"reading and writing."[210] There are also two emendations of the sentence as it appears in the Cairo Geniza manuscript. The first is the addition of a conjunction, "and," before the word מוסר. Although the conjunction is not present in the Cambridge fragment, it does appear in the same phrase in 4Q213 6 i 8; thus it is provided in our text of *Aramaic Levi*. The second emendation, the switch of אפילו to אליפו, does not appear in the TEXT since it lacks textual support. But that it is the result of a scribal error seems certain, and so the correct form is reflected in the translation.[211]

Ar. Levi 88-89. ליקר עלם די אליף חוכמתא ויקר. 4Q213 6 i 9 gives virtually the same text, although חוכמה is not emphatic, and the final יקר lacks the *waw*.

Ar. Levi 89. שאיט חוכמתא לבשרון מתיהב חזו בני. In 4Q213 6 i 10 שאים, "despise," of the Cambridge fragment appears between לבשרון, "for shame" and מתיהב, "he is given," as ולשימו, "and to his rejection." The sentence thus reads, "to shame and to his rejection he is given." The verbal form of the Cambridge fragment is a noun in the Qumran text. This may be treated as a variant vis-à-vis the Geniza manuscript reading; neither text is manifestly superior. Note also that between חזו and בני the Qumran scroll provides לכן.

Ar. Levi 90. On Cambridge f, line 3, there is]∘חש∘[. It is not possible to locate this in relationship to 4Q213 6 i 11-14.

Ar. Levi 90b-91c. The first two lines of Cambridge f are missing completely, and lines three through ten all lack substantial portions. Hence one may rely on the fuller text of 4Q213 6 i 11-14, filling in the lacunae with material present in the Cambridge fragment, but absent from the Qumran manuscript.[212]

Ar. Levi 91. למאלף. Charles and Greenfield and Stone read the two underlined letters, from Cambridge f 4, to be לב.[213] However the second is just as easily a *mem*, and the Qumran manuscript confirms that reading.

Ar. Levi 91. גבר די ∘∘∘[. Cambridge f 5 provides the underlined text, and the final letter of the previous word, probably a final *nun*. Greenfield and Stone read the גבר, but do not see the following *dalet*, while Charles only transcribed גבר.[214]

---

[210] See Greenfield and Stone, "Remarks," 226-27, where they note the use of the same word for this pair of terms in Isa 29:11-12.

[211] So also Pass and Arendzen, "Fragment of an Aramaic Text of the Testament of Levi," *JQR* 12 (1900) 659.

[212] For the portions of the lacunae that are reconstructed in this section the suggestions of Michael Wise, in Eisenman and Wise, *The Dead Sea Scrolls Uncovered*, 138, have been used, with a few adjustments.

[213] Charles, *Greek Versions*, 256; Greenfield and Stone, "Remarks," 230.

[214] Charles, ibid.; Greenfield and Stone, ibid.

Ar. Levi 91. אלף. Cambridge f 5 provides the first two letters plainly. The third letter is less plain. Greenfield and Stone read אלן;[215] Charles reads את. The latter reading is impossible, while Greenfield and Stone's is plausible. However the Qumran manuscript suggests most strongly the final *pe*.

Ar. Levi 91. וסנה לה שמע[ה לכל מח. Cambridge f 6 shows the underlined portion. There is also a trace of an ʾ*aleph* after the *mem* of מח. Hence it is likely that the word was spelled מאח in the Cairo Geniza manuscript. This would be in keeping with the manuscript's typically fuller orthography.

Ar. Levi 91. מדינה די יהך לה [אחא. Cambridge f 7 gives the underlined section of text, with the exception of the final *kap* of יהך. Instead it appears to have had a *lamed* in that space. The manuscript probably read יעל in place of יהך.

Ar. Levi 91. הוי בה ולא מתנכר הוא[בה. The underlined text appears also in Cambridge f 8. Examination of the Cairo Geniza manuscript shows that Charles is likely mistaken when he separates the *taw* in תנכר[from the rest of the word, and reconstructs the text as כוא[ת נכר, "like a stranger." The *taw* and the following *nun* are part of the same word; hence our reconstruction.

Ar. Levi 91. Cambridge f 9-11 provide the remaining underlined portions of *Ar. Levi* 91, with no significant variation from the Qumran manuscript.

Ar. Levi 91. לכילני. The translation "scoundrel," is suggested by Stone and Greenfield.[216]

Ar. Levi 92. רחמוה[י] סגיאין ושאלי שלמיה רברבין. The underlined portion of the verse appears also in 4Q213 6 i 17.

Ar. Levi 93. למשמע מילי חוכמתה. This portion of the verse appears also in 4Q213 6 i 18.

Ar. Levi 94. וסימא מאבא. 4Q213 6 i 19 reads here [ידעיה ושימה טבה. It seems likely that the Qumran manuscript has ל[ידעיה. Thus it would read for the first part of *Ar. Levi* 94, "Great abundance of glory is wisdom, *to all who know it.*"

Ar. Levi 95. It is apparent that the underlined portion through וחיל appears in 4Q213 6 i 20, although the ink traces are very faint. The word ומדינה is visible in 4Q214 6 ii 1. And the last word of the verse is the first word visible on 4Q213 6 ii.

Ar. Levi 96-106. Throughout this section we differ often in our reading of the Qumran manuscript from the reading by Stone and Greenfield. For a detailed comparison see their treatment.[217] We discuss only those variations between our treatments where substantial differences in meaning arise.

---

215 Ibid., 230.
216 Stone and Greenfield, "The First Manuscript," 266.
217 Ibid., 269-78.

Ar. Levi 96. ולא ישכחון. The underlined text is probably the occurrence of this phrase that appears in 4Q214 6 ii 2, although it is also
possible that is is the the earlier occurrence. Line 3 of the same fragment gives the underlined portion of איתי כל מחיר, also from *Ar. Levi*
96.

Ar. Levi 96. שידתה שימתה. Translate the phrase as "treasure box,"
although strictly speaking it ought to be rendered "its box, its treasure."[218]

Ar. Levi 96. נגדה. Stone and Greenfield translate this as "He who
acquires it . . . ."[219] It seems more likely that it is the preposition נגד,
and that it expresses the notion of "corresponding to" in this sentence.
Thus one might read, "There is not any price corresponding to her."

Ar. Levi 97. כ]ל[אנ]ש דין. The ʾ*aleph* and the *nun* appear in part on
the first line of visible ink on 4Q213 7.

Ar. Levi 97. מ]נה [ולא] ממטרה מנה. The entire lemma appears also in
4Q214 6 ii 4.

Ar. Levi 98. וכען בני]ספר ומוסר ח[כ]מה. The underlined text is from
4Q214 6 ii 5. Although we provide it only as reconstructed text, the
וכען בני prior to ספר may also be visible on 4Q214 6 ii 5.

Ar. Levi 100. אף כהנין ומלכין תא]לפון. The first two letters of the
last word are not clear enough to grant much confidence in the otherwise striking claim. In fact, only the *taw* is visible, with the slightest
bit of ink following it. We provide the reconstruction on the basis of
Ar. Levi 91 and 93, where it appears that Levi's children will instruct
others in wisdom. Note also that Eisenman and Wise think there is an
additional line preserved on 4Q213 6 ii beyond what we propose.
While our line 14 begins with ודאנין (which corresponds to their [ודי]ו), and
our line 16 begins with תא]לפון, it is not until line 17 that they find additional ink traces which they render as תהוה. They were deceived, apparently, by the way in which the leather of 4Q213 6 ii rests on PAM
43.241. It is sewn on the right margin to the preceding column, and
the section containing the beginning of lines 16ff. angles downward
slightly from the rest of the fragment, giving the impression that there
is space enough between the line that begins with ודא]ן and the one start-
ing with תא]ן for two missing lines. In fact, were the fragment adjusted,
what is clear from careful examination of the photograph would be
obvious: there is room only for one lost line between our lines
designated as 14 and 16.

Ar. Levi 100. מלכותכן. Compare the use of the phrase
מלכות כהנותא in 1Q21 1 and the apparent adaptation of Exod 19:6 in *Ar.
Levi* 67. The reference is probably to a priestly dominion.

---

[218] Eisenman and Wise, *The Dead Sea Scrolls Uncovered*, 138, give the unlikely
שיחתה, "its fodder," in this case. Stone and Greenfield, "The First Manuscript," 272,
read the first and second words as שימתה.

[219] Stone and Greenfield, "The First Manuscript," 274, 280.

Ar. Levi 101-102. 4Q213 6 ii–7 breaks off a few lines short of the bottom of the column. The following text is from a new column made up of three pieces of leather. Although there is no physical evidence granting certainty that 4Q213 8–10 gives the text from the following column, the content is suggestive of *Testament of Levi* 14-15, thus prompting the placement.[220]

Ar. Levi 102-104. Milik offers bold restorations for the lacunae of this section.[221] While his suggestions are interesting, their reliance on *Testament of Levi* 14–15 counsels that one treat them with caution. Thus the gaps remain for the most part empty in our transcription.

Ar. Levi 105-106. Approximately six lines are missing between 4Q213 9 and 10.

COMMENT

After announcing that he died at age one hundred thirty-seven (*Ar. Levi* 81), Levi begins the new section by recalling that when he was one hundred eighteen he gave a speech to his children (*Ar. Levi* 82).[222] In *Ar. Levi* 83 he summons them, and he describes the value of truthfulness in *Ar. Levi* 84-87. Then in *Ar. Levi* 88 he enjoins his children to learn wisdom, with *Ar. Levi* 89-101 serving as an exposition on the value of learning and teaching wisdom.[223] The final section of *Aramaic Levi* that is preserved continues Levi's speech to his children (*Ar. Levi* 102-106). However the tenor of the speech changes considerably, with Levi focusing his attention on the future sins of his children, and the consequences such behavior will have for them and for others.

Without indulging in an exhaustive commentary on the passage,[224] the following individual items ought to be noted before investi-

---

[220] See Milik, *Books of Enoch*, 23-25.

[221] Ibid.

[222] Beyer, *Die aramäischen Texten*, 189, 204, n. 1, considers the reference to Joseph's death to be an indication that the speech is actually Joseph's testament. He seems to rely on Milik for the insight, accepting Milik's identification of a tiny Aramaic fragment from Qumran as a testament of Joseph (see "Écrits," 101-2), and linking it with this speech. As indicated below it seems that the author of *Aramaic Levi* has actually mined and supplemented Isaac's blessing for Levi to create the wisdom speech.

[223] For a very similar breakdown of vv. 82-95, see Max Küchler, *Frühjüdische Weisheitstraditionen*, (OBO 26; Göttingen: Vandenhoeck & Ruprecht, 1979) 496-97. Haupt, "Testament," 87, also notes the two foci of the first part of the speech on truth and wisdom.

[224] For one of the few attempts to address this material, available at least in part since the publication of the Cairo Geniza fragments, see Küchler, *Frühjüdische Weisheitstraditionen*, 494-99. Küchler's treatment is ultimately flawed by his narrow definition of how wisdom could be understood at the various stages in the development of early Judaism: he thinks that the treatment of wisdom in *Aramaic Levi* requires

gating its use of existing texts and traditions. The first and most noteworthy item is the premium the author places on wisdom. Levi's claim
that possession of wisdom will win one honor and favor, even in foreign lands (*Ar. Levi* 91-93), shows the elevated role the author gives
the concept. In addition its possession seems to be linked to the future
success of Levi's children in leadership roles and to their possession of
a priestly kingdom. Yet he never connects the notion of wisdom to
Torah as do *Testament of Levi* 13 and other texts of Hellenistic-era
Judaism.[225] The sort of wisdom promoted here is "secular," focused on
the skills of reading, writing, instruction, and truthful judgment.

A second item of particular interest is the changed tenor of the
last section of Levi's speech. From *Ar. Levi* 102 to the end of the extant document Levi directs his attention to indicating the ways in which
his children will someday depart from his instructions about exercising
wisdom; instead they will fall into lives of disobedience and acts of evil.
Their behavior will bring darkness upon themselves and upon others.

A third detail that catches the reader's attention is Levi's claim
that Enoch had already made a complaint related to his own against his
children regarding their future misbehavior. From the context one can
guess that it has something to do with failure to exercise good judgment
and wisdom. Unfortunately we lack the continuation of thought in
Aramaic Levi and have no clear idea regarding Enoch's accusation;
therefore it is impossible to associate the reference to Enoch's sayings
with any particular passage in the literature bearing his name, and to
determine more precisely of what Levi's descendants stood accused.[226]

A fourth, and perhaps most interesting aspect of this speech is its
connection to Joseph. Levi begins the address by indicating that he
made it in the year that Joseph died (*Ar. Levi* 82), and he notes that
Joseph is a model for anyone who wishes to pursue wisdom (*Ar. Levi*
90). Beyond such explicit references Joseph cannot be far from the
reader's mind when Levi tells his children that they will be able to
make their way in foreign lands best if they value reading, writing, and
instruction in wisdom most of all; in fact, if they follow such advice
they will never be treated as strangers, but instead will be made to sit in
the seat of honor (*Ar. Levi* 91-94; cf. Gen 41:39-40). It is surely significant that Levi aligns himself with wisdom by making reference to

---

that it be dated between 100 BCE and 100 CE (499); the date of the Qumran fragments
assures us that cannot be the case. See also H. W. Hollander, *Joseph as an Ethical
Model in the Testaments of the Twelve Patriarchs* (SVTP 6; Leiden: Brill, 1981) 57-
62.

[225] Cf. Sir 24:23; Bar 4:1-3. See Hollander, *Joseph*, 60-1.

[226] The difficulty of linking quotations of purported words of Enoch with known
material that bears his name is familiar. See, for example, James VanderKam, "Enoch
Traditions in Jubilees and Other Second-Century Sources," *SBLSP* 13 (1978) 1:229-
51.

the tradition that his younger brother Joseph was known for insight.[227] Indeed, considering the Samaritan self-description as having descended from the tribes of Joseph and Levi,[228] it seems wise on our part to consider these positive references to the younger brother in a document that glorifies the older sibling as a strong indication of its origin.[229]

Due in part to the fragmentary character of the section, and also to its tendency toward broad, general statements, the number of clearly identifiable biblical allusions are few. A first may be Levi's rather unusual self-designation as ידיד אל, "God's friend" (*Ar. Levi* 83). The phrase occurs only once in the Hebrew Bible as the term Moses uses with reference to Benjamin in his blessing of the tribe that bore his name (Deut 33:12; note, however, that God is designated with the word יהוה in this verse). Then in *Ar. Levi* 87 the image of sowing and reaping goodness calls to mind Job 4:8; Prov 11:21; Hos 8:7; 10:12. The repeated use of the term ספר for "reading and writing" recalls Isa 29:11-12 (*Ar. Levi* 88, 90, and 98). *Ar. Levi* 90 reflects Joseph's elevation to a role of leadership in Pharaoh's government as a result of his wisdom (Gen 41:39-40). The theme of strangers honoring a wise person with well-wishing and homage reminds the reader once again of Joseph, and of the description of Solomon in 1 Kgs 5:14.

It has long been evident to critics that the author relied not only on biblical traditions for the speech, but also on another, pseudepigraphic source. Levi announces in *Ar. Levi* 81 that he lived to one hundred thirty-seven, but then he remarks in v. 82 that when he was one hundred eighteen he gave a speech to his children. On account of this awkward seam many commentators have concluded that the original document ended with v. 81, and that the author relied on a separate source for the speech, attaching it clumsily to the rest of *Aramaic Levi*.[230] It might be overly hasty, however, to conclude that the speech was entirely borrowed material. While the evidence of the seam between the life-history and the wisdom speech may imply that the latter

---

[227] Cf. LXX Ps 104:22; *Jub.* 40:5; Philo, *De Jos.* 106; Josephus *Ant.* 2 §87.

[228] See the various Samaritan chronicles and their account of the group's origins in the two brothers (see the convenient list of chronicles and references to their *edition princeps* in Lester L. Grabbe, *Judaism from Cyrus to Hadrian* [2 vols.; Minneapolis: Fortress, 1992] 2:502-7).

[229] Milik has long held this view (see Milik, "Fragment," 403-5; "Écrits préesséniens," 96, 106; *Books of Enoch*, 56, 252; "Problèmes de littérature hénochique à la lumière des fragments araméens de Qumran," *HTR* 64 [1971] 345). For more on this, see below, 3.3.4.

[230] See Becker, *Untersuchungen*, 94-95, 102-3; Haupt, "Testament," 84; Ulrichsen, *Grundschrift*, 186. But see Hultgård, *L'eschatologie*, 1:28. An alternative explanation is that the speech was added later to the original author's version of *Aramaic Levi* by a redactor. However the appearance of the speech in reduced form in *Testament of Levi* 13 and its attestation at Qumran speaks against a theory of redaction, and for the originality of the speech.

is an addition to an existing textual tradition, it is not necessary to assume that it was also an independent *source*. Instead it could be a *fresh composition* constructed from existing resources by the author of *Aramaic Levi*. Comparison of the language, themes, and concepts of the speech with Isaac's blessing of Levi as it appears in *Jub*. 31:13-17 suggests that the author of the passage knew Isaac's blessing and used it for Levi's speech. The language of *Ar. Levi* 90 and 99 is very similar to phrases in *Jub*. 31:14-15.[231] And in spite of its purpose of conferring the priestly office on Levi, the focus of a substantial part of Isaac's blessing is on Levi's exercise of good judgment and effective blessing (*Jub*. 31:15), both of which are especially prominent in Levi's speech to his children. These indications (taken together with the observation made above that *Aramaic Levi* apparently knew a tradition wherein Levi received a blessing from Isaac, but did not preserve the content of the blessing) suggest once again that our author shared a source with the writer of *Jub*. 30:1–32:9, but used it differently.[232] Not allowing the blessing of Isaac to stand, he reduced it to a single sentence which states that a benison was given. But also not allowing the contents of the blessing to go to waste, he put it to use in Levi's speech to his children.[233]

The principal aim of the first half of Levi's speech is to encourage the cultivation of wisdom among its readers and to add to the document's model priesthood the roles of scribe and sage. There can be no missing the fact that the author considers wisdom—the sort that is characterized by the skills of reading, writing, and good judgment—to be of considerable value. Thus it seems the wise person of God described in the passage is a person charged with the responsibility of having typical scribal skills and of making judgment on various matters.[234] It is also to be noted that wisdom is understood to serve one especially well when one is in a strange land. This focus on the practice of wisdom as a stranger may suggest something of the context of

---

[231] Compare *Ar. Levi* 90 with *Jub*. 31:14a; *Ar. Levi* 99 with *Jub*. 31:15.

[232] See 4.2.1 and 4.3.4.

[233] The author of *Aramaic Levi* no doubt undertook this rearrangement and expansion of material from the apocryphon so as to give to Levi the privilege of foretelling his descendants' future. This would have been especially important were his overall objective to exalt his own branch of the Levitical descendants over others.

[234] Michael Stone, "Ideal Figures and Social Context: Priest and Sage in the Early Second Temple Age," in *Ancient Israelite Religion* (ed. P. D. Miller, P. D. Hanson, and D. S. McBride; Philadelphia: Fortress, 1988) 578-80, suggests that it is the focus on the "instructional function of the priesthood" that "attracted sapiential motifs" (580). It is more likely, however, that the author began with an interest in sapientializing the priesthood, and that along with that came the emphasis on the priest's teaching role. Moreover, the use of Joseph as a generative figure for the speech indicates a certain predisposition toward wisdom motifs.

the document as a whole. We return to this below when we address the purpose of the work.

The second half of Levi's speech in which he predicts the evil actions of later generations may be the author's explanation of how a later part of the Levitical line failed in its stewardship of the office. In that sense it is necessary once more to to entertain the possibility that the document was intended as a polemic against a branch of the priesthood with which its author was at odds. Again, we will return to this aspect of the speech when we speak of the document's purpose.

The relationship of the speech to the rest of *Aramaic Levi* has been addressed above, at least from a formal standpoint: it is a new creation of the author of *Aramaic Levi* fashioned from part of the Levi-apocryphon, and then added to it. The speech's functional relationship with the rest of the document is somewhat simpler. First, the positive part of the address casts its light back over the rest of the document, inasmuch as the sort of priest embodied by Levi is made to be not only a sacerdotal functionary, but now also a scribal figure. Second, Levi's speech of condemnation for his future apostate descendants indicates that some of Levi's seed would not conform to the model priesthood laid out in the preceding sections.

The connection of the speech with the other texts in the LPT is also clear. A creation of the author of *Aramaic Levi*, it appears here for the first time, although it is at least in part a reuse of Isaac's blessing that was probably known by the author from a Levi-apocryphon which was also used by the author of *Jub.* 30:1–32:9. After *Aramaic Levi* the exhortation to wisdom reappears in *Testament of Levi* 13 in abbreviated form, and the warnings about future iniquity seem to lie at the heart of *Testament of Levi* 14–15.

3.2. The place of *Aramaic Levi* in the LPT

After the long look at the individual parts of *Aramaic Levi* it is time now to turn to the question of its relationship to the other parts of the LPT. Because we have only begun to assess the parts of the tradition our comments here must be preliminary in character.

The question of *Aramaic Levi*'s connection to antecedent texts in the LPT is at once easy and difficult to answer. It is clear that *Aramaic Levi* relies on many Hebrew Bible passages, including Mal 2:4-7 and the key Hebrew Bible Levi traditions discussed in chapter one.[235] What remains difficult to pinpoint is its relationship to a no-longer extant source that may also have been employed by the author of *Jubilees*. So far the evidence does indicate that the author of *Aramaic Levi* used a Levi-apocryphon; the obvious abbreviation of an existing narrative in *Ar. Levi* 8 provides substantial evidence for the assertion. In addition,

---

[235] See especially *Ar. Levi* 1-3, 6.

the fuller account in *Jub.* 31:4-32 of the events alluded to in *Ar. Levi* 8, the reuse of parts of Isaac's blessing from *Jub.* 31:12-17 in *Ar. Levi* 90, 99, and the other similarities between the two documents suggest that their authors shared a Levi-apocryphon, but used it differently. As for what the source contained, and what *Aramaic Levi* added to it, we may say only the following for now (while examination of *Jubilees* in chapter four will allow greater certainty and broader understanding). Because Levi's speech to his children appears to have been added to an existing text, and employs some of the elements found in Isaac's blessing of Levi in *Jub.* 31:12-17, it may probably be eliminated as part of the the Levi-apocryphon; it is instead, as we have already suggested, a new composition by the author of *Aramaic Levi*, though built from parts of the apocryphon.[236] Meanwhile, the different location of the cultic instructions need not lead to the conclusion that they were not part of the source; instead their placement in *Jub.* 21:7-20 is perhaps explained by the penchant of *Jubilees'* author for narrative consistency.[237] The complete absence of Levi's prayer and life history in *Jubilees* does lead one to doubt their presence in the Levi-apocryphon.[238]

The single text in the LPT that follows *and relies* on *Aramaic Levi* is almost assuredly *Testament of Levi*. The similarities between the two evident in the life histories preserved in *Ar. Levi* 62-81 and *Testament of Levi* 11–12, the wisdom speeches in *Ar. Levi* 82-106 and *Testament of Levi* 13, and the cultic instructions in *Ar. Levi* 13-61 and *T. Levi* 9:6-14 all support this conclusion. Nevertheless, as we indicate in chapter five, there are significant differences between the two works resulting from the compositional efforts of *Testament of Levi's* author.

3.3. The date, purpose, and provenance of *Aramaic Levi*

We close our discussion of *Aramaic Levi* with a tentative consideration of the date, purpose, and provenance of *Aramaic Levi*. More complete assessment of these questions can be undertaken only in conjunction with a fuller commentary on the document.

3.3.1. Previous views on the date, purpose, and provenance of *Aramaic Levi*

After Charles and Cowley asserted in 1907 that *Aramaic Levi* was written before 150 BCE at the latest since it served as a source for

---

[236] In fact, its poor connection with passages like the account of the incident at Shechem (see 3.1.1) indicate that it was integrated into an already established literary work.

[237] See 3.1.5, 4.2.1, and 4.3.6.

[238] See 4.2.1 for a more complete and confident assessment of the relationship between *Aramaic Levi, Jubilees*, and the apocryphon. There we have the benefit of closer examination of *Jub.* 30:1–32:9.

Jubilees,[239] the next substantive contribution to the question of date is Milik's view that it may be assigned a very early date in the late fourth century or early third century.[240] Most critics have received his suggestion with skepticism, but have awaited full publication of the Qumran fragments before judging its reliability.[241] In fact, the reconstructed text adds nothing decisive. As for the purpose of *Aramaic Levi*, Milik has stated that it was part of a larger body of priestly literature aimed at passing on sacerdotal traditions and instruction, and that it may have been part of a priestly-testamentary literature at Qumran that included testaments of Amram and Kohath as well.[242]

In his 1956 article Pierre Grelot stated that Levi's possession of a kingdom of the sword alongside his priestly reign "invite à place la rédaction de cette œuvre dans le contexte maccabéennes."[243] So Grelot finds a pro-Hasmonean flavor in *Aramaic Levi*, and therefore dates it in the second century BCE. His conclusion rests on the claim that Bodl. a 1-7, in tandem with 1Q21 1, describe the nature of a kingdom of the sword that Levi would permanently possess. If one reads that section of text differently—that is, as the grant of the priesthood to the exclusion of the exercise of military power—then Grelot's view is hardly tenable.

A similar view is taken by Beyer in the introduction to his edition of *Aramaic Levi*.[244] He suggests that since Levi and his descendants are assigned the roles of priests, kings, and warriors—all indications of a pro-Hasmonean perspective—the document may be understood as legitimation for their dynasty; hence, he says, it was composed in the second century BCE. Writing after the publication of 4Q213 8-10 (*Ar. Levi* 103-105), Beyer suggests that the lines were meant to condemn pre-Hasmonean attempts at hellenizing the priesthood.[245] Yet Beyer's contention that Levi and his descendants are granted the offices of priest, king, and warrior is not easily supported with evidence from the document itself. The text often cited as evidence of royal rule for the levitical line is preserved only in the Greek, in Mt. Athos 18:2, (*Ar. Levi* 67), and is absent from the Aramaic.[246] As for his contention that *Aramaic Levi* depicts Levi as a warrior, Beyer relies on Grelot's de-

---

239 Charles and Cowley, " An Early Source," 567.
240 See J. T. Milik, "Écrits préesséniens," 96; see also *Books of Enoch*, 24.
241 See, for example, Hollander and de Jonge, *Commentary*, 22-23.
242 Milik, "Écrits préesséniens," 103. See now the publication of the Kohath text by Émile Puech, "Le Testament de Qahat en araméen de la Grotte 4 (*4QTQah*)," *RevQ* 15 (1992) 2-54.
243 Grelot, "Notes," 406.
244 Beyer, *Die aramäischen Texten*, 188-209.
245 Ibid., 188-89.
246 See the discussion of the phrase in 3.1.6.

batable reconstruction of *Ar. Levi* 4ff. using 1Q21 and Bodl. a 1-7,[247] and implicitly on the faulty assumption that like *Testament of Levi*, *Aramaic Levi* records an angelic double-commission to the exercise of the power of the sword and the priesthood. We have demonstrated that in *Aramaic Levi* Levi dreams of heavenly angels only *after* he has slain the offending Shechemites.

Meanwhile, Anders Hultgård urges an early second-century BCE date for *Aramaic Levi*.[248] He believes *Aramaic Levi* was written by the Zadokite Jerusalem-temple clergy who were opposed to the lay and priestly efforts to hellenize cult and society in the pre-Maccabean era, and who wanted to legitimate the Zadokite ascendancy as it had evolved in post-exilic Judaism.[249]

> They use the theme of the exaltation of Levi and his descendants to confirm the post-exilic development in which the high priest and the sacrificial cult of the Zadokite priesthood were given an increasing importance. Already in this stage there is an idealiza- tion of the high priest and the priesthood. The stress laid on displaying them as models of purity, of zeal for the Torah, and as bringers of divine wisdom reveals this tendency.[250]

Hultgård explains the obvious difficulty of understanding a text that idealizes Levi as a legitimation document for Zadokites by noting that Gershom's rejection from the priesthood in the life history suggests marginalization of the Levites.[251] As evidence for the author's opposi- tion to hellenizing Zadokites he cites 4Q213 8–10 (*Ar. Levi* 103-105) published by Milik in his *The Books of Enoch*. There Hultgård finds an attack on accommodationist priests.[252] Clearly the greatest weakness with his position is the inadequate way in which he explains the ideal- ization of Levi for the sake of Zadokite legitimation.

Michael Stone has offered very restrained reflections on the date and purpose of *Aramaic Levi*. He cites Milik's paleographic dating of

---

[247] Both Hultgård and Beyer might find support in *Ar. Levi* 99 (see 3.1.7), with its mention of priests and kings. However, the text is so fragmentary that it is impos- sible to tell whether Levi is telling his children that they will fill those roles, teach such figures, or be favored by such figures.

[248] Hultgård, *L'eschatologie*, 1:29, 44. He allows for redaction during the Maccabean era when pro-Hasmonean editors co-opted the text as support for Jonathan and/or Simon's control of the throne and the altar.

[249] Ibid., 1:43-45; also see his article "The Ideal 'Levite,' the Davidic Messiah, and the Saviour Priest in the Testaments of the Twelve Patriarchs," in *Ideal Figures in Ancient Judaism* (ed. J. Collins and G. W. E. Nickelsburg; Chico: CA: Scholars Press, 1980) 94-95.

[250] Ibid.

[251] Ibid., *L'eschatologie*, 1:40-41; cf. Mt. Athos 18:2, 64.

[252] Ibid., 1:43-45.

4Q213 to the late second or early first century BCE,[253] what he considers
to be *Jubilees'* reliance on *Aramaic Levi* and the composition of the
former in the first half of the second century BCE, and *Aramaic Levi's*
non-polemical use of a solar calendar as signs that it may not be dated
much later than the third century BCE.[254] He resists the temptation to
state a firm view on the purpose of the document. Instead he limits
himself to noting its emphasis on the instructional character of the
priesthood, the unusual cultic prescriptions, and its elevation of Levi
over Judah.[255] He and Greenfield think also that Isaac's bestowal of a
blessing only on Levi (*Ar. Levi* 8), and the application of Gen 49:10 to
Kohath (*Ar. Levi* 67) are indications that Judah's royal prerogatives
have been transferred to Levi;[256] Stone draws from these facts the additional conclusion that *Aramaic Levi* depicts Levi as a priestly messiah.[257]

As for the question of provenance, it is apparent that most have
simply assumed a Palestinian origin for the document. However, J. T.
Milik has also advanced the view that *Aramaic Levi* is of Samaritan
origin. So far his published defense of this view has relied mainly on
the concentration of northern place names in the book, and especially
on the occurrence of Abelmain/Abelmaul.[258] Few have been convinced
by his suggestion.

3.3.2. The date of *Aramaic Levi*

The conclusion that *Aramaic Levi* was composed in the third century
BCE stands. In addition to the reasons Stone offers for the date, there is
also the character of the dualism found in the document. Resting
somewhere between the incipient dualism of the late biblical psalms and
the full-blown form appearing in the texts composed by the sectarians
of Qumran, it could fit in the early third century BCE.[259] Of course,
this sort of evidence is obviously imprecise.

---

[253] See now the results of the Carbon-14 tests administered on the leather of
4Q213 by G. Bonani, M. Broshi, I. Carmi, S. Ivy, J. Strugnell, and W. Wölfi,
"Radiocarbon Dating of the Dead Sea Scrolls," *Atiqot* 20 (1991) 27-32; their results
provide a date for 4Q213 consistent with Milik's paleographic assessment.

[254] Michael Stone, "Enoch, Aramaic Levi, and Sectarian Origins," *JSJ* 19 (1988)
160, n. 2. See also his *Scriptures, Sects and Visions* (Philadelphia: Fortress, 1980)
37-38, 75, 138; and "Ideal Figures," 578, n. 20.

[255] The emphasis on the teaching function of the priesthood is evinced by Levi's
wisdom speech. For the unusual cultic prescriptions, see 3.1.5.

[256] Greenfield and Stone, "Remarks," 219, 223-24

[257] Stone, "Enoch," 168-69; "Ideal Figures," 580-81.

[258] Milik, "Fragment," 403-5; "Écrits préesséniens," 96, 106; *Books of Enoch*,
56, 252; "Problèmes de littérature hénochique à la lumière des fragments araméens de
Qumran," *HTR* 64 (1971) 345.

[259] See section 3.1.2.

An additional indicator regarding the date of *Aramaic Levi* is perhaps the subtle nature of the book's attack on the purity of the priesthood and the genteel character of its proposal for an alternative form. Lacking the intense rhetoric of the sectarian literature from Qumran, *Aramaic Levi* seems to come from a period when there was a dispute regarding the proper character of the priestly office, but when the discussion was still quite tame, and there was yet room for differences of opinion. Once Jason and Menelaus took office authors like the one responsible for *Aramaic Levi*—people concerned for the purity of cult and community—would likely have been less restrained and subtle. Hence the argument for a date at least sometime before the early second century is bolstered.[260]

3.3.3. The purpose of *Aramaic Levi*

We may begin by laying one tendency among previous commentators to rest. Observing in *Aramaic Levi* what they think is the attribution of royal characteristics and prerogatives to Levi, and constructing the document along the lines of *Testament of Levi* (wherein Levi is commissioned to be a priest and to wield the sword in one angelic command), some scholars have suggested that the work intends to legitimate the combination of the priest's, king's, and warrior's roles in one individual.[261] We have suggested that the accretion of royal attributes to Levi is less significant than usually thought, especially inasmuch as the apparently royalist portion of the Greek text of *Ar. Levi* 67 appears to be a gloss from the translator. As for his role as a warrior, those who view him as such have been influenced by Grelot's reconstruction of *Ar. Levi* 4ff., and by the notion that *Aramaic Levi* contains the same sort of vision that we find in *T. Levi* 2:5–5:4, where in the same heavenly encounter he is made a priest and commanded to bear the sword against Shechem. But Grelot's hypothesis is subject to considerable doubt,[262] and our reconstruction of *Aramaic Levi* makes it clear that Levi acted to avenge his sister's rape *before* the vision and his elevation to the priesthood.[263]

On the positive side, there are several motifs that emerge time and again in a reading of *Aramaic Levi* that give a hint of its author's intention. The first and most evident theme is Levi's suitability for the priestly office owing to his passion for his own purity and that of the

---

[260] Of course, this assumes that literary subtlety is a reliable indication of low-level historical tensions. To the extent that that assumption may be challenged, the argument for dating *Aramaic Levi* on the basis of it is weakened.

[261] See above, 3.3.1.

[262] In fact, our analysis demonstrated that *Ar. Levi* 4 may be part of a comparison between the reigns of the sword and the priesthood in which the latter emerges as the preferable dominion; see 3.1.3.

[263] See 2.3.2 above.

community.[264] The second is the characterization of the ideal priesthood as different in its practices vis-à-vis the Torah's requirements for
clergy.[265] A third motif is the attachment of the roles of sage and
scribe to the priesthood.[266] Yet another characteristic of *Aramaic Levi*
that shows up repeatedly is its dualism.[267] Together with the narrative
flow of the document these themes suggest something of its purpose.[268]
By moving from an account of the Shechem episode that depicts Levi's
action as a righteous response to the the proposal of marriage between
Jews and non-Jews, to his plea for elevation to the priesthood, and on to
the fulfillment of his request by heavenly agents and by Levi's father,
the author makes known his view regarding the proper character of the
priesthood—it is to be an office marked by a passion for purity. Then
by continuing with Isaac's instructions for priestly service that differ so
from the norms required by the Torah, and by adding to the priestly
office the exercise of wisdom and scribal skills, the author enlarges his
definition of the priestly office—its character is to differ considerably
from the clergy who practice according to the norms of the Pentateuch,
and its practitioners are to have scribal attributes as well. Concluding
with bitter condemnation of Levi's descendants who would one day fail
to heed Levi's advice and conform to his model, the author gives notice
that some of Levi's descendants have indeed failed. They are, perhaps,
the priests of his own day. Throughout the book the author's dualism
appears over and over again; there are forces that seek purity and
righteousness, and wisdom and learning, while there are others that
promote impurity and iniquity, and foolishness and ignorance.

Altogether the themes and the narrative pattern suggest that the
author is engaged in a constructive polemic against some form of the
priesthood, and in the promotion of his own notion of the office's
proper character. On one hand there are priests who do not realize the
ideal evinced by Levi with his passion for purity and attachment to the
roles of scribe and sage; they are, probably, the priests of the author's
day who are implicitly indicted by the model of Levi that varies from
the Pentateuchal norms, and who are explicitly accused by Levi's
warnings about his apostate descendants. On the other hand there are
priests who accept the norms established in Levi, the most ancient
priest of all; they are the adherents to the author's views, those who
prize purity, wisdom, and learning as traits proper to the priesthood.

---

[264] See, for example, *Ar. Levi* 1-3; *Ar. Levi* supp. 1-19, 22-27; *Ar. Levi* 17-21.

[265] See the cultic instructions in *Ar. Levi* 13–61, and the discussion of them in
3.1.5.

[266] See *Ar. Levi* supp. 8; *Ar. Levi* 82-101.

[267] See especially Levi's prayer, *Ar. Levi* supp. 1-19.

[268] For the moment we assume that the scope of *Aramaic Levi* as it has been
reconstructed here accounts for its contents, or at least for its beginning.

Aramaic Levi is a rejection of the former kind of priest, and a plea for acceptance of the latter type.

3.3.4. The provenance of *Aramaic Levi*

Who would have written this sort of work? Milik's proposal that it comes from the hand of a Samaritan author turns out to be remarkably attractive. We have already noted the significance for the possibility of a Samaritan origin of combining in one document exaltation of Levi and Joseph.[269] Milik has made the case for Samaritan provenance on the basis of the place names.[270] And we have also seen that there is reason to believe the author relied on a text for Leviticus that is similar to the so-called Samaritan Pentateuch.[271] Perhaps the priests responsible for this work sought to lay the historical foundation for a Samaritan priesthood, one explicitly differentiated from the sacerdotal leadership in Jerusalem. Of course, even when these indications are taken together it is difficult to be extremely confident that the document is Samaritan. We must recognize that, without additional evidence and further study of *Aramaic Levi*, Samaritan provenance is only a possibility.

There is yet another view regarding provenance which is also more in the realm of speculation than of the possible. Nevertheless, it deserves to be mentioned, if for no other reason than its tantalizing character. Josephus tells us that during the period of the Diadochoi Ptolemy captured Samaritans and exiled them to Egypt, where they were in conflict with Jews of Judea regarding which temple ought to receive their sacrifices (*Ant.* 12 §§ 3-10). One wonders in light of this report if it were not such Samaritans, exiled in a foreign land, who composed a document like this. Certainly they would have disputed with their Jewish brothers from Judea as to which priests—ones descended from the Jerusalem priesthood, or ones from Samaria—were proper clergy; hence the at times apparently intentional self-differentiation from Pentateuchal law regarding proper priestly behavior (see especially the cultic instructions, *Ar. Levi* 13-61). And most certainly they would have found the traditions regarding their ancestor Joseph and his exaltation for wisdom in a foreign land an irresistible resource as they sought to make the best of their situation (*Ar. Levi* 88, 90-94). Unhappily, apart from the fact that the document turns up in the Cairo Geniza centuries later, we have little more to go on to substantiate this interesting speculation. All the same, this view regarding provenance fits nicely with what we have concluded regarding the date and purpose of the work. If it were written by Samaritans in Egypt, one would not be surprised were the document to have a third-century origin and an

---

[269] See 3.1.7.

[270] See note 258 above.

[271] See note 155 above, and the caveat we offer in this regard.

overall aim of promoting a model priesthood that is based on Levi and differentiated from the one dictated strictly by Pentateuchal legislation.

3.4. Conclusion

Our study of *Aramaic Levi* has provided us with an understanding of the text necessary for a continuation of our study of the LPT, and it has turned up some surprising results. As for the surprises, it has suggested that *Aramaic Levi* is only the first *extant* work in the LPT, and that before it there existed a Levi-apocryphon which served as a resource for the author of *Jubilees* as well. And it has led us to consider with renewed appreciation J. T. Milik's suggestion that *Aramaic Levi* comes from a Samaritan author. But most of all our analysis has established a sense of the text and contents of *Aramaic Levi* necessary for us to continue our analysis of the LPT. Armed with that information we turn now to the next phase of the study.

CHAPTER 4 THE LEVI-PRIESTLY TRADITION IN
JUB. 30:1–32:9

The LPT continues in *Jub* 30:1–32:9. Here Levi avenges Dinah's rape, and after a speech against exogamy by the angel-author of *Jubilees*, Levi's elevation to the priesthood is promised as a reward for his zeal (30:1-23). Then his impending election to the priesthood is foreshadowed again, this time by Isaac's blessing (31:12-17). Next, in a third forecast of his appointment, Levi dreams of his elevation to the priesthood (32:1-2). After awakening from the dream Levi is tithed to God's service by his father, and the threefold prediction is fulfilled (32:3). Then Levi, the new priest, makes offerings on his father's behalf (32:4-9). All of this is interwoven with other material focused on Jacob and Judah.

Even such a brief recitation of the events relating to Levi in *Jub* 30:1–32:9 shows that it is very similar to *Aramaic Levi*, yet that it differs from it on several important points. Therefore a principal concern will be to determine the precise relationship between the two documents. This will be achieved through commentary on the text of *Jub.* 30:1–32:9, and comparison of its contents with those of *Aramaic Levi*. But first it is necessary to reflect on the date and purpose of the book. We must consider the matter of date because we need to confirm the view that *Jubilees* is later than *Aramaic Levi*, and so deal with the recent suggestion that *Aramaic Levi* relied on *Jubilees* (among other sources), and not vice-versa.[1] And it is necessary to address the question of purpose so as to set the LPT in *Jubilees* in context.

4.1. Establishing the context of the LPT in *Jubilees*

The date of *Jubilees* has long been a troublesome question, while the issue of its purpose is less in dispute. For the date of the book, however,

---

[1] James Kugel, "Levi's Elevation to the Priesthood in Second Temple Writings," *HTR* 86 (1993) 1-64, esp. 52-58.

we may rely for the most part on James VanderKam.[2] As for the book's purpose, review of critical studies shows that opinion varies, but within a narrow range; therefore the matter requires minimal attention.

4.1.1. The date of *Jubilees*

Before discovery of the scrolls from Qumran the range of opinion regarding the book's date was immense. At one extreme *Jubilees* was thought to have been composed in the fifth or fourth century BCE,[3] and at the other end of the spectrum are those who thought *Jubilees* was composed in the first century CE.[4] Others believed there to be a close association between the themes of *Jubilees* and the concerns of the period immediately before and during the Hasmonean era.[5] But recently a manuscript of *Jubilees* from Qumran was dated by James VanderKam and J. T. Milik to ca. 150-100 BCE; thus the late date for *Jubilees* can be discarded completely.[6] Meanwhile, adherents of the early date were contradicted by the verification from the scrolls that conflicting legal texts abounded even into the late period of the Second Commonwealth, and they either retracted their views in light of the Qumran evidence,[7]

---

[2] James C. VanderKam, *Textual and Historical Studies in the Book of Jubilees* (HSM 14; Missoula: Scholars, 1977) 214-85.

[3] Solomon Zeitlin, "The Book of Jubilees, Its Character and Its Significance," *JQR* 30 (1939-40) 8-16; and "The Book of 'Jubilees' and the Pentateuch," *JQR* 48 (1957) 218-35. Zeitlin held this position because *Jubilees* contains views contrary to Pentateuchal law. Solomon Zeitlin reasoned that such bold contradictions could not persist after the Torah had acquired normative status.

[4] August Dillmann, "Das Buch der Jubiläen oder die kleine Genesis," *JBW* 3 (1851) 3, 88-94, cited by VanderKam, *Textual and Historical Studies*, 208, n. 2. Dillmann noted that *Jubilees* presupposes Enoch (a book which he believed was composed around the middle of the first century), yet *Jubilees* had to have been written before the fall of Jerusalem, concerned as it was with the cult; therefore it must have come into existence sometime shortly before 70 CE. Other commentators asserted that its fascination with the law signals anti-Christian polemic, or even a stand against a Pauline theology of justification by faith alone (see H. Rönsch, *Das Buch der Jubiläen oder die Kleine Genesis* [Leipzig: Fues's Verlag, 1874] 523-29; and Wm. Singer, *Das Buch der Jubiläen oder die Leptogenesis* [Stuhlweissenburg, Hungary: Ed. Singer'sche Buchhandlung, 1898] 264-322, cited by VanderKam, *Textual and Historical Studies*, 209, nn., 4 and 5).

[5] See those listed by James Charlesworth, "The Date of Jubilees and of the Temple Scroll," *SBLSP* 24 (1985) 193.

[6] James VanderKam and J. T. Milik, "The First *Jubilees* Manuscript from Qumran Cave 4: A Preliminary Publication," *JBL* 110 (1991) 243-70, especially 246. VanderKam, *Textual and Historical Studies*, 216, had already established a *terminus ad quem* of 100 BCE by means of other manuscript evidence from Qumran.

[7] W. F. Albright, *From Stone Age to Christianity*, (2nd ed.; New York: Doubleday, 1957) 20.

or they continued to hold an increasingly untenable position.[8] In the wake of the proof of a *terminus ad quem* only the "centrist view" that *Jubilees* was composed in the half century from just before the Maccabean revolt to the last decade of the second century BCE remains. Proponents of this dating are divided between supporters of a pre-Maccabean date and advocates of a post-167 BCE date.[9]

There are reasons to believe that *Jubilees* was composed before the Maccabean revolt, and prior to the putative suspension of the Hellenization of Judaism. The concerns addressed in *Jubilees* indicate that at the time of its composition its author thought traditional Judaism to be under assault from encroaching Hellenism, and that the beliefs and practices of Jews required defense. The emphasis on sabbath observance (2:1, 17-33; 50:6-13), circumcision (15:25-34; 16:14, 25; 20:3), festival celebration (6:17-22; 16:20-31; 34:18-19; 49), avoidance of exogamy (20:4; 22:16-18; 30:5-15; 41:2), and the stern prohibition of public nudity (3:30-31) all point toward a pre-Maccabean date.[10] At least one scholar cites as further evidence the silence of the apocalyptic material in 23:8-32 regarding Antiochus IV Epiphanes' desecration of the temple.[11] Taken together these are impressive indications of a pre-Hasmonean date.[12]

There are, however, more compelling indications in favor of a date sometime during the early-Maccabean period. VanderKam has shown that the battle accounts in *Jub.* 34:2-9; 37:1–38:14 are allusions

---

[8] Zeitlin, "The Book of Jubilees," passim.

[9] See Charlesworth's list, cited in note 5 above. There is one other possibility represented by Robert Doran, "The Non-Dating of Jubilees: Jub 34–38; 23:14-32 in Narrative Context," *JJS* 20 (1989) 1-12, who basically asserts that the elements in *Jubilees* which are usually thought to give some indication of date may not be historical allusions at all, and even so are too general to allow association of the document with a very specific point in time. While his observations have some merit we remain convinced that the range and variety of indicators mentioned here do allow some confidence about the work's date.

[10] *Pace* Doran, "The Non-Dating of Jubilees," 11-12.

[11] G. W. E. Nickelsburg, "The Bible Rewritten and Expanded," 103; *Resurrection, Immortality, and Eternal Life in Intertestamental Judaism* (HTS 26; Cambridge: Harvard University, 1972) 46-47.

[12] Of course, this position assumes that the Hasmoneans were actually opposed to Hellenism in large measure. As such it is a view that may be overly credulous with respect to the chief source for our understanding of the Hasmonean dynasty, namely 1 Maccabees. Few doubt that it was principally propaganda for the Hasmonean family's control over affairs in Palestine and the surrounding region. One ought also to remember the point of Bickerman's landmark work, *Der Gott der Makkabäer* (Berlin: Schocken, 1937; ET Leiden: Brill, 1979)—in spite of the indications to the contrary, the Hasmoneans were surely more adept at managing the phenomenon of Hellenism to their own advantage than they were at turning back its inevitable tide.

to early Maccabean wars.[13]   Even if all of VanderKam's arguments may not be defended, most would still agree that the references in *Jub.* 37:1–38:14 to Edomite wars provide testimony to early Maccabean battles.[14] Additionally VanderKam has noted the author's reliance on the Enochic Book of Dreams, a document composed shortly after Judas Maccabee's victory at Bethsur (cf. *Jub.* 4:20 and *1 Enoch* 85:3; *Jub.* 5:9 and *1 Enoch* 88:2; *Jub* 5:10 and *1 Enoch* 88:3; *Jub.* 7:22 and *1 Enoch* 87:4; 88:2; 89:6).[15] Hence *Jubilees* must have been composed in 164 BCE or after.   VanderKam adds that its positive view of the priesthood urges a date before Jonathan usurped the office of the high priest; so it must have been written before the Maccabean high priesthood began in 152 BCE.[16] VanderKam also points out that even though *Jubilees* shares key ideas and concepts with the Qumran sectarian literature, at least three things set them apart: while two messiahs are expected at Qumran, none is mentioned in *Jubilees*; while the Qumran community relaxes the penalties for Sabbath violations (e.g., CD 12:3-6), *Jubilees* preserves the Pentateuch's requirement of capital punishment for such offences (2:25-27; 50:13; cf. Exod 31:14-15; 35:2; Num 15:32-36); and while the Qumran community sees itself as set apart from the rest of Israel and cut off from the Jerusalem cult, *Jubilees* still centers attention on the entire people and emphasizes participation in the temple cult (see *Jub.* 49:16-21 where it is required that Passover observations take place in the temple; cf. Deut 16:7).[17] So although the author of *Jubilees* stands in the same intellectual tradition as the Qumran sectarians, his views appear to precede theirs by at least a few years.   From these observations VanderKam concludes that the document came into existence after 164 BCE, but before 152 BCE.[18]

The arguments for a post-167 BCE date are superior.   While support for a pre-Maccabean date derives from the presence or absence of certain themes in *Jubilees*, the later date is anchored by the author's knowledge of the Book of Dreams, which requires that he wrote after 164 BCE.   Moreover, to the extent that they are still defensible,

---

[13] VanderKam, *Textual and Historical Studies*, 217-38. But on the identification of 34:2-9 with Judas' battles against Nicanor, see Nickelsburg's review in *JAOS* 100 (1980) 83-84, and Robert Doran, "The Non-Dating of Jubilees," passim.

[14] *Pace* Doron Mendels, *The Land of Israel as a Political Concept in Hasmonean Literature: Recourse to History in Second Century B.C. Claims to the Holy Land* (Tübingen: J. C. B. Mohr, 1987) 78-79.

[15] For the date of the Book of Dreams, see J. T. Milik, *The Books of Enoch* (Oxford: Oxford University, 1976) 44. James VanderKam makes his argument in "Enoch Traditions in Jubilees and Other Second Century Sources," *SBLSP* 13 (1978) 1:229-51. For others who have made the connection between the two books see the notes in VanderKam's article.

[16] VanderKam, *Textual and Historical Studies*, 249-52.

[17] Ibid., 280-82.

[18] Ibid., 283-85.

VanderKam's observations about the wars narrated in *Jubilees* 37–38 also require composition after known events. Hence we join with those who say that *Jubilees* was written after the beginning of Maccabean influence on Judean affairs, and we remain satisfied with VanderKam's range of dates, 164 to 152 BCE.[19] Moreover, we remain convinced that the composition of *Jubilees* followed that of *Aramaic Levi*. Now one may ask what the author's purpose was in writing a text like *Jubilees*

---

[19] We can narrow the date even farther if we accept VanderKam's observation that *Jub.* 23:21-23 may reflect Alcimus' apostate priesthood and the battles between Judas and the invading Syrian forces during Alcimus' reign (VanderKam, *Textual and Historical Studies*, 253-54; cf. Charles, *The Book of Jubilees or the Little Genesis* [London: Adam and Charles Black, 1902] 148; VanderKam also notes the possibility that vv. 22-23 refer to the slaughter of the Hasidim by Alcimus [cf, 1 Macc 7:17-18; Josephus, *Ant.* 12 § 396]). This suggests that *Jubilees* was written sometime after the beginning of Alcimus' priesthood in 162. It also accords well with the document's concern over continued Hellenization, and with its implicit polemic against assimilationist Jews. Alcimus probably promoted the process of Hellenization; after all, he was hand-picked by the Seleucids to assume the office of high priest, and he demonstrated his loyalty to them, and his disregard for pious Jews and their concerns, when he had sixty of the Hasidim slain (1 Macc. 7:1-18). However, it is just as possible that *Jubilees* was written after Alcimus passed from the scene, during the so-called *intersacerdotium* (Josephus, *Ant.* 20 § 237; 1 Macc 10:21; compare *Ant.* 12 § 413). Though we have too little information to be certain, it is likely that Hellenization continued apace then. Especially in such a period one can expect that priestly groups would have made known their views regarding the office's proper character as they vied for control at its restoration. Indeed, if VanderKam's suggestion that Josephus' assignment of the high priesthood to Judas (Josephus, *Ant.* 12 § 414) has some truth to it, and that Judas possessed the office in competition with Alcimus ("People and High Priesthood in Early Maccabean Times," in *The Hebrew Bible and its Interpreters* [ed. W. H. Propp, B. Halpern, and D. N. Freedman; Biblical and Judaic Studies from the University of California, San Diego 1; Winona Lake, IN: Eisenbrauns, 1990] 219-22), one can easily see how the complicated situation may have compelled debate about the office's proper character, and generated such texts as the one we find in *Jub.* 30:1–32:9.

It is also necessary to note that while it is rather certain that *Jubilees* was written after 164 BCE, it can still be argued that it was composed later in the second century, rather than earlier. Doron Mendels has suggested that it was written sometime in the twenties (*The Land of Israel as a Political Concept in Hasmonean Literature* [Tübingen: J.C. B. Mohr, 1987] 57-88). Besides coming perilously close to the date of the oldest manuscripts of *Jubilees* from Qumran, Mendels relies too heavily on the notion that the major—if not sole—purpose of *Jubilees* was to settle the question of "what border the Jewish state is to have, what is to be its political authority, and what exactly should be done with the foreigners settled on the land" (59). Such a narrow definition of the purpose of *Jubilees* forces Mendels to ignore the considerable evidence for the book's other interests which situate it so much more readily in the fifties of the same century.

then in Israel's history. To that question we now turn, as its answer has significance for how we construe the LPT in *Jubilees*.

4.1.2. The purpose of *Jubilees*

There is a generous literature on the theology, religious ideas, and purpose of *Jubilees*.[20] The details of the literature need not detain us. Instead, we may focus attention on the rhetorical character of the book and the themes it evinces as indications of its purpose.

The rhetorical strategy of *Jubilees* is well known. It is Moses' transcription of an angelic account of the events depicted in Genesis 1 to Exodus 14; to say it another way, it is a heavenly speech about a fundamentally determinative period in Jewish history mediated through the most authoritative figure of Israel's past.[21] In addition, appended to the stories are numerous laws that go beyond what is found in the Torah.[22] The author, it seems, set out to compose a new charter for Hasmonean-era Judaism that would have great credibility, founded as it was on a claim to antiquity, heavenly revelation, and transcription by one of Israel's greatest heroes.

The aim of the proposal was chiefly to preserve Jewish unity and identity in the face of Hellenization.[23] For instance, in a midrash on

---

[20] See, for example, R. H. Charles, *The Book of Jubilees*; Klaus Berger, *Unterweisung in erzählender Form: Das Buch der Jubiläen* (JSHRZ II.3; Gerd Mohn: Gütersloher Verlagshaus, 1981); Gene Davenport, *The Eschatology of the Book of Jubilees* (Studia Post Biblica 20; Leiden: Brill, 1971); Annie Jaubert, *La notion d'alliance dans le Judaïsme* (Paris: Editions du Seuil, 1963) 89-115; F. Martin, "Le Livre de Jubilés: But et procedes de l'auteur. Ses doctrines," *RB* 8 (1911) 321-44, 502-33; Doron Mendels, *The Land*; Eberhard Schwarz, *Identität durch Abgrenzung: Abgrenzungsprozesse in Israel im 2. vorchristlichen Jahrhundert und ihre Traditionsgeschichtlichen Voraussetzungen. Zugleich ein Beitrag zur Erforschung des Jubiläen Buches* (Europäische Hochschulschriften 162; Frankfurt am Main: Peter Lang, 1982); M. Testuz, *Les idées réligieuses du Livre des Jubilés* (Geneva: Droz, 1960); and Solomon Zeitlin, *The Book of Jubilees: Its Character and Significance* (Philadelphia: Dropsie College, 1939). As with the date of *Jubilees*, the views on its purpose before the discovery of the scrolls were abundant and far reaching; however, once the scrolls came to light and the close similarities they share with *Jubilees* were known, it became impossible to hold the more extreme positions on *Jubilees'* purpose. Instead, the possibilities were focused on options that accounted for the closeness between *Jubilees* and the scrolls.

[21] For resolution of the difficulties the Ethiopic text poses with respect to the author of *Jubilees*—at times Moses writes, and in other places the angel of the presence is the scribe—see James VanderKam, "The Putative Author of the Book of Jubilees," *JSS* 26 (1981) 209-17.

[22] Many of these laws are introduced by the phrase, "And for this reason it is written on heavenly tablets . . ." (cf. *Jub.* 3:10, 31; 4:5, 32; 5:13; 6:17, etc.).

[23] This theme is highlighted by, among others, Schwarz, *Identität durch Abgrenzung*, passim. See also A. Jaubert, *La notion d'alliance*, 95-97, where she

Genesis 1 to Exodus 14 one expects figures like Abraham and Moses to take very central roles; yet the author focuses most intensively on Jacob, no doubt because Jacob is the quintessential "all Israel" figure.[24] Also the emphasis on circumcision and Sabbath observance, the virulent rejection of exogamy, and the prohibition of the Greek practice of public nudity indicate deep concern over Hellenization.

The author also shows signs of having been "a member of the priestly caste."[25] Indications of his occupation are his preoccupation with proper sacrifice (e.g., *Jub.* 21:7-20), his concern to declare Levi's ascendancy in the priestly role (*Jub.* 31:12-17; 32:1-9), and his implicit claim to possess secret principles of sacerdotal practice (*Jub.* 45:16). At the same time some of his priestly and cultic norms differ from those espoused by the Pentateuch; see, for example, the book's promotion of a solar calendar (*Jub.* 6:29-38).

One other element that defines the book's purpose is the small apocalypse in chapter 23. Although the events to which it alludes can be situated at a variety of junctures in Jewish history, the chapter's function within *Jubilees* seems clear enough. It works to convey the author's sense that while Judaism had suffered distractions, persecutions, and difficulties in the past, at the time he wrote it was on the verge of a golden, if not messianic age. Thus the book grounds Judaism's contemporary glory in the distant past, and indicates that its unique vision of the proper character of Judaism was both responsible for and able to sustain Judaism's smashing success under the Maccabees. The fact that *Jub.* 23:26 suggests that the new age will be (or had been) brought into existence by a select group's zealous reading and keeping of the law is significant; the statement probably reflects the author's self perception, and indicates something of his own community's character. They were not mere priests—they were the class of priests who were occupied with the learning, teaching, and doing of the law, and they considered themselves to be responsible for Judaism's success, and the guarantors of its continued prosperity.

Recalling the date of composition assigned to *Jubilees* sheds considerable light on its purpose. It was a time when possession of the office of the high priesthood, the position of power from which the character of Jewish society in the Second Temple period was shaped, was in dispute. Hence, as a priestly document that proposed a unique set of legal guidelines for life in Judea, *Jubilees* was meant to give voice to its

---

emphasizes the book's insistence on the holiness and purity of the people of Israel (in particular Jacob) over against the "peoples."

[24] This view is articulated especially by Jaubert, *La notion d'alliance*, 99. The recognition that Jacob assumes the ascendant role in *Jubilees* is seconded by John C. Endres, *Biblical Interpretation in the Book of Jubilees* (CBQMS 18; Catholic Biblical Association of America, 1987) 19.

[25] Charles, *Book of Jubilees*, li.

author's views in the debate over the character Judaism ought to have in the wake of the political liberation achieved by the Maccabees. It was probably intended also to give the author a role in the competition for the power of the high priesthood.[26] This is the context for the LPT in *Jubilees*.

4.2. The place of *Jub.* 30:1–32:9 in the LPT

The similarities between *Jub.* 30:1–32:9 and *Aramaic Levi* have long been noted, and have fueled speculation that the two documents are related. Our identification of *Ar. Levi* supp. 22-27 as a close parallel to *Jub.* 30:5-17 strengthens that suspicion considerably. Nevertheless, scholars have also isolated many differences between the two documents which indicate that they are only rather distantly related. Hence the question of *Jubilees*' place in the LPT is particularly engaging.

4.2.1. *Jub.* 30:1–32:9 and *Aramaic Levi*

Jürgen Becker, Pierre Grelot, Anders Hultgård, Marinus de Jonge, and James Kugel have offered substantial answers to the question of *Jubilees'* relationship to *Aramaic Levi*. Becker concluded that *Aramaic Levi*, *Testament of Levi*, and *Jubilees* relied separately on a common oral tradition.[27] Grelot stated that *Jubilees* and *Aramaic Levi* used a common written source, a midrash on Genesis centered on the person of Levi.[28] Hultgård also decided that *Jubilees* and *Aramaic Levi* relied independently on a shared written source.[29] In 1953 de Jonge suggested that both *Aramaic Levi* and *Testament of Levi* went back to a haggadic source which he called "Original Levi;" *Jubilees*, he concluded, probably also used the source.[30] Finally, Kugel has taken a very different approach, suggesting that the complete form of *Aramaic Levi* incorporated parts of *Jubilees*.[31] All but Kugel are fairly confi-

---

[26] For a similar view, see A. Jaubert, *La notion d'alliance*, 115.

[27] Jürgen Becker, *Untersuchungen zur Entstehungsgeschichte der Testamente der zwölf Patriarchen* (AGJU 8; Leiden: Brill, 1970) 77-87. See now also Jarl Henning Ulrichsen, *Die Grundschrift der Testamente der zwölf Patriarchen: eine Untersuchung zu Umfang, Inhalt und Eigenart der ursprünglichen Schrift* (Acta Universitatis Upsaliensis; Historia Religionum 10; Uppsala: Almqvist & Wiksell, 1991) 182.

[28] Pierre Grelot, "Notes sur le Testament araméen de Lévi," *RB* 63 (1956) 402-406.

[29] Anders Hultgård, *L'eschatologie des Testaments des Douze Patriarches*, vol. 1, *Interpretation des textes* (Acta Universitatis Upsaliensis; Historia Religionum 6; Uppsala: Almqvist & Wiksell, 1977) 23-25.

[30] Marinus de Jonge, *Testaments of the Twelve Patriarchs* (Assen: Van Gorcum, 1953) 39, 167.

[31] Kugel, "Levi's Elevation," 52-58. For a fuller treatment of Kugel's suggestion, see the conclusion of this section.

dent, at any rate, that *Aramaic Levi* predates *Jubilees*.[32] Unfortunately none of these scholars had access to the full range of evidence for *Aramaic Levi*, and so each one proceeded on the assumption that *Aramaic Levi* contained two visions. Naturally this affected their evaluation of the relationship between *Aramaic Levi* and *Jubilees*; therefore the issue merits reassessment in light of the complete evidence for *Aramaic Levi* and of our reconstruction of its scope and structure.

Comparison of *Jub* 30:1–32:9 with the same series of events in *Aramaic Levi* reveals striking parallels between the two works, along with equally noticeable differences in order and content.[33]

Jub. 30:1–32:9 and *Aramaic Levi* Compared

Jub. 30:1–32:9	*Aramaic Levi*
§1 *Jub.* 30:1-4—The rape of Dinah and the sack of Shechem by Levi and Simeon.	*Ar. Levi* 1-3—The rape of Dinah and the sack of Shechem by Levi and Simeon (and other brothers?).
§2	*Ar. Levi* supp. 1-19—Levi's prayer.
§3	*Ar. Levi* supp. 20—Levi's travel between his prayer and his vision.
§4	*Ar. Levi* supp. 21—The beginning of Levi's vision, with ascent (?) and encounter with an angel.[34]
§5 *Jub.* 30:5-17—The angel's speech against exogamy.	*Ar. Levi* supp. 22-27—The angel's speech against exogamy.

[32] Although his comment is made only in passing, one must add to the list Michael Stone, "Enoch, Aramaic Levi and Sectarian Origins," *JSJ* 19 (1988) 159, n. 2, who thinks that the author of *Jubilees* relied directly on *Aramaic Levi*, using it as a source. As our discussion of *Aramaic Levi* and of *Jub.* 30:1–32:9 makes clear, this is rather unlikely.

[33] For this chart we depend in part on Becker, *Untersuchungen*, 80-81; we supplement his chart with the added portions of *Aramaic Levi* known now through the complete evidence from Qumran. "Cf." before an entry denotes the fact that it differs from the corresponding material by reason of location or content.

[34] Cf. *Jub.* 32:1, Levi's vision.

§6	*Jub.* 30:18-20—The angelic narrator indicates that Levi was made a priest as a reward for his zeal [cf. 32:1]	*Ar. Levi* 4-6—Levi is made a priest (as a reward for his zeal?) by the heavenly angels.
§7	*Jub.* 30:21-23—"Thus it is written on the heavenly tablets" that no one should engage in exogamy.	
§8	*Jub.* 30:24-26—Conclusion of the Shechem episode.[35]	
§9	*Jub.* 31:1-3—Jacob and his family travel to Bethel.[36]	
§10	*Jub.* 31:4—Isaac calls Jacob for his deathbed blessing.	
§11	*Jub.* 31:5—Jacob and his family travel to Isaac.	*Ar. Levi* 8a—Levi and his family travel to Isaac.
§12	*Jub.* 31:6-25—Isaac blesses Levi and Judah.	*Ar. Levi* 8b—Isaac blesses Levi.
§13	*Jub.* 31:26-32—Jacob asks Isaac to travel with him to Bethel; only Rebekah agrees to accompany him.	
§14	*Jub.* 32:1—Levi has a vision in which he is made a priest.[37]	
§15	*Jub.* 32:2—Jacob tithes all of his possessions.	*Ar. Levi* 9a—Jacob tithes all of his possessions through Levi.
§16	*Jub.* 32:3a—Rachel is pregnant with Benjamin.	
§17	*Jub.* 32:3b—By including him in his tithe, Jacob ordains Levi as a priest and invests him with priestly garments.	*Ar. Levi* 9b—Jacob ordains Levi as a priest and invests him with the priestly garments.

[35] Cf. *Ar. Levi* 1-3

[36] Cf. *Ar. Levi* supp. 20, where we may have the remains of a narration of the travel to Bethel.

[37] Cf. *Ar. Levi* 4-6.

§18	*Jub.* 32:4-9—Offerings are made by Levi.	*Ar. Levi* 9c—Offerings are made by Levi.
§19		*Ar. Levi* 9d-10—Levi blesses his father and brothers and they bless him.
§20	*Jub.* 33:1, 21, 23—The family travels to Isaac and he rejoices and blesses them upon their arrival.	*Ar. Levi* 11-12—The family travels to Isaac and he rejoices and blesses them upon their arrival.

After §20 the two accounts part. While *Aramaic Levi* goes on to give Isaac's instructions to Levi, Levi's family history, and Levi's speech, *Jubilees* continues with an element of the following biblical narrative, Reuben's sin with Bilhah.

Study of the table above reveals the following. First, *Aramaic Levi* and *Jub.* 30:1–32:9 have some items in common: the rape of Dinah and the sack of Shechem (§1); the angelic speech against exogamy, followed by the angelic proclamation that Levi would be a priest (§§5–6); a trip to Isaac, on the occasion of which Isaac blesses Levi (§§11–12); Jacob's tithe of his possessions (§15); the account of Jacob's ordination and investiture of Levi, and of Levi making offerings after his elevation to the priesthood (§§17–18); and another family trip to Isaac in Hebron (§20).

Items in *Jub.* 30:1–32:9 that are absent from *Aramaic Levi* include: the indication that the laws against exogamy have been inscribed on heavenly tablets, and the corresponding engraving of Levi's family name forever in heavenly books (§7); the tidy conclusion of the Shechem episode and mention of the trip from Shechem to Bethel (§§8–9); Isaac's summons of Jacob to Hebron (§10); the blessing of Judah (§12); Jacob's request that Isaac accompany him to Bethel, Isaac's refusal, Rebekah's assent, and the return once more to Bethel (§13); and the notice that because of Rachel's pregnancy with Benjamin the role of tithe-son fell to Levi (§§16–17). The lauding of Levi at the conclusion of the speech against exogamy, the end of the Shechem episode, and the mention of a trip from Shechem to Bethel, were perhaps all part of *Aramaic Levi* in its complete form, though we cannot be certain, since they may now be lost due to the fragmentary nature of the manuscript witnesses. Furthermore, even though *Aramaic Levi* does not explicitly mention the return trip to Bethel after Isaac's blessing of Levi, it is apparent the author knew of the trek, since the events that follow take place there (*Ar. Levi* 9-10).

Material that appears in *Aramaic Levi*, but is lacking in *Jub.* 30:1–32:9, includes the following items: Levi's prayer (§2); Levi's blessing of his father and brothers, and their reciprocation (§18); Isaac's cultic instructions (*Ar. Levi* 13-61); Levi's family history (62-81); and Levi's speech to his children (82-106).

Some of the episodes shared by both books are retold differently, either by reason of location, or because the episodes, though basically the same, are still recounted in variant ways. These include: the two different loci for the vision (§§4-6 and §14); the transformation of the angelic speech within the dream in *Aramaic Levi* into commentary on the Shechem incident and the basis for the law of exogamy in *Jubilees* (§5); the fuller account of the first family trip to Isaac and his blessing of Levi in *Jubilees*, in contrast with the short account in *Aramaic Levi* (§§11-12); and the introduction of a rationale for Jacob's ordination of Levi (§§14, 17).

How is this complex set of relationships to be explained? The most likely answer is that both books relied independently on a similar source. The chief evidence for this claim is the way in which each re-counts Levi's first visit to Isaac. *Ar. Levi* 8 summarizes the entire event in a few words, while *Jubilees* 31 provides a complete account. While one might conclude from this that *Jubilees* is the earlier book, and that *Aramaic Levi* relied on it, and summarized the longer account of the family's trek,[38] paleographic dating of the oldest *Aramaic Levi* manuscript from Qumran makes that view unlikely; it is almost certain that *Aramaic Levi* is the older document.[39] Meanwhile, the journey in *Ar. Levi* 8 and *Jubilees* 31 is not described in the biblical account, and may therefore be considered part of the pseudepigraphic tradition. Thus it is unlikely that *Aramaic Levi*, with its abbreviated report, came first, and was relied upon later by the author of *Jubilees*; it is difficult to imagine circumstances under which an author who creates a work that expands a biblical narrative would mention in passing a journey not recorded in the scriptural tradition, but offer no explanation for its significance. Hence the only remaining way to explain the relationship between the two accounts is to posit a common source which the au-thors used differently.[40]

A glance down the list of items found in both accounts indicates that the common source, which we label the "Levi-apocryphon," con-tained at least the following: the Shechem incident (*Ar. Levi* 1-3; *Jub.* 30:1-4, 24-26); the trip to Bethel (*Ar. Levi* 20 [?]; *Jub.* 31:1-3); the vi-sion with an angelic speech against exogamy and Levi's elevation to the priesthood (*Ar. Levi* supp 21-27, *Ar. Levi* 4-6; *Jub.* 30:5-23; 32:1); a journey to Hebron (*Ar. Levi* 8a; *Jub.* 31:5); Isaac's blessing (*Ar. Levi* 8b; *Jub.* 31:12-17); the return to Bethel (cf. *Ar. Levi* 10; *Jub.* 31:30); and Jacob's ordination and investiture of Levi, and his tithe-offering (*Ar. Levi* 9a-b, 10b; *Jub.* 32:1-9). The apocryphon probably also con-

---

[38] This is the view of Kugel, "Levi's Elevation," *passim*.

[39] See 3.3.1 for a discussion of *Aramaic Levi*'s date.

[40] Of course, it is still possible that *Jubilees* relied directly on *Aramaic Levi*

tained an account of the return to Hebron and Isaac's priestly instructions (*Ar. Levi* 11-61; *Jub.* 33:1, 21, 23; 21:7-20).[41] What remains is
to explain the additions, minuses, and other divergences exhibited by
Ar. Levi and *Jubilees* vis-à-vis the apocryphon.

To begin we review the conclusions reached tentatively in chapter three regarding the divergent material in *Aramaic Levi*, since comparison with *Jubilees* now allows more confidence in judgment. First
the complete form of Isaac's blessing in *Jub.* 31:12-17, in contrast with
its mere mention in *Ar. Levi* 8, underscores the view that the apocryphon contained such a blessing and that *Aramaic Levi*'s author used
only parts of it, probably in order to re-employ its themes in a new
composition, Levi's wisdom speech.[42] Second, the omission from
Jubilees of Levi's prayer (*Ar. Levi* supp. 1-19), his life history (*Ar.
Levi* 62-81), and his speech on wisdom and the fate of his descendants
(*Ar. Levi* 82-106) indicates that they were not part of the apocryphon,
and that they were composed by the author of *Aramaic Levi*, or were
added by him to the Levi-apocryphon from other sources. In fact, one
expects that the author of *Jubilees* would have preserved the prayer,
with its expression of piety and concern for purity, had he known it.
And the tidy beginning and conclusion of the life history in *Aramaic
Levi*, with the announcement of Levi's death at age one hundred thirty-
seven, indicate that it was a freestanding tradition which *Aramaic
Levi*'s author awkwardly incorporated into his own composition. And
as we have seen, the wisdom speech in *Aramaic Levi* seems to have
been composed, in part, from pieces of Isaac's blessing of Levi.[43]

The changes wrought by the author of *Jubilees* on the apocryphon are equally explicable. The most significant difference is the
writer's removal of the vision from its place after the Shechem episode,
his placement of it immediately before Levi's ordination by Jacob, and
his evisceration of its contents for use as a commentary on the Shechem

---

[41] Cf. Grelot, "Notes," 403, where the notion of a Levi-apocryphon that served as
the source for *Aramaic Levi* and *Jubilees* was first proposed. Grelot also attempts to
describe the contours of the Levi-apocryphon. Convinced that two visions were a part
of the Levi-tradition from its beginning, he concludes that the apocryphon must have
included "arrivée de Jacob à Sichem et enlévement de Dina; premier songe de Lévi,
tandis qu'il séjourne aux sources du Jourdain; arrivée de Lévi et de Siméon près de
Sichem; massacre des Sichémites; pèlerinage de Jacob à Béthel; second songe de Lévi;
visite chez Isaac où Lévi (et Juda?) recoivent la bénédiction de leur aïeul; retour à
Béthel; investiture sacerdotale de Lévi et remise des dîmes."

[42] Additional evidence that the author of *Jubilees* did not know the wisdom speech
in *Aramaic Levi* is the fact that it would have been very attractive to him, and surely
would have been included, had he known it. It will be recalled that the author of
Jubilees was likely an intellectual of the priestly caste (see 4.1.2 above). Levi's
speech would have served such an author well.

[43] For discussion of the purpose of these sections in *Aramaic Levi* see 3.1.2;
3.1.6; and 3.1.7.

incident. The author probably made the change for two reasons. First, transfer of the angel's discourse transformed what was a speech-act that elevated Levi to the priesthood into an explanation of the law against exogamy and a recollection of one of the reasons Levi was later made a priest.[44] Second, it preserved for Jacob, the central figure in *Jubilees*, the act of ordaining Levi to the priesthood.

The author of *Jubilees* made another large adjustment of the apocryphon by moving Isaac's instructions from their location after Jacob's ordination of Levi to *Jub.* 21:7-20. In spite of substantial differences, the similarities shared by the cultic instructions in *Jub.* 21:7-20 and in *Ar. Levi* 13-61 suggest a common source. Especially significant are their nearly identical list of wood-types suitable for the altar-fire and their common assertion that the guidelines were first given by Abraham to Isaac. The different location of the regulations in *Jubilees* is explained perhaps by the author's penchant for narrative consistency. In *Ar. Levi* 22, 50, 57 it is said that Abraham gave the instructions first to Isaac. Their removal to *Jub.* 21:7-20 allows them that context, since the chapter relates Abraham's speech to Isaac. Perhaps the changed location for the instructions also required that they take on slightly different content, since Abraham prepared Isaac on that occasion to make sacrifice for the Feast of Shabuoth (cf. *Jubilees* 22).

A third substantial adjustment of the apocryphon appears in chapter 31, with the addition of the blessing for Judah and of much of the material about Jacob and Isaac. The blessing, though somewhat difficult to understand as a part of *Jubilees*,[45] is at any rate an addition to the apocryphon and a stranger to the LPT. Meanwhile, the further material relating to Jacob and Isaac reflects the interest of *Jubilees'* author and so may be deemed unique to that book as well.

Among the minor changes the author of *Jubilees* made in appropriating the apocryphon is the failure to mention the Shechemites' circumcision. It was almost certainly part of the apocryphon; after all it appears in *Ar. Levi* 1-3, and is an integral part of the biblical account. But unwilling to depict Jacob, the key figure in his nationalistic epic, as being open to the inclusion of non-Jews in the covenant of circumcision, the author probably omitted all mention of it.[46]

Other small adjustments made by the author of *Jubilees* in adapting the apocryphon include the addition of heavenly tablets on which the laws against exogamy are written, and on which the names and deeds of the righteous and wicked are etched (*Jub.* 30:9, 19, 20, 22, 23). The addition is typical of *Jubilees*, and further evinces the au-

---

[44] *Pace* Kugel, "Levi's Elevation," 6, where *Jub.* 30:18-20 is depicted as an actual elevation.

[45] See, for example, the views expressed in Charles, *Book of Jubilees*, 188-89; Berger, *Buch der Jubiläen*, 479.

[46] But see note 56 below.

thor's determination to transform a story of Levi's elevation to the priesthood into another episode in the account of how the laws at the heart of his proposal for Hasmonean-era Judaism came into existence in the distant past. The author also added notice of Rachel's pregnancy with Benjamin and the explicit notion that Jacob tithed Levi. Treating Levi as a part of Jacob's tithe explains Jacob's elevation of one of his sons to the priesthood; and Jacob's knowledge that Benjamin was *in utero* clarifies how Levi could be the tithe-son.[47] The exegetical consistency the additions provide is typical of the author of *Jubilees*.[48] Finally, Levi's blessing of Jacob and his brothers and their response were probably omitted by the author of *Jubilees* because he did not want to elevate Levi over Jacob so completely. Jacob is allowed to remain the central figure.

We reiterate an important point. The evidence indicates that *Jub.* 30:1–32:9 and *Aramaic Levi* were only indirectly related, having been built from a common source, a Levi-apocryphon. That they are related is evident from the many similarities they share. Yet that their relationship is not direct is suggested by the differences between them. Most telling are the variations between the accounts of Levi's journey to Isaac and Isaac's blessing for Levi in *Ar. Levi* 8 and *Jubilees* 31. *Ar. Levi* 8 is a single line which mentions a non-biblical journey to Isaac and a blessing of Isaac for Levi; it is clearly the summary of an existing story. Yet *Ar. Levi* 8 cannot be a summary of *Jubilees* 31, since the latter text is the later of the two. Meanwhile, *Jubilees* 31 is a complete report of the journey and of Isaac's blessing, a report its author is not likely to have developed solely from awareness of *Ar. Levi* 8. The only other possible explanation for the appearance of the non-biblical trek to Isaac in both documents, in such varying forms, is their independent reliance on the same source.

---

[47] For the origin of these insights, see 4.3.5 below, and the accompanying notes.

[48] John Endres, *Biblical Interpretation*, passim, has cogently demonstrated this tendency on the part of *Jubilees'* author. Especially concerned to show why Jacob chose Levi as his priest, the author may have also taken a cue from the phrase in the Levi-apocryphon which is preserved in *Ar. Levi* supp. 27, מעשר קודש קרבן לאל, "a holy tithe, an offering to God." From that phrase he developed the notion that Jacob fulfilled his vow to tithe all of his belongings (Gen 28:22) by tithing his sons as well, thus creating a priest through whom he could make the sacrifices associated with vow-fulfillment. Of course, this suggestion regarding the origin of the tithe-son notion relies on a reading of *Ar. Levi* supp. 27 different from the one offered in 3.1.3 above. The explanation assumes that by the end of the 4Q213 2, the fragment bearing *Ar. Levi* supp. 22-27, the angel had already shifted attention from the sin of exogamy to the elevation of Levi, and that the references to offerings and tithes to God were allusions to Levi's relationship to the Lord. As our discussion of the passage indicates, however, the language of sacrifice at the end of the fragment is better explained by comparison with *Jub.* 30:16.

As noted above, this view runs counter to the position taken by James Kugel in his study of the relationships among *Aramaic Levi*, *Jubilees*, and *Testament of Levi*. It is worth taking a moment at this point to respond more fully to Kugel. As for the basic details of his view, he posits the growth of the tradition in the following manner. First there was a Levi-apocryphon which contained but one account of Levi's appointment to the priesthood, the one evident in our version of *Ar. Levi* supp. 20-27; *Ar. Levi* 4-7. Kugel calls this version the "Priestly Initiation" of Levi. A "Levi Apocalypse," which appears in its most complete form in *T. Levi* 2:5–5:7, developed around the same time, but separately from the Levi-apocryphon. The merger of these two made up a stage in the composition of *Aramaic Levi*. Meanwhile *Jubilees* was composed in reliance on the Levi-apocryphon with its Priestly Initiation. The author/editor of *Aramaic Levi* then consulted a completed form of *Jubilees* as yet another resource for his work, even including episodes from the latter work which serve no purpose in his own, apparently because he considered *Jubilees* to be authoritative. This, says Kugel, explains why *Jubilees* does not know Levi's prayer and two visions as does *Aramaic Levi*; it also clarifies the presence in *Jubilees* of evidence only for the Priestly Initiation (cf. 32:1; 31;15-16); and it makes clear why there is material shared by *Jubilees* and *Aramaic Levi* for which there is a clear rationale in *Jubilees* and no similar justification in *Aramaic Levi* (e.g., the blessing of Isaac; chain of priests tradition; and references to Noah's book about the blood).[49]

In addition to the most basic problem of the relative dates of the two works—*Aramaic Levi* seems almost certainly to have been considerably older than *Jubilees*—there are still other factors which militate against easy acceptance of Kugel's proposal. The foremost is its unnecessary complexity. For instance Kugel's explanation requires a concern for logical consistency on one author's part (*Jubilees*) while allowing the other the freedom to include material for no apparent reasons (*Aramaic Levi*). A much more economical explanation of the presence of shared items which seem to Kugel to fit better in *Jubilees* than they do in *Aramaic Levi* is to assume that the two works used a common source, items from which the author of *Jubilees* integrated into his own work better than the author of *Aramaic Levi*. Kugel's model also assumes an overly convoluted developmental history for the Levi-Priestly tradition, one that creates more hypothetical sources than seem necessary to explain the relationships among those which we do possess. For instance, while our approach requires that we posit only a Levi-apocryphon that served as a source for *Jubilees* and *Aramaic Levi*, Kugel forces one to imagine at least two documents which we do not possess, that is, the "Priestly Initiation" and the "Levi Apocalypse." And if his view is that there was for a time a "Proto-*Aramaic Levi* "

---

[49] See Kugel, "Levi's Elevation," passim; esp. 52-58.

made up of those two appointment accounts but lacking the material eventually borrowed from *Jubilees*, his approach requires one to imagine yet a *third* hypothetical source. Anyway, Kugel's multiplication of sources also stumbles on the question of two visions in *Aramaic Levi*. If one accepts our version of *Aramaic Levi* as having contained but one dream (the one called Levi's "Priestly Initiation" by Kugel), it is no longer necessary to posit the independent existence of the "Levi Apocalypse." Indeed, the presence of only a single vision in *Aramaic Levi and* in *Jubilees* reflects the likelihood that the Levi-apocryphon they shared as a source also contained only one vision. So, in the final analysis it seems that the dynamics of the growth of the Levi-Priestly tradition as it appears in *Aramaic Levi* and *Jubilees* are most easily explained by our approach, while the forces that must be posited to accommodate Kugel's view make necessary the construction of more hypothetical documents than are required.

4.2.2. *Jub.* 30:1–32:9 and *Testament of Levi*

Almost all commentators agree that the differences between *Testament of Levi* and *Jub.* 30:1–32:9 indicate that the former did not use the latter as a source.[50] Instead, *Aramaic Levi* and *Testament of Levi* exhibit very close similarities, and are assumed to be related.[51] Whether the author of *Testament of Levi* knew *Jubilees*, but chose to ignore it, cannot be determined. What is certain is the fact that *Testament of Levi* did not follow the pattern developed in *Jubilees*.

4.3. The Levi-Priestly Tradition in *Jub.* 30:1–32:9[52]

We turn now to comment on the LPT in *Jubilees*. We limit our discussion to those portions of 30:1–32:9 that repeat known sections of the Levi-apocryphon,[53] and dedicate only a few words to the sections most

---

[50] For a graphic comparison of the two, see the charts in Becker, *Untersuchungen*, 80-81, 89-90.

[51] See 5.1 and 5.3.

[52] Since there are no Hebrew manuscripts of *Jub.* 30:1–32:9 (no Qumran fragments of the section survive), we are fortunate that a number of full, fairly trustworthy Ethiopic manuscripts of *Jubilees* are available. The reliability of the Ethiopic manuscripts as witnesses to a more original Hebrew text was shown by VanderKam in the first half of his study, *Textual and Historical Studies*. More recently he has confirmed his views regarding the textual history of *Jubilees*, and has provided a critical edition of the Ethiopic text in James VanderKam, *The Book of Jubilees* (Corpus Scriptorum Christianorum Orientalium 510-511; Louvain: E. Peeters, 1989). Hence, for the following discussion of the LPT in *Jubilees* we rely on James VanderKam's Ethiopic text and English translation.

[53] They include 30:1-4, 24-26, the story of Dinah's rape and Levi's revenge; 30:5-17, 21-23, an angelic speech against exogamy; 30:18-20, the angelic statement that Levi was rewarded with the priesthood for his zeal against Shechem; 31:12-17, Isaac's

certainly added by the author of *Jubilees*.[54] In the case of the latter
group of texts, it is necessary only to indicate how they reflect the author's unique aims in appropriating the Levi-apocryphon. We also restrict the scope of our comments on the LPT material, as our goal is
principally to underscore how *Jubilees*' author appears to have relied
on a source used also by the author of *Aramaic Levi*, but with very different intentions. To that end, treating the text section by section, we
describe its contents; we note its author's reliance on biblical and LPT
traditions and the manner in which he appropriates his sources; and in
light of the latter observations we address the purpose of the LPT in
Jubilees.

4.3.1. *Jub*. 30:1-4, 24-26: The rape of Dinah and Levi's revenge

The retelling of Genesis 34 is spare and to the point,[55] eliminating
many of the elements found in the biblical account, most notably any
mention of the bargain with the Shechemites and their agreement to
circumcision.[56] It adds that Dinah was twelve at the time of the rape.
The narrative itself moves rapidly, announcing in quick succession the
family's arrival in Salem (v. 1), the rape of Dinah (v. 2), Hamor's desire to marry Dinah (v. 3a), Jacob and his sons' anger with the
Shechemites and their deceitful dealings with them (v. 3b), and Levi
and Simeon's revenge (v. 4). After the intervening speech against exogamy and the promise of Levi's future priesthood the passage concludes with Dinah's removal from Shechem (v. 24a), the completion of
the sack of the city (v. 24b), Jacob's reproach (v. 25), and the family's
departure in peace (v. 26).

There are good reasons to assume that the author used and
adapted a source for his account. First, the statement that Dinah was
only twelve at the time of the rape (reinforced by the remark that she
was but a small girl) goes beyond what appears in Genesis, and does not
necessarily serve any purpose of the author.[57] Second, the revised

---

blessing of Levi; and 32:1-9, Levi's dream that he was made a priest, Jacob's ordination and investiture of Levi, and Levi's sacrifices.

[54] The parts of *Jub*. 30:1–32:9 not discussed at any length include 31:1-11, the
family's travel to Bethel where Jacob prepares to make sacrifice, Isaac's summons of
Jacob and his family to his side, and the clan's travel to Hebron; and 31:18-32, Isaac's
blessing for Judah, the conclusion of the visit with Isaac, and Jacob's travel with his
family back to Bethel.

[55] Verses 2-3 duplicate the facts from Gen 34:2, 4, 7, 13; vv. 4 and 24 repeat Gen
34:25-29; v. 25 reflects Gen 34:30; and v. 26 mirrors Gen 35:5.

[56] Nevertheless v. 4 states that Levi and Simeon "killed them all in torments."
Perhaps this is the author's subtle nod in the direction of the tradition from Genesis.

[57] One might argue, as does Endres, *Biblical Interpretation*, 125-27, that her age
suggests the "heinous nature of the crime" (127). In fact he admits that the statement
is odd, and others have attempted to clarify it and have also failed to arrive at a

portrait of Levi's act as righteous is not original to *Jubilees*, surfacing among extant texts first in the *Aramaic Levi* narrative. Finally, Jacob's rebuke of Simeon and Levi in v. 24 contradicts his willing participation in the plan, noted in v. 3. Thus the reprimand was also evidently part of the author's source.[58]

Meanwhile, the writer adjusted his sources in a variety of ways. First, *Jub.* 30:2 erases any notion of Dinah's fault in the incident (contrary to what is implied in Gen 34:1, and stated explicitly by Josephus, *Ant.* 1 § 337; *Bereshit Rabbah* 80:1) by indicating that she was forcibly abducted; yet, the laws against exogamy that follow, clearly from a source shared by *Aramaic Levi*, hardly inspire confidence that their author would absolve her of all guilt (30:7-8). The same verse alters still more the biblical account by implying that the entire people of Shechem abducted Dinah. Both adjustments reflect the author's interest in vilifying non-Jews who oppose Israel, and making the Israelite characters populating his narrative largely faultless.[59] And *Jub* 30:3b introduces Jacob into the plan of deception, a role he does not have in Genesis 34, *Testament of Levi*, or *Aramaic Levi*. Becoming a participant in the plan he is made a partner in his sons' opposition to exogamous marriages. In a related vein, the story omits mention of the Shechemites' circumcision, something which was surely unacceptable to our xenophobic author (cf. *Ar. Levi* 1-3).[60]

The manner in which *Jubilees* appropriated its sources—Genesis 34, and the pseudepigraphic retelling of that account from the Levi-apocryphon—is indicative of the passage's intent: the focus is especially

---

satisfactory explanation (e.g., L. Finkelstein, "The Book of Jubilees and the Rabbinic Halaka," *HTR* 16 [1923] 55, n. 69, discussed by Endres, *Biblical Interpretation*, 126). In short, the most plausible view is that the notice regarding Dinah's age came from an inherited source.

[58] Indeed, as 4.2 demonstrates, *Aramaic Levi* served as a source for *Testament of Levi*, which also contains the rebuke (cf. *T. Levi* 6:5–7:4). Thus one can conclude that the author of *Jubilees* either adapted *Aramaic Levi* or a source both writers held in common.

[59] Endres, *Biblical Interpretation*, 124-25 notes this as well. R. H. Charles, *APOT* II, 6, thinks that the account in 30:2-4 reflects John Hyrcanus' attack on Shechem. However his view is not widely accepted, and for good reason. As a midrash on Genesis, which at this point in its development leads it to retell Genesis 34, *Jubilees* can be expected to recount these events, regardless the contemporary historical occurences the author may have known.

[60] Compare *T. Levi* 6:3. Josephus, *Ant.* 1 §§ 337-340, also omits any mention of circumcision. Charles, *Book of Jubilees*, 179 (echoed by Endres, *Biblical Interpretation*, 129), thinks that the omission is due to the author's revulsion at the notion that Levi and Simeon slew brothers in the covenant of circumcision. However, that explanation seems less likely than our author's greater revulsion at the idea of non-Israelites sharing in the covenantal sign of God's people. Endres agrees that the concern might be a factor (129).

on clarifying and upgrading Jacob's role in the affair. By giving Jacob
a part in the plan to destroy Shechem he is made into a fellow guardian
of the integrity of the people. By eliminating his equivocation and
openness to integration with the Shechemites, the author transformed
Jacob from an insecure and indecisive patriarch into a hero of Israel
and gave him a share in Levi's glory.

Because of this objective, the Shechem incident plays a different
role in *Jubilees* than it does in the other texts of the LPT. In *Aramaic
Levi* and *Testament of Levi* the Shechem incident is essential for
defining Levi's character. But due to the author's special interest in
depicting Jacob favorably, concern for Levi's identity recedes into the
background in favor of a greater emphasis on his father.

4.3.2. *Jub.* 30:5-17, 21-23: Laws against exogamy

The legal pronouncement against exogamy is like most of the other
laws in *Jubilees*—it is narrative-based in that it arises from an episode
in Israel's distant past.[61] First, vv. 5-6 serve as a bridge between the
Shechem incident and the laws. Then vv. 7-8 follow with the law of
punishment for the man who gives his daughter in marriage to a
Gentile, and for the woman who marries a foreigner; vv. 9-10 indicate
that the law is written in the heavenly tablets,[62] and that there is no
limit to its application;[63] and vv. 11-17 give the angel's command that
Moses instruct the people in following the law, with elaboration on the
consequences for keeping and breaking it.[64] Then, after an interlude in
which the angelic narrator says that Levi merits appointment to the
priestly office for his opposition to exogamy (v. 18-20), the legislation
concludes, warning Israel to learn from the lesson of the Shechemites:
if they violate the laws, they too will lose their lives by removal from
maṣḥafa ḥeyawan, "the book of life," and be placed instead among those
to be destroyed (v. 22b). As for the sons of Jacob, the merit of their
deed was also entered in the heavenly record (v. 23).

---

[61] For other instances of this phenomenon see 3:31; 4:5-6.

[62] For a recent discussion of the heavenly tablets in *Jubilees* see Florentino García
Martínez, "Las tablas celestes en el Libro de los Jubileos," in *Palabra y vida:
Homenaje a José Alonso Díaz en su 70 cumpleaños* (ed. A. Vargas-Machuca y G.
Ruiz; Madrid: Universidad Pontifica Comillas, 1984) 333-49. While the motif is
common in Second Temple literature (see the list of occurrences collected in R. H.
Charles, *The Book of Enoch or 1 Enoch translated from the Editor's Ethiopic Text*
[Oxford: Oxford University, 1912] 91-92), it is particularly prominent in *Jubilees*.
Charles, *Book of Jubilees*, 24-25, notes that there are three types of information
recorded on heavenly tablets: laws, contemporary events, and predictions.

[63] For an example of a similar construction, see *Jub* 16:29-30.

[64] For a passage that begins in almost identical fashion, see 49:15, 22 where the
angel uses the same language to command Moses to instruct the people with regard to
the law of Passover.

Passages from Leviticus regarding marriage and sexual intercourse with non-Jews, and the sacrifice of offspring to Molech lie at the heart of this set of injunctions; at the same time, however, the biblical material is considerably intensified and expanded in its application.[65] First, in *Jub.* 30:7 the author apparently connected giving a daughter in marriage to a Gentile with sacrificing a child to the god Molech (cf. 30:10). The biblical injunction against Molech worship that appears within a long list of prohibited sexual relations in Lev 18:21 is surely the basis for the connection.[66] With that association in mind, the author indicates in v. 7 the punishment for the father who arranges an exogamous union, and for the woman who undertakes such a relationship: the man is to be stoned according to Lev 20:2 which decrees the penalty for the father who sacrifices a child to Molech, and the woman is to be burned according to Lev 21:9 which dictates the consequences for the daughter of a priest who "plays the harlot."[67] *Jubilees'* interpretation, intensification, and generalization of the injunctions from the Torah are clear.

A second instance of interpretive, intensifying, and generalizing use of the Pentateuch is in *Jub.* 30:15 where the author further applies Lev 20:3-5 to the matter of exogamy. In Lev 20:3 sacrifice to Molech pollutes God's sanctuary; *Jub.* 30:15b indicates that exogamy pollutes the worship place *and* God's own name. Similarly, Lev 20:4-5 points out that when others in the community ignore their neighbor's false worship, God sees to it that the violator and his kin are punished through exclusion from the cult and community; meanwhile *Jub.* 30:15a suggests that those who ignore the sin will be punished too.[68]

---

[65] One must keep in mind that the entire theme of exogamy echoes Ezra 9–10; and Neh 13:23-31. Indeed, the notion that any occasion of exogamy within the community threatens the whole people (cf. *Jub.* 30:13-14) has roots in the attitude expressed in Ezra-Nehemiah. Yet none of the language characteristic of those well-known passages appears here. That fact may indicate that the author's concern was not motivated by an interest in biblical exegesis as much as it was by contemporary events.

[66] Others who note the importance of Lev 18:21 include Ch. Albeck, *Das Buch der Jubiläen und die Halacha* (Berlin: Druck von Siegfried Scholem, 1930) 27-8; Charles, *Book of Jubilees*, 181 (see also Charles' collection of similar Targumic and Rabbinic interpretations of Lev 18:21); S. Cohen, "From the Bible to the Talmud: The Prohibition of Intermarriage," *HAR* 7 (1983) 26; Finkelstein, "Book of Jubilees," 57; and Florentino García Martínez, "Las tablas celestes," 347-48.

[67] The only other occasion on which it is commanded by the Hebrew Bible that a woman be burned is Gen 38:24. There Judah proclaims that Tamar, the victim of his own sexual folly, is to be burned for "playing the harlot."

[68] Among commentators surveyed on this issue, only A. S. Hartom, "The Book of Jubilees," in *The Apocryphal Literature* (3rd ed.; Tel Aviv: Yavneh, 1969) (Hebrew) 1:95, notes this intensification. Note also that *Jub.* 30:15b intensifies the notion that all Israel suffers punishment for the exogamy of one. A. Jaubert, *La notion d'alliance*, 97, n. 25, links this with Mal 2:11.

The author of *Jubilees*, however, is not entirely responsible for all of this exegetical sophistication: comparison of *Jub.* 30:5-17, 21-23 with *Ar. Levi* supp. 22-27 reminds us that *Jubilees* inherited this pericope from the Levi-apocryphon. The *Jubilees* passage is an angelic speech against exogamous relationships, and a description of the punishment dealt to those who violate the prohibition of such unions. Likewise, *Ar. Levi* supp. 22-27 condemns exogamy, and seems to describe the disciplinary measures brought against transgressors. Mention of plagues or blows and of guilty persons in *Ar. Levi* supp. 23 recalls *Jub.* 30:7, 15. Reference to a woman who profanes her own name, her father's name, and her brothers' names, and to burning in *Ar. Levi* supp. 24-25 also remind the reader of *Jub.* 30:7, where the same language is used to describe what a woman's exogamy brings upon her family and herself. The enduring character of the woman's shameful reputation noted in *Ar. Levi* supp. 26 resonates with *Jub.* 30:14 where it is said that Israel will not be cleansed from the defilement stemming from the presence of such unions in its midst. References to a holy tithe and an offering to God in *Ar. Levi* supp. 27 probably are reflected in *Jub.* 30:16, where the angel announces that no sacrifices will be accepted from violators of the law against exogamy. The two words for shame or revilement used in *Ar. Levi* supp. 24 and 26 (אבההתחא and חסרא) have mirror images in the use of the parallel Ethiopic term in *Jub.* 30:5, 7 (*xafrat*, "shame"). Hence it is reasonable to conclude that the author of *Jubilees* relied on a source similar to the one used by the writer of *Ar. Levi* supp. 22-27.[69]

That the passage was part of a vision in the Levi-apocryphon, as we believe it is in *Aramaic Levi*, is apparent from the intervening portion, *Jub.* 30:18-20. Its language is reminiscent of the heavenly election to priesthood Levi received in the vision known from *Ar. Levi* 4-7, and secondarily from *Testament of Levi* 8. It appears that *Jubilees'* author adapted the angelic address to Levi in his post-Shechem vision so as to make it an address to Moses *about* Levi on the occasion of narrating the Shechem incident.[70]

What is the aim of this passage? Obviously it condemns marriage with non-Jews. But even more, when compared with *Ar. Levi* supp. 22-27, it appears the author intended also to raise the stakes regarding the issue. By intensifying the penalties for exogamy, and laying their consequences on all of Israel, the author made clear his view

---

[69] In that regard it is noteworthy that there is no evidence in *Ar. Levi* supp. 22-27 of heavenly tablets, or of the sort of explicit connection between narration of the Shechem incident and the law of exogamy that appears in *Jubilees*. Both motifs are characteristic of the latter book, and probably reflect the writer's redaction of his source.

[70] For additional reflection on why this section was taken from Levi's vision, see 4.2.1 above.

on the matter: it was a great threat to the community and was to be avoided at all costs.[71] Implied here (and made explicit in vv. 18-20), of course, is the merit of all who stood in opposition to exogamous practices, and the evil of those who approved of such unions.

4.3.3. *Jub*. 30:18-20: Levi and the priesthood

Here the angel-narrator of *Jubilees* announces that Levi won a promise of the priesthood by his sack of Shechem (30:18). His deeds are inscribed on the heavenly tablets, as is the fact that he is to be remembered as a friend and a righteous man (30:19-20).

The same biblical texts that form the nucleus of Levi's elevation to the priesthood in *Aramaic Levi* are at work here. In addition to Levi's behavior at Shechem in Genesis 34, Phinehas' action in Num 25:1-13, the Levites' zeal in Exod 32:25-29, Moses' appointment of Levites as priests in Deut 33:8-11, and Malachi's decree that God made a covenant for priestly services with Levi in Mal 2:4-7 cannot have been far from the author's mind.[72]

Comparison with *Ar. Levi* 6 demonstrates that our author preserves the angelic announcement of Levi's elevation to the priestly office, indicating use of a common source by the authors of *Aramaic Levi* and *Jubilees*. But the passage in *Jubilees* reveals also the unique perspective of its author. While it may be assumed from comparison of *Ar. Levi* 6 and *Jub*. 30:18-20 that the Levi-apocryphon recorded the angelic elevation of Levi to the priesthood, the Jubilees version is carefully nuanced. The form of the angel's speech, as it is redacted by the author of *Jubilees*, supports this view. In 30:18 he says, *wataxarya zarʾa lēwi lakehnat*, "Levi's descendants were chosen for the priesthood." Relying on the rhetorical device of the angelic narrator speaking to Moses of past events allows the author to transform the apocryphon; instead of stating that Levi has just been elevated by heavenly beings, the angel simply indicates that Levi became a priest—at an unnamed point in time—because of the events just narrated (the slaughter at Shechem). Indeed, the event of Levi's elevation appears elsewhere in the narrative. Contrary to those who believe that this verse marks Levi's elevation to the priesthood,[73] it is perhaps more appropriately

---

[71] For this reason Schwarz, *Identität durch Abgrenzung*, passim, makes much of this passage throughout his study.

[72] For this list of passages see James VanderKam, "Jubilees and the Priestly Messiah of Qumran," *RevQ* 13 (1988) 361-63. VanderKam also mentions Deut 7:2-4, which prohibits marriage with certain foreigners, and Mal 2:11, which also condemns exogamy. For the notion that Levi and his descendants are made to minister before God as angels—that is, that they are assimilated to angelic status—see 1QSb 11 7; 1QSb 4 24-26; and 1QH 3 20.

[73] See, for example, Kugel, "Levi's Elevation," 6, where Kugel expresses well the traditional view that 30:18-20 is an announcement of Levi's elevation.

understood as the angelic announcement that his eventual elevation was
due to his righteousness at Shechem. Careful reading of 30:1–32:9 reveals that according to *Jubilees* the actual elevation took place when
Jacob's ordination of Levi (32:3) confirmed what had been presaged in
the present passage (30:18), in Isaac's blessing (31:12-17), and in Levi's
vision (32:1).[74] So the angel's statement merely confirms that Levi was
rewarded with the priestly office for his ferocious commitment to
communal purity.

After the conclusion of the Shechem incident in 30:26, and before the next LPT material in 31:12-17, the reader hears of Jacob's
decision to go to Bethel to sacrifice (vv. 1-3a), his invitation to Isaac to
join him (v. 3b), Isaac's refusal and his invitation to Jacob to come to
him (v. 4), Jacob's travel to Hebron (v. 5), Rebekah's reception and
blessing of Levi and Judah (vv. 6-7), and the meeting between Isaac,
Jacob, and Jacob's two sons (vv. 8-11). Verses 5-11 seem to provide a
more detailed version of *Ar. Levi* 8a which says only ועלנא על אבי יצחק,
"And we went to my father Isaac" (while vv. 12-17 correspond to *Ar.
Levi* 8b, ואף הוא כדן ברכני, "And he too blessed me thus"). Due to the
truncated form in which the author of *Aramaic Levi* preserved this
section, we cannot know how the author of *Jubilees* transformed the
corresponding part of the Levi-apocryphon.

4.3.4. *Jub.* 31:12-17: Isaac blesses Levi

Verse 12 establishes for the reader the superiority of Levi's blessing
over Judah's (which appears in 31:18-20): Levi is at Isaac's right, and
Isaac offers him the first benison. In v. 13 Isaac expresses his hope that
the Lord will bless Levi and his sons forever. Then in v. 14 Isaac asks
that Levi receive extremely great honor; that only Levi and his descendants have the priestly vocation of approaching God in sacerdotal service; that Levi be able to serve like the angels of the presence and the
holy ones;[75] and that he receive like them honor, greatness, and holiness. As a result, Levi and his descendants will be *wamakwānenta
wamasāfenta, wamalāᵓekta*, "princes, judges, and leaders" of all the descendants of Jacob's sons (v. 15a).[76] In those roles Levi's children will
declare the word of the Lord with justice, make righteous judgments,
tell God's ways to Jacob and his paths to Israel, and speak the Lord's

---

[74] See below for comment on those passages.

[75] Once more the theme of Levi's assimilation to the angelic role appears; this time,
however, the author adds reference to the two kinds of angels mentioned elsewhere in
Jubilees (cf. Charles, *Book of Jubilees*, 12, on *Jub.* 2:2 and the two types of angels).

[76] See VanderKam's note on this translation in *Book of Jubilees*, 2:204. Also see
Charles, *Book of Jubilees*, 187, where he defends his widely disputed view that this
putative reference to three offices reflects the reign of John Hyrcanus.

blessing to all descendants of the beloved.[77] Isaac states that Leah named Levi appropriately, since he would be joined to the Lord, and become a companion of Jacob's sons, and a table partner for God; indeed, says Isaac, Levi's table will be full forever (v. 16). Isaac concludes the blessing with the hope that Levi's foes would be accursed, and his friends would be blessed (v. 17).

A wealth of biblical passages have influenced Isaac's blessing. Isaac's hope, expressed in v. 14, that Levi be designated the only figure charged with priestly service to God calls to mind the constellation of passages noted in association with 30:18-20 (cf. Exod 32:25-29; Num 25:6-13; Deut 33:8-11; Mal 2:4-7). In addition Zech 3:6-7 may play a part in the notion that Levi would be like the heavenly angels. That Levi should declare God's word, make judgments, tell God's ways to Jacob and Israel, and pronounce blessings (v. 15) all point to Deut 33:8-11 and Mal 2:4-7;[78] Num 6:24-26 may also be behind the reference to a priestly blessing. The first half of v. 16 is based on Gen 29:34 where Leah names Levi in an apparent play on the word לוה, "join"; here the word-play is extended by Isaac's pronouncement that Levi would be joined to the Lord, and be a companion to Jacob's sons.[79] The latter half of v. 16 is based on Num 18:20ff. Finally one can detect faint echoes of Deut 33:11 in v. 17.

Once again it is appropriate to note that while the author of *Jubilees* may exhibit considerable exegetical skill in marshalling such a wide range of biblical traditions in one passage, in fact, the blessing is, at least in part, an inherited tradition. In addition to the evidence of *Ar. Levi* 8, which indicates that the Levi-apocryphon contained a blessing of Isaac for Levi, *Ar. Levi* 99 provides a similar set of terms to describe Levi's descendants as those employed in *Jub.* 31:15. *Ar. Levi* 90 emphasizes the greatness that Levi's descendants will enjoy, just as does Isaac's blessing (*Jub.* 30:14). And Levi's speech to his children in *Aramaic Levi* and Isaac's blessing in *Jubilees* emphasize learning, wisdom, and the exercise of good judgment. These indications suggest that the authors had before them the same source, but used it differently.

The aim of Isaac's blessing in this narrative context is to take another step toward Jacob's actual act of ordaining Levi to the priest-

---

[77] It is not certain to whom the term "the beloved" refers. However, given the emphasis on Jacob, and the other references to Jacob and Jacob's sons throughout Isaac's blessing for Levi, he seems the most likely candidate. Berger, *Das Buch der Jubiläen*, 478, also suggests Abraham with his citation of Isa 41:8, אברהם אהבי זרע, "the offspring of Abraham, my friend."

[78] Especially see VanderKam, "Priestly Messiah," 363-64, for a complete discussion of the place of Deut 33:8-11 in vv. 15, 17.

[79] Charles, *Book of Jubilees*, 186 also suggests that Num 18:2, 4 stand behind this text.

hood in 32:3. While Jacob's ordination of Levi remains the deed which effects Levi's exaltation to the priesthood, the benison of Isaac is important: Jacob does nothing in the biblical account to indicate he was a priest, while Isaac does (Gen 26:25); hence his affirmation of Levi's destiny is necessary for the sake of continuity.[80] The blessing also functions to demonstrate that Levi would be a priest who is equally at home in the roles of cultic official, teacher, and judge. As part of the author's overall plan of offering a charter for Maccabean-era Judaism, Isaac's blessing establishes the great antiquity and sound character of Levi's priesthood, the priesthood preferred by the author.

Prior to the next section of the LPT is *Jub.* 31:18-32; it includes Isaac's blessing for Judah, an extended account of Isaac and Jacob's further discussions during the family visit to Hebron, and the family's trip back to Bethel. The first two items are almost surely not part of the Levi-apocryphon, as they both serve principally the interests of the author of *Jubilees*;[81] and the last item makes explicit what is assumed in *Ar. Levi* 8. As we see below, the latter difference, more than anything else, indicates that *Aramaic Levi* and *Jubilees* used a common source in different ways.

4.3.5. *Jub.* 32:1-9: Levi's dream, Jacob's tithe, and Levi's first sacrifice

At home once more in Bethel, Levi had a dream in which he and his descendants are designated priests "of the Most High God forever" (v. 1).[82] According to v. 2 Jacob then tithed all of his belongings and

---

[80] It is Kugel, "Levi's Elevation," 19-24, who has the wisdom to see this as the reason for Isaac's role in the affair. However, we disagree with Kugel when he indicates that Isaac's blessing therefore causes Levi's elevation to the priesthood. Indeed, unlike *Aramaic Levi*, *Jubilees* does not recount Isaac's instruction of Levi in priestly arts, perhaps because in the author's mind Isaac only foretells the elevation, but does not accomplish it; thus he would be out of order in offering instruction.

[81] It is readily apparent that the conversation between Isaac and Jacob is part and parcel of the author's overarching focus on the figure of Jacob: the conversation lends added legitimacy to his character. As for the blessing of Judah, it is no doubt present both as an affirmation of the importance of the tribe of Judah, and as the author's means of confirming his desire that a reconstituted Israel be ruled by prince and priest. Some speculate that the priority of blessing for Levi indicates the author's sense of who should be preeminent in a government constituted by a king and a high priest (see, for example, Endres, *Biblical Interpretation*, 161). There is an additional degree of interest attached to the blessing for Judah thanks to the messianic overtones in 31:18b; however, as Endres, *Biblical Interpretation*, 161, n. 10, indicates, "in view of the lack of consensus on the issue," we may forego further consideration of the matter (but see Davenport, *Eschatology of the Book of Jubilees*, 64-66, cited by Endres, ibid., for some of the discussion of the verse and its problems).

[82] VanderKam, *Book of Jubilees*, 2:208, indicates that the Latin text reads *quasi*, "as, as it were, as if." This strengthens the motivation to believe that Levi was not

his children to complete the unfulfilled vow he had made at Bethel (cf. Gen 28:22).[83] Verse 3 offers an explanation of how Levi could be the tithe-son among Jacob's twelve male offspring.[84] Verses 4-5 describe the details of Jacob's tithe, and affirm that the sacrifice was made in satisfaction of his unpaid debt (Gen 28:22). The narrator goes on to explain the family's celebration of the feast of Sukkoth (vv. 6-7). Verse 8 states that Jacob tithed, giving clean animals to Levi for sacrifice. The same verse adds that Jacob also gave the unclean animals and all persons over to him.[85] The passage concludes in v. 9 with the af-

---

actually elevated to the role within the dream. Meanwhile most commentators think of this as an actual elevation; see, for example, Kugel, "Levi's Elevation," 5, 48. In fact Kugel posits the prior existence of a separate document, "Levi's Priestly Initiation," that is adapted by the author of *Jubilees* with this one sentence. The purpose for reducing the source to a single line, says Kugel, is to avoid clashing with Isaac's initiation in 31:12-17.

Also of note in v. 1 is the use of the unusual name for God. Although it appears often in *Jubilees* (7:36; 12:19; 13:29; 16:18, 27; 20:9; 21:20, 22, 23, 25; 22:6, 11, 13, 19, 23, 27 [2x]; 25:3, 11, 21; 27:15; 32:1; 36:16; 39:6; cf. Charles, *The Book of Jubilees*, 213, n. 16 for indication of the regularity with which the title appears in second-century sources), it is also the name associated with Levi as a priest in *Ar. Levi* 13 and 30, and perhaps comes from the Melchizedek tradition in Gen 14:18-20.

[83] Charles, *Book of Jubilees*, 191, is somewhat misleading when he says that v. 2 borrows language from Gen 14:20. In the latter instance Abraham gives *to* Melchizedek a tithe; in this verse Jacob gives Levi *as* the tithe. The parallel with Gen 14:20 emerges only in vv. 1 and 4ff.

[84] For discussion of this ingenious exegetical move see Charles, *Book of Jubilees*, 191-92; and Kugel, "Levi's Elevation," 13-17. Both point out the parallels for this explanation of Levi's role as a priest in the Targumim and Rabbinic literature. Also see Kugel's discussion of what he calls the "Jacob Counts Backwards" motif, and his indication that it is a late addition (49-51). He bases his view on the different methods of celebrating Sukkoth in this passage and in 16:20-25. Yet the difference may not be as significant as he suggests. James VanderKam, "The Temple Scroll and the Book of Jubilees," in *Temple Scroll Studies* (ed. G. Brooke; Sheffield: JSOT, 1989) 362, points out that but for the sheep, all of the sacrificial measures in chapter 16 relate to those in chapter 32 at a ratio of 1:7; thus *Jub.* 32:4 seems to give the numbers needed for all seven days of the feast described in chapter 16.

[85] The difficulty of Jacob giving to Levi *unclean* animals is resolved by Charles, *Book of Jubilees*, 193, with the addition of the negative, ʾi, "not," to accompany the verb. However VanderKam, *Book of Jubilees*, 2:211, points out that there is no textual support for Charles' emendation. The alternative is to explain the statement as do E. Littmann, "Das Buch der Jubiläen," in *Die Apocryphen und Pseudepigraphen des Alten Testaments* (ed. E. Kautzsch; 2 vols.; Tübingen: J. C. B. Mohr, 1900) 2:95; and Berger, *Das Buch der Jubiläen*, 482, saying that Levi receives authority over the unclean animals and human beings. See 5Q13 2 6-7, cited by VanderKam and Berger, where Jacob, Bethel, and the gift to Levi of the right to bind are all mentioned together (*DJD* 3, 182).

firmation that Levi served as Jacob's priest in Bethel, that Jacob vowed, and that Jacob made a second tithe.

The passage relies on a number of biblical texts. Gen 28:22 serves as the basis for Jacob's act of tithing;[86] reference to Benjamin's impending birth, and the count of Jacob's sons that puts Levi in the tenth place rely on Gen 35:16-18, 22-26; the notion of tithing to a priest of the "Most High God" has its foundation in Gen 14:18-20; rules for observance of the Feast of Booths appear in Num 29:13-34; and the second tithe is probably related to Deut 14:22-23.[87]

Unlike the previous sections, this one is probably almost wholly a creation of the author of *Jubilees*. Although the dream mentioned in v. 1 was probably known to the writer from a source used by *Aramaic Levi*, or from *Aramaic Levi* itself, on the whole the innovations are from the author of *Jubilees*.[88] So, whereas the accounts of the vision and of Jacob's ordination of Levi in *Aramaic Levi* are focused almost entirely on Levi, this report pushes him to the periphery; it is principally interested in showing how Jacob brought to fruition the three "prophecies" of the elevation,[89] how he was able to fulfill his tithe, and how the law of the second tithe came into existence. Hence the LPT was used at this juncture in *Jubilees* as a means of addressing another of the author's agenda items—the glorification of Jacob, and the revelation of new laws.

Jub. 32:1-9 discloses the character and purpose of the LPT in *Jubilees* as a whole. Although the narrative is concerned to communicate something about Levi and his special priestly position, it is even more interested in revealing how Jacob plays a key role in Levi's ele-

---

[86] Note that Amos 4:4 also mentions tithing at Bethel; cf. James VanderKam, "Jubilees and the Priestly Messiah," 364.

[87] Albeck, *Das Buch der Jubiläen*, 31, suggests the last connection. R. H. Charles, *Book of Jubilees*, 193, links the notion of a second tithe in v. 9 to Num 18:25-26. Hartom, *Book of Jubilees*, 100, joins Charles, although he also goes on to say that v. 10 alludes to Deut 14:22-23. A. Caquot, "Jubilés," in *La Bible. Écrits intertestamentaires* (eds. André Dupont-Sommer, Marc Philonenko, and D. A. Bertrand; Paris: Gallimord, 1987) 760, handles the matter in an unusual way: he merges the second half of v. 9 with v. 10 so there is no doubt that the biblical basis is Deut 14:22-23. Finally Berger, *Das Buch der Jubiläen*, 482, simply spares himself the difficulty by not commenting on v. 9 and linking v. 10 with the Deuteronomy passage. At any rate, Albeck must be right: the second tithe of Num 18:25-26 is given to priests by Levites from the tithe they receive. In this narrative Levi has no priest beyond himself to whom he can make a tithe, and it is plain from the text that Jacob, the lay person, is the actor in v. 9b.

[88] Kugel, "Levi's Elevation," 56-58, would seem to oppose this view.

[89] The first two are the angel's statement that Levi and his sons were appointed priests (30:18-20), and Isaac's blessing that asked for Levi's appointment (31:12-17), and the third is Levi's dream (32:1). Note that neither of the first two actually results in Levi becoming a priest, and his dream only foreshadows the event that followed.

vation, and in adding to Jacob's image as the exemplary Israelite. Everything Jacob does with respect to Levi contributes to Jacob's reputation. Thus the author enhances his role in the Shechem episode by placing him in league with the zealots whose action leads to the angelic assurance that Levi merited his priestly office. Likewise, Jacob's faithfulness as a son, demonstrated in his responsiveness to Isaac's wish that the family visit him in Hebron, is the reason Isaac is able to address Levi with a blessing for priestly service. And it is Jacob's devout fulfillment of a vow that finally results in Levi's elevation. While the LPT is used in *Jubilees* to say a little about Levi and his exemplary character vis-à-vis the priesthood, its primary function is to contribute to the book's portrait of Jacob. The LPT appears in *Jubilees* to further the author's aim of establishing a charter for Hasmonean-era Judaism in which he thinks a priesthood modelled on Levi will be important, but in which Jacob's example will be most important of all.

4.3.6. Excursus on *Jub.* 21:7-20: Priestly instructions

Among the many differences between *Aramaic Levi* and *Jub.* 30:1–32:9 is the absence of priestly instructions in the latter passage. Nevertheless commentators often say that *Jub.* 21:7-20 is connected to *Ar. Levi* 13-61.[90] But while there are general agreements between the two sets of instructions, and there is a close parallel between the two lists of acceptable types of wood for the altar-fire (*Ar. Levi* 22-25a; *Jub.* 21:12),[91] and both sets of guidelines were given first by Abraham to Isaac (cf. *Ar. Levi* 22, 50, 57), there are also numerous differences. Isaac's instructions to Levi deal with the holocaust offering of Leviticus 1, but Abraham's instructions to Isaac reflect more readily the peace offering described in Leviticus 3. The directives in *Ar. Levi* 13-61 are detailed, but the rules set out in *Jub.* 21:7-20 are cursory. So if, as we suggest above, the two recipes for cultic success derive from a common source, one or the other must have undergone considerable adjustment to achieve its present condition.[92]

---

[90] For example, Charles, *Book of Jubilees*, 132, asserted that *Testament of Levi* 9 used *Jubilees* 21, or a text like it, as a source; more recently Berger, *Buch der Jubiläen*, 429, makes the connection between *Jub.* 20:7-20 and *Ar. Levi* 13-61. Berger's judgement is typical of recent scholarship. See also the more unusual and intriguing view of Kugel, "Levi's Elevation," 17-19, 54; see also chapter 3, note 173.

[91] For a convenient comparison of the lists of trees, see R. H. Charles, *The Greek Versions of the Testaments of the Twelve Patriarchs* (Oxford: Oxford University, 1908) 249. For more on the wood-types listed in both books, see the secondary literature cited in note 152 in chapter three.

[92] See 4.2.1.

4.3.7. Excursus on *Jub.* 45:16: Levi, the guardian of knowledge

In *Jub.* 45:16 Israel gives "his books and the books of his fathers to Levi his son so that he could preserve them and renew them for his sons today." Does the sentence come from the LPT, or is it peculiar to *Jubilees*? It is tempting to say that it appears here only because the author was of levitical lineage,[93] and that he used the literary conceit to explain his knowledge (as a descendant of Levi) of the matters covered in *Jubilees*. Yet a similar statement occurs in 4Q Visions of Amram, suggesting it was common to depict Levi as the transmitter of tradition.[94] Related is the "priestly testament" of Kohath from Qumran.[95] Additionally there is an Abraham-Isaac-Jacob-Levi genealogy in 4Q225 and 4Q227, suggestive of a tradition connecting these figures with one another for reasons transcending family ties.[96] Unfortunately the phrase in *Jub.* 45:16 appears nowhere else in the LPT. Thus the true nature of its relationship to the other texts in the trajectory must remain in the realm of speculation.

4.4. Conclusion

The contents of *Jub.* 30:1–32:9 tell much regarding its place in the LPT. While the passage is concerned in large part with accounting for the origin of the priesthood in Levi's ordination to the office in the period of the ancestors, it also betrays the author's broader interests in elevating Jacob and developing a complete proposal for Jewish life in the wake of the Maccabean successes. The reduction of Levi's vision in particular signals that the author has a different agenda than the one served by the other texts in the LPT. Although Levi and his election to the priesthood were of great interest to the author of *Jubilees*, broader issues took pride of place, and necessitated restraint in re-presenting the LPT.

The author's use of the Levi-apocryphon as a source supports the last statement. While preserving the storyline contained in the apocryphon, it has been severely truncated and adjusted to meet the writer's needs. There is no surprise in this, however, since he treated the biblical record—his principal source—in a similar fashion. Furthermore, just as he was willing to adjust the biblical record to create strict logical

---

[93] See, for example, the statement to this effect in Charles, *Book of Jubilees*, 244.

[94] 4QVision of Amram 2 11-12, according to J. T. Milik, "4Q Visions de ʿAmram et une citation d'Origène," *RB* 79 (1972) 97.

[95] J. T. Milik, "Écrits préesséniens de Qumrân; d'Hénoch à ʿAmram," in *Qumrân. Sa piété, sa théologie et son milieu* (ed. M. Delcor, BEThL 46; Gembloux: Duculot, 1978) 103. See now the publication of the Kohath text by Émile Puech, "Le Testament de Qahat en araméen de la Grotte 4 (*4QTQah*)," *RevQ* 15 (1992) 2-54.

[96] The reason for such a suspicion, of course, is the fact that Levi is the son among the many selected as the figure with which to continue the genealogy. 4Q225 and 4Q227 are found in *DJD* 13, 141-55 and 171-75 respectively.

consistency otherwise absent from the narrative, he felt free to tinker with the Levi-apocryphon to lend his own logic to it as he incorporated it into his work. The outstanding example of this is the transformation of the apocryphon and of *Aramaic Levi*'s three instances[97] of Levi's elevation to the priesthood to three incidents of foreshadowing, and a single instance of appointment by the hero of *Jubilees*, Jacob.

In terms of the intent of the LPT in *Jubilees*, it may be noted that while *Aramaic Levi* was somewhat polemical in its portrayal of Levi as the most acceptable priest, *Jubilees* is not combative. The author was chiefly intent on showing the origins of his notion of a proper priesthood. The manner of his incorporation of the LPT is in keeping with the probable historical conditions under which the text was composed, and the broader purpose of the entire book. The concern of *Jubilees* with the priesthood was controlled by a historical context in which there was probably a mood of optimism about the future, and in which literature like *Jubilees* articulated hopes and aspirations for that future.

Finally, the relationship of *Jub.* 30:1–32:9 to the other entries in the LPT places it somewhat at the periphery of the tradition. While it relied upon the Levi-apocryphon as a source, as did *Aramaic Levi*, it demonstrates no direct knowledge of *Aramaic Levi*, and there is no significant trace of its influence on *Testament of Levi*. Meanwhile, it does carry on many of the biblical traditions embodied in the other LPT texts. Indeed, its strongest connection with the rest of the tradition is its abiding concern with the purity of the Jewish community and with promoting Levi as the model priest. Hence, in spite of its isolation from other texts in the tradition, *Jub.* 30:1–32:9 must be counted a full partner in the LPT.

---

[97] This number assumes that Isaac's blessing in the apocryphon, preserved by a mere mention in *Ar. Levi* 8, entailed also an elevation.

CHAPTER 5 THE LEVI-PRIESTLY TRADITION IN TESTAMENT OF LEVI

Among the texts of the LPT, the fact that there is a relationship between *Aramaic Levi* and *Testament of Levi* has long been obvious to scholars. Meanwhile few discern any close connections between the testament and *Jubilees*. As a result interest in defining the sources of *Testament of Levi* has focused on the link between the Greek and Aramaic documents. And while some continue to say there is only a distant traditio-historical connection between them,[1] or that they are

---

[1] Jürgen Becker, *Untersuchungen zur Entstehungsgeschichte der Testamente der zwölf Patriarchen*, (AGJU 8; Leiden: Brill, 1970), 103-5; and Jarl Henning Ulrichsen, *Die Grundschrift der Testamente der zwölf Patriarchen: Eine Untersuchung zu Umfang, Inhalt und Eigenart der ursprünglichen Schrift* (Acta Universitatis Upsaliensis, Historia Religionum 10; Uppsala: Almqvist & Wiksell, 1991) 177-86. Ulrichsen states with respect to *Aramaic Levi* and *Testament of Levi*, "Sie schöpfen alle beide aus den vorliegenden Levitraditionen, die sie je getrennt verwenden und gestalten" (186). This judgment speaks for his view of *Jubilees'* relationship to *Testament of Levi* as well. Especially noteworthy is Ulrichsen's separate treatment of *Aramaic Levi's* individual manuscript witnesses. He also seems to share Becker's opinion that the common tradition was oral, because, with respect to *Jubilees, Aramaic Levi*, and *Testament of Levi* on Levi's encounter with Jacob he says, "Die Versionen sind alleinstehende Darstellungen einer mündlichen Tradition" (*Grundschrift*, 182); and again, about Isaac's instructions in *Aramaic Levi* and *Testament of Levi* he says, "Man darf eher damit rechnen, daß die drei Texte (TL 9:6–14; Jub; der aramäisch-griechische Text) schriftliche Fixierungen verwandter mündlicher Traditionen sind" (184). Yet he does not apply that judgment consistently to all of the *Aramaic Levi* texts he examines, and avoids such language in his concluding statement. Chr. Burchard, "Zur armenischen Überlieferung der Testamente der Zwölf Patriarchen," *BZNW* 36 (1969) 4-5, n. 25, also says that *Aramaic Levi* and *Testament of Levi* share no close connections, and contain similar traditions only. See also Burchard's review of an edition of *T12P* from Marinus de Jonge in *RevQ* 5 (1964/66) 283, n. 2.

related only by common reliance on a Levi-apocryphon,[2] most agree that their relationship is very close, and that the later text is based on some form of the earlier work.[3] In light of the conclusions reached already in this study regarding the relationships among *Aramaic Levi*, *Jubilees*, and *Testament of Levi* it should be clear that we favor the latter view.[4]

Of course, the value of the connection between texts is heightened considerably when we can show it to be direct. Comparison of a document with its source text affords the possibility of isolating very precisely the ways in which existing material was altered, and so yields excellent evidence for the intent of the author of the later document. Hence, as comparison of *Jubilees* with the reconstructed Levi-apocryphon and *Aramaic Levi* assisted us in discerning *Jubilees'* unique contribution to the LPT, measuring *Testament of Levi* against *Aramaic Levi* will greatly aid us in understanding the Greek testament's place in the tradition.

Unfortunately two impediments have stood in the way of attaining the full benefit of comparing *Aramaic Levi* with *Testament of Levi*. The first was the bygone inaccessibility of the Qumran manuscripts of *Aramaic Levi*. Without them it was impossible for scholarship to assess adequately the scope and shape of the earlier doc-

---

[2] Pierre Grelot, "Notes sur le Testament araméen de Lévi," *RB* 63 (1956) 404. See also Pierre Grelot, "Le Livre des Jubilés et le Testament de Lévi," in *Mélanges Dominique Barthélemy: études bibliques offertes a l'occasion de son 60e anniversaire* (ed. P. Casetti, O. Keel and Adrian Schenker; OBO 38; Göttingen: Vandenhoeck & Ruprecht, 1981) 110-33, especially 111.

[3] J. T. Milik, "Le Testament de Lévi en araméen: Fragment de la Grotte 4 de Qumrân," *RB* 62 (1955) 404-406. See also Charles' pre-Qumran view in R. H. Charles and A. Cowley, "An Early Source of the Testaments of the Patriarchs," *JQR* 19 (1907) 566-69; and *The Greek Versions of the Testaments of the Twelve Patriarchs* (Oxford: Oxford University, 1908) liii-lviii. He believed then that *Aramaic Levi*, known to him only from the Cairo Geniza manuscript and the Mt. Athos additions, was "a work which formed a common source both of the Testaments and the Book of Jubilees" (*Greek Versions*, liv). Others who hold this view include Marinus de Jonge, *The Testaments of the Twelve Patriarchs. A Study of their Text, Composition, and Origin* (Assen: Van Gorcum, 1953) 38-52, 129-31, who in his more recent statements on the matter has indicated that reliance was on a form of *Aramaic Levi* somewhat different from the extant version (see for example, Marinus de Jonge, "Main Issues in the Study of the Testaments of the Twelve Patriarchs," *NTS* 26 [1980] 515); Detlev Haupt, "Das Testament des Levi. Untersuchungen zu seiner Entstehung und Überlieferungsgeschichte" (Ph.D. diss., Halle, 1969) 123, who is also of the opinion that the form of *Aramaic Levi* used was different from the document preserved in the manuscripts; and Anders Hultgård, *L'eschatologie des Testaments des Douze Patriarches*, vol. 2,*Composition de l'ouvrage textes et traductions* (Acta Universitatis Upsaliensis; Historia Religionum 7; Uppsala: Almqvist & Wiksell, 1982) 106.

[4] See our affirmation of this position in 5.1 and 5.3 below.

ument, and as a result commentators typically reconstructed it on the basis of its similarities with the testament. Clearly that procedure rendered comparison rather useless, inasmuch as it became an exercise of examining mirror images. Chapters two and three of our study have addressed this problem for the first time. When it is reconstructed using the full range of textual evidence, *Aramaic Levi* no longer appears as a pale image of *Testament of Levi*; instead it stands as an independent document which is very different from the extant Greek text.

The second obstacle to realizing the full potential of a comparison between *Aramaic Levi* and the testament is the long-standing uncertainty regarding the proper form of *Testament of Levi* with which to make comparisons.[5] There is little doubt that in its present form it is a Christian document.[6] Among those who accept the notion that its author relied directly on a Semitic *Vorlage*,[7] there are some who say that

---

[5] This issue is subordinate to the broader problematic of *Testaments of the Twelve Patriarch*'s (*T12P*) Jewish or Christian origin. However, contrary to common practice, one's conclusion regarding the origin of *Testament of Levi* is not a good standard by which to measure the origin of *T12P* as a whole. As we see throughout this study, we have strong evidence that *Testament of Levi*, in some way, is derived ultimately from a Jewish document. Yet the evidence for pre-*T12P* forms of any of the other testaments is in no case as good. Although Milik says that Semitic manuscripts of several of the testaments appear at Qumran (J. T. Milik, "Écrits préesséniens de Qumrân; d'Hénoch à ᶜAmram," in *Qumrân. Sa piété, sa théologie et son milieu* [ed. M. Delcor; BEThL 46; Gembloux: Duculot, 1978] 96), closer examination of each leads to considerable doubt. Only scattered fragments of the manuscripts in question survive, and those that do share only vague connections with the Greek testaments with which they are said to correspond. As a consequence the shape of the text on which the author of *Testament of Levi* relied must be considered apart from the wider problem of *T12P*'s origin.

[6] The leading proponent of the Christian origin of *T12P* is Marinus de Jonge ("Christian Influence in the Testaments of the Twelve Patriarchs," *NT* 4 [1960] 182-235; "Once More: Christian Influence in the Testaments of the Twelve Patriarchs," *NT* 5 [1962] 311-19; "The Testaments of the Twelve Patriarchs: Christian and Jewish. A Hundred Years After Friedrich Schnapp," *NedTTs* 39 [1985] 265-75). There are those who still contest this view, holding to the notion that *T12P* is in its entirety of Qumran, or Essene, origin (see, for example, the work of M. Philonenko, *Les interpolations chrétiennes des Douze Patriarches et les manuscrits de Qoumrân* [Paris: Presses universitaire de France, 1960]). For a history of scholarship dealing with *T12P* in general, and with the question of its Jewish, Essene, or Christian origin, see H. Dixon Slingerland, *The Testaments of the Twelve Patriarchs: A Critical History of Research* (SBLMS 21; Missoula, MT: Scholars Press, 1977).

[7] We exclude from consideration those who think that the author of the extant *Testament of Levi*, or of a pre-Christian form, relied solely on disparate traditions about Levi. As we indicate below, that seems an indefensible view in light of the close parallels between *Testament of Levi* and *Aramaic Levi*, and in view of the evidence *Jubilees* offers regarding the likely content of any Levi-apocryphon.

Aramaic Levi is that work.[8] Thus for them comparison may be made between the reconstructed form of the Aramaic text and *Testament of Levi* as it appears in *Testaments of the Twelve Patriarchs* (henceforth, *T12P*). Others accept the notion of dependence on *Aramaic Levi*, but claim that there are one or more intermediate stages between the extant Aramaic text and the Greek *Testament of Levi*.[9] They say the author of the Christian testament edited an existing document that is at least one step removed from the text of *Aramaic Levi*. If one accepts the latter view, as do we, reliable comparison of *Aramaic Levi* with *Testament of Levi* must await determination of the pre-Christian form of the testament.

So we begin this chapter with a brief comparison of *Aramaic Levi* and the Greek testament. This is meant simply to reaffirm our contention that the author of the Greek text relied on some form of the Aramaic work. In the second part of the chapter we analyze the Greek *Testament of Levi* to determine what it contained prior to its conversion to a Christian document. What emerges from this exercise is Original *Testament of Levi*,[10] the pre-Christian testament that was clearly based on *Aramaic Levi*, but that was not yet the Greek testament that is part of *T12P*, and that may be most legitimately compared with *Aramaic Levi*. The third part of the chapter undertakes that comparison. The fourth part comments on the individual sections of Original *Testament of Levi*, focusing in particular on the variations vis-à-vis *Aramaic Levi*. On the basis of the commentary we offer an initial impression of the document's date and purpose as the final portion of the chapter.

5.1. *Testament of Levi* and *Aramaic Levi* Compared

Aramaic Levi is most easily compared with *Testament of Levi* by means of the following parallel columns. They provide a graphic indication of where the two documents share the most in common, and where they are significantly different.

---

[8] In fact, Milik may be the only remaining critic who seems to hold this view (see note 3 above).

[9] See, for example, Haupt, "Testament," 123. Some of those who take this view nevertheless think it impossible to isolate the pre-Christian form of the testament. The most prominent proponent of this view is Marinus de Jonge. Consult the many works he has devoted to the origin of the testaments, many of which are cited in the notes of this chapter.

[10] Or at least an earlier form of the testament that stands closer to the source text, *Aramaic Levi*.

Testament of Levi and *Aramaic Levi* Compared

§1	*T. Levi* 1:1–2:2—Introduction to the testament.	
§2	*T. Levi* 2:3-4—Levi tends sheep, reflects on the human condition, and prays for deliverance (cf. *Ar. Levi* supp. 1-19).	
§3	*T. Levi* 2:5–6:2—Levi dreams, he sees (or hears described) several heavens, his prayer is answered as he is made a priest, and he is commissioned to avenge his sister's rape (cf. *Ar. Levi* supp. 20-27; *Ar. Levi* 4-7).	
§4	*T. Levi* 6:3–7:4—The sack of Shechem, Jacob's reproach, Levi's self defense.	*Ar. Levi* 1-3—The sack of Shechem.
		Ar. Levi supp. 1-19—Levi prays (cf. *T. Levi* 2:3-4).
§5	*T. Levi* 8:1-19—Levi's second vision and a second ordination and elevation to the priesthood, including investiture.	*Ar. Levi* supp. 20-27; *Ar. Levi* 4-7—Levi has a vision in which he is elevated to the priesthood and he hears a speech against exogamy.
§6	*T. Levi* 9:1-5—Travel to Isaac where Isaac blesses Levi, travel to Bethel where Jacob has a vision concerning Levi and appoints him to the priesthood, and travel back to Isaac.	*Ar. Levi* 8-11—Travel to Isaac where Isaac blesses Levi, travel to Bethel where Jacob appoints Levi to the priesthood, and travel back to Isaac.
§7	*T. Levi* 9:6-14—Isaac instructs Levi in cultic matters.	*Ar. Levi* 13-61—Isaac instructs Levi in cultic matters.
§8	*T. Levi* 10:1-5—Levi predicts the fate of his descendants.	
§9	*T. Levi* 11:1–12:7—Levi narrates his life history.	*Ar. Levi* 62-81—Levi narrates his life history.

| §10 | *T. Levi* 13:1-9—Levi instructs his children on the value of wisdom and learning, and on their relationship to the law of God. | *Ar. Levi* 82-101—Levi instructs his children on the value of truth, wisdom, and the value of learning. |
| §11 | *T. Levi* 14:1–15:4—Levi warns his children regarding their future. | *Ar. Levi* 102-106—Levi warns his children regarding their future. |

Testament of Levi continues with additional speech material in chapters 16–18. Unfortunately *Aramaic Levi* breaks off in the middle of v. 106, so comparison beyond that point is impossible.

It is plain that from the Shechem incident onward the two documents are structurally identical. In addition it is worth recalling that our study of *Ar. Levi* 8-11 revealed a striking resemblance between that passage and *T. Levi* 9:1-5.[11] Even more compelling as evidence for the closeness of the two documents was the parallel between *Ar. Levi* 78 and *T. Levi* 12:5.[12] Moreover, examination of the priestly instructions (*Ar. Levi* 13-61; *T. Levi* 9:6-14) and the wisdom speeches (*Ar. Levi* 82-101; *T. Levi* 13:1-9) in both works indicates that the author of the Greek testament edited a text like *Aramaic Levi* to create his own document.[13] Another indication that *Testament of Levi* is based on *Aramaic Levi* are the results of our comparison of *Aramaic Levi* and *Jubilees*. They demonstrate that both documents relied independently on a Levi-apocryphon, a text that lacked Levi's prayer, life history, and wisdom speech. Those three items appear for the first time in *Aramaic Levi*, and are apparently innovations in the LPT made by the author of the Aramaic work. Inasmuch as *Testament of Levi* also contains evidence of all three,[14] we may assume that the author of the Greek testament relied on a text like *Aramaic Levi*.

We discover also from examination of the parallel columns the principal ways in which *Testament of Levi* differs from *Aramaic Levi*. The testament contains one large adjustment of *Aramaic Levi*'s structure, shifting Levi's prayer from its place after the Shechem incident to just before his act of revenge.[15] The scope of *Aramaic Levi* was also expanded significantly on at least one occasion by the insertion of a second vision between the prayer and the Shechem incident. Hence the focal point of any attempt to determine whether the author of the

---

[11] See 2.3.1.

[12] See 3.1.6.

[13] See discussion of these sections below, in 5.4.1, 5.4.5 and 5.4.7.

[14] *T. Levi* 2:4; 4:2-6; 11:1–12:5; 13:1-9.

[15] Another immediately apparent adjustment is the addition of chapter 10 between the encounters with Isaac and with Jacob and Levi's life history. For discussion of this chapter and its Christian character, see 5.2.9 below.

Christian form of *Testament of Levi* used *Aramaic Levi* or a document based on *Aramaic Levi* must be *Testament of Levi* 2–5. If after the Christian additions have been identified and other obvious late accretions to the testament have been isolated we still have an internally coherent document with two visions and the mention of Levi's prayer in first place, then we may be certain that *Testament of Levi* was not based directly on *Aramaic Levi*, but on a modified version of the Aramaic work, an Original *Testament of Levi*. So we turn now to analysis of the testament that addresses this topic.

5.2. The scope of Original *Testament of Levi*

Much of the literature devoted to *Testament of Levi* attempts to isolate the *Urschrift* used by the author of *T12P*. The results of those studies vary widely.[16] Several factors account for the variety. First, as we have noted, to the present no study has been able to take into account the full evidence for *Aramaic Levi* as one measure of what Original *Testament of Levi* contained. We no longer face that obstacle, and so hope to provide here a substantial advance on previous treatments of the shape of Original *Testament of Levi*, at least with respect to what a new and fuller understanding of *Aramaic Levi* has to offer. Second, scholars have often been overzealous in identifying Christian additions to an earlier document. While de Jonge's view that we can no longer isolate with confidence any sense of the Original *Testament of Levi* seems too conservative,[17] the position that goes to the opposite extreme and eliminates entire chapters because they contain hints of Christian

---

[16] For the most recent attempt, complete with comprehensive notes directing the reader to previous studies, see Ulrichsen, *Grundschrift*, 176-206. Ulrichsen decides that the earliest form of the testament contained only 1:1a, 2–2:2; 6:3–7:4; 9:1, 3-5, 7-17; 10:1; 11:1–13:9; 19:1, 4-5. The first to engage the question in depth was F. Schnapp, *Die Testamente der zwölf Patriarchen untersucht* (Halle: Max Niemeyer, 1884) 5-43. Followed closely by Ulrichsen, Schnapp says that 2:3–6:2 cannot be original (see our discussion of 2:3-5 in 5.2.3 for Schnapp's and Ulrichsen's reasoning on this matter), nor can much of chapters 8, 10, and 14–19. In fact, he indicates that the original testament ended after chapter 13. Schnapp first developed the notion that the testament was originally Jewish paranesis, and was then redacted by a Jewish editor interested in future matters, and finally by a Christian author. J. M. S. Baljon, "De testamenten der XII patriarchen," *ThStud* 4 (1886) 208-31, follows Schnapp, offering only a more precise definition of the Jewish and Christian additions. Some of the others who have attempted to isolate Original *Testament of Levi* include Jürgen Becker, who eliminates 2:11; 4:1, 4, 6; 8:12-15; 10:2-3; 14:2; 16:3-4; 18:3, 6-7, 9 as Christian additions; and 2:6-12; 3:1–4:1; 10; 16; 17;18; 19:1-3 as other interpolations (*Untersuchungen*, 306); and Detlev Haupt, who says that the original testament contained 1:2 (?)–2:1, 3-6; 4:2-6; 6:2-7; 7:1-3 (?), 4; 8:1-13, 16-19; 9:1-5; 11:1–12:7; 13:1-9; 14:1–15:4 ("Testament," 123).

[17] See the citations in note 6 to some of the principal works in which de Jonge makes known his view.

interpolation in one or more verses is also not acceptable. We prefer a moderate approach which acknowledges that some items that appear Christian could just as easily have emerged from a Jewish background.[18]   Third, unless there is unequivocal evidence within the text that it has been edited, we will not engage in minuscule dissection of *Testament of Levi* into various editorial levels.   While it has been fashionable to dismiss even half-verses as interpolations into a pristine form of the testament, our objective is only to gain a sense of Original *Testament of Levi's* broad outline, not of the exact number of words it contained.[19]

5.2.1. *T. Levi* 1:1-2

It is clear that these verses are the same sort of introduction as one finds in the other testaments, and so may be counted as an addition to Original *Testament of Levi*.[20]   Noteworthy is the use of the word κρισις, "judgment." Ulrichsen points out that it occurs with this eschatological sense again only in *T. Levi* 3:2a, 3; 4:1; and 18:2.[21]   While he takes this as indication of the secondary character of those sections as well, a more likely alternative is that the present verses are the latest addition, one that consciously takes into account the character of the document to which it was attached.

5.2.2. *T. Levi* 2:1-2

These two verses indicate that Levi was born in Haran, that he came with his father to Shechem around the age of twenty, and that at that time he avenged his sister's rape with his brother Simeon. The verses' originality is hotly contested, and the position one takes in their regard is determinative of how 2:3–6:2 is treated. According to Schnapp, Baljon, and Ulrichsen, accepting the section as part of Original *Testament of Levi* requires dismissal of 2:3–6:2 as an interpolation, since 2:2 announces the beginning of the Shechem episode, and 6:3 is its

---

[18] See, for example, *T. Levi* 17:2c, which falls under suspicion for some because it speaks of the priest of the first jubilee arising for the salvation of the world on the day of his gladness. As Hollander and de Jonge, point out, each element of the phrase—day of gladness, arising, and the salvation of the world—has some precedent in Jewish literature (*The Testaments of the Twelve Patriarchs. A Commentary* [SVTP 8; Leiden: Brill, 1985] 175-76).

[19] Anyway, as Schnapp noted already in 1884, the transmission processes that the testaments underwent assure us that we cannot be as exact in our identification of accretions to the earlier form of *Testament of Levi* as we might want to be. Instead, we must be satisfied with only a general sense of the document's shape (*Testamente*, 41).

[20] So Ulrichsen, *Grundschrift*, 187, n. 73; Becker, *Untersuchungen*, 257; and Haupt, "Testament," 7. Cf. *T. Reuben* 1:1-2; *T. Simeon* 1:1-2; *T. Jud.* 1:1.

[21] Ulrichsen, *Grundschrift*, 187.

continuation.[22] But if we reject 2:1-2 as an addition made to integrate Original *Testament of Levi* into *T12P*, then the following verses which are concerned with Levi's prayer and announce the beginning of his first vision begin the earlier form of the document quite naturally, especially considering the fact that they appear in that order in *Aramaic Levi*. The latter seems to be the more probable view. Indeed, 2:1-2 is disruptive, it speaks of an event otherwise ignored in the testament (Levi's birth at Haran), and it differs from *T. Levi* 12:5 which gives Levi's age at the time of the Shechem episode as eighteen.[23] Moreover, the presence of these intrusive verses may be explained by Hultgård's observation that other testaments begin also with "une légende aggadique de la naissance," and "une aggadah biographique."[24] Hence the author responsible for the composition or collection of *T12P* provided 2:1-2 (along with 1:1-2) as introductory material that made Original *Testament of Levi* conform with the pattern evinced otherwise by the testaments.[25] Thus we may reject 2:1-2. In fact, if we accept Original *Testament of Levi's* dependence on *Aramaic Levi* and expect from it a modicum of narrative consistency, abandonment of the verses is recommended, since we can assume that 2:3-6 was part of Original *Testament of Levi*; after all it refers to the prayer and then gives a vision, a sequence known thus far only from *Aramaic Levi*.

5.2.3. *T. Levi* 2:3-5

As we indicated in the foregoing paragraphs, a group of scholars reject this section, as well as everything else to 6:2 as an addition. Accepting 2:1-2 as authentic, they reason that the announcement that Levi avenged Dinah's rape must be followed by 6:3, the continuation of that account. Moreover, following the so-called β text of *Testament of Levi*, which lacks the α text's resumptive phrase μετα δε τουτο, "After these things," Ulrichsen says that 6:3 follows quite naturally on 2:2. Apart from the arguments we have made already for the rejection of 2:1-2, one may recall that using text-critical judgments to isolate earlier stages of com-

---

[22] Schnapp, *Testamente* 15-18; Baljon, "De testamenten," 208-10; Ulrichsen, *Grundschrift*, 187-89. See 5.2.3.

[23] James Kugel, "Levi's Elevation to the Priesthood in Second Temple Writings," *HTR* 86 (1993) 39-40, n. 39, suggests that this is "an editorial attempt to blur somewhat the obvious contradiction between *T. Levi* 12.5 . . and *T. Levi* 5.3." He is probably correct; we only add that it is also the editor's effort to integrate this work into *T12P* as a whole, and that the redaction took place much later than Kugel seems to suggest.

[24] Hultgård, *L'eschatologie*, 2:107-108; 138-39. Cf. *T. Simeon* 2:2-4; *T. Jud.* 1:3–2:1; *T. Naphtali* 1:6–2:1; and *T. Gad* 1:2.

[25] See also the comments of Haupt, "Testament," 7; "TL 2, 1-2 trägt einen zusammenfassenden, überschriftartigen Charakter, der mit dem erzählenden Stil von 6,3ff. nichts zu tun hat."

position in *T12P* is notoriously difficult and ill-advised. As Marinus de Jonge has amply demonstrated, the history of the testaments' textual transmission is much too long and tortured to draw from what little we know of it any firm literary-critical conclusions.[26]

However, Ulrichsen and those who hold his position have other arguments in favor of discounting 2:3-5. First, he claims that 2:3–6:2 has nothing to do with the Shechem incident, even though he must acknowledge that 5:3 is the angelic command to execute vengeance on Shechem, and reject it as an interpolation.[27] Unfortunately for him there is nothing about 5:3 that suggests it is secondary in its context, and so it remains as a vital link between part of 2:3–6:2 and the following retelling of Genesis 34. Second, Ulrichsen says that the entire section is structurally dissimilar with the rest of the testaments. By his accounting *Testament of Levi* would be like other testaments if it began with a *Lebensdarstellung* in 2:1-2—›6:3ff.; indeed, says Ulrichsen, 2:3–6:2 interrupts the standardized beginning in *Testament of Levi*, and must therefore be an interpolation.[28] However, if *Testament of Levi* is based on a source or sources of a slightly different character from the rest of *T12P* (something Ulrichsen admits[29]), then one expects it to depart from the standard. In fact, if one accepts the author's reliance on *Aramaic Levi* we know where the author derived the order of events that places a vision after Levi's prayer (*Ar. Levi* supp. 1-27; *Ar. Levi* 4-7), and we recognize again that 2:1-2 is the interpolation, not 2:3ff.

5.2.4. *T. Levi* 2:6–6:2

A first step in sorting out the authentic portions of Levi's first vision is to identify those sections that duplicate material from *Aramaic Levi*, the document on which *Testament of Levi* was based. Such passages may be assumed to have been part of Original *Testament of Levi*.[30] The mention of open heavens in *T. Levi* 2:6 reflects *Ar. Levi* supp. 21, and 4:2-6 recalls Levi's prayer in *Ar. Levi* supp. 1-19.[31] Likewise, the angelic elevation of Levi to the priesthood and references to the

---

[26] See especially Marinus de Jonge, "Textual Criticism and the Analysis of the Composition of the *Testament of Zebulun*," in *Studies on the Testaments of the Twelve Patriarchs. Text and Interpretation* (SVTP 3; Leiden: Brill, 1975) 120-39.

[27] Ulrichsen, *Grundschrift*, 188.

[28] Ibid.

[29] Ulrichsen, *Grundschrift*, 186.

[30] For the argument that *Aramaic Levi* was Original *Testament of Levi*'s principal source, and for a table giving the parallels between the two, see 5.1 above and 5.3 below.

[31] See Jonas Greenfield and Michael Stone, "Two Notes on the Aramaic Levi Document," in *Of Scribes and Scrolls*, eds. H. Attridge, J. Collins, T. Tobin (Lanham, MD: University Press of America, 1990) 157-58, for analysis of the correspondence between of *T. Levi* 4:2 and the Aramaic prayer of Levi.

Shechem incident in 5:1-7 demonstrate the author's knowledge of *Ar.
Levi* 1-3, 4-7.[32] Meanwhile, almost nothing between *T. Levi* 2:6 and
4:2 resembles *Aramaic Levi*. Hence 2:7–4:1 falls under suspicion as a
passage added to Original *Testament of Levi*. But it must be shown
from the passage itself that there is reason to believe it to have been
added to an existing document before labeling it an addition to the
original testament.

Portions of three verses evince the hand of a Christian redactor,
and may be eliminated as interpolations. The second half of *T. Levi*
2:11 exhibits Christian influence with its reference to salvation for all
of humankind.[33] In 4:4b and 5b there are also Christian additions that
indicate Jewish opposition to Jesus, and turn the intellectual gifts of the
priesthood into the knowledge necessary for avoiding the mistake of an
unfavorable response to him.

Beyond these few identifiable Christian additions, another apparently
ently secondary passage is 2:7-9.[34] While *T. Levi* 5:1 announces that
Levi entered a single heaven (the angel opens τας πυλας ουρανου, "the
gates of heaven"), as though he traveled into celestial space for the first
time, *T. Levi* 2:7-9 requires that he had already traveled through three
heavens. Inasmuch as 5:1 closely resembles *Ar. Levi* supp. 21, and
may therefore be considered original to *Testament of Levi*,[35] it appears
that 2:7-9, with its three- (or seven-) heaven cosmology, was clumsily
inserted into Original *Testament of Levi* sometime after the document's
initial composition.[36] Second, the following verses in *T. Levi* 2:10, 12

---

[32] Marinus de Jonge, "Notes on Testament of Levi II-VII," in *Travels in the World
of the Old Testament* (eds. H. van Voss, H. ten Cate and N. A. van Uchelen; Assen:
Van Gorcum, 1974) 142-43.

[33] Becker, *Untersuchungen*, 265-66; de Jonge, *Testaments*, 50; but see Haupt,
"Testament," 36-37, 124, who thinks it is from a Jewish interpolator. Ulrichsen,
Grundschrift, 192-93, 206, remains uncertain, but does assign it to the hand of a later
redactor.

[34] For a list of those who share this view of 2:7-9, see Jarl Henning Ulrichsen,
Die Grundschrift, 190-91.

[35] The relationship between *T. Levi* 5:1 and *Ar. Levi* supp. 21, and the conflict
between the number of heavens in 2:7-10 and 5:1 were noted by de Jonge, "Notes,"
142-43; Greenfield and Stone, "Two Notes," 156.

[36] The non-α manuscripts of *T. Levi* 2:7-9 present a seven-heaven cosmology,
while the α manuscript mentions three. See de Jonge, "Notes," 133-36, for a discussion
of the non-α and α manuscripts for this section of *Testament of Levi*. De Jonge
thinks that the α text, with its three-heaven cosmology, is probably a clarifying recension
of a non-α text. Whatever the case, the textual tradition does not easily allow one
to date either schema relative to the other, since all texts are themselves so late. All that
may be said is that one scheme was original, and the other was imposed later. The
impetus for adding the three- or seven-heaven cosmology here may have been the reference
to ουρανοι, "heavens," in 2:6 (Ulrichsen, *Grundschrift*, 190), which was likely
a translation of שמיא/שמים.

are also customarily attributed to a later hand.[37] They amount to completion of the passage begun in 2:7-9 with the announcement of Levi's installation as a priest.[38] Third, others dismiss *T. Levi* 3:1-8 as an addition because it appears to be an expansion on 2:7-9, repeating the number of heavens, and describing them, though in a rather confused fashion, more completely than 2:7-9.[39] Beyond the fact that both descriptions of the celestial realms never lead to anything more in *Aramaic Levi*, mention of seven heavens appears in Jewish and Christian literature for the first time only in the first century CE, well after the time when most date *Testament of Levi*.[40] And following the description of the heavens is another apparently intrusive section, 3:9-4:1. A judgment scene that describes the poor relationship between God and humanity, it was probably intended as a conclusion to 3:5-8,[41] and so its only connection with the rest of *Testament of Levi* is the immediately preceding secondary material; thus it too may be dismissed as an interpolation.[42]

After deleting all of 2:7–4:1, and reading 4:2 immediately following 2:6, the narrative flow of Levi's first vision is coherent, and the problem of proliferating heavens is solved.[43] First the angel invites

---

[37] See Ulrichsen, *Grundschrift*, 192-93. Recall that 2:11 has already been identified as a Christian addition.

[38] See Ulrichsen, *Grundschrift*, 192-93. Note the similarities between these verses and *T. Levi* 4:2-6; 8:10, 16-17. It appears that the redactor reworked existing material.

[39] Becker, *Untersuchungen*, 260; Haupt, "Testament," 38; and de Jonge, *Testaments*, 46-48. For a brief discussion of the text-critical problems in the passage, and references to the literature dealing with them, see Ulrichsen, *Grundschrift*, 191-92.

[40] Of course, this adds significant weight to the argument that the section from 2:7 to 3:8 is an addition. For the view that the seven-heaven cosmology first entered Jewish thought in the first century, see Martha Himmelfarb, *Ascent to Heaven in Jewish and Christian Apocalypses* (Oxford: Oxford University, 1993) 32-33, and the works cited there.

[41] Ulrichsen, *Grundschrift*, 193. Many think 4:1 is a separate Christian addition (see Ulrichsen, *Grundschrift*, 193, n. 99). However, it completes the judgment scene that commences in 3:9, and contains no elements that require it to be considered Christian in origin.

[42] See Becker, *Untersuchungen*, 260-61; Haupt, "Testament," 44; de Jonge, *Testaments*, 142, n. 45; and Ulrichsen, *Grundschrift*, 193, for a similar assessment.

[43] Haupt, "Testament," 47, 122, also determines this to be the scope of *Testament of Levi* 2–5 at its earliest stage of development beyond *Aramaic Levi*. But see Ulrichsen, *Grundschrift*, 19, n. 81, for the view that this was the shape of *Testament of Levi* at an intermediate stage. Ulrichsen takes this view because he holds to the notion that at its inception Original *Testament of Levi* contained no visions, and that *Aramaic Levi* was known only to the first redactor who added 2:3-6; 4:2–6 (and chapter 8). Finally, see Becker, *Untersuchungen*, 264, 306, for yet another perspective, one that is very close to our own.

Levi to ascend with him (2:5-6), whereupon he tells Levi that his prayer has been heard (4:2-6). Then he ushers him into heaven where God confirms the angel's judgment regarding the prayer's effectiveness, saying that Levi has already been given the blessings of the priesthood (5:1-2). Having thus been commissioned to the priesthood, Levi is told by the angel that he must avenge Dinah's rape (5:3-4).[44] After asking the angel's name and receiving an answer, Levi is then delivered from his vision to carry out his violent mandate (5:5-6).

5.2.5. *T. Levi* 6:3–7:4

There is no argument regarding the place of the Shechem episode in Original *Testament of Levi*, although some points about the account trouble critics enough that they suggest that it grew in stages. For instance, Haupt believes there to have been three steps in the development of the episode: 6:3-7, 8-11, and 7:1-3.[45] But his analysis relies on indications too subtle to be taken as true indicators of disunity in the text.[46] Others note the apparent contradiction between 5:3, where Levi is commanded by a heavenly being to undertake his act of vengeance, and

---

[44] Ulrichsen, *Grundschrift*, 188, thinks that the heavenly command was not part of the early form of *Testament of Levi*, since Levi does not use the angelic commission as a defense of his action against Jacob's disappointment and anger in 6:6-7. However, Ulrichsen fails to see that Levi does acknowledge his commission, saying in 6:8, αλλ εγω ειδον οτι αποφασις θεου ην εις κακα επι Σιχιμα, "But I saw that God's judgment was for evil against Shechem." Ulrichsen also asserts that it is Levi who becomes ill after the Shechem incident in 6:7, and that this matches *T12P*'s theme of sickness striking a sinner for his or her misbehavior (188-89; for the passages he cites for the theme of sickness in *T12P*, see 237-38); this, he says, is additional evidence that the divine command to execute vengeance on Shechem in chapter 5 must be an addition. Yet Ulrichsen must ignore a textual tradition that indicates it was Jacob who sickened, and he must turn a blind eye to the fact that if it was Levi who became ill, the text in no way indicates that his illness resulted from his action at Shechem. Hollander and de Jonge, *Commentary*, 146-47, are surely correct in reading with the texts that make sickness Jacob's response, not Levi's. For additional discussion of Ulrichsen's treatment of 5:3, see above.

[45] Haupt, "Testament," 23-27.

[46] For example, Haupt, "Testament," 25, agrees with de Jonge, *Testaments*, 50, that vv. 8-11 are at odds with vv. 3-7 and with 7:1-3. But he holds also that each passage expresses differing emotions on the part of the actors in the drama; this he takes as a sign of narrative inconsistency, which in turn he understands as an indicator of disunity. Yet it may be more sensible to read the passage as a whole to see if the changes in attitude are signs of a broader narrative plan. In this case they surely are. Levi begins with zeal for his task, befitting one who has been appointed by heaven (5:3; 6:1-5). Jacob responds in anger, as he does in the biblical narrative, and Levi, the dutiful son, accepts a measure of his father's judgment (6:6-7). But then Levi reminds his father that in spite of his disappointment with the immediate outcome, it was proper in light of earlier events, and a harbinger of things to come (6:8-11; 7:1-3).

6:6-7, where his father is angry with him for having slain the circumcised Shechemites, and Levi acknowledges his sin. They conclude from this that it is possible to assign the two passages to different sources, or to see in chapter 6 some disharmony.[47] Yet the biblical account on which the episode is based makes it clear that Jacob was perturbed by his sons' action, and that they incurred Jacob's anger (Gen 34:30; 49:5-7). In sum, it seems best, lacking additional evidence to the contrary, to accept the account as it stands as basically representative of what appeared in Original *Testament of Levi*.[48]

5.2.6. *T. Levi* 8:1-19

Levi's second vision is especially nettlesome to those who are inclined to see evidence of a Christian redactor, since the liturgical garb and elements are often identified with both Jewish and Christian ritual practices.[49] Additionally, some of those who reject the authenticity of the first dream are compelled to say that this one too may not be deemed original, especially since its narration makes reference to the first (8:1, 18).[50] Yet if one acknowledges the fact that Jewish authors could have used comfortably much of the ritual vocabulary of the passage, and if one accepts the originality of at least parts of the first vision, as do we, the reasons for doubting the place of most of this chapter in Original *Testament of Levi* are reduced considerably.

Nevertheless, there are two points at which the unity of the chapter is suspect. The first is in vv. 1-10, where vv. 1-3 and 4-10 give two slightly different accounts of Levi's ordination to the priesthood. Some say this indicates that the text has been adjusted over time. Of course, it is possible that there was once only a single account. However, to decide which is earliest is beyond the power of discernment granted us by the available evidence. And since neither account

---

[47] See, for example, Ulrichsen, *Grundschrift*, 188, 194.

[48] Another noteworthy item is the parallel between 6:11 and 1 Thess 2:16. Scholars are undecided as to which came first, the testament passage, or the Christian text. See the comments of Ulrichsen, *Grundschrift*, 194; Haupt, "Testament," 25, n. 68; and the lengthy treatment by T. Baarda, "The Shechem Episode in the Testament of Levi," in *Sacred History and Sacred Texts* (eds. J. N. Bremmer and Florentino García Martínez; Kampen: Pharos, 1992) 11-73.

[49] See de Jonge, *Testaments*, 43-46; Hollander and de Jonge, *Commentary*, 150-55. One of the best known passages in *T12P*, chapter 8 has drawn considerable attention. See the many studies that attempt to illuminate its Christian elements noted by Slingerland, *Testaments*, passim. Yet see G. R. Beasley-Murray, "The Two Messiahs in the Testaments of the Twelve Patriarchs," *JTS* 48 (1947) 1-12, who thinks that the whole passage is original and that it promises a Levitical messiah. Then, of course, there are those who assign the testament a Qumran provenance; of course, they understand this passage with its possible messianic overtones in a rather unique fashion.

[50] This is the view of Schnapp, *Testaments*, 18-21; and Ulrichsen, *Grundschrift*, 194-96. See also Baljon, "De testamente," 218-19.

presents itself as particularly Christian (and therefore a likely addition), it is best simply to note that there is a conflation of two accounts of the angelic investiture of Levi, neither of which can claim priority.

Meanwhile, at least part of *T. Levi* 8:11b-15 is suspect as an addition primarily because the seven angels who appear in the rest of chapter 8 are absent from these verses.[51] Among the numerous attempts to comprehend the redactional history of this passage Pierre Grelot provides a most helpful analysis in his study of *Ar. Levi* 4-6, concluding that a Christian redactor had before him a text that probably described the threefold division of Levi's seed into high priest, priests, and Levites.[52] Grelot offers no explanation for the Christian redactor's intentions, although Hollander and de Jonge are probably right when they suggest that 8:11b-15 was intended as a threefold periodization of history, with the first being the age of Abraham, the second the life of Israel, and the third, with its "king from Judah," the period that dawns with Jesus.[53] At any rate, if Grelot is correct, 8:11b-15, 16-17, in its earlier form, was little more than a description of the future division of Levi's seed into the familiar three branches. Nevertheless, the Christian (and perhaps Jewish) redaction is so thorough as to render the passage that lay behind it unrecognizable. So in spite of Charles' well-known opinion that 8:11-15 refers to the Hasmonean priest-kings,[54] and still other attempts to isolate its pre-Christian form,[55] it is best to set it aside as a substantially Christian portion of *Testament of Levi*.[56]

---

[51] Haupt, "Testament," 51. It is also possible that the reference in v. 14 to the "king from Judah" indicates a Christian origin for the passage.

[52] Grelot, "Notes," 394-97.

[53] Hollander and de Jonge, *Commentary*, 153-54.

[54] See Charles, *Testaments*, 44-46. It is important to remember that his understanding of the text hinges on the textually-baseless emendation of the phrase εκ του Ιουδα, "from Judah," so that it reads εν τω Ιουδα, "in Judah." In the alternative he suggests that it is a Christian addition (45). See Becker, *Untersuchungen*, 277, n. 7, for others who reject Charles' conjectural emendation.

[55] See for example, Haupt, "Testament," 66, who thinks that vv. 14-15 were added during the Hasmonean period when their dynasty consciously linked itself with the Davidic line (at least from Aristobulus I). For others who think this section suffered redaction, but that the original text can be isolated, see Becker, *Untersuchungen*, 276-80, and his extensive summary of previous opinions. We are simply not as confident as Haupt and others of literary criticism's ability, assisted liberally by historical speculation, to sift out the "original" text in this instance.

[56] An alternative is to see only 8:11a, 16-17 as the original text, and all intervening material as a Christian composition (de Jonge, *Testaments*, 45). However, such an approach ignores the parallel between 8:11b and 1Q21 1 noted by Grelot, "Notes," 395, and before him, by J. T. Milik, *DJD* 1, 88.

5.2.7. *T. Levi* 9:1-5

There is little in this passage that one may easily question regarding its
place in Original *Testament of Levi*. Only the reference in 9:2 to
Levi's visions receives attention from Ulrichsen because he considers
both dreams as interpolations.[57] As we have seen, the dreams are, in
fact, both part of Original *Testament of Levi*, and so there is no reason
to doubt the authenticity of the reference to them in 9:2.

5.2.8. *T. Levi* 9:6-14

The same can be said for this section as was said for the preceding part.
There is little doubt regarding its place in Original *Testament of Levi*.
It is only Ulrichsen who finds reason to question a small portion of it.
Citing again his view that the early form of the document contained no
visions, he thinks Isaac's reference to an angelic figure and the "law of
the Lord" in 9:6 is out of place. Not only that, he also thinks the statement inexplicable inasmuch as Levi encounters not a single heavenly
being, but *seven* angels in chapter 8, and the referent of "law of the
Lord" is not clear.[58] As we see below in our discussion of the passage,
the verse is an integral part of the earliest form of the testament, and is
clearly an allusion to Levi's first vision, where a single angel does appear.[59]

5.2.9. *T. Levi* 10:1-5

Chapter 10 is understood almost universally as a Christian addition.[60]
For the purpose of our study it suffices to note that *Aramaic Levi* lacks
anything like chapter 10 between its parallel material for 9:6-14 (*Ar.
Levi* 13-61) and 11:1–12:7 (*Ar. Levi* 62-81), and that 10:2-3 exhibit
strong Christian characteristics.[61] Moreover, it resembles *Testament of
Levi* 14–15, a "Sin-Exile-Return" passage which *is* paralleled in
Aramaic Levi.[62] Especially on the basis of the latter observation, de
Jonge's thesis that chapter 10 is a Christian reworking of chapters

---

[57] Ulrichsen, *Grundschrift*, 196.

[58] Ibid.

[59] See 5.4.5.

[60] See the convenient listing of those who hold this view in Ulrichsen,
Grundschrift, 197, n. 115. In the same note he also mentions those who reject this
view of chapter 10. See, for instance, Charles, *Testaments*, lvii-lix, who thinks that
Testament of Levi 10, 14–16 were added by anti-Hasmonean Pharisees after the
breach between the two groups during the first century BCE.

[61] See, for example, the discussions of Becker, *Untersuchungen*, 281-82; Haupt,
"Testament," 100-1; de Jonge, *Testaments*, 41-42; Hultgård, *L'eschatologie*, 1:93-95.

[62] For the literature in which de Jonge identifies the "Sin-Exile-Return" passages,
see "Levi, the Sons of Levi," 522, n. 13.

14-15 has some merit.[63] The only item that might appear to weigh against his theory is the reference to "the Book of Enoch the Righteous" in v. 5, but that could have been added by the Christian editor in imitation of 14:1.[64]

5.2.10. *T. Levi* 11:1–12:7; 13:1-9

Levi's life history and speech regarding wisdom are both paralleled in *Aramaic Levi*. Furthermore, they do not show any significant signs of Christian redaction. In fact, the two versions of the life history are in places virtually the same,[65] and the differences in the speech are explained easily with reference to a Jewish editor's interests. Hence we accept this lengthy section as it stands as part of Original *Testament of Levi*.[66]

5.2.11. *T. Levi* 14:1–15:4

We are inclined to accept Marinus de Jonge's judgment that these chapters are part of the Original *Testament of Levi*, and that chapter 10 is the reworked version of them.[67] There is one particularly sound indication in favor of this view, namely the connection between these two chapters and *Ar. Levi* 102-106. Milik brought attention to the relationship with his first discussion of 4Q213 8-10.[68] Specific similarities include references to Enoch in *T. Levi* 14:1 and *Ar. Levi* 103; references to Levi's children as heavenly luminaries in *T. Levi* 14:3 and *Ar. Levi* 102; mention of Gentiles in *T. Levi* 14:4 and "the peoples" in *Ar. Levi* 102; and indication that the light of Levi's children will be darkened by their own misbehavior in *T. Levi* 14:4 and *Ar. Levi* 103. *Ar. Levi* 102 preserves a general condemnation of the ways of Levi's children which, although in no way matching the specificity of *T. Levi* 14:5-8, parallels that passage's condemnation of Levi's descendants for ill-considered choices and action.

Of course, several verses from chapters 14 and 15 must be excluded from consideration because they show signs of Christian redac-

---

[63] De Jonge, *Testaments*, 40-42; "Levi, the Sons of Levi," 518-19. But see Ulrichsen, *Grundschrift*, 198, for a brief critique.

[64] Note also that the title "Enoch the Righteous" occurs elsewhere in *T12P*; *T. Jud.* 18:1; *T. Dan* 5:6; *T. Benjamin* 9:1. Hollander and de Jonge, *Commentary*, 39-40, point out that Enoch is often the source cited by the Christian compiler for a patriarch's knowledge of Israel's sin, exile, and return.

[65] See especially *T. Levi* 12:5 and *Ar. Levi* 78.

[66] For a similar view see Ulrichsen, *Grundschrift*, 198, with references to others. Ulrichsen treats this section as the "Kern des Testaments" (198).

[67] De Jonge, *Testaments*, 40-42; "Levi, the Sons of Levi," 518-19. See 5.2.9 above.

[68] J. T. Milik, "Problèmes de la littérature hénochique à la lumière des fragments araméen de Qumrân," *HTR* 64 (1971) 333-78.

tion. *T. Levi* 14:2b reads οιτινες επιβαλουσι τας χειρας αυτων επι τον σωτηρα του κοσμου, "who laid their hands upon the savior of the world." This apparent reference to Jewish opposition to Jesus interrupts the thought begun in v. 2a, which is resumed in v. 3.[69] In the same chapter v. 4b is also probably from a Christian hand, and was meant to capitalize on the context that condemns some of Levi's descendants for their corruption of the law; the addition says τουτον θελοντες ανελειν, "him you seek to kill." The phrase identifies Jesus with the essence of the law, and links its corruption with attempts to end Jesus' life.[70]

5.2.12. *T. Levi* 16:1–17:11

While we lack any parallel Aramaic text for this section,[71] Milik is probably correct that the Aramaic document contained at one time something like what appears in *T. Levi* 16:1–17:11, and that it focused on the decline of the priesthood.[72] Christian redaction of an existing Jewish text is once again evident,[73] confirmation at least that the text had an existence prior to its incorporation into the Christian testament. Yet we may say little with certainty about the text in its original form, since it has evidently undergone considerable adjustment. Note, for instance, that 16:1 mentions seventy weeks while the chapter goes on to ignore their narration in any clear way, and yet 17:1 states confidently that the reader received a good accounting of the weeks.[74] So although we may express some confidence that Original *Testament of Levi* contained material like this, we are also hindered in our comprehension of it by the absence of parallel evidence from the Aramaic side. Without comparative material we may acknowledge only that the early form of the text gave Levi's speech about the eventual decline of the priesthood, a decline that would lead to its utter desolation.[75]

---

[69] Marinus de Jonge, "Levi, the Sons of Levi and the Law in the Testament of Levi X, XIV-XV and XVI," in *De la Tora au Messie* (eds. J. Doré, P. Grelot, M. Carrez; Paris: Tournai, 1981) 517.

[70] Ibid. However, de Jonge includes everything to the end of the verse.

[71] But see the view of Milik and Puech, addressed in 2.2.6 above. We do not share their opinion that parts of 4Q540 and/or 4Q541 may be linked with chapters 17 and 18.

[72] J. T. Milik, *The Books of Enoch: Aramaic Fragments from Qumrân Cave 4* (Oxford: Oxford University, 1976) 252-53.

[73] See especially 16:3, and the discussions offered by Schnapp, *Testamente*, 34; Becker, *Untersuchungen*, 284-86; Haupt, "Testament," 102-3.

[74] See J. T. Milik, "Milkî-ṣedeq et milkî-rešaʿ dans les anciens écrits juifs et chrétiens," *JJS* 28 (1972) 119; and *The Books of Enoch*, 252-53, on 4Q180-181 and their resemblance to chapter 16.

[75] Of course, the lack of comparative evidence will severely limit our ability to tease out indications from this part of the document regarding Original *Testament of Levi*'s overall character. See 5.4.9 below.

5.2.13. *T. Levi* 18:1-14

Because of its content this is one of the most examined chapters in all of *T12P*.[76] With respect to its place in Original *Testament of Levi*, some say that it is a Christian composition based on disparate Jewish material,[77] while others think it was a Jewish composition that underwent Christian redaction.[78] The latter seems to be the case. While there are evident Christian additions,[79] they do not predominate, and the remainder of the passage can be easily understood as the prediction of the emergence of an ideal priest. Regrettably, we lack parallel Aramaic evidence, and the received Greek text is surely the end-result of a considerable history of transmission and adjustment. And so once more we must acknowledge that the earlier version of the testament probably contained the portion in question, but that we can know little more than the fact that the chapter announced the rise of a new ideal priest after the failure of the priesthood described in chapters 16 and 17.

5.2.14. *T. Levi* 19:1-5

We treat *Testament of Levi* 19 as a substantially Christian passage. Notwithstanding Slingerland's theory that the chapter shows the levitical hallmark of *T12P* as a whole,[80] and Milik's view that 4Q548 is a fragment of this chapter in Aramaic,[81] we agree with Marinus de Jonge

---

[76] See the literature listed in note 155 below.

[77] See, for example, de Jonge, *Testaments*, 90; A. J. B. Higgins, "The Priestly Messiah," *NTS* 13 (1966-1967) 224-25.

[78] Becker, *Untersuchungen* 291-300; Haupt, "Testament," 107-20; Schnapp, *Testamente*, 36-38.

[79] *T. Levi* 18:3c, 7c, 9b. *T. Levi* 18:3c says that the new priest will be magnified εως αναληψεως αυτου, "until his assumption." The notion lacks sufficient Jewish parallels to be considered anything but a Christian addition. At the end of v. 7 in the same chapter there is a small Christian addition (εν υδατι) that makes the glorification of the new priest an announcement of Jesus' baptism. In v. 9 appears a typical, late expansion that condemns Israel's ignorance vis-à-vis Jesus.

[80] H. Dixon Slingerland, "The Levitical Hallmark within the Testaments of the Twelve Patriarchs," *JBL* 103 (1984) 531-37. He claims that the first person plural response to Levi's exhortation to keep his word—compared with the third person plural response in the closing chapters of the other testaments—indicates that the authors are the sons of Levi who respond in faith to their (fore)father's plea. See the critical comments of Marinus de Jonge, "The Testament of Levi and 'Aramaic Levi,'" *RevQ* 13 (1988) 384, n. 65.

[81] For the fragment, see J. T. Milik, "4Q Visions de ꜥAmram et une citation d'Origène," *RB* 79 (1972) 90, where he first identified it tentatively as 4Q Visions of Amram[f]. Émile Puech, "Fragments d'un apocryphe de Lévi et le personnage eschatologique. 4QTestLévi[c-d](?) et 4QAJa," in *The Madrid Congress: Proceedings of the International Congress on the Dead Sea Scrolls, Madrid 18–21 March 1991* (eds. Julio Trebolle Barrera and Luis Vegas Montaner; Studies on the Texts of the Desert of Judah 11; Leiden: Brill, 1993) 2:491, n. 48, informs us that Milik has changed his mind, and

that in its present form it amounts to the Christian redactors' self-identification as "true servants of the true highpriest [Jesus] announced by Levi in chapter 18."[82]

5.3. The place of Original *Testament of Levi* in the LPT

Now that we have established in general the contours of Original *Testament of Levi* we may turn to an analysis of its relationship to the other texts of the LPT. While we are inclined by previous comparison of *Testament of Levi* with *Aramaic Levi* to think that the Aramaic text served as the principal source for Original *Testament of Levi*, that remains to be shown with greater confidence.

Most commentators assess the relationships among the three principal parts of the LPT with the assumption that *Aramaic Levi* contained two visions, and without the benefit of access to all of the *Aramaic Levi* material from Qumran. As a result they have been hampered in their attempts to sort out the relationship between Original *Testament of Levi* and the other texts of the tradition. Moreover, almost no one first established the parameters of Original *Testament of Levi* as a distinctive document which stood between *Aramaic Levi* and *T12P*. Therefore, with full access to the Qumran manuscripts, a different understanding of *Aramaic Levi*, and a new definition of Original *Testament of Levi*, we offer a fresh analysis of the relationship between Original *Testament of Levi* and its predecessors in the LPT.[83]

The following table forms the basis for the analysis. In the left column are the parts of Original *Testament of Levi*, and in the right column are the corresponding portions of *Aramaic Levi* and *Jub.* 30:1–32:9. Where Original *Testament of Levi* is associated only loosely with *Aramaic Levi* or *Jubilees*, the citations of the latter texts are preceded with "Cf." When *Aramaic Levi* or *Jubilees* virtually matches Original *Testament of Levi* in content and location, or differs in small, but occasionally still significant details, the entry is preceded by no markings. Of course, where there is no parallel material, the right column remains blank. A dagger on entries in the left column indicates that some verses underwent Christian redaction.

---

now thinks that the fragment reflects *Testament of Levi* 19. See 2.2.6 above for further discussion of Milik's identification.

[82] De Jonge, "Testament of Levi and 'Aramaic Levi'," 383-85, esp. 385.

[83] Neither in the following table, nor in the summary of its contents below, do we offer detailed notes indicating where previous scholars agree with and differ from our assessment; instead we mention only the most significant similarities and differences among the various views. Ulrichsen, *Grundschrift*, 177-86, provides very complete references which require no duplication here.

Original *Testament of Levi, Aramaic Levi,* and *Jub.* 30:1–32:9
Compared

Part One: *Levi's First Vision*

---

§1	2:3-4—Levi tends sheep at Abelmaul, reflects on the human condition, and prays for deliverance.	Cf. *Ar. Levi* supp. 1-19—Levi prays.
§2	2:5-6—Levi sleeps, he sees a high mountain, the heavens are opened, and an angel of God invites him to enter.	Cf. *Ar. Levi* supp. 21—Levi sleeps, he sees a mountain (?) reaching up; gates of heaven are mentioned, as is an angel.
§3	4:2-6†—The angel tells Levi that his prayer has been heard: he will be separated from unrighteousness; he will be made a servant of God in God's presence; he will be a heavenly luminary for Jacob and Israel; a blessing will be given to him and his descendants; he has received counsel and understanding; and his enemies will perish and his friends will be blessed.	Cf. *Ar. Levi* supp. 7, 11, 17—Levi prays for separation from evil, and that he be appointed to God's service; *Ar. Levi* 102—Levi tells his children that they are like the sun and stars; *Jub.* 31:15—Levi's descendants will instruct Jacob and Israel; *Ar. Levi* 8, 10—Isaac blesses Levi, and his father and brothers bless him; *Jub.* 31:13—Isaac tells Levi that he will receive a blessing; *Ar. Levi* supp. 8—Levi prays for counsel, wisdom, knowledge, and strength; *Jub.* 31:17—Isaac tells Levi that his opponents will be cursed and his friends blessed.
§4	5:1-2—The angel opens the gates of heaven so that Levi sees the temple and God upon a throne of glory; God announces that he has given Levi the blessings of the priesthood.	Cf. *Ar. Levi* supp. 21—Levi sees the gates of heaven open; *Ar. Levi* 4a, 6, 18—Angels and Isaac tell Levi that he will be a priest, and enjoy the first fruits, and that he is close to God's holy ones.

§5	5:3-4—The angel takes Levi to earth to avenge Dinah's rape, and Levi recalls that the deed is recorded in the heavenly tablets.	Cf. *Ar. Levi* 1-3 and *Jub.* 30:1-4—Accounts of the sack of Shechem; *Jub.* 30:12, 19, 23—Levi's deeds are recorded in the heavenly tablets; *Ar. Levi* 4—Mention of a kingdom of the sword.
§6	5:5-6—Levi asks the angel's name and the angel replies.	
§7	5:7–6:2—Levi awakens, blesses God and the angel, travels to Jacob (finding on the way a shield), and reveals nothing of the dream to anyone.	Cf. *Ar. Levi* 7a—Levi awakens from a vision; *Ar. Levi* supp. 20—After praying Levi travels to his father from a place called Abelmain; *Ar. Levi* 7b—After awakening from a vision Levi reveals nothing of it to anyone.

Part Two: *The Sack of Shechem*

§8	6:3-5—Levi uses Reuben and his father to trick the Shechemites, and he and Simeon slay Shechem and Hamor.	Cf.*Ar. Levi* 1-3 and *Jub.* 30:1-4—Accounts of the sack of Shechem.
§9	6:6–7:3—Jacob reproves Levi, and Levi excuses himself with an attack on the character of the Shechemites.	
§10	7:4—The family departs for Bethel.	Cf. *Ar. Levi* supp. 20—Levi travels to his father in Bethel after prayer.

Part Three: *Levi's Second Vision*

§11	8:1—A second vision commences.	Cf. *Ar. Levi* supp. 21—A vision commences.

§12	8:2-3—Seven men invest Levi with the garments of the priesthood and command him and his descendants to be priests forever.	Cf. *Ar. Levi* 6—Angels tell Levi that they have made him a priest forever; cf. *Ar. Levi* 7—Seven angels (?) depart from Levi; cf. *Ar. Levi* 48-49, 51—Isaac tells Levi he and his seed will be priests forever.
§13	8:4-10—The angels invest Levi with the priesthood a second time.	Cf. *Ar. Levi* 6—Angels tell Levi that they have made him a priest forever.
§14	8:11a, 16-17—The angels tell Levi that he and his descendants will enjoy the good produce of Israel, and eat at the table of the Lord, and that high priests, judges, and scribes will come from his seed.	Cf. *Ar. Levi* 99—Levi tells his children that they will be rulers, judges and magistrates; *Jub.* 31:15-16—Isaac tells Levi that his children will be rulers, judges and messengers and eat at the table of the Lord; cf. *Ar. Levi* 4—The angels tell Levi his seed will enjoy the produce of Israel.
§15	8:18-19—Levi awakens, recognizes the similarity between the two visions, and tells no one.	*Ar. Levi* 7—Levi awakens, is amazed that he should have a vision, and tells no one.

Part Four: *Levi with Isaac and Jacob*

§16	9:1-2a—Levi, Judah, and Jacob go to Isaac, and Isaac blesses Levi.	*Ar. Levi* 8—Levi and his family go to Isaac, and Isaac blesses Levi; *Jub.* 31:1-32—Levi and his family go to Isaac, and Isaac blesses Levi and Judah.
§17	9:2b—The family sets out for Bethel, and Isaac declines to accompany them.	*Jub.* 31:27—The family sets out for Bethel, and Isaac declines to accompany them.

§18	9:3-4—Jacob has a vision concerning Levi and his appointment to the priesthood, and he pays his tithes through Levi.	*Ar. Levi* 9-10—Jacob makes tithes through Levi, and ordains him as a priest; Levi makes sacrifice for his father, blesses his father and brothers, and they bless him; *Jub.* 32:2-9—Jacob tithes all of his possessions, including Levi as a servant of God, and Levi makes Jacob's offerings to fulfill his vow.
§19	9:5—The family travels to Isaac.	*Ar. Levi* 11—The family travels to Isaac.

Part Five: *Isaac's Priestly Instructions for Levi*

§20	9:6-14—Isaac instructs Levi in cultic matters.	*Ar. Levi* 13-61—Isaac instructs Levi in cultic matters

Part Six: *Levi's Life History*

§21	11:1–12:4—Levi recalls the birth of his children.	*Ar. Levi* 62-77—Levi recalls the birth of his children.
§22	12:5—Levi recites the key events of his lifetime.	*Ar. Levi* 78-80—Levi recites the key events of his lifetime.
§23	12:6-7—Levi says his children are a third generation, and indicates that Joseph died in his one hundred and eighteenth year.	*Ar. Levi* 81-82a—Levi says that he lived one hundred and thirty-seven years, that he saw a third generation, and that in his one hundred and eighteenth year (in which Joseph died), he called his children together to instruct them.

Part Seven: *Levi's Wisdom Speech*

§24	13:1-9—Levi instructs his children on the value of wisdom and learning and on their relationship to the law of God.	*Ar. Levi* 82b-101—Levi instructs his children on the value of wisdom and learning.

Part Eight: *Levi's Predictions for His Children*

§25 14:1–15:4†—Levi warns his children regarding the future of the priesthood.	Cf. *Ar. Levi* 102-106—Levi foretells his descendants' varied future.

Part Nine: *The Seven Weeks and Seven Jubilees of the Priesthood*

§26 16:1–17:11—Levi describes the seven weeks and seven jubilees of the priesthood	No extant *Aramaic Levi* material; however, cf. 4Q540?[84]

Part Ten: *Prophecy of the New Priest*

§27 18:1–14†—Levi describes the coming of a messianic priest.	No extant *Aramaic Levi* material; however, cf. 4541?[85]

The close relationship between Original *Testament of Levi* and *Aramaic Levi* is apparent. First, from the standpoint of structure, they are virtually the same.[86] Both contain two principal parts: an account of events in Levi's life (*T. Levi* 2:3-6; 4:2–9:14; 11:1–12:7; *Ar. Levi* 1-81),[87] and Levi's speeches regarding wisdom and the future of his children and of the priesthood (*T. Levi* 13:1–15:4; *Ar. Levi* 82-106).[88] Second, although the first part of Original *Testament of Levi* differs from *Aramaic Levi* by the addition of a new vision (*T. Levi* 2:5–5:7) and the transfer and redaction of the prayer,[89] the new dream seems to have been composed from individual elements taken from *Aramaic Levi*'s vision, prayer, and speech.[90] Third, from the end of Levi's second vision in Original *T. Levi* 8:19, to Levi's warnings to his children in Original *T. Levi* 14:1–15:4, where *Aramaic Levi* breaks off, Original *Testament of Levi* closely parallels *Aramaic Levi*.[91] In spite of small differences that reflect the specific exegetical interests of

---

[84] Émile Puech, "Fragments d'un apocryphe de Lévi," 490. For a more extensive discussion of the possible relationship between this Qumran manuscript and *Aramaic Levi* and *Testament of Levi*, see 2.2.6.

[85] Ibid.

[86] Haupt, "Testament," 7, 84-85.

[87] See §§1-23.

[88] See §§24-25.

[89] The prayer is mentioned only twice (2:3; 4:2), and it appears before the Shechem episode, rather than after it as in *Aramaic Levi*.

[90] See §§2-7. Parts of Original *Testament of Levi*'s second dream also appear in *Aramaic Levi*'s single vision and Levi's wisdom speech; see §§11-15.

[91] See §§16-25.

Original *Testament of Levi*'s author,[92] the broad sweep of the narrative is identical in both documents. This striking parallel in content and order contrasts sharply with *Jubilees*, which apparently contained nothing more after Levi's encounter with Jacob. In short, Original *Testament of Levi*'s author knew and followed the pattern established in *Aramaic Levi*, and even used elements of *Aramaic Levi* to forge the new material he composed for his own work.

One could argue that the preceding observations require only that the author of Original *Testament of Levi* relied on a source that was also known by *Aramaic Levi*'s author.[93] Yet there is strong evidence that it was precisely some form of *Aramaic Levi* that inspired the author. In *Ar. Levi* 78b-79a the reader is told that Levi slew the Shechemites at eighteen, and was made a priest at nineteen. *T. Levi* 12:5 provides the same order of events, and even appears to be a nearly verbatim reproduction of the older passage.[94] Yet according to the narrative order of Original *Testament of Levi*, Levi became a priest before he sacked Shechem (cf. 4:2; 5:2 and 6:3-4). The author of Original *Testament of Levi* preserved *Aramaic Levi*'s recital of the key events in Levi's life, but reversed that order by his own rewriting of the tradition. This internal contradiction indicates that Original *Testament of Levi*'s author used a source that had the narrative order implied in *T. Levi* 12:5, as well as that very verse. *Aramaic Levi* has both.

Meanwhile, comparison of Original *Testament of Levi* with *Jubilees* reveals that the latter was probably not a significant source for the former. Three times Original *Testament of Levi* preserves information that appears only in *Jub.* 30:1–32:9 among the LPT texts; but in each instance, except one, the material could also have been known from no-longer extant portions of *Aramaic Levi*, or it could have derived from the author's use of other sources. First, in Levi's two visions there are hints of Isaac's blessing for Levi (cf. 4:4a and *Jub.* 31:13; 4:3 and 31:15; 4:6 and 31:17; 8:16 and 31:17; and 8:17a and 31:15).[95] In fact, these are only faint traces of the blessing, and they are references that could have derived from many other texts and traditions known to the author.[96] Moreover, it is clear from *Ar. Levi* 8

---

[92] For discussion of the significance of the differences for understanding Original *Testament of Levi*, see 5.4.1-10 and 5.5 below.

[93] See especially Grelot, "Notes," 405-6. For the view that the common tradition was only oral see Becker, *Untersuchungen*, 69-105; and Ulrichsen, *Grundschrift*, 177-86.

[94] The Aramaic text has only the additional statement, ונמרת עבדי חמסא, "and I destroyed the doers of violence."

[95] See §§3 and 14.

[96] For instance, the reference in 4:4a to a blessing for Levi and his seed is also found in 1QSb 1 3; 3 5. 4:4 is a variation on part of Moses' blessing for Levi in Deut

that the Levi-apocryphon, upon which the author of *Aramaic Levi* relied, also contained Isaac's blessing, and that the author of *Aramaic
Levi* scattered parts of the blessing about in his own composition. Thus
acquaintance with *Aramaic Levi*, apart from *Jubilees*, can explain the
appearance of fragments of Isaac's blessing.

A second instance in which it appears *Jubilees* may have served
as a source is *T. Levi* 5:4. Levi recalls his destruction of Shechem, and
concludes, saying καθως γεγραπται εν ταις πλαξι των ουρανων, "as it is
written in the heavenly tablets." Similarly, *Jub.* 30:12, 19, and 23
mention that a record of Levi's deed was entered in the heavenly
tablets. While recording events in the heavenly tablets is a characteristic theme in *Jubilees*, it is not alien to *T12P*, nor to other Second
Temple literature.[97] Moreover, it is conceivable that *Aramaic Levi*
contained the phrase, but that the portion containing it has been lost or
damaged. The author of Original *Testament of Levi* need not have relied on *Jubilees* for this item.

The third occasion on which Original *Testament of Levi* seems to
be related to *Jubilees* is in 9:2b-3a, where Isaac declines to accompany
Jacob and his sons to Bethel.[98] Absent from *Aramaic Levi*, this appears
to be unique in *Jubilees*, although it may ultimately derive from the
Levi-apocryphon. At any rate, the significance of the parallel should
not be overrated. It is, after all, the sole piece of reasonable evidence
for the reliance of Original *Testament of Levi* on *Jubilees*. As such, it
suggests only that the author of Original *Testament of Levi* knew of
references to Isaac refusing to travel with the family back to Bethel,
perhaps from *Jubilees*, perhaps from a separate tradition,[99] or perhaps
from a more developed form of *Aramaic Levi* than the one preserved
in the Cairo Geniza fragments.[100]

Finally it may be added that Original *Testament of Levi* 17 and
18 bear some similarity to texts found at Qumran (4Q540 and 4Q541,
respectively). Nevertheless, the similarities are scant at best, and

---

33:8-11. Divine blessing for Levi's friends, and divine wrath for his enemies (4:6) are
also found in Deut 33:11. Mention in 8:16 of dividing the table of Lord is likely a
simple allusion to the priestly prerogative of the first fruits and tithes; cf. Num 18:8-
32; Deut 18:1-8. The reference to high priests, judges, and scribes may also derive
from *Ar. Levi* 99.

[97] For a list of the occurrences of the term, see R. H. Charles, *The Book of Enoch
or 1 Enoch translated from the Editor's Ethiopic Text* (Oxford: Oxford University,
1912) 91-92. Also see the recent discussion of the heavenly tablets in *Jubilees* by
Florentino García Martínez, "Las tablas celestes en el Libro de los Jubileos," in
Palabra y vida: Homenaje a José Alonso Díaz en su 70 cumpleaños (ed. A. Vargas-
Machuca y G. Ruiz; Madrid: Universidad Pontifica Comillas, 1984) 333-49.

[98] Cf. the discussion of this passage in Hultgård, *L'eschatologie*, 2:98.

[99] This is the view of Becker, *Untersuchungen*, 82-84; and Ulrichsen, *Grundschrift*, 181-82.

[100] Such is the position of Haupt, "Testament," 70-71.

claiming them as proof of a relationship between the Qumran manuscripts and Original *Testament of Levi* involves more speculation than is acceptable.[101] In the final analysis it is necessary to treat Original *Testament of Levi* 17–18 as creations of the document's author, even if they have antecedents in older, unknown texts.

So it is clear that there was a very close relationship between Original *Testament of Levi* and *Aramaic Levi*. In fact, one can say with confidence that the author of the testament used some text-form[102] of *Aramaic Levi* as his principal source: *Aramaic Levi* provided the overall structure for his work; when the author of the testament added a second vision, he used elements of the older book to create it; and he left proof of his reliance on *Aramaic Levi* by reproducing *Ar. Levi* 78b–79a unchanged, while contradicting its chronology with his adjustments to the first section of the work. As for *Jub.* 30:1–32:9, the author of Original *Testament of Levi* may have known it, but he did not use it to any significant extent.

5.4. The LPT in Original *Testament of Levi*

Now we may turn our attention to Original *Testament of Levi*'s place in the LPT. Doing so we focus on the ways in which the author adjusted *Aramaic Levi* as a measure of his intentions; after all, as we noted at the outset of this chapter, comparison of a text with its primary source is an excellent means of gaining insight into an author's purpose in writing. Hence we limit our comment on Original *Testament of Levi* to describing the content of the document, noting the differences between it and *Aramaic Levi*, and drawing from these observations some notion of the purpose of Original *Testament of Levi* as a text within the LPT. It is important to note, however, that attention will be given only to the broad variations between the two documents; closer comparison, although desirable, would necessitate greater comprehension of the exact contours of Original *Testament of Levi* than is possible.[103]

---

[101] For a fuller discussion of the relationship between 4Q540-541 and *Testament of Levi* 17–18, and of a possible connection between 4Q548 and *Testament of Levi* 19, see 2.2.6 above.

[102] That Original *Testament of Levi* relied on a slightly different textual tradition of *Aramaic Levi* than the one(s) reflected in the Cairo Geniza manuscript, the Qumran manuscripts, and the Mt. Athos text additions is evident from a comparison of *Ar. Levi* 71 and *T. Levi* 11:8. The two different explanations of Jochebed's name presuppose different *Vorlagen*; see Becker, *Untersuchungen*, 100; Grelot, "Le Testament araméen de de Lévi est-il de l'hebreu?" *REJ* 14 (1955) 91-99; Haupt, "Testament," 81-82; and Ulrichsen, *Grundschrift*, 185.

[103] For one recent attempt to be fairly precise in comparing part of *Testament of Levi* with *Aramaic Levi*, see, de Jonge, "The Testament of Levi and 'Aramaic Levi,'" 374-78.

5.4.1. *T. Levi* 2:3-6; 4:2–6:2: Levi's prayer and first vision[104]

This section of Original *Testament of Levi* is the most divergent from
Aramaic Levi. It adds a vision (2:5-6; 4:2–5:6), and all but removes
Levi's prayer. Only two fleeting references to the petition remain (2:4;
4:2).[105] As for the dream, its content varies considerably from what
we know of *Aramaic Levi's* vision. It consists of the angel's invitation
to Levi to enter the heavens (2:6); the announcement that Levi's prayer
for separation from unrighteousness and appointment to the priesthood
had been heard (4:2-6); Levi's entry into heaven itself where he sees
the temple and God upon a throne, and hears God say that he had been
given the blessings of the priesthood (5:1-2); the angel's command to
Levi, the new priest, to destroy Shechem (5:3-4); and an exchange between Levi and the angel regarding the angel's name (5:5-6).

The addition of the vision gave heavenly sanction to Levi's action
at Shechem, and depicted him as a priestly figure who also exercised
the power of the sword. While according to its reconstructed order
Aramaic Levi recounts Levi's zeal against Shechem and his piety in
prayer before God as the reasons for his elevation to the the priestly
office, Original *Testament of Levi* assures the reader that Levi's violent
behavior against Shechem was first commissioned by heaven, and accomplished only *after* Levi's elevation to the priesthood. This is also in
sharp contrast to the disparagement of the מלכות חרבא, "the reign of the
sword," and the elevation of the kingdom of the priesthood in *Ar. Levi*
4. Here sacerdotal and military power are apparently considered to be
of equal merit.

The notion that the vision was "new" can be questioned. It could
be argued once more that it and the later vision we encounter in
T. Levi 8:1-19 were original to *Aramaic Levi*, and this one was only
edited to meet the author's needs. Indeed, the opening of the vision
(2:5-6), and Levi's entry into heaven (5:1) resemble *Ar. Levi* supp. 21,
in that the passages share in common an angel, open heavens, and the
gates of heaven. Yet we have seen already that *Aramaic Levi* could
almost certainly have contained only one vision.[106] So what appears to
have been the case is this: the author of Original *Testament of Levi*
took on loan elements of the single vision in *Aramaic Levi*, and constructed from them the basic building blocks of a second, pre-Shechem
vision for his own work. We can see this especially with respect to the

---

[104] For discussion of this passage see Becker, *Untersuchungen*, 257-65; Charles,
Testaments, 26-40; Haupt, "Testament," 8-23, 27-49; Hollander and de Jonge,
Commentary, 132-34, 136, 140-45; Hultgård, *L'eschatologie*, 2:95-96; G. W. E.
Nickelsburg, "Enoch, Levi, and Peter: Recipients of Revelation in Upper Galilee,"
JBL 100 (1981) 588-90; Ulrichsen, *Grundschrift*, 187-94.

[105] See Greenfield and Stone, "Two Notes," 157-58, for an affirmation of the
connections between the testament and the Aramaic prayer.

[106] See 2.2.5 and 2.3.

beginning of the vision. The contents of 2:5-6; 5:1, key introductory elements of the only vision in *Aramaic Levi*, were borrowed from the original single vision to provide a beginning for this one. Indeed, while there were eventually seven angels in *Aramaic Levi*'s vision (*Ar. Levi* 7; cf. Original *Testament of Levi* 8), here only the one angel-guide mentioned in the introduction to the original dream ever materializes (*Ar. Levi* supp. 21; cf. *T. Levi* 2:5).[107] Similarly, while Levi is described as leaving the site of his prayer, Abelmain, *before* dreaming in *Aramaic Levi* (*Ar. Levi* supp. 20),[108] to distinguish this dream from the second he is forced by the narrator of Original *Testament of Levi* to remain in that place for the completion of this new vision (*T. Levi* 2:3).[109] And as the exegetical basis of Mal 2:4-7 for the single vision of *Aramaic Levi* appears mostly in its introduction, so it turns up here, in the first vision of Original *Testament of Levi*, but is absent from the second vision.[110] Finally, while the single vision of *Aramaic Levi* ends in a fulsome fashion, replete with Levi's exclamation of surprise and emphatic statement that he never revealed it to anyone, this vision ends abruptly, as though its author lacked the equivalent resources for its completion he had for its introduction. As it turns out, he left them for the completion of the second vision.[111]

Meanwhile, there is one element of this vision—certainly its central element—which sets it decisivley apart from anything that might have appeared in *Aramaic Levi*, and marks it as a new composition. It is the divine mandate that Levi avenge his sister's rape, coupled with elevation to the priesthood. It must be an innovation from the author of Original *Testament of Levi*, and could not have been in the single vision in *Aramaic Levi*, since we know that the latter dream *followed* the episode at Shechem.

---

[107] Kugel, "Levi's Elevation," 27, says that, among other things, the mention of a single angel in *Ar. Levi* supp. 21, compared with seven beings in *Ar. Levi* 7, is a distinction between two visions in *Aramaic Levi*. However it is precisely at the point of saying "one angel" that 4Q213 1 ii breaks off, leaving us uncertain as to whether the text would have gone on to enumerate more angels.

[108] See 3.1.3 for our discussion of *Ar. Levi* supp. 20, and the probability that Levi was at Bethel on the occasion of his dream.

[109] In fact, the place name is changed from Abelmain in *Aramaic Levi* to Abelmaul in *Testament of Levi*. Ulrichsen, *Grundschrift*, 179, notes the different locations in *Aramaic Levi* and *Testament of Levi*, but concludes only that therefore *Aramaic Levi* and *Testament of Levi* may not be drawn too closely into relationship with one another. Kugel, "Levi's Elevation," 60, offers another explanation, suggesting that in *Aramaic Levi* the place name serves to distance what he posits as a first dream from the second, and the change to Abelmaul in *Testament of Levi* functions to put Levi closer to the scene of the action that follows. On the latter point he is probably correct.

[110] See 3.1.3. For the significance of the lack of evidence for an exegetical basis for the second vision of *Testament of Levi*, see 5.4.3 below.

[111] See 5.4.3 below.

The reasoning behind Original *Testament of Levi*'s reduction of Levi's prayer to little more than a cipher is less transparent. However, if Original *Testament of Levi* turns out to be a document that aimed, like this section, to legitimate simultaneous possession of military *and* priestly powers, then a possible answer is that the prayer undermined that aim. By portraying Levi as especially zealous for the priestly office, the petition enfeebles the impact of the purely divine legitimation of his elevation communicated by the first vision. Inclusion of the prayer would make it appear that Levi coveted the office for himself, thus compromising the notion that he was appointed to the priesthood purely on God's initiative. Another possibility is that the prayer's emphasis on purity issues was objectionable to Original *Testament of Levi*'s author. Marinus de Jonge has noted that, while the prayer concerns itself with impurity, *T. Levi* 2:3-4; 4:2-6 lack that interest, expressing only Levi's desire to be separated from evil.[112] A reduced emphasis on purity—a prominent issue in *Aramaic Levi*—is also evident in Original *Testament of Levi*'s appropriation of Isaac's priestly instructions.[113] Of course, yet another explanation of the prayer's diminution in Original *Testament of Levi* is suggested by Milik's judgment of the author of Original *Testament of Levi* as an abbreviator of sources.[114]

5.4.2. *T. Levi* 6:3–7:4: The Shechem episode[115]

This passage narrates Levi and Simeon's act of revenge at Shechem for the rape of Dinah, Jacob's anger over the murder of the just-circumcised Shechemites, Levi's acknowledgement of a measure of guilt and his defense of the action taken, and the departure of the family for Bethel.

Due to the tattered condition of the Cairo Geniza manuscript of *Aramaic Levi*, it is almost impossible to describe any differences, much less similarities, between the accounts of this incident that appear in Aramaic and Greek.[116] There is the odd appearance of Reuben in both texts (*Ar. Levi* 1, 3; *T. Levi* 6:3), suggesting a common source; yet the double-appearance of his name in *Aramaic Levi* exceeds what is known

---

[112] De Jonge, "Notes," 255.

[113] See 5.4.5 below.

[114] Milik, "Testament," 406.

[115] Baarda, "The Shechem Episode," 11-73; Becker, *Untersuchungen*, 269-70; Charles, *Testaments*, 40-42; John J. Collins, "The Epic of Theodotus and the Hellenism of the Hasmoneans," *HTR* 73 (1980) 91-104; Haupt, "Testament," 23-27; Hollander and de Jonge, *Commentary*, 146-49; Hultgård, *L'eschatologie*, 2:96-97; James Kugel, "The Story of Dinah in the *Testament of Levi*," *HTR* 85 (1992) 1-34; R. Pummer, "Genesis 34 in Jewish Writings of the Hellenistic and Roman Periods," *HTR* 75 (1982) 177-85; and Ulrichsen, *Grundschrift*, 194.

[116] See the discussion of the manuscript in 2.2.2.

from Original *Testament of Levi*. Meanwhile, the older text is more intent on giving the details of the bargain for circumcision (*Ar. Levi* 2), and may give a fuller description of the attack itself (*Ar. Levi* 3). But in the end, the fragmentary remains simply prohibit substantial comparison.

In any case, Original *Testament of Levi's* account of the event provides some very good clues as to its purpose in the document. Particularly helpful in this regard are several details that transcend those known from the biblical account.[117] Levi claims in his speech of self-justification that he knew God destined Shechem for destruction because its inhabitants were inveterate rapists (6:8), persecutors of Abraham (v. 9a), abusers of livestock (v. 9b), and poor hosts to strangers in general, and specifically to an unknown home-born slave of Abraham named Jeblae (vv. 9c-10). James Kugel points out that this list of crimes can, for the most part, be traced to existing biblical motifs, the sum of which suggest that what is taken aim at here is—surprisingly—not the individual act of Shechem against Dinah, Shechem's foreignness, or even the threat of exogamy, but the moral turpitude and generally objectionable character of the Shechemites, and of the broader group to which they belonged, namely all Canaanites.[118] This collection of invectives against and judgments on Shechem (and Canaan in general) suggests that the author was concerned to denigrate the reputation of the Shechemites and of all Canaanites and to demonstrate that they were deserving of the treatment they received. Thus it is possible that the passage reflects the well-known negative perception of Shechem on the part of Hellenistic-era Jews in Judea, and an interest in

---

[117] For a complete treatment of these details see Kugel, "The Story of Dinah," passim. While we agree with Kugel that most of the details can be traced to imaginative exegesis of curious turns in the biblical text, we would add, as we do in what follows, that some of them were developed or adopted by the author of our text for reasons extending beyond sheer exegetical interests. At the same time some other details are no doubt present in the testament because they simply answered questions posed by biblical statements or silences. For instance, Kugel is almost certainly correct in his view that Levi is said to have killed Shechem while Hamor was left to Simeon (*T. Levi* 6:4-5) because Gen 49:6 states that each one killed *a* man (12-15; cf. Theodotus in Eusebius, *Praeparatio Evangelica* 9.22.4-12).

[118] See Kugel, "The Story of Dinah," 18-22, for the passages he thinks serve as the scriptural foundation for Levi's speech. For instance, the rapacious character of all of Shechem is based on the reference to "they" in Gen 34:27; and the crime of persecuting Abraham, strangers, and livestock is connected to Gen 13:7-8, read in conjunction with Gen 34:30. It is in the latter instance that the accusation is broadened to include Canaanites in general. See also Kugel's explanation of the reference to Shechem as a city of fools (7:1-3), and his suggestion that it is a late entry into the list of reasons for Shechem's punishment reflecting an attempt to make sense of the view that the Samaritans—later inhabitants of the Shechem region—were the non-people and foolish nation of Deut 32:21 ("The Story of Dinah," 23-25; cf. Sir 50:26).

legitimating violent action taken against that city and region, and against other non-Jewish inhabitants of Canaan, without relying on themes of foreignness or exogamy.

5.4.3. *T. Levi* 8:1-11a, 16-19: Levi's second vision[119]

Chapter 8 records Levi's second vision in which he is twice invested with the accoutrements of priesthood by a group of angels, after which he is addressed regarding the character of the office and his descendants' role within it. He then awakens, recalls the first dream and its likeness to this one, and tells the reader that he told no one of what he had experienced.

Once more, comparison of Original *Testament of Levi* with *Aramaic Levi* is difficult due to the fragmentary condition of the surviving *Aramaic Levi* manuscripts.[120] Nevertheless, the following can be noted. The texts are similar in that both mention seven angels (*T. Levi* 8:2; *Ar. Levi* 7), each announces Levi's elevation to the priesthood (*T. Levi* 8:3; *Ar. Levi* 6), in both Levi is rewarded with the desirable things of Israel (*T. Levi* 8:16; *Ar. Levi* 4), and each one has a fulsome conclusion which includes Levi's claim that he kept silent about his vision (*T. Levi* 8:19; *Ar. Levi* 7b).[121] Beyond these similarities, the destiny of Levi's descendants as high priests, judges, and scribes in *T. Levi* 8:17 is paralleled in the speech to his children in *Ar. Levi* 99.

There are also some clear differences between the two visions. This vision begins abruptly, lacking the introductory material found in *Ar. Levi* supp. 20 (cf. *T. Levi* 2:5-6; 5:1). Also absent is an exegetical justification for this nonbiblical dream (cf. *Ar. Levi* supp. 21; Mal 2:4-7; *T. Levi* 2:5-6; 5:1).[122] And just as the first vision in Original

---

[119] Some think this chapter is heavily Christianized; see, for example, de Jonge, *Testaments*, 44-46; and T. W. Manson, "Miscellanea Apocalyptica," *JTS* 48 (1947) 59-61, cited by de Jonge. Manson thinks that 8:4-10 describes a Syrian Christian baptism, emphasizing especially vv. 4-5. While it may be true that the Christian redactor of *Testament of Levi* meant the passage to be understood in that fashion, there is nothing that requires chapter 8 to be a Christian composition. Instead it appears to be the "description of the installation of a highpriest" (de Jonge, *Testaments*, 44; see especially his list of Old Testament texts that pertain to the actions undertaken on Levi's behalf in this chapter). Other comment on the text may be found in Becker, *Untersuchungen*, 270-80; Charles, *Testaments*, 42-46; Haupt, *Testament*, 49-66; Hollander and de Jonge, *Commentary*, 149-55; Hultgård, *L'eschatologie*, 2:97-98; Ulrichsen, *Grundschrift*, 194-96.

[120] See 2.2.1 and 2.2.2.

[121] Others link 8:18 with *Ar. Levi* 7a, but only because of Charles' inaccurate translation of the Aramaic text and its perpetuation in the scholarly literature; see the discussion of this passage in 2.2.5 and 3.1.3.

[122] Thanks are due James Kugel, "Levi's Elevation," 36, 41, for this insight. Of course we use it differently, assuming it to be further evidence that the introduction of a second vision came only with composition of Original *Testament of Levi* and the

Testament of Levi does not preserve any of the angelic speech against exogamy found in *Aramaic Levi*, this one lacks it also. Similarly, as Original *Testament of Levi*'s first vision promoted Levi's role as a bearer of weapons (5:2), this one omits the mild polemic against the dominion of the sword found in *Ar. Levi* 4b-5 (cf.*T. Levi* 8:16).

These observations lead to several conclusions. First, they underscore the suspicion that the two visions of Original *Testament of Levi* are made up, at least in part, of bits and pieces of the single vision in *Aramaic Levi*; the motif of seven angels, the appointment of Levi and his descendants as an eternal priesthood, and the promise of his enjoyment of every desirable thing in Israel are all elements taken from the vision in *Aramaic Levi*. And while the first vision in Original *Testament of Levi* took over the introduction to the original single vision from *Aramaic Levi* (including its scriptural foundation in the allusions to Mal 2:4-7) and had none of the earlier dream's concluding elements, this one has the concluding elements and none of the introductory material of the dream from the Aramaic text. Additionally, Original *Testament of Levi* uses material from other parts of *Aramaic Levi* to create the dream, drawing in a bit of Levi's speech to his children (see *T. Levi* 8:17 and *Ar. Levi* 99). Second, these observations reveal some of the interests of Original *Testament of Levi*'s author. He does not share the preoccupation with purity issues found in *Aramaic Levi*; the complete omission of the angelic speech against exogamy reflects not only disinterest in, but perhaps also suppression of that theme. And in Original *Testament of Levi* none of *Aramaic Levi*'s interest in mildly condemning the reign of the sword appears; in fact, the first vision gives quite the opposite impression.

Assuming the last statement to be true, can anything be said in general about the purpose of the vision? Without becoming involved in the question of the chapter's unity,[123] or becoming entangled in the de-

---

division of the earlier single vision into two dreams. Meanwhile, Kugel understands this datum in the context of his view that there were two visions in *Aramaic Levi*, that they were composed separately by different authors, and that they existed indpendently before being merged in *Aramaic Levi*. He explains the second vision's (*T. Levi* 8:1-19) lack of a biblical basis by saying it was composed with the first in mind, and so its author let the roots of the first in Mal 2:4-7 serve as the unspoken "scriptural justification" for his new dream. Our view that this absence of a scriptural foundation in the second vision results from the division of an original single vision into two dreams seems much more plausible than the notion that the second vision's author created his nonbiblical work to replace and be independent from an earlier dream-account, yet also to rely on that account's biblical roots.

[123] We do not share the view that one or the other of the investitures can be identified as Christian (*pace* Manson, "Miscellanea Apocalyptica," 59-61). Perhaps the most sensible assessment is that of Haupt, "Testament," 58-59, who says it is now impossible to tell which account is more original, and who draws attention to the precedent for doubling in Exodus 28–29. Haupt also calls attention to Ludin Jansen,

tails of the complex relationships among the various items of investiture in *T. Levi* 8:2, 4-10 and their Hebrew Bible references,[124] one can say at least the following. First, the structure of the passage sandwiches the angelic proclamation that Levi was made fully a priest between two acts of investiture, and probably followed the second installation with a description of the Levites' threefold destiny as high priests, priests, and Levites who served as scribes, judges, and guards (*T. Levi* 8:11b-15).[125] Thus, at the very least, the vision functioned to assure the reader regarding the legitimacy of Levi's appointment to the high priesthood, and of the grant of that office to his descendants.[126] And, following the Shechem incident and the dream before it that mandated Levi's priestly status and his military role, this dream serves to confirm his right to an office that might have been put in question by his violent behavior.[127]

"The Consecration in the Eighth Chapter of Testamentum Levi," *StHR* (=Supp. to *Numen*) 4 (1955) 356-65, who thinks that the double investiture is a portrayal of an enthronement ceremony (Haupt, "Testament," 57-58). However, both Jansen and Haupt admit that there is no evidence that the ritual of enthronement ever occurred during the time in which they place *Testament of Levi* 8, during the reign of John Hyrcanus I. For a very different view on the meaning of the double investiture, a perspective that is located in the Qumran-origins school of thought regarding *T12P*, see A. Caquot, "La double investiture de Lévi," *StHR* (=Supp. to *Numen*) 21 (1972) 156-61.

[124] See Hollander and de Jonge, *Commentary*, 151-53, for an exhaustive list of possible connections between chapter 8 and various articles of priestly clothing mentioned in the Old Testament, Apocrypha, and Pseudepigrapha.

[125] See discussion of this passage and its present Christian form in 5.2.6.

[126] Without greater certainty regarding the contents of the pre-Christian form of 8:11b-15, one should reject the view of R. H. Charles, *Testaments*, 45-46, that the entire passage was a legitimation of the elevation of John Hyrcanus I to the role of prince and priest.

[127] Kugel, "Levi's Elevation," 27-30, concludes that the very different emphases in content between the two visions and their lack of coordination are evidence that the dreams were composed separately, and "*not* . . . to be part of a single document" (29); he can thus call the first "Levi's Apocalypse" (30-32), and the second "Levi's Priestly Initiation" (36-39) This conclusion assumes that the content of *T. Levi* 2:5-5:7; *T. Levi* 8:1-19 reflects essentially what was in *Aramaic Levi* as well. Yet as we have seen, much of 2:5-5:7 must be attributed to later Christian redactors. When that material is left out of consideration and we posit the sort of first vision we have for Original *Testament of Levi* differences remain, but they are less intense and are attributable to the different aims of the two visions. As for the lack of coordination between the two, while one might hope for such, it is not necessary that some be evident in order to posit the "composition" of two visions by a single author. Anyway, coordination of a sort *is* evident in the complete introduction and truncated conclusion for the first vision and the abbreviated introduction and fulsome conclusion for the second, and in the presence of a scriptural foundation in the first and absence of any in the second. These data certainly suggest that the two visions originated from a single vision, the parts of

We must address here a question that in fact relates to both visions. If the goal was to legitimate simultaneous wielding of the sword and priestly power by means of a vision, why did the author not simply place the single vision of *Aramaic Levi* before the Shechem incident, and adjust it so that it reflected heavenly appointment to both roles? Apart from the obvious fact that the presence of two visionary appointments offers considerable assurance of the propriety of Levi's priestly elevation, it is noteworthy that the second focuses solely on the priestly office, as if to confirm that someone who has exercised violence on behalf of Israel's purity is especially deserving of such an elevated office and may legitimately hold it. While the first vision only served to *announce* Levi's appointment as a priest, the second enacts the elevation again, as if to say, the violent zealot for the Lord can also serve at the altar of sacrifice. And we may not forget that there is also a well-known tradition of two visions providing certainty that a promise will be fulfilled or a predicted action taken.[128]

Finally we note that there was already an exegetical hook in *Aramaic Levi* on which the author of Original *Testament of Levi* could hang the second vision. In *Ar. Levi* 7b וטמרת אף דן בלבי ולכל אינש לא גליתה he had a basis for a new dream. Rather than read it as do we, and as we think its original author meant it ("And I hid this very thing in my heart, and I did not reveal it to anyone"), he understood it as most modern commentators have, as an allusion to the occurrence of more than one dream.[129]

5.4.4. *T. Levi* 9:1-5: Isaac's blessing and Jacob's tithe[130]

After his vision Levi, Judah, and Jacob travel to Isaac where the last-mentioned blesses Levi in accord with Levi's vision. The father and sons return to Bethel where Jacob has a vision indicating that Levi is to possess the priesthood. The following morning he rises and pays his tithes through Levi.

---

which are now distributed between the two. And some form of coordination was also provided by the treatment of *Ar. Levi* 7 in Original *T. Levi* 8:19 (see below in this section).

[128] See *Testament of Naphtali* 6–7; Artemidorus, *Oneirocr.* 4:27; Herodotus I.107f (cited in Hollander and de Jonge, *Commentary*, 151). See also de Jonge, "Notes," 256, n. 30.

[129] We recall that even if the אף means "also," the sentence still may not be taken with great confidence to require a second dream. Levi could have referred to any number of things that he kept in his heart, things unknown to us due to the loss of text. See 2.2.5 above.

[130] Becker, *Untersuchungen*, 280; Charles, *Testaments*, 46-47; Haupt, "Testament," 66-71; Hollander and de Jonge, 155-57; Hultgård, *L'eschatologie*, 2:98-99; Kugel, "Levi's Elevation," 66-68, 72-73; Ulrichsen, *Grundschrift*, 180-82.

At this point the two accounts begin to run closely parallel with one another, at least in terms of the general narrative. Yet significant and telling details separate them. In this section Original *Testament of Levi* adds a chronological note (9:1), the statement that Isaac blessed Levi "according to all the words" of his visions (9:2a),[131] and Isaac's refusal to come to Bethel (9:2b).[132] It deletes Jacob's ordination, investiture, and consecration of Levi as a priest to the Most High God (*Ar. Levi* 9a), Levi's subsequent offerings, and his blessing of his father and brothers (*Ar. Levi* 9b), and Jacob's and his sons' blessing for Levi (*Ar. Levi* 10). Original *Testament of Levi* also introduces Jacob's vision through which he comes to know of Levi's priestly status (9:3; cf. *Ar. Levi* 9).

The differences of greatest interest are the addition of Jacob's dream and the elimination of Levi's ordination, investiture, and consecration to the priesthood by Jacob. Both moves function to preserve the divinely-ordained character of Levi's election. Presumably Jacob's vision was heaven-sent, and served as celestial confirmation of Levi's second dream. And by taking the act of election away from Jacob, the completely divine legitimation of Levi's elevation was preserved.[133]

A third change, omission of the fuller description of Levi's sacrificial activity on behalf of Jacob and the exchange of blessings, is not as easily explained. However, if Original *Testament of Levi* was intended, at least in part, as an apologetic for the exercise of sacerdotal and secular rule by a single individual, the focus had to be on legitimation of those roles, and not necessarily on their actual function; thus extended references to Levi's cultic actions were expendable. This seems to be confirmed by the treatment Original *Testament of Levi*'s author gave to the next major section of *Aramaic Levi*, Isaac's cultic instructions.

5.4.5. *T. Levi* 9:6-14: Isaac's cultic instructions for Levi[134]

T. Levi 9:6-14 gives a brief account of Isaac's comprehensive priestly instructions for Levi. Beginning with his affirmation of what the single angel had commanded Levi to do in the first vision, Isaac goes on to

---

[131] It appears that the author of Original *Testament of Levi* felt it necessary to add the statement to explain why Isaac blessed Levi, and to conform that blessing to the essential focus of the document—Levi's elevation to the priesthood.

[132] For a discussion of this last notice in Original *Testament of Levi* and *Jubilees*, see 5.3 above.

[133] In fact, one wonders whether Original *Testament of Levi* did not build parts of Levi's second vision from Jacob's acts. Unfortunately, due to the poor preservation of *Aramaic Levi*, that suspicion cannot be confirmed or denied.

[134] Becker, *Untersuchungen*, 280; Charles, *Testaments*, 47-48; Haupt, "Testament," 71-76; Hollander and de Jonge, *Commentary*, 155, 157-58; Hultgård, *L'eschatologie*, 2:99-101; Ulrichsen, *Grundschrift*, 182-84.

teach him how to make offerings, be they sacrifices, holocausts, voluntary offerings of the first fruits, or peace offerings. He also exhorts Levi to avoid impurity in matters of marriage, and to maintain proper cleanliness in the act of sacrifice. He concludes by indicating that Levi should use the proper kinds of wood for the sacrificial fire, present the appropriate beasts, see to the offering up of all first produce, and provide salt with all offerings.

At first sight the relationship between *T. Levi* 9:6-14 and *Ar. Levi* 13-61 seems very distant. Just the sheer difference in the size of each suggests vast dissimilarities between the two accounts. Yet closer examination reveals considerable similarities of structure: in large part the younger text turns out to be an abbreviation and simplification, but in several significant instances, also an expansion, of the older document.[135]

The first noteworthy expansion on *Ar. Levi* 13-61 appears in *T. Levi* 9:6. Levi states that Isaac was continually reminding him of the νομον Κυριου, καθως εδειξε μοι ο αγγελος του θεου, the "law of the Lord, just as the angel of the Lord had shown me." The phrase νομον Κυριου, the "law of the Lord," is to be distinguished from the νομον ιερωσυνης, the "law of the priesthood" (9:7). Levi's aside that he had received the law of the Lord from a single angel explains what law he meant. The singular ο αγγελος, "the angel," recalls Levi's first vision, where a single angel spoke the νομος Κυριου that was Levi's commission as priest and warrior. Thus Isaac is portrayed as knowing and approving of Levi's appointment to priestly and military roles.

A second expansion appears in *T. Levi* 9:7 which indicates that Isaac also taught Levi the νομον ιερωσυνης, the "law of the priesthood." The phrase parallels *Ar. Levi* 13b, דין כהונתא, "the law of the priesthood." However, added to the law of the priesthood are the qualifiers θυσιων, ολοκαυτωματον, απαρχων εκουσιου, σωτηριου, "of cereal offerings, burnt offerings, first fruits, and peace offerings." An addition to *Aramaic Levi*, the list was provided probably to fill out an incomplete set of instructions; as noted above, in spite of their length, Isaac's instructions in *Aramaic Levi* teach only the burnt offering and its accom-

---

[135] Becker, *Untersuchungen*, 87-93; and Ulrichsen, *Grundschrift*, 182-84, deny *Testament of Levi*'s dependence here on *Aramaic Levi*, saying once more that the two documents relied independently on a common Levi-tradition. Haupt, "Testament," 75, n. 51, rightfully expresses disbelief that such a position could be held in this regard. Yet he concludes that *T. Levi* 9:6-14 is understandable as a "Produkt der Kürzung einer aTL nahestehenden Quelle" (75). De Jonge, meanwhile, unequivocally stated his position, saying that "T.L. IX 7-14 is a bad extract from a source [*Aramaic Levi*] which gave Isaac's instructions in a fuller and more readable form" (*Testaments*, 40). As we indicate below, although de Jonge is correct that *T. Levi* 9:7-14 is an extract of the corresponding Aramaic material, he misses the point with his adjective "bad." In fact, it is a skillful extract of the earlier text.

paniments.[136] In contrast, the testament, although shorter on the whole, actually expanded Isaac's instructions so that they took on the appearance of a complete and practicable set of guidelines for cultic use.

The remaining portion of Isaac's instructions, *T. Levi* 9:9-14, is an outline-form abbreviation of *Ar. Levi* 13-47. *T. Levi* 9:9-10 summarize *Ar. Levi* 14-18;[137] 9:11 gives a summary of *Ar. Levi* 19-21; 9:12 abbreviates *Ar. Levi* 22-25a; 9:13 condenses *Ar. Levi* 25b-30; and 9:14 digests in one sentence *Ar. Levi* 31-47. In spite of the extensive abbreviation of the instructions in *Aramaic Levi*, virtually all of Isaac's cultic guidelines are summarized in these few verses. However, the concluding exhortation (*Ar. Levi* 48-50), the abbreviated set of instructions (*Ar. Levi* 51-57), and the final commendation (*Ar. Levi* 58-61) are omitted by Original *Testament of Levi*.[138]

The purpose of this passage in Original *Testament of Levi* vis-à-vis *Ar. Levi* 13-47 is clear. It is meant to encompass all of the instructions Isaac gave to Levi in *Aramaic Levi* without presenting them in their entirety. Not only that, it also supplements those instructions by indicating that Isaac did not restrict his guidelines to the burnt offering; he also taught Levi the art of making the other kinds of sacrifice (9:7). Furthermore, Isaac is depicted as exhorting Levi to fulfill his entire commission mandated by the first vision, that of being both priest and prince (9:6). So while Original *Testament of Levi*'s author was apparently not interested in the details of sacrifice, he did want to show his readers that such details were known by Levi, and by his descendants; this passage assured readers that they were competent in cultic matters. It also served notice that Levi's forefather in the faith knew and approved of his exercise of the power of the priesthood and of the sword.

---

[136] See 3.1.5.

[137] The single departure in content and theme on the part of *Testament of Levi* is the addition of the phrase, τουτο γαρ ενδελεχη εστιν και μελλει μιαινειν δια του σπερματος σου τα αγια, "for this will continue and will defile the holy things by your seed." It seems likely that this is a redactional pointer to chapter 10, as suggested by Hollander and de Jonge, *Commentary*, 157.

[138] See 3.1.5, n. 169, on the implications of this omission for understanding the apparently composite character of *Ar. Levi* 13-61.

5.4.6. *T. Levi* 11:1–12:7: Levi's life history[139]

These chapters provide the material in Original *Testament of Levi* closest to the surviving text of *Aramaic Levi*. Differences from *Ar. Levi* 62-81 are probably, for the most part, the result of Original *Testament of Levi*'s source text having undergone a long process of textual transmission.[140] Only in a few instances do the disparities amount to anything affecting the meaning of the text, and then in a very minor way. For instance, while *Ar. Levi* 65 indicates that Gershom's fate was to be cast out of the priesthood, *T. Levi* 11:3 says only that ουκ εσται εν πρωτη ταξει, "he would not be in the first rank." While Kohath's exalted status is indicated in *Ar. Levi* 67 with the promise that he would have a gathering of all the people to him, and that he and his seed would be the beginning of the priesthood,[141] in *T. Levi* 11:4-6 very different terms are used to express the same notion. In *Ar. Levi* 71 Jochebed's name is explained with the epithet, ליקר ילידת לי לכבוד לישראל, "For glory she was born to me, for glory for Israel." Meanwhile *T. Levi* 11:8 explains her name by saying simply, ενδοξος γαρ ην τοτε εν μεσω των αδελφων, "For I was renowned then in the midst of my brothers." Mention of the family's descent into Egypt in *Ar. Levi* 73a is omitted between *T. Levi* 11:8 and 12:1. Similarly, the explanation of Amram's name, preserved in *Ar. Levi* 76, is missing from Original *Testament of Levi*. Most conspicuous is the transfer of Levi's announcement that he lived to one hundred and thirty-seven years of age from just after the single-verse recital of the key events in Levi's life history (*T. Levi* 12:5; *Ar. Levi* 78-81a), to *T. Levi* 19:4, the conclusion of the testament. Taken together, these variations create

---

[139] T. Baarda, "Qehath—'What's in a name'," *JSJ* 19 (1988) 215-29; Becker, *Untersuchungen*, 282; Charles, *Testaments*, 50-51; P. Grelot, "Le Livre des Jubilés et le Testament de Lévi," in *Mélanges Dominique Barthélemy: études bibliques offertes a l'occasion de son 60e anniversaire* (eds. P. Casetti, O. Keel, A. Schenker; OBO 38; Göttingen: Vandenhoeck & Ruprecht, 1981) 110-33; Haupt, "Testament," 76-84; Hollander and de Jonge, *Commentary*, 161-64; Hultgård, *L'eschatologie*, 2:101-104; Ulrichsen, *Grundschrift*, 184-85.

[140] See, for example, the confusion already apparent within the *Aramaic Levi* textual tradition regarding the origin of Merari's name (*Ar. Levi* 69-70; see 3.1.6). Baarda, "Qehath," 228-29, probably makes too much of the differences he notes; they lead him to think that the author of *Testament of Levi* engaged in *Notarikon* exegesis in reflecting on Kohath's name. (For *Notarikon* exegesis, see H. L. Strack and G. Stemberger, *Introduction to the Talmud and Midrash* [Minneapolis: Fortress, 1992] 33.)

[141] Against Greenfield and Stone, "Remarks," 223-24; and Hollander and de Jonge, *Commentary*, 466, n. a, it is probable that the notice in the addition at Mt. Athos 18:2 that Kohath would also be the beginning of kings is a gloss; see further discussion above in 3.1.6.

only small differences between Original *Testament of Levi* and *Aramaic Levi* in the section describing Levi's life history.

Much more significant are the similarities, and chief among them is the parallel between *T. Levi* 12:5 and *Ar. Levi* 78-80. As noted above,[142] the two brief recitals of key events in Levi's life match the narrative order in *Aramaic Levi* and contradict the narrative order in Original *Testament of Levi*. Hence they demonstrate the reliance of the testament on *Aramaic Levi*.[143]

5.4.7. *T. Levi* 13:1-9: Levi's wisdom speech[144]

Here Levi recites a speech to his children encouraging them to learn and keep the law, indicating that its observance will keep them in good stead, be they in their own land or another. Moreover, when tragedy strikes or when captivity occurs, wisdom gained in fear of the Lord— that is understanding achieved by observance of the law—cannot be taken away. Anyone, says Levi, who teaches these things and does them will be enthroned with monarchs, just as was Joseph.

Unlike the previous two chapters, this one differs markedly in its details from the corresponding material in *Ar. Levi* 82-101. Nevertheless, there are significant repetitions of text from *Aramaic Levi* which support the view that Original *Testament of Levi*'s author used the speech from *Ar. Levi* 82-102 as source material for this chapter.[145]

In addition to considerable abbreviation of *Ar. Levi* 82-102, the author of *T. Levi* 13:1-9 made three significant changes in his source. First, the focus shifts from wisdom and its acquisition, to Torah and its study and enactment. The opening verse echoes Deut 4:29; 6:5; 10:12; 11:13, with Levi saying to his children εντελλομαι υμιν ινα φοβεισθε τον κυριον ημων εξ ολης καρδιας, "I command you to fear our Lord from

---

[142] See 5.3.

[143] Ibid.

[144] Becker, *Untersuchungen*, 282; Charles, *Testaments*, 52-53; Haupt, "Testament," 84-90; H. W. Hollander, *Joseph as an Ethical Model in the Testaments of the Twelve Patriarchs* (SVTP 6; Leiden: Brill, 1981) 57-62; Hollander and de Jonge, *Commentary*, 164-67; Hultgård, *L'eschatologie*, 2:104-105; Max Küchler, *Frühjüdische Weisheitstraditionen* (OBO 26; Göttingen: Vandenhoeck & Ruprecht, 1979) 491-99; M. Philonenko, "Paradoxes Stoïciens dans le Testament de Lévi," in *Sagesse et Religion* (ed. E. Jacob; Paris: Bibliothèque des centres d'études supérieures spécialés, 1979) 99-104; H. Dixon Slingerland, "The Nature of *Nomos* (Law) within the *Testaments of the Twelve Patriarchs*," *JBL* 105 (1986) 42; Michael Stone, "Ideal Figures and Social Context: Priest and Sage in the Early Second Temple Age," in *Ancient Israelite Religion* (eds. P. D. Miller, P. D. Hanson, and D. S. McBride; Minneapolis: Fortress, 1988) 578-79; Ulrichsen, *Grundschrift*, 185-86.

[145] Compare *T. Levi* 13:2 and *Ar. Levi* 88; 13:3-4 and 91; 13:5-6 and 87; 13:7 and 95; 13:9 and 90.

(your) whole heart." The verse concludes with Levi's exhortation to his children: πορευσθε εν απλοτητι κατα παντα τον νομον αυτου, "Walk in simplicity according to all his law." Then, adapting the command from *Ar. Levi* 88 that Levi's children teach their offspring reading and writing, *T. Levi* 13:2 adds the reason for doing so: ινα εχωσι συνεσιν εν παση τη ζωη αυτων, αναγινωσκοντες αδιαλειπτως τον νομον του θεου, "So that they may have understanding all their life, reading unceasingly the law of God" (cf. Deut 17:18-20). *T. Levi* 13:3 adapts the theme of *Ar. Levi* 91 that the wise person is never a stranger in strange places, and always a recipient of honor, by replacing wisdom with νομος, "law." Similarly, while *Ar. Levi* 91 says that many will flock to hear a sage's wisdom, *T. Levi* 13:4 states that many will serve the one who knows God's law so that they can ακουσαι νομον εκ του στοματος αυτου, "hear (the) law from his mouth." And even though *T. Levi* 13:5-9 shifts away from Torah-language, and exhorts righteous action (vv. 5-6) and the acquisition of wisdom in the fear of God (vv. 7-9), the preceding verses, with their emphasis on Torah, assure the reader that the author still has the law in mind.

The second noteworthy change *T. Levi* 13:1-9 made in adapting *Ar. Levi* 82-102 is the imposition of a structure on what appears at best to be a loosely organized piece of literature. *T. Levi* 13:1-4 exhorts study and learning of the law, and describes the consequences of doing so; 13:5-6 commands action in accordance with the law; and 13:7-9 takes up the theme of acquiring wisdom. The structure implies that right action and the acquisition of wisdom are rooted in knowledge of God's law.[146]

A third change is the transformation Joseph undergoes from *Ar. Levi* 90 to *T. Levi* 13:9. In the earlier document he was an example of the glory gained from seeking wisdom; in the later book he becomes a figure who wins a king's throne by teaching the wisdom of the law.[147]

Why did the author of Original *Testament of Levi* adapt the wisdom speech in this manner? Apparently he was interested in promoting the law, proving Levi's concern for it, and showing that its pursuit is appropriate to kings (cf. Deut 17:18-20), and that its keeping even wins them their seat of honor. And he argues forcefully for the view that Levi, his offspring, and all of his descendants could be expected to be deeply engaged with the study, practice, and love of Torah.

---

[146] See Küchler, *Weisheitstraditionen*, 492-93, for a similar structure.

[147] Hollander, *Joseph*, 61-62.

5.4.8. *T. Levi* 14:1–15:4: Levi's warnings to his children[148]

In this first section foretelling the future apostasy of his children Levi indicates that generations will corrupt the priesthood through various abuses, and that through their corruption the whole people of Israel will suffer greatly and the temple itself will be desecrated. In the end their demise will be a thing of joy to those oppose them.

This is the last section for which any *Aramaic Levi* text is preserved. Unfortunately, due to its very fragmentary condition and limited scope, comparison of *Ar. Levi* 102-106 with *T. Levi* 14:1–15:4 is problematic. The difficulty of comparison is exacerbated by the number of Christian elements in chapter 14.[149]

The only specific similarities that can be described include references to Enoch in *T. Levi* 14:1 and *Ar. Levi* 103; references to Levi's children as heavenly luminaries in *T. Levi* 14:3 and *Ar. Levi* 102; mention of Gentiles in *T. Levi* 14:4 and "the peoples" in *Ar. Levi* 102; and indication that the light of Levi's children will be darkened by their own misbehavior in *T. Levi* 14:4 and *Ar. Levi* 103. Otherwise *Ar. Levi* 102 preserves a general assault on the ways of Levi's children which, although in no way matching the specificity of *T. Levi* 14:5-8, parallels that passage's condemnation of Levi's descendants for ill-considered choices and action. Nothing in the remaining fragments of *Aramaic Levi* preserves material like *T. Levi* 15:1-4; however little should be made of this, since the extant remains of the parallel material in *Aramaic Levi* have become almost completely useless.

5.4.9. *T. Levi* 16–17: The seven weeks and seven jubilees of the priesthood[150]

In spite of the evident Christian additions to this material it is clear that at one time it recited the seventy weeks and seven jubilees of the priesthood with the aim of describing in a diachronic fashion what Levi circumscribed in chapters 14 and 15—the decline of the priesthood to a dismal nadir. Unfortunately it is now very difficult, if not impossible, to declare what events the author referred to with each passing period. In fact, the author may never have intended an exact referent for each statement; instead he may have sought to deliver simply the overall im-

---

[148] Becker, *Untersuchungen*, 283-87, 300-304; Charles, *Testaments*, 52-59; Haupt, "Testament," 90-100; Hollander and de Jonge, *Commentary*, 167-71; Hultgård, *L'eschatologie*, 2:105-106; Marinus de Jonge, "Levi, the Sons of Levi," 513-23; Ulrichsen, *Grundschrift*, 199-201.

[149] See 5.2.11 above.

[150] Becker, *Untersuchungen*, 287-90; Charles, *Testaments*, 60-62; Haupt, "Testament," 105-106; Hollander and de Jonge, *Commentary*, 173-77; Hultgård, *L'eschatologie*, 2:118-121; Ulrichsen, *Grundschrift*, 202-204.

pression of a priesthood that would become ever more corrupt with the passage of time.

Original *Testament of Levi* 16–17 preserves text that is not attested in *Aramaic Levi*. Although Milik and Puech claim that the Aramaic fragment of 4Q540 reflects *T. Levi* 17:8-10, and connect it with *Aramaic Levi*, their arguments are not convincing.[151] While there may at one time have been something like this chapter in *Aramaic Levi*, we have no reliable evidence to support an assumption in that regard. Hence we proceed on the view that chapters 16 and 17 were part of Original *Testament of Levi*.

While Original *Testament of Levi* 16 is very general in its description, chapter 17 is considered by some to be a history of the Aaronite priesthood,[152] which culminates with the pollution of the clergy in the seventh jubilee, one that is described with special reference to its fifth and seventh periods of weeks.[153] Some consider the seventh jubilee a description of the hellenizing priests on the eve of the Maccabean revolt.[154] If this is so, and if one accepts that *Aramaic Levi* did not contain material similar to chapters 16 and 17, the author of Original *Testament of Levi* has changed his source in a new, and significant way: he has added a section that describes the decline of the priesthood since its glorious beginning in Levi until it reached its low in the reign of the apostate high priests Jason, Menelaus, and Alcimus. With the addition of one chapter he has set the stage for the next supplement, announcement of a new, Levi-like priest.

---

[151] See 2.2.6.

[152] Benedikt Otzen, "Die neugefundenen hebräischen Sektenschriften und die Testamente der zwölf Patriarchen," *ST* 7 (1953) 146-47.

[153] For the view that chapter 17 is a single "apocalypse" that includes seven jubilees, with the last being described in greatest detail in 17:10-11, see Milik, "Milkî-ṣedeq et milkî-rešaʿ," 123; and "*The Books of Enoch* (Oxford: Oxford University, 1976) 252-53.

[154] See John J. Collins, "The Testaments of the Twelve Patriarchs," in *Jewish Writings in the Second Temple Period* (ed. Michael Stone; CRINT II, 2; Philadelphia: Fortress, 1984) 343.

5.4.10. *T. Levi* 18:1-14: The new priest[155]

In the final chapter the author announces through Levi the dawn of a new age with the rise of a new priest. In nearly messianic terms his rule is described; he will bring peace and prosperity to a world marred by the preceding generations of apostate priests.

As is the case with chapter 17, it seems wise to resist the temptation of positing an *Aramaic Levi Vorlage* for this chapter. Although Puech thinks that 4Q541 resembles Original *Testament of Levi* 18, the similarities are so few and general that one should reject his claim of having identified an Aramaic precursor.[156]

Meanwhile, a plausible case can be made that the author of Original *Testament of Levi* composed the chapter, using themes and phrases already developed elsewhere in his own work. Peter Macky has pointed out that the notion of a πνευμα συνεσεως, a "spirit of understanding" (18:7) turns up already in 2:3;[157] the opening of the heavens in 18:6 appears also in 2:6; the notion of a figure becoming like an astral light (18:4) is known from 4:2; and the claim that the new priest will ανοιξει τας θυρας του παραδεισου, "open the gates of paradise"

---

[155] The questions at issue in this chapter are numerous, and the literature responding to them is immense. We must forego grappling with any of the critical questions, apart from the chapter's relationship to *Aramaic Levi*, and we can cite only a representative sample of the secondary literature dealing with it. A fuller treatment must await another study. See Becker, *Untersuchungen*, 291-300; M. Black, "The Messiah in the Testament of Levi XVIII," *ET* 60 (1948-1949) 321-22; F.-M. Braun, "Les Testaments des XII Patriarches et le problème de leur origine," *RB* 67 (1960) 516-49; Charles, *Testaments*, 62-67; M.-A. Chevallier, *L'esprit et le messie dans le bas judaïsme et le Nouveau Testament* (Paris: Presses universitaires de France, 1958) 126-30; Haupt, "Testament," 106-120; Higgins, "The Priestly Messiah," 229-30; Hollander and de Jonge, *Commentary*, 177-82; Hultgård, *L'eschatologie*, vol. 1, *Interprétation des textes* (Acta Universitatis Upsaliensis; Historia Religionum 6; Uppsala: Almqvist & Wiksell, 1977) 268-70, 287-90; Marinus de Jonge, "Two Messiahs in the Testaments of the Twelve Patriarchs?" in *Tradition and Re-Interpretation in Jewish and Early Christianity* (eds. J. W. Henten, P. T. van Rooden, J. W. Wesselius; Leiden: Brill, 1986) 157-59; M.-J. Lagrange, *Le judaïsme avant Jésus-Christ* (Paris: Libraire Lecoffre, 1931) 122-30; Peter Macky, "The Importance of the Teaching on God, Evil and Eschatology for the Dating of the Testaments of the Twelve Patriarchs" (Ph.D. diss., Princeton, 1969) 336-49; J. R. Porter, "The Messiah in the Testament of Levi XVIII," *ET* 61 (1949-1950) 90-91; André Dupont-Sommer, *Nouveaux aperçus sur les manuscrits de la mer morte* (Paris: Maisonneuve, 1953) 78-83; R. A. Stewart, "The Sinless High Priest," *NTS* 14 (1967-1968) 128-29, 135; Ulrichsen, *Grundschrift*, 204-205; B. Vawter, "Levitical Messianism and the New Testament," in *The Bible in Current Thought* (ed. John L. McKenzie; New York: Herder, 1962) 90-92.

[156] See 2.2.6.

[157] Of course, it is also possible that the author simply relied on Isa 11:2 for the phrase.

(18:10), recalls 5:1.[158] All of these parallels are within another section of Original *Testament of Levi*, Levi's first vision, that has proved to be a new composition of the author, and was not borrowed from *Aramaic Levi*. Indeed, a successive reading of the first vision in *T. Levi* 2:5-6; 4:2–5:6 and Original *Testament of Levi* 18 shows that just as in his dream future glory was promised to Levi and his children, the final chapter is Levi's prediction of the fulfillment of those promises in one of his descendants.

What does Original *Testament of Levi* 18 provide that exceeds the material already found in *Aramaic Levi*? What is the aim of the additional material? The obvious answer to the first question is that chapter 18 adds the expectation of a unique priest, whose advent will herald the beginning of a new age that is qualitatively different from the period immediately preceding.[159] As for the aim of the chapter, Original *Testament of Levi* 18 is intended as Levi's ancient pledge that a new priesthood—one in keeping with the glorious beginning the office had in him—will commence after the office's long decline.

5.5. The date and purpose of Original *Testament of Levi*

What do all of these differences between *Aramaic Levi* and Original *Testament of Levi* indicate about the date and purpose of the latter text? The chief difference—the addition before the Shechem incident of a second vision in which Levi is commissioned as a priest and a warrior—strongly indicates that the author's principal aim was to legitimate the simultaneous exercise of the power of the priesthood and of the sword, and to offer a defense of the possession of the priestly office. Among the proposed dates for Original *Testament of Levi*, the

---

[158] Macky, "Importance," 365. Macky also draws the references to a voice, Abraham, and Isaac in 18:6 into connection with 9:2. However, the text of 18:6 is disputed, and is probably best rendered as "a voice of a father, as from Abraham, Isaac's father," with Isaac having been added only because of the patriarchal context (Hollander and de Jonge, *Commentary*, 177). On that reading Macky's suggestion is without foundation.

[159] There has been a lively debate regarding the character of the new priest. Some think that he is a Jewish messianic figure (e.g., Porter, "The Messiah in the Testament of Levi XVIII"), while others opine that he is only a unique priestly figure (e.g., Stewart, "The Sinless High Priest"). Of course, still others think he is the Christian Messiah (de Jonge, "Two Messiahs?"). Since we accept the Jewish origin of the text, the last option is not acceptable, at least prior to *Testament of Levi*'s Christian redaction. Of the first two, we find the second the more plausible explanation of the evidence. M.-J. Lagrange's study (*Le judaïsme avant Jésus-Christ*, 122-30) notes that it was rather common to use elevated terminology in praise of someone who was in power—and it is Lagrange's contention that this document was meant to glorify the Hasmoneans—and so one ought to resist interpreting this chapter as prophecy of a messiah. In the absence of further evidence in the rest of Original *Testament of Levi* for messianic pretensions, it seems best to accept Lagrange's cautionary warning.

suggestion that best fits this observation is Detlev Haupt's view that it was composed to legitimate the rule of John Hyrcanus I.[160] While Haupt's choice of Hyrcanus' reign as the time of Original *Testament of Levi*'s origin may be too narrow in its scope, it is plausible to think that the book has some relationship to the broader phenomenon of the Hasmonean exercise of priestly and princely power.[161] Do the other changes made by the author of Original *Testament of Levi* support the notion?

We cannot be certain that the caricature of the Shechemites, and of Canaanites in general, appeared first in Original *Testament of Levi*, but if it did, it seems that the telling of the tale was aimed at legitimating an action taken against the northern neighbors, and/or against other non-Jewish inhabitants of Canaan. Moreover, as James Kugel has noted, unlike other texts in this tradition of recounting the violence at Shechem, the justification in *Testament of Levi* does not rest on countering the threat of exogamy or on the foreignness of Shechem, but on biblically-based notions of the flaws in the Shechemite/Canaanite character.[162] Indeed, John Hyrcanus I, a treaty partner with Rome and an employer of mercenaries—thus also one unlikely to defend violent action against foreigners because of their status or the threat of intermarriage with them—defeated Shechem around 128 BCE,[163] and some years later, perhaps between 113 and 107 BCE, he conquered Samaria.[164] And throughout his period of influence he campaigned against non-Jewish neighbors to expand his territory. Any or all such military actions may have been associated with the recollection of Genesis 34. And although one must acknowledge that the account, based as it is on a biblical story, may not allude to anything more than that, the vitriol reserved for Shechemites in Levi's self-defense suggests there is more here than the mere recollection of a biblical incident.

---

[160] Haupt, "Testament," 122-24. This recalls R. H. Charles' view on the matter (*Testaments*, l-lvi). However, the critical difference between Charles' hypothesis and the one put forward by Haupt is that the latter approach does not make the implausible suggestion that all of *T12P* was composed as a Hasmonean legitimation document. *Testament of Judah* 24, with its expectation of a non-priestly king from Judah's lineage, is difficult to reconcile with the Hasmonean merger of the roles of king and priest.

[161] That there was not complete acceptance of the Hasmonean high priesthood is suggested by the stela set up in honor and defense of Simon's elevation (1 Macc 14:27-47); this is noted by Joseph Sievers, *The Hasmoneans and Their Supporters: From Mattathias to the Death of John Hyrcanus I* (USFSJ 6; Atlanta, GA: Scholars, 1990) 119-27.

[162] See 5.4.2 and associated notes above.

[163] Josephus, *J. W.* 1 §§ 63-64; *Ant.* 13 §§ 255-256; see the discussion of Hyrcanus' actions in Sievers, *The Hasmoneans*, 142-43.

[164] Josephus, *J. W.* 1 §§ 65-66; *Ant.* 13 §§ 275-281; again, see Sievers, *The Hasmoneans*, 144-46, for the suggested dates.

The traits of Levi's second dream in Original *Testament of Levi* also tend to support the notion that the book ought to be dated to the Hasmonean period, and be treated as a legitimation document for Hasmonean princely and priestly rule. The absence of the speech against exogamy, which is so prominent in *Aramaic Levi*, could be explained as part of a general reduction of interest in purity issues over against *Aramaic Levi*.[165] The diminished attention to purity may be related to the Hasmonean openness to external influences, especially those that may have assisted them in achieving their goals.[166] The disappearance of the gentle polemic against the rule of the sword from *Ar. Levi* 4-6 is particularly understandable, given the possible aim of the document. And the twofold investiture of Levi, along with the simple fact that it is the second dream in which he was appointed a priest, may have reassured readers of the trustworthiness of the Hasmonean claim to the priesthood.

Removal of Jacob's act of ordination and investiture of Levi, along with the addition of Jacob's dream by which he was apparently informed of Levi's elevation, also guaranteed the reader that the heavenly authorization of Levi's priesthood was in no way compromised. While *Aramaic Levi* presents Levi's appointment to the priestly office as something accomplished by heavenly and human powers working in concert, Original *Testament of Levi* eliminated any human agency; only God's choice of Levi remained. This too may indicate Hasmonean origin: it would not have helped their case to allow the faintest suspicion that their claim to the priestly office was not entirely God's idea, but was in part the result of a mortal's decision and action, even if that mortal were one of Israel's great patriarchs. If there were questions about the propriety of the Hasmonean exercise of the power of the altar and of the sword—and the evidence says there were[167]—it would have been to their advantage to claim legitimation solely from heaven.

Particularly suggestive in this regard are the expansions the author of Original *Testament of Levi* made in his adaptation of *Aramaic Levi*'s priestly instructions. First, Isaac's exhortation to Levi to re-

---

[165] A reduced interest in issues of purity is also evident in the failure to preserve the prayer in its entirety, and the abbreviation of Isaac's exhortations to personal purity in *Ar. Levi* 13ff.

[166] See the references to known and suspected alliances made by the Hasmoneans with Seleucid, Roman, and other leaders in Sievers, *The Hasmoneans*, passim. For instance, see Josephus, *J. W.* 1 § 61; *Ant.* 13 § 249, where Hyrcanus uses money from David's tomb to bribe the Seleucid ruler Antiochus VII, and to hire foreign mercenaries. For other evidence of the cordial relationship between Hasmoneans and the Hellenistic world, see Shimon Applebaum, "Jewish Urban Communities and Greek Influences," in *Judea in Hellenistic and Roman Times: Historical and Archaeological Essays* (Leiden: Brill, 1989) 30-46.

[167] See Josephus, *Ant.* 13 §§ 288-299, the story of the banquet with the Pharisees, and the subsequent revolt put down by Hyrcanus.

member the νομος Κυριου, the "law of the Lord," appears to be an allusion to the heavenly commission to service at the altar and with the sword in the first vision. Placing such words in Isaac's mouth put the oldest surviving patriarch in the role of affirming Levi's double-appointment, and urging him to understand it as the law of God, a mandate that could not be ignored lightly. Second, the expanded list of the kinds of sacrifice in which Levi was instructed proves to the reader that Levi was a fully trained and qualified occupant of the priestly office. Both changes would have gone a long way toward underscoring a claim to the priestly office.

The shift of focus in Levi's speech from secular wisdom to law also supports the idea that the book was composed to defend Hasmonean claims to priestly power. By depicting the ancestor of all Hasmoneans as someone who was deeply concerned with the law, the author indicated to a skeptical audience that their doubt, associated with questions concerning the family's piety, was unfounded. Levi had instructed his children and their descendants in the proper attitude toward the law, so there was no need for concern. Moreover, portrayed in *Aramaic Levi* as someone who had achieved glory by his possession of secular wisdom, Joseph appears in Original *Testament of Levi* as a king who had won his throne by exercising wisdom that was grounded in honoring the law (Deut 17:18-20). Similarly, one can conceive of a supporter of the Hasmoneans suggesting that they came to power because of their Joseph-like piety, and because they followed the law of the king in Deut 17:18-20, and occupied themselves with reading of the law.

Next, it is possible that *T. Levi* 14:1–15:4; 16:1–17:9 foretold the failure of some of Levi's priestly descendants to act appropriately and prophesied the concomitant decline of the priesthood, and the seventh jubilee of the priesthood in 17:10-11 portrayed the period of the hellenizing priests Jason, Menelaus, and Alcimus. Thus the stage was set for Original *Testament of Levi* 18 to follow naturally with the announcement, made in prophetic fashion by Levi, of the dawn of the Hasmonean priesthood. And with that the book could end, having accomplished its purpose of saying to a skeptical audience that the simultaeous Hasmonean possession of the high priestly office and military authority had been ordained in heaven long before it had come to pass; hence the doubters had nothing to worry about. The temple, with its wealth and power, was in good hands.

5.6. Conclusion

This survey of the key differences between *Aramaic Levi* and Original *Testament of Levi* as evidence for a Hasmonean-era date for Original *Testament of Levi* is clearly provisional. Although a fair interpretation of the evidence, it remains to be seen whether it can stand up under closer scrutiny.[168]

Whatever the precise date and purpose of Original *Testament of Levi*, it remains a capstone on the LPT. It extended the depiction of an idealized version of the priesthood that had its origin in Levi; it upheld the linkage of Levi's special honor with his zeal at Shechem; and it continued the tradition of honoring wisdom as a key trait exercised by Levi. And, like the other parts of the tradition, it probably developed from a debate over the proper occupants of the priestly office.

---

[168] For instance one could interpret differently our earlier observation that Original *Testament of Levi* tones down the emphasis on purity found in *Aramaic Levi*. One might say that a defender of Hasmonean ascendancy would have preserved that emphasis as another means of legitimating the family's claim to power.

CONCLUSION

The foregoing study was devoted to describing and analyzing the LPT. Materially the focus throughout was on establishing the content of the tradition's texts, determining the connections among them, and making a preliminary assessment of their date and their view respecting the proper character of the priestly office. We summarize the results of the last two undertakings, and refer the reader to the body of the study for a description of the texts' contents.

6.1. The relationships among the texts of the LPT

Our study has allowed us to sort out the complex relationships among the texts of the LPT. We have seen that the biblical foundation for the notion that Levi was an ideal priest is a synoptic reading of Genesis 34; Exod 32:25-29; Num 25:6-13; and Deut 33:8-11. Mal 2:4-7 provides a first example of how those Pentateuchal passages, read synoptically, create Levi, the ideal priest. In turn Mal 2:4-7 became a resource for later authors in the LPT who also sought to create an idealized version of the priesthood embodied by Levi.

Because our reconstruction of *Aramaic Levi* is new and considerably different from preceding understandings of the document, it was possible to assess the relationships among the remaining three texts of the LPT from a fresh perspective.[1] On the basis of the similarities and differences between *Aramaic Levi* and *Jub.* 30:1–32:9 we affirmed the view that both relied independently on a Levi-apocryphon. The apocryphon probably contained the Shechem incident; a vision in which Levi is elevated to the priesthood and hears an angel's speech against exogamy; a journey to Hebron where Isaac blesses him; a return trip to

---

[1] In chapter three we developed a new definition of the scope and structure of *Aramaic Levi*. It includes (1) an account of the Shechem episode; (2) a prayer of Levi for elevation to the priesthood; (3) a vision in which his prayer was answered, and in which he heard an angelic speech condemning exogamy; (4) an encounter with Isaac and Jacob; (5) Isaac's priestly instructions for Levi; (6) Levi's life history; and (7) Levi's speech to his children.

Bethel where Jacob ordains him; and another trek to Hebron where Isaac instructs Levi in the law of the priesthood. The author of *Aramaic Levi* summarized the first trip to Hebron and Isaac's blessing in one line (*Ar. Levi* 8), and used some of the contents of Isaac's speech to create Levi's address on wisdom (*Ar. Levi* 82-101). And he added Levi's prayer (*Ar. Levi* supp. 1-19), life history (*Ar. Levi* 62-81), and warnings regarding his apostate descendants (*Ar. Levi* 102-106). Meanwhile the author of *Jubilees* also changed the apocryphon. He transferred Levi's vision from its location after the Shechem incident to just before the ordination by Jacob (*Jub.* 32:1); but he left the angelic speech regarding exogamy and Levi's elevation in place after the Shechem episode, treating it as an address by the book's angel-narrator (*Jub.* 30:5-17). And in accordance with Isaac's own claim that the priestly instructions originated from Abraham (cf. *Ar. Levi* 22, 50, 57), he moved them to *Jub.* 21:7-20, where the regulations could be spoken by Abraham to Isaac. In addition he probably expanded the account of the first trip to Isaac with a blessing for Judah and with additional material concerning Jacob (*Jub.* 31:18-32).[2]

Our new reconstruction of *Aramaic Levi* allowed us to confirm the view that an early version of *Testament of Levi* relied on *Aramaic Levi*, but it also indicated the significance of the ways in which Original *Testament of Levi*'s author transformed his source. For the first time it is possible to see that this author adjusted *Aramaic Levi* in ways that allow Levi, the ideal priest, to legitimate unification of the offices of priest and prince. The principal change is the addition of a second vision before the Shechem incident in which Levi is commissioned as a priest and as the sword-bearing agent of retribution against Shechem (*T. Levi* 2:3-6; 4:2–6:2). In addition this author reduced the emphasis on purity found in *Aramaic Levi*, and replaced the focus on wisdom in Levi's speech to his children with an emphasis on law.

So, to summarize, the relationships among the texts of the LPT are as follows. The authors of *Aramaic Levi* and *Jub.* 30:1–32:9 used independently a Levi-apocryphon to create their own portraits of Levi; they both adjusted the apocryphon to meet their own requirements. Then the author of Original *Testament of Levi* took up *Aramaic Levi* as his primary source, transforming it to develop his unique picture of the patriarch-become-priest.

6.2. The dates and views respecting the priestly office of the LPT texts

Aramaic Levi is probably a third-century BCE document. As for its views regarding the priesthood, there are several motifs that emerge time and again, which, along with the narrative flow, tell the story of

---

[2] For the remaining smaller changes the author of *Jubilees* made in adapting the apocryphon, see 4.2.

the book's position on the clergy. The first and most evident theme is Levi's suitability for the priestly office owing to his passion for the purity of cult and community.[3] The second is the characterization of the ideal priesthood as different in its practices vis-à-vis the Torah's requirements for clergy.[4] A third motif is the attachment of the roles of sage and scribe to the priesthood.[5] Yet another characteristic is the book's dualism.[6] The author weaves these themes into a narrative that moves from an account of Levi's zealous rejection of exogamy in the Shechem episode, to his plea for elevation to the priesthood, and on to the fulfillment of his request by heavenly agents and by his father. It continues with his grandfather's commendation of his purity, and instruction in preserving and exercising that purity in daily life and in cultic administration. After recounting Levi's family history the book concludes with Levi's own speech in favor of wisdom and against the impure and inadequate priestly leadership that some of his descendants would someday provide. This series of events and set of themes make known the author's view regarding the proper character of the priesthood. It is to be an office occupied by individuals who passionately protect communal and cultic purity and ferociously attack the sources of evil; they are to live by norms that transcend those prescribed by the Torah; and they are to be known for their wisdom. The tapestry woven from the narrative flow and the themes of the document also suggests that there are priests who do not meet these requirements among Levi's descendants, clergy who are unconcerned about purity, rules of conduct, and wisdom. *Aramaic Levi* is perhaps a rejection of the latter kind of priest, and a plea for acceptance of the former type. Interestingly, we are led by certain indications in the text to consider with renewed seriousness Milik's longstanding and much maligned suggestion of Samaritan provenance.[7]

Jubilees 30:1–32:9, dating from the middle of the second century BCE, was composed as part of *Jubilees'* larger agenda of proposing a new constitution for Judaism in the wake of the Maccabean revolt and its early successes. The view of the priesthood in the passage is highlighted by the angelic speech against exogamy (30:7-15), Isaac's blessing of Levi (31:12-17), and Levi's legitimation as a priest by his father's act of ordination (32:2-9). The abhorrence of marriage outside the community may reflect the author's concern that some of the competing proposals for the shape of Judaism and of the priestly office

---

[3] See, for example, *Ar. Levi* 1-3; *Ar. Levi* supp. 1-19, 22-27; *Ar. Levi* 17-21.

[4] See the cultic instructions in *Ar. Levi* 13–61, and the discussion of them in 3.1.5.

[5] See *Ar. Levi* supp. 8; *Ar. Levi* 82-101.

[6] See especially Levi's prayer, *Ar. Levi* supp. 1-19.

[7] See 3.3.4 above.

were too open to such unions among the clergy and the people.[8] Isaac's speech is a rather generic blessing, expressing his desire that Levi and his seed be priests forever, and his anticipation that they will be leaders among the people. The emphasis on Jacob's role in elevating Levi to the priesthood reflects the author's special interest in putting Jacob forward as the model Israelite. All in all, *Jub.* 30:1–32:9 has the character of one voice among many in a lively debate about the proper character of Judaism in general, and about the appropriate shape of the priesthood in particular.

Study of the LPT as it appears in *Testament of Levi* leads to some surprising conclusions. At least on the basis of the differences between *Testament of Levi* and its chief source, *Aramaic Levi*, it seems clear that one of its principal concerns was to legitimate the joint possession of military and sacerdotal power. Hence it is possible to imagine that it was composed during the period of Hasmonean rule as a defense of their simultaneous occupation of the offices of prince and priest. If so, for the first time in the tradition the depiction of Levi as the ideal priest was used to legitimate the view of the office's incumbents, rather than the perspective of the challengers.

6.3. The LPT and the history of the priesthood from Malachi to *Testament of Levi*

While it has not at all been the aim of this study to address the history of the priesthood in Second Temple Judaism, but only to provide new literary evidence for constructing that history, we dare to close with a few reflections on what the LPT might mean for our understanding of the office from Malachi to *Testament of Levi*. First, and above all, it confirms the view that there were tensions among many groups during the Second Temple period over the possession and definition of the priestly office. The texts reveal their author's dissatisfaction with the status quo (Mal 2:4-7; *Aramaic Levi*), their yearning for a chance to take up the office themselves (*Jub.* 30:1–32:9), or their defense of the way they defined the office in their own possession (*Testament of Levi*). There has never been much doubt that there was constant discussion about who should serve at the altar, and what their qualifications ought to be. These texts simply remind us that at times the debate became acrimonious, and at other times it quieted. But it never ceased completely.

Our study has also suggested the variety of views from the period regarding the priestly office. Although the authors who contributed to the LPT relied on similar traditions, nevertheless they all expressed unique concerns. Beginning with Mal 2:4-7 we see an author who was particularly preoccupied with the priests' failure to adhere to

---

[8] See the well-known passages, Ezra 9–10; Neh 13:23-31; Mal 2:10-16 for similar expressions of concern from an earlier period.

the Pentateuchal norms for sacrifice and teaching, and who was clearly an outsider attacking incumbents. Meanwhile, *Aramaic Levi*'s author had a broader range of worries regarding the occupants of the priestly office that included sacrifice, teaching, marriage, and the general purity of the clergy. Moreover, he was intent on proposing a more complete model of the priesthood than Malachi's, a model that he seemed to intentionally differentiate from the one prescribed by the Pentateuch. The author of *Jubilees* had far less to say about the clergy, being satisfied with addressing the issue of exogamy, establishing the origins of the priesthood in Levi, and securing a connection between Jacob and the model priest. If our preliminary assessment is correct, the writer of *Testament of Levi* wrote from a perspective entirely different from the one taken by the first three authors. He was interested in proving the piety and righteousness of incumbent priests who also exercised the power of the sword. He was a defender of clergy who were probably under fire from critics with many of the same interests as the authors of Malachi, *Aramaic Levi*, and *Jubilees*.

The last comment points to a final lesson our literary study may yield regarding the priesthood in the Second Temple period. Given what we have learned, it would seem to be a mistake to conjure the historical significance of these texts wiht the aid of the overly-simplified, but well-worn notion that the priestly hierarchy consisted of dispossessed Levites and powerful Aaronites/Zadokites. Were one to do so it is easy to imagine that these texts would be attributed to a movement from the side of the descendants of their central figure, Levi, to enhance their priestly power. But one should consider carefully the fact that *Testament of Levi* may have been forged from *Aramaic Levi* by pro-Hasmoneans at the very same time the Qumran sectarians were preserving *Aramaic Levi* as an expression of their self-definition and of their negative assessment of the Hasmonean high priesthood. Indeed, the sectarians may have fled to the desert to escape the power of the Hasmonean high priesthood which merged secular and sacerdotal power.[9] That scenario indicates that documents idealizing Levi and Levites as priestly figures were not always the texts of Second Temple Levites yearning for more priestly power. They may also have been the documents of a wide range of opponents of the incumbent priesthood, as well as the texts favored by some of the occupants of the office. This reminds us that not only were there many views regarding the priestly office; it also cautions us against designating the different views too readily with the names of the literary figures used by their authors to express them. The common descriptive terms "Levites,"

---

[9] See James VanderKam, "People and High Priesthood in Early Maccabean Times," in *The Hebrew Bible and its Interpreters* (eds. W. H. Propp, B. Halpern, and D. N. Freedman; Biblical and Judaic Studies from the University of California, San Diego 1; Winona Lake, IN: Eisenbrauns, 1990) 205-225.

"Aaronites," and "Zadokites," may not suffice to denote all of the factions that fought for priestly power in Second Temple Judaism. They may, with further study, only succeed in revealing that there were those who held power, and those who did not, and that the two kinds of groups legitimated their positions by telling their foundational stories in the names of the few priestly ancestors known to them from the Bible. Of course, these reflections are our most speculative and require considerably more investigation on the basis of the texts studied here, as well as others with which we have not dealt. But for now we let our reflections stand as an invitation to further consideration of the significance of the literary tradition we have traced.

APPENDIX 1 THE MANUSCRIPT WITNESSES TO
ARAMAIC LEVI

The manuscript witnesses to *Aramaic Levi* include 1Q21, 4Q213, 4Q214, the Cairo Geniza manuscript, and additions to the Mt. Athos manuscript of *T12P*. Unfortunately 4Q214 remains unpublished, and 4Q213 has appeared only in part.

1Q21

Milik produced a transcription and French translation of 1Q21 shortly after its discovery. The sixty fragments give very little that is useful in reconstruction of *Aramaic Levi*. Only frg. 3 provides text that one can confidently associate with known material in *Aramaic Levi*.

D. Barthélemy, O.P. and J. T. Milik. *Discoveries in the Judaean Desert I: Qumran Cave 1*. Oxford: Clarendon Press, 1955, 87-91

4Q213

The prayer of Levi in 4Q213 1 i, ii was published in 1955 (and was re-published in 1993), and a small portion of Levi's speech to his children in 4Q213 8–10 appeared in 1976. Most recently fragments of what we call 4Q213 were published by Jonas Greenfield and Michael Stone under the name "4QLevi[a] aram." It is apparent that the latter two scholars have divided the former 4Q213 into several manuscripts. The listing in *The Dead Sea Scrolls Catalogue* would indicate that they now discern three manuscripts where Milik saw but one.[1] The fragments of

---

[1] *The Dead Sea Scrolls Catalogue: Documents, Photographs and Museum Invetory Numbers* (comp. Stephen A. Reed; rev. and ed. Marilyn Lundberg and Micahel B Phelps; SBL Resources for Biblical Study 32; Atlanta: Scholars Press, 1994) 82. Note that Greenfield and Stone have divided 4Q214 into two manuscripts as well (ibid. 82-83), leaving five manuscripts of *Aramaic Levi* from Cave 4.

Milik's 4Q213 assigned to the manuscript published by Greenfield and Stone include 4Q213 6 i, ii; 7; 8 i; 9; and 10.[2]

Greenfield, Jonas and Michael Stone. "The First Manuscript of *Aramaic Levi Document* From Qumran (4QLevi[a] aram)." *Museon* 107 (1994) 257-81.
        . "The Prayer of Levi." *JBL* 112 (1993) 247-66.
Milik, J. T. *The Books of Enoch. The Aramaic Fragments of Qumrân Cave 4*. Oxford: Clarendon, 1976, 23-25.
        . "Le Testament de Lévi en araméen: Fragment de la Grotte 4 de Qumrân." *RB* 62 (1955) 398-406.

The Cairo Geniza Manuscript

Before the turn of the century two fragments of an *Aramaic Levi* manuscript were discovered in the Cairo Geniza. Unfortunately they were separated and distributed to different libraries before it was recognized that they belong to the same manuscript. Preliminary publication of the fragment housed in the library at Cambridge occurred in 1900. A preliminary edition of the Oxford fragment followed in 1907. Then in 1908 R. H. Charles brought the two together in a single edition. In addition Jonas Greenfield and Michael Stone have given revised readings for much of the manuscript.

Charles, R. H. *The Greek Versions of the Testaments of the Twelve Patriarchs*. Oxford: Oxford University, 1908, 245-56.
Charles, R. H. and A. Cowley. "An Early Source of the Testaments of the Patriarchs." *JQR* 19 (1907) 566-83.
Greenfield, Jonas, and Michael Stone. "Remarks on the Aramaic Testament of Levi from the Geniza." *RB* 86 (1979) 216-30.
Pass, H. L. and J. Arendzen. "Fragment of an Aramaic Text of the Testament of Levi." *JQR* 12 (1900) 651-61.

The Mt. Athos Additions

The additions to the Mt. Athos manuscript of *T12P* at *T. Levi* 2:3; 5:2; 18:2 were announced by Charles in his preliminary publication of the Oxford fragment (see above), and published officially in his 1908 edition of *T12P*. More recently the same additions have received publication again in de Jonge's edition of *T12P* which is intended to replace Charles' 1908 publication.

Charles, R. II. *The Greek Versions of the Testaments of the Twelve Patriarchs*. Oxford: Oxford University, 1908, 29, 37, 247-53.
De Jonge, Marinus. *The Testaments of the Twelve Patriarchs: A Critical Edition of the Greek Text*. PVTG I, 2. Leiden: Brill, 1978, 25, 30, 46-48.

---

[2] The corresponding fragments are as follows, with our numbering first and Greenfield and Stone's second: 4Q213 6 i = frg. 1 i; 4Q213 6 ii = frg. 1 ii; 4Q213 7 = frg. 2; 4Q213 8 i = frg. 3; 4Q213 9 = frg. 4; 4Q213 10 = frg. 5. Greenfield and Stone think 4Q213 8 ii does not even belong to *Aramaic Levi*, much less to this manuscript.

The Syriac Fragment

In addition to the manuscript witnesses mentioned above, there is a Syriac fragment of *Aramaic Levi* located in the British Museum (MS Add. 17,193). Associated first with *Aramaic Levi* by Pass and Arendzen in 1900, and then published officially by Charles in his 1908 edition, it parallels Oxford d 14–e 1, and provides nothing beyond the Aramaic text.

Charles, R. H. *The Greek Versions of the Testaments of the Twelve Patriarchs.* Oxford: Oxford University, 1908, 254.
Pass, H. L. and J. Arendzen. "Fragment of an Aramaic Text of the Testament of Levi." *JQR* 12 (1900) 651-57.

Other publications of the *Aramaic Levi* texts

Klaus Beyer has edited the Cairo Geniza manuscript together with the Qumran fragments to produce a text of *Aramaic Levi* for his collection of Aramaic documents from Qumran. Fitzmyer and Harrington also published the available Aramaic materials in their collection of Aramaic texts. Michael Wise and Robert Eisenman included much of 4Q213 and 4Q214 in their 1992 volume.

Beyer, Klaus. *Die aramäischen Texten vom Toten Meer.* Göttingen: Vandenhoeck & Ruprecht, 1984, 188-209; *Ergänzungsband,* 1994, 71-78.
Fitzmyer, Joseph, and D. J. Harrington. *A Manual of Palestinian Aramaic Texts.* Rome: Biblical Institute Press, 1978, 80-90.
Eisenman, Robert, and Michael Wise. *The Dead Sea Scrolls Uncovered.* Rockport, MA: Element, 1992, 136-41.

APPENDIX 2 A RECONSTRUCTION OF THE CAIRO GENIZA MANUSCRIPT

The surviving portions of the Cairo Geniza manuscript allow its partial reconstruction. On the basis of the reconstruction one can speculate on the original scope and structure of *Aramaic Levi*, and provide further support for the view that the book contained but one vision.

The remains of the Cairo Geniza manuscript permit certainty on several counts.[1] First, we know that the manuscript was made up of double-leaf pieces of vellum folded in the middle, with four columns of text on each single leaf; the leaves on the right side give text from the early part of the document and the leaves on the left side provide text from the later portion. One might doubt this judgment, considering the fact that we have a single-leaf piece preserved in Oxford fragment. Fortunately, though, direct examination of the edge adjacent columns a and c reveals the indisputable evidence that the fragment was torn from a double leaf. The manuscript was dry-lined for ease of writing. On the fold of the Cambridge fragment one discerns cracks and openings in the vellum where the dry-lining crosses it, while there are no corresponding cracks on the fragment's outside edges. One does find the cracks on the left edge (columns a and c) of the Oxford fragment, above lines 1, 6, 8, 13, 15, and 15, and no such cracking on the right edge.[2] Thus one can be sure that the single leaf was once part of a

---

[1] For the terminology that follows, as well as for additional information regarding the construction of medieval Hebrew manuscripts, see Malachi Beit-Arié, *Hebrew Codicology: Tentative Typology of Technical Practices Employed in Hebrew Dated Medieval Manuscripts* (Jerusalem: Israel Academy of Sciences and Humanities, 1981).

[2] For this simple and all-important observation I thank the American Philosophical Society, which provided the grant enabling me to travel to Cambridge and Oxford. Without direct examination of the Oxford fragment this judgment would not have been possible, since the fragment suffers from extremely poor preservation dating to the time of its purchase for the library in 1896. Thanks also go to the staff of the Manuscript Reading Room at the Unversity Library at Cambridge and to Dr. Richard

double-leaf piece of vellum. Similarly, it is reasonable to assume that the single leaf represented by part of Mt. Athos 18:2 (columns 17-20) was also part of a double leaf, now entirely lost to us in Aramaic.[3]

Second, because of the overlap between the Cairo Geniza fragments and Mt. Athos 18:2 we can be certain of the order of twelve columns in the manuscript.[4]

Third, the account of the Shechem incident must precede the twelve consecutive columns since it is the right side of the double-leaf Cambridge fragment that provides the final four columns of the dozen.

One vexing uncertainty remains. If the *Aramaic Levi* manuscript from the Geniza was part of a codex—as it appears to have been—we can be almost positive that *Aramaic Levi* was not the only book that occupied the codex. A codex is made up of several quires, which in turn are composed of a number of double leaves folded together. The implications of this observation are clear. We cannot know what preceded and followed the surviving portions of the Cairo Geniza manuscript of *Aramaic Levi*, nor how much of such material was part of *Aramaic Levi*. Hence we are limited in our reconstruction to speculating on the scope and structure of what lay between an account of the Shechem episode and Levi's speech to his children. That much may be reconstructed as follows.

A Reconstruction of the Cairo Geniza Manuscript of *Aramaic Levi*

Column and double-leaf number in original MS	Contents	Surviving column
Column 1, right side of double leaf 1	Shechem incident	Cambridge a
Column 2, right side of double leaf 1		Missing
Column 3, right side of double leaf 1		Missing
Column 4, right side of double leaf 1	Shechem incident	Cambridge b

Judd, Hebrew Specialist for the Bodleian Library in Oxford, for their generous assistance.

[3] It is not possible that the Oxford fragment and the portion of Mt. Athos 18:2 lacking Aramaic parallel formed a double leaf. Were that so Oxford a (column 13), the end of a vision, would have to follow Cambridge b (column 4), the account of the Shechem incident. Some material had to come between the two fragments.

[4] See columns 13 to 24 in the table below and the fuller description of how the overlapping witnesses allow the reconstruction of twelve consecutive columns of text in 2.3.1.

Columns 5–12, right side of double leaves 2-3		Missing
Column 13, left side of double leaf 3	End of vision, encounter with Isaac and Jacob	Oxford a
Column 14, left side of double leaf 3	Isaac's instructions	Oxford b/Mt. Athos 18:2
Column 15, left side of double leaf 3	Isaac's instructions	Oxford c/Mt. Athos 18:2
Column 16, left side of double leaf 3	Isaac's instructions	Oxford d/Mt. Athos 18:2
Columns 17–20, left side of double leaf 2	Isaac's instructions and Levi's life history	Mt. Athos 18:2
Column 21, left side of double leaf 1	Levi's life history	Cambridge c/Mt. Athos 18:2 (through Oxford a 13)
Column 22, left side of double leaf 1	Levi's life history	Cambridge d
Column 23, left side of double leaf 1	Levi's wisdom speech	Cambridge e
Column 24 left side of double leaf 1	Levi's wisdom speech	Cambridge f

The reconstruction supports the proposal for *Aramaic Levi's* scope and structure offered in 2.2 to 2.3. The eight columns missing between Cambridge b (the Shechem incident) and Oxford a (the end of the vision) are too many for the single vision that one would have to place there were the model of *Testament of Levi* followed. Instead, the prayer in 4Q213 1 i 1–ii 14 (about two columns of Geniza Aramaic) and the vision-report material in 4Q213 1 i 15–2 22 (about one and a half columns of Geniza Aramaic), provide three and a half of the missing columns.[5] When one allows for perhaps three more columns to complete the account of the Shechem incident and narrate the transition to Levi's prayer, and another one and a half columns to complete the vision report, the eight column gap is easily filled.

---

[5] Even though we do not have a complete one and a half columns of vision text from Qumran, since 4Q213 1 ii shows the bottom of a column, as does 4Q213 2, the estimate is possible. The vision-report material must be continuous, since there is only one dream in *Aramaic Levi*. Hence we can be certain that all of the column that occupied the leather of 4Q213 2 gave an account of a dream, since the beginning of the vision occupies the end of a preceding column. Note that the estimate does not assume that 4Q213 2 is necessarily the bottom of the column following 4Q213 1 ii. There could be intervening material which is now lost.

INDEX OF PRINCIPAL ANCIENT CITATIONS

Only the most significant discussions of the main texts dealt with in this study are indexed. Also note that for the sake of simplicity, citations of *Testament of Levi* and Original *Testament of Levi* passages are not differentiated in the index. All are listed under the heading "*Testament of Levi.*"

Biblical and Apocryphal Passages

Ancient Texts

	n. 145, 212
90	129, 163, 212
90-94	137
91	211, n. 145, 212
95	211, n. 145
99	129, 163, 197, n. 96, 203, 204
102	187, 213
103	187, 213
102-106	187, 213
103	187
103-105	132, 133

Josephus

Ant. 1 §§ 337-40	10, n. 3, 66, n. 23, 157, n. 60
Ant. 12 §§ 3-10	137
Ant. 13 §§ 249	218, n. 166
Ant. 13 §§ 255-56	217, n. 163
Ant. 13 §§ 275-81	217, n. 164
Ant. 13 §§ 288-99	218, n. 167
J. W. 1 §§ 61	218, n. 166
J. W. 1 §§ 63-64	217, n. 163
J. W. 1 §§ 65-66	217, n. 164

Jubilees

16:20-25	165, n. 84
21	110-11
21:7-20	131, 152, 167
21:12	104, n. 152
30:1–32:9	30-31, 147-55, 191-98
30:1-4	67-68, 156-58
30:5-17	36-37, 87, 158-61
30:12	197
30:18	36, n. 77
30:18-20	37, 161-62, 166, n. 89
30:19	197
30:21-23	158-61
30:23	197
30:24-26	67-68, 156-58
31:4-32	91-92, 130-31, 150, 153
31:1-11	156, n. 54, 162
31:12-17	129, 131, 162, 166, n. 89
31:13	196
31:15	196
31:17	196
31:18-32	156, n. 54, 164
32:1	82, 87, 162, 166, n. 89
32:3	162, 164
32:3-9	92
45:16	168

Testament of Levi

	169, 175-77, 191-98
1:1-2	178
2–5	46-47, 205, n. 127
2:1-2	178-79
2:3-4	82
2:3-5	179-80
2:3-6	199-201
2:4	76-77, 176, n. 4
2:6–6:2	180-83, 199-201
4:2	32
4:2-6	76-77, 176, n. 4
5:2-4	54-55
6–7	66-68, 157, n. 58, 183-84, 201-3
6:3	157, n. 60
8	46, 160, 184-85
8:1-2	82
8:1-11	203-6
8:11-15	85, n. 91, 185
8:16-19	203-6
8:18-19	29, 49-51
9	167, n. 90
9:1-3	93
9:1-5	186, 206-7
9:3	29, 40, 88, n. 100, 89, n. 101
9:3-4	50
9:6-14	110, 131, 176, 186, 207-9
9:12	104, n. 152
11–12	117, 131, 176, n. 14, 187, 210-11
11-13	25
11:8	198, n. 102
12:5	54-55, 176, 187, n. 65, 196
13	127, 130, 176, 187, 211-12
14–15	27, 126, 130, 186-88, 213
16–17	30, 188, 213-14
16–18	46-47
17:8-10	51
18	189, 215-16
18:2, 4, 9	51
19	189-90

Mt. Athos Maunscript Additions

INDEX OF MODERN AUTHORS

BIBLIOGRAPHY

Albeck, Ch. *Das Buch der Jubiläen und die Halacha*. Berlin: Scholem, 1930.

Allegro, John. *Discoveries in the Judaean Desert* V. Oxford: Clarendon Press, 1968.

Applebaum, Shimon. "Jewish Urban Communities and Greek Influences." In *Judea in Hellenistic and Roman Times: Historical and Archaeological Essays*, 30-46. Leiden: Brill, 1989.

Baarda, T. "Qehath—'What's in a name?'" *JSJ* 19 (1988) 215-29.

Baarda, T. "The Shechem Episode in the Testament of Levi." In *Sacred History and Sacred Texts*, eds. J. N. Bremmer and Florentino García Martínez, 11-73. Kampen: Pharos, 1992.

Baentsch, B. *Exodus, Leviticus, Numeri*. HKAT 2. Göttingen: Vandenhoeck & Ruprecht, 1903.

Baldwin, Joyce G. *Haggai, Zechariah, Malachi*. London: Inter-Varsity Press, 1972.

Barthélemy, D., and J. T. Milik. *Discoveries in the Judaean Desert* 1. Oxford: Clarendon Press, 1955.

Barthélemy, D. *Preliminary Interim Report on the Hebrew Old Testament Text Project*. 2nd rev. ed. New York: United Bible Society, 1979-80.

Beasley-Murray, G. R. "The Two Messiahs in the Testaments of the Twelve Patriarchs." *JTS* 48 (1947) 1-12.

Becker, Jürgen. *Untersuchungen zur Entstehungsgeschichte der Testamente der Zwölf Patriarchen*. AGJU VIII. Leiden: Brill,1970.

Beit-Arié, Malachi. *Hebrew Codicology: Tentative Typology of Technical Practices Employed in Hebrew Dated Medieval Manuscripts*. Jerusalem: Israel Academy of Sciences and Humanities, 1981.

Berger, Klaus. *Unterweisung in erzählender Form: Das Buch der Jubiläen*. JSHRZ II.3. Gerd Mohn: Gütersloher Verlagshaus, 1981.

Beyer, Klaus. *Die aramäischen Texten vom Toten Meer*. Göttingen: Vandenhoeck & Ruprecht, 1984.

Beyerlin, W. "Der *nervus rerum* in Psalm 106." *ZAW* 86 (1974) 50-64.

Bickerman, E. *Der Gott der Makkabäer*. Berlin: Schocken, 1937.

Binns, L. E. *The Book of Numbers*. London: Methuen, 1927.

Black, M. "The Messiah in the Testament of Levi XVIII." *ET* 60 (1948-1949) 321-22.

Blenkinsopp, Joseph. *A History of Prophecy in Israel*. Philadelphia: Westminster, 1983.

Blum, Erhard. *Die Komposition der Vätergeschichte*. WMANT 57. Neukirchen: Neukirchener, 1984.

Bonani, G., M. Broshi, I. Carmi, S. Ivy, J. Strugnell, and W. Wölfi. "Radiocarbon Dating of the Dead Sea Scrolls." *Atiqot* 20 (1991) 27-32.

Bousset, Wilhelm. "Ein aramäisches Fragment des Testamentum Levi." *ZNW* 1 (1900) 344-46.

_____. "Die Testamente der XII Patriarchen: I. Die Ausscheidung der christlichen Interpolationen." *ZNW* 1 (1900) 187-209.

_____. "Die Testamente der XII Patriarchen: II. Composition und Zeit der jüdischen Grundschrift." *ZNW* 1 (1900) 187-209.

Böhme, W. "Zu Maleachi und Haggai." *ZAW* 7 (1887) 210-17.

Braun, F.-M. "Les Testaments des XII Patriarches et le problème de leur origine." *RB* 67 (1960) 516-49.

Budd, Philip J. *Numbers*. WBC 5. Waco, TX: Word Books, 1984.

von Bulmerincq, Alexander. *Der Prophet Maleachi*. 2 vols. Tartu: J. G. Krüger, 1926/1932.

Burchard, Chr. "Zur armenischen Überlieferung der Testamente der Zwölf Patriarchen." *BZNW* 36 (1969) 1-29.

_____. Review of *Testamenta XII Patriarchum*, by Marinus de Jonge. In *RevQ* 5 (1964/66) 283.

Caquot, A. "Les bénédictions de Moïse (Deutéronome 33, 6-25)." *Sem* 32 (1982) 75-79.

_____. "La double investiture de Lévi." *StHR* (=Supp. to *Numen*) 21 (1972) 156-61.

_____. "Jubilés." In *La Bible. Écrits intertestamentaires*, eds. André Dupont-Sommer, Marc Philonenko, and D. A. Bertrand, 716-19, 750-60, 797. Paris: Gallimord, 1987.

Charles, R. H. *The Apocrypha and Pseudepigrapha of the Old Testament in English*. 2 vols. Oxford: Clarendon, 1913.

_____. *The Book of Enoch or 1 Enoch translated from the Editor's Ethiopic Text*. Oxford: Oxford University, 1912.

_____. *The Book of Jubilees or the Little Genesis*. London: Adam and Charles Black, 1902.

_____. *The Greek Versions of the Testaments of the Twelve Patriarchs*. Oxford: Oxford University, 1908.

Charles, R. H. *The Testaments of the Twelve Patriarchs*. London: Adam and Charles Black, 1908.

Charles, R. H., and A. Cowley. "An Early Source of the Testaments of the Patriarchs." *JQR* 19 (1907) 566-83.

Charlesworth, James. "The Date of Jubilees and of the Temple Scroll." *SBLSP* 24 (1985) 193-97.

Chary, Théophane. *Aggée-Zacharie, Malachie*. Paris: Gabalda, 1969.

Chevallier, M.-A. *L'esprit et le messie dans le bas judaïsme et le Nouveau Testament*. Paris: Presses universitaires de France, 1958.

Cody, A. *A History of the Old Testament Priesthood*. AnBib 35. Rome: Pontifical Biblical Institute, 1969.

Coggins, R. J. *Haggai, Zechariah, Malachi*. OTG. Sheffield: JSOT Press, 1977.

Cohen, Shaye. "From the Bible to the Talmud: The Prohibition of Intermarriage." *HAR* 7 (1983) 23-39.

Collins, John J. *The Apocalyptic Imagination*. New York: Crossroad, 1987.

_____. "The Epic of Theodotus and the Hellenism of the Hasmoneans." *HTR* 73 (1980) 91-104.

_____. "The Testaments of the Twelve Patriarchs." In *Jewish Writings in the Second Temple Period*, ed. Michael Stone, 331-44. CRINT II, 2. Philadelphia: Fortress, 1984.

Craigie, Peter. *The Book of Deuteronomy*. NICOT. (Grand Rapids, MI: Eerdmans, 1976).

Cross, F. M. *Ancient Library of Qumran*. 2nd ed. New York: Anchor, 1961.

Cross, F. M. *Canaanite Myth and Hebrew Epic*. Cambridge, MA: Harvard University, 1973.

Davenport, Gene. *The Eschatology of the Book of Jubilees*. Studia Post Biblica 20. Leiden: Brill, 1971.

The Dead Sea Scrolls Catalogue: Documents, Photographs and Museum Invetory Numbers. Comp. Stephen A. Reed; rev. and ed. Marilyn Lundberg and Micahel B Phelps; SBL Resources for Biblical Study 32; Atlanta: Scholars Press, 1994.

de Jonge, Marinus. "Christian Influence in the Testaments of the Twelve Patriarchs." *NT* 4 (1960) 182-235.

_____. "Levi, the Sons of Levi and the Law in the *Testament of Levi* X, XIV-XV and XVI." In *De la Tora au Messie*, eds. J. Doré, P. Grelot, M. Carrez, 513-23. Paris: Tournai, 1981.

_____. "Notes on Testament of Levi II-VII." In *Travels in the World of the Old Testament*, eds. H. van Voss, H. ten Cate, and N. A. van Uchelen, 132-45. Assen: Van Gorcum, 1974.

de Jonge, Marinus. "The Main Issues in the Study of the Testaments of the Twelve Patriarchs." *NTS* 26 (1980) 508-24.

_____. "Once More: Christian Influence in the Testaments of the Twelve Patriarchs." *NT* 5 (1962) 311-19.

_____. "The Testament of Levi and 'Aramaic Levi.'" *RevQ* 13 (1988) 367-88.

_____. *Testaments of the Twelve Patriarchs*. Assen: Van Gorcum, 1953.

_____. *The Testaments of the Twelve Patriarchs: A Critical Edition of the Greek Text*. PVTG I, 2. Leiden: Brill, 1978.

_____. "The Testaments of the Twelve Patriarchs: Christian and Jewish. A Hundred Years After Friedrich Schnapp." *NedTTs* 39 (1985) 265-75.

_____. "Textual Criticism and the Analysis of the Composition of the *Testament of Zebulun*." In *Studies on the Testaments of the Twelve Patriarchs. Text and Interpretation*, 120-39. SVTP 3. Leiden: Brill, 1975.

_____. "Two Messiahs in the Testaments of the Twelve Patriarchs?" In *Tradition and Re-interpretation in Jewish and Early Christian Literature*, eds. J. W. Henten, H. J. de Jonge, P. T. van Rooden, J. W. Wesselius, 150-62. Leiden: Brill, 1986.

Dillmann, August. "Das Buch der Jubiläen oder die kleine Genesis." *JBW* 3 (1851) 1-96.

Doran, Robert. "The Non-Dating of Jubilees: Jub 34–38; 23:14-32 in Narrative Context." *JJS* 20 (1989) 1-12.

Driver, S. R. *A Critical and Exegetical Commentary on Deuteronomy*. ICC. New York: Charles Scribner's Sons, 1895.

_____. *An Introduction to the Literature of the Old Testament*. 3rd ed. New York: Charles Scribner's Sons, 1913.

Dumbrell, W. J. "Malachi and the Ezra-Nehemiah Reforms." *Reformed Theological Review* 35 (1976) 42-52.

Dupont-Sommer, André. *Nouveaux aperçus sur les manuscrits de la mer morte*. Paris: Maisonneuve, 1953.

Durham, John I. *Exodus*. WBC 3. Waco, TX: Word Books, 1987

Eisenman, Robert, and Michael Wise. *The Dead Sea Scrolls Uncovered*. Rockport, MA: Element, 1992.

Endres, John C. *Biblical Interpretation in the Book of Jubilees*. CBQMS 18. Catholic Biblical Association of America, 1987.

Finkelstein, L. "The Book of Jubilees and the Rabbinic Halaka." *HTR* 16 (1923) 39-61.

Fitzmyer, Joseph, and D. J. Harrington. *A Manual of Palestinian Aramaic Texts*. Rome: Biblical Institute Press, 1978.

Flusser, David. "Qumran and Jewish 'Apotropaic' Prayers." *IEJ* 16 (1966) 194-206.

García Martínez, Florentino. "*4QMess Ar* and the *Book of Noah.*" In *Qumran and Apocalyptic: Studies on the Aramaic Texts from Qumran*, 24-44. Leiden: Brill, 1992.

_____. "Las tablas celestes en el Libro de los Jubileos." In *Palabra y vida: Homenaje a José Alonso Díaz en su 70 cumpleaños*, ed. A. Vargas-Machuca y G. Ruiz, 333-49. Madrid: Universidad Pontifica Comillas, 1984

Glazier-McDonald, Beth. *Malachi: The Divine Messenger.* SBLDS 98. Atlanta: Scholars Press, 1987.

Gray, G. B. *A Critical and Exegetical Commentary on Numbers.* ICC. Edinburgh: T. & T. Clark, 1903.

Greenfield, Jonas. "The Words of Levi, Son of Jacob in Damascus Document IV, 15-19." *RevQ* 13 (1988) 319-22.

Greenfield, Jonas, and Michael Stone. "The First Manuscript of *Aramaic Levi Document* from Qumran." *Museon* 107 (1994) 257-81.

_____. "Two Notes on the Aramaic Levi Document." In *Of Scribes and Scrolls*, eds. Harold Attridge, John J. Collins, and Thomas Tobin, 153-61. Lanham, MD: University Press of America, 1991.

_____. "Remarks on the Aramaic Testament of Levi from the Geniza." *RB* 86 (1979) 216-30.

Grelot, Pierre. "Le coutumier sacerdotal ancien dans le Testament araméen de Lévi." *RevQ* 15 (1991) 253-63.

_____. "Le Livre des Jubilés et le Testament de Lévi." In *Mélanges Dominique Barthélemy: études bibliques offertes a l'occasion de son 60e anniversaire*, ed. P. Casetti, O. Keel and Adrian Schenker, 110-33. OBO 38. Göttingen: Vandenhoeck & Ruprecht, 1981.

_____. "Une mention inaperçue de 'Abba' dans le Testament araméen de Lévi." *Sem* 33 (1983) 101-108.

_____. "Notes sur le Testament araméen de Lévi." *RB* 63 (1956) 391-406.

_____. "Quatre cents trente ans (Ex XII, 34): du Pentateuque au Testament araméen de Lévi." In *Hommages à André Dupont-Sommer*, eds. A. Caquot et M. Philonenko, 383-94. Paris: Adrien-Maisonneuve, 1971.

_____. "Quatre cents trente ans (Ex 12,40): du Testament de Lévi aux visions de ʿAmram." in *Hommenaja a Juan Prado*, ed. Alvarez Verdes, 559-70. Madrid, 1975.

_____. "Le Testament araméen Lévi est-il traduit de l'hébreu?" *REJ* 14 (1955) 91-99.

Gunneweg, A. H. J. *Leviten und Priester: Hauptlinien der Traditionsbildung und Geschichte des israelitisch-jüdischen Kultpersonals.* Göttingen: Vandenhoeck & Ruprecht, 1965.

Hartom, A. S. "The Book of Jubilees." In *The Apocryphal Literature*, 1:72-73, 93-100. 3rd ed. Tel Aviv: Yavneh, 1969 (Hebrew).

Haupt, Detlev. "Das Testament des Levi. Untersuchungen zu seiner Entstehung und Überlieferungsgeschichte." Ph.D. diss., Halle, 1969.

Higgins, A. J. B. "The Priestly Messiah." *NTS* 13 (1966-1967) 229-30.

Martha Himmelfarb. *Ascent to Heaven in Jewish and Chrisitan Apocalypses*. Oxford: Oxford University, 1993.

Holladay, William. *Jeremiah 2. A Commentary on the Book of the Prophet Jeremiah, Chapters 26–52*. Hermeneia. Minneapolis: Fortress, 1989.

Hollander, H. W. *Joseph as an Ethical Model in the Testaments of the Twelve Patriarchs*. SVTP 6. Leiden: Brill, 1981.

Hollander, H. W., and M. de Jonge. *The Testaments of the Twelve Patriarchs: A Commentary*. SVTP 8. Leiden: Brill, 1985.

Horton, F. L. *The Melchizedek Tradition*. Cambridge: Cambridge University, 1976.

Hultgård, Anders. *L'eschatologie des Testaments des Douze Patriarches*. 2 vols. Acta Universitatis Upsaliensis, Historia Religionum 6 & 7. Uppsala: Almqvist & Wiksell, 1977/1982.

_____. "The Ideal 'Levite,' the Davidic Messiah, and the Saviour Priest in the Testaments of the Twelve Patriarchs." In *Ideal Figures in Ancient Judaism*, ed. John J. Collins and G. W. E. Nickelsburg, 93-100. Chico: CA: Scholars Press, 1980.

Hyatt, J. P. *Exodus*. NCBC. London: Oliphant, 1971.

Jacobson, Howard. "The Position of the Fingers During the Priestly Blessing." *RevQ* 9 (1977) 259-60.

Jansen, Ludin. "The Consecration in the Eighth Chapter of Testamentum Levi." *StHR* (=Supp. to *Numen*) 4 (1955) 356-65.

Jastrow, Marcus. *Dictionary of the Targumim, Talmud Babli, Yerushalmi and the Midrashic Literature*. New York: Judaica Press, 1989.

Jaubert, Annie. *La notion d'alliance dans le Judaïsme*. Paris: Editions du Seuil, 1963.

Jones, D. R. *Jeremiah*. NCBC. Grand Rapids: Eerdmans, 1992.

Keil, C. F. *Die zwölf kleinen Propheten*. Leipzig: Dörflin und Franke, 1888.

Kobelski, Paul. *Melchizedek and Melkireša⁽*. CBQMS 10. Washington, D. C.: Catholic Biblical Association of America, 1984.

Kraeling, E. G., ed. *The Brooklyn Museum Aramaic Papyri*. New Haven: Yale University, 1953.

Kuenen, A. "Dina und Sichem." In *Gesammelte Abhandlungen zur biblischen Wissenschaft*, 255-76. Freiburg: J. C. B. Mohr, 1894.

Kugel, James. "Levi's Elevation to the Priesthood in Second Temple Writings." *HTR* 86 (1993) 1-64.

_____. "The Story of Dinah in the *Testament of Levi*." *HTR* 85 (1992) 1-34.

Küchler, Max. *Frühjüdische Weisheitstraditionen*. OBO 26. Göttingen: Vandenhoeck & Ruprecht, 1979.

Lagrange, M.-J. *Le Judaïsme avant Jésus-Christ*. Paris: Libraire Lecoffre, 1931.

Lehming, S. "Versuch zu Ex XXXII." *VT* 10 (1960) 16-50.

Lévi, Israel. "Encore un mot sur le texte araméen du Testament de Lévi récemment découvert." *REJ* 55 (1907) 285-87.

_____. "Notes sur le texte araméen du Testament de Lévi récemment découvert." *REJ* 54 (1907) 166-80.

Liddell, H. G., and Robert Scott. *A Greek-English Lexicon*. Rev. ed. Oxford: Clarendon, 1940/1968.

Littmann, E. "Das Buch der Jubiläen." In *Die Apocryphen und Pseudepigraphen des Alten Testaments*, ed. E. Kautzsch, 2:31-119. Tübingen: J. C. B. Mohr, 1900.

Macky, Peter. "The Importance of the Teaching on God, Evil and Eschatology for the Dating of the Testaments of the Twelve Patriarchs." Ph.D. diss., Princeton, 1969.

Manson, T. W. "Miscellanea Apocalyptica." *JTS* 48 (1947) 59-61.

Marti, Karl. *Das Dodekapropheton*. KHAT XIII. Tübingen: J.C.B. Mohr, 1904.

Martin, F. "Le Livre de Jubilés: But et procedes de l'auteur. Ses doctrines." *RB* 8 (1911) 321-44, 502-33.

Mayes, A. D. H. *Deuteronomy*. NCBC. Grand Rapids: Eerdmans, 1979.

McKenzie, Steven L. and Howard N. Wallace. "Covenant Themes in Malachi." *CBQ* 45 (1983) 549-63.

Mendels, Doron. *The Land of Israel as a Political Concept in Hasmonean Literature: Recourse to History in Second Century B.C. Claims to the Holy Land*. Tübingen: J. C. B. Mohr, 1987.

Meyers, Eric. "Priestly Language in the Book of Malachi." *HAR* 10 (1986) 225-37.

Milgrom, Jacob. *Numbers*. JPS Torah Commentary. Philadelphia: Jewish Publication Society, 1990.

Milik, J. T. *The Books of Enoch: Aramaic Fragments of Qumrân Cave 4*. Oxford: Clarendon, 1976.

_____. "Écrits prééséniens de Qumrân; d'Hénoch à ʿAmram." In *Qumrân. Sa piété, sa théologie et son milieu*, ed. M. Delcor, 91-106. BEThL 46. Gembloux: Duculot, 1978.

Milik, J. T. "Fragment d'une source du Psautier (4Q Ps 89)." *RB* 73 (1976) 94-106.

_____. "Milkî-ṣedeq et milkî-rešaʿ dans les anciens écrits juifs et chrétiens." *JJS* 28 (1972) 95-144.

_____. "Problèmes de la littérature hénochique à la lumière des fragments araméen de Qumrân." *HTR* 64 (1971) 333-78.

_____. "Le Testament de Lévi en araméen: Fragment de la Grotte 4 de Qumrân." *RB* 62 (1955) 398-406.

_____."4Q Visions de ʿAmram et une citation d'Origène." RB 79 (1972) 77-97.

Neubauer, O., and A. E. Cowley. *Catalogue of the Hebrew Manuscripts in the Bodleian Library.* 2 vols. Oxford: Clarendon, 1906.

Nickelsburg, George. "Enoch, Levi, and Peter: Recipients of Revelation in Upper Galilee." *JBL* 100 (1981) 575-600.

_____. *Resurrection, Immortality, and Eternal Life in Intertestamental Judaism.* HTS 26. Cambridge: Harvard University, 1972.

_____. Review of *Textual and Historical Studies in the Book of Jubilees*, by James VanderKam. In *JAOS* 100 (1980) 83-84.

Noth, Martin. *Numbers: A Commentary.* OTL London: SCM Press, 1968.

O'Brien, Julia. *Priest and Levite in Malachi.* SBLDS 121. Atlanta: Scholars Press, 1990.

Otzen, Benedikt. "Die neugefundenen hebräischen Sektenschriften und die Testamente der zwölf Patriarchen." *ST* 7 (1953) 125-57.

Pass H. L., and J. Arendzen. "Fragment of an Aramaic Text of the Testament of Levi." *JQR* 12 (1900) 651-61.

Perlitt, Lothar. *Bundestheologie im Alten Testament.* WMANT 36. Neukirchen: Neukirchener, 1969.

Philonenko, M. *Les interpolations chrétiennes des Douze Patriarches et les manuscrits de Qoumrân.* Paris: Presses universitaire de France, 1960.

_____. "Paradoxes Stoïciens dans le Testament de Lévi." In *Sagesse et Religion*, ed. E. Jacob, 99-104. Paris: Bibliothèque des centres d'études supérieures spécialés, 1979.

Porter, J. R. "The Messiah in the Testament of Levi XVIII." *ET* 61 (1949-1950) 90-91.

Powell, Marvin A. "Weights and Measures." In *Anchor Bible Dictionary*, ed. D. N. Freedman, VI:897-908. New York: Doubleday, 1992.

"A Preliminary Concordance to the Hebrew and Aramaic Fragments from Qumran Caves II–X Including Especially the Unpublished Material from Cave IV." Privately printed, Göttingen, 1988.

Puech, Émile. "Fragments d'un apocryphe de Lévi et le personnage eschatologique. 4QTestLévi^c-d(?) et 4QAJa." In *The Madrid Congress: Proceedings of the International Congress on the Dead Sea Scrolls, Madrid 18–21 March 1991*, eds. Julio Trebolle Barrera and Luis Vegas Montaner, 2:449-501. Studies on the Texts of the Desert of Judah 11. Leiden: Brill, 1993.

_____. "Le Testament de Qahat en araméen de la Grotte 4 (*4QTQah*)." *RevQ* 15 (1992) 2-54.

Pummer, Reinhard. "Genesis 34 in Jewish Writings of the Hellenistic and Roman Periods." *HTR* 75 (1982) 177-88.

Reif, S. C. "What Enraged Phinehas?—A Study of Numbers 25:8." *JBL* 90 (1971) 100-6.

Renker, Alwin. *Die Tora bei Maleachi*. FTS 112. Freiburg: Herder, 1979.

Rivkin, Ellis. "Aaron, Aaronites." *IDBSup*, 1-3.

Rönsch, H. *Das Buch der Juiläen oder die Kleine Genesis*. Leipzig: Fues's Verlag, 1874.

Rudolph, Wilhelm. *Haggai-Sacharja-Maleachi*. KAT XIII 4. Gütersloh: Gütersloher Verlagshaus, 1976.

Ruppert, L. "Das Motiv der Versuchung durch Gott in vordeuteronomischer Tradition." *VT* 22 (1972) 56-69.

Sanders, James A. *Discoveries in the Judaean Desert* IV. Oxford: Oxford University, 1965.

Sanderson, Judith. *An Exodus Scroll from Qumran: 4QpaleoExod^m and the Samaritan Tradition*. HSS 30. Atlanta: Scholars Press, 1986.

Schnapp, Friedrich. *Die Testamente der zwölf Patriarchen untersucht*. Halle: Max Niemeyer, 1884.

Schwarz, Eberhard. *Identität durch Abgrenzung: Abgrenzungsprozesse in Israel im 2. vorchristlichen Jahrhundert und ihre traditionsgeschichtlichen Voraussetzungen. Zugleich ein Beitrag zur Erforschung des Jubiläen Buches*. Europäische Hochschulschriften 162. Frankfurt am Main: Peter Lang, 1982.

Sievers, Joseph. *The Hasmoneans and Their Supporters: From Mattathias to the Death of John Hyrcanus I*. USFSJ 6. Atlanta, GA: Scholars, 1990.

Singer, Wm. *Das Buch der Jubiläen oder die Leptogenesis*. Stuhlweissenburg, Hungary: Ed. Singer'sche Buchhandlung, 1898.

Skehan, P. W., E. Ulrich, and J. Sanderson. *Discoveries in the Judaean Desert* IX. Oxford: Clarendon, 1992.

Slingerland, H. Dixon. "The Levitical Hallmark within the Testaments of the Twelve Patriarchs." *JBL* 103 (1984) 531-37.

_____. "The Nature of *Nomos* (Law) within the *Testaments of the Twelve Patriarchs*." *JBL* 105 (1986) 39-48.

Slingerland, H. Dixon. *The Testaments of the Twelve Patriarchs: A Critical History of Research.* SBLMS 21. Missoula, MT: Scholars Press, 1977.

Smith, J. M. P. *Malachi.* ICC. Edinburgh: T. & T. Clark, 1912.

Smith, Ralph L. *Micha–Malachi.* WBC 32. Waco, TX: Word Books, 1984.

Smyth, H. W. *Greek Grammar.* Cambridge: Harvard University, 1920.

Snaith, N. H. *Leviticus and Numbers.* London: Nelson, 1967.

Stewart, R. A. "The Sinless High Priest." *NTS* 14 (1967-1968) 126-35.

Stone, Michael, and Jonas Greenfield. "The Prayer of Levi." *JBL* 112 (1993) 247-66.

Stone, Michael. "Enoch, Aramaic Levi, and Sectarian Origins." *JSJ* 19 (1988) 159-70.

_____. "Ideal Figures and Social Context: Priest and Sage in the Early Second Temple Age." In *Ancient Israelite Religion*, eds. P. D. Miller, P. D. Hanson, and D. S. McBride, 575-86. Philadelphia: Fortress, 1988.

_____. *Scriptures, Sects and Visions.* Philadelphia: Fortress, 1980.

Strack, H. L., and G. Stemberger. *Introduction to the Talmud and Midrash.* Minneapolis: Fortress, 1992.

Strugnell, John. "Notes en marge du Volume 5 des 'Discoveries in the Judaean Desert of Jordan.'" *RevQ* 7 (1970) 225.

Testuz, M. *Les idées réligieuses du Livre des Jubilés.* Geneva: Droz, 1960.

Thomas, J. "Aktuelles im Zeugnis der Zwölf Väter." In *Studien zu den Testamenten der zwölf Patriarchen*, ed. Walther Eltester, 62-150. Berlin: Töpelmann, 1969.

Ulrichsen, Jarl Henning. *Die Grundschrift der Testamente der zwölf Patriarchen: Eine Untersuchung zu Umfang, Inhalt und Eigenart der ursprünglichen Schrift.* Acta Universitatis Upsaliensis, Historia Religionum 10. Uppsala: Almqvist & Wiksell, 1991.

Utzschneider, Helmut. *Künder oder Schreiber? Eine These zum Problem der "Schriftprophetie" auf Grund von Maleachi 1,6–2,9.* Beiträge zur Erforschung des Alten Testaments und des Antiken Judentums 19. Frankfurt am Main: Lang, 1989.

_____. "Die Schriftprophetie und die Frage nach dem Ende der Prophetie." *ZAW* 104 (1992) 377-94.

VanderKam, James. *The Book of Jubilees.* Corpus Scriptorum Christianorum Orientalium 510-511. Louvain: E. Peeters, 1989.

_____. "Enoch Traditions in Jubilees and Other Second-Century Sources." *SBLSP* 13 (1978) 1:229-51.

_____. "Jubilees and the Priestly Messiah of Qumran." *RevQ* 13 (1988) 353-65.

VanderKam, James. "People and High Priesthood in Early Maccabean Times." In *The Hebrew Bible and its Interpreters*, eds. W. H. Propp, B. Halpern, and D. N. Freedman, 205-225. Biblical and Judaic Studies from the University of California, San Diego 1. Winona Lake, IN: Eisenbrauns, 1990.

_____. "The Putative Author of the Book of Jubilees." *JSS* 26 (1981) 209-17.

_____. "The Temple Scroll and the Book of Jubilees." In *Temple Scroll Studies*, ed. G. Brooke, 211-36. Sheffield: JSOT, 1989.

_____. *Textual and Historical Studies in the Book of Jubilees*. HSM 14. Missoula: Scholars, 1977.

VanderKam, James, and J. T. Milik, "The First *Jubilees* Manuscript from Qumran Cave 4: A Preliminary Publication." *JBL* 110 (1991) 243-70.

Vawter, B. "Levitical Messianism and the New Testament." In *The Bible in Current Thought*, ed. John L. McKenzie, 83-99. New York: Herder, 1962.

Verhoef, Pieter. *The Books of Haggai and Malachi*. NICOT. Grand Rapids, MI: Eerdmans, 1987.

Vuilleumier, René. *Aggée, Zacharie 1–8, Zacharie 9–14, Malachie*. Paris: Delachaux & Niestlé, 1981.

Wellhausen, Julius. *Die kleine Propheten übersetzt und erklärt*. Skizzen und Vorarbeiten 5. Berlin: G. Reimer, 1892.

_____. *Prolegomena zur Geschichte Israels*. Sechste Ausgabe. Berlin: DeGruyter, 1927.

Westermann, C. *Genesis 37–50*. Minneapolis: Augsburg, 1986.

Zeitlin, Solomon. "The Book of 'Jubilees' and the Pentateuch." *JQR* 48 (1957) 218-35.

_____. "The Book of Jubilees, Its Character and Its Significance." *JQR* 30 (1939-40) 8-16.

_____. *The Book of Jubilees: Its Character and Significance*. Philadelphia: Dropsie College, 1939.